ABOUT THIS BOOK!

PLEASE NOTE: IF YOU ARE A VICTIM OF ABUSE WHO HAS PURCHASED THIS BOOK, PLEASE PLACE IT IN A SAFE PLACE, AWAY FROM YOUR ABUSER.

It'sNot Okay Anymore, Your Personal Guide to Ending Abuse, Taking Charge, and Loving Yourself

Featuring the Cycle of Personal Responsibility
created by survivors of domestic violence.

This book is a practical and artistic step-by-step path out of abuse and into life management and self-care. Written with sensitivity and respect by two life coaches, Greg Enns and Jan Black, the reader is guided through the process of living abuse-free. It is highly recommended by victims, survivors, and helping professionals of all disciplines.

Who is this book for?

- Victims wanting help in identifying their abuse and moving from insight to action
- Survivors wanting to stay safe and create a life of love and well-being
- Groups wanting an effective discussion and action tool. (The *Coaching Guide for Leaders* is also available.)
- Shelters wanting a practical guide to help victims begin a new way of living
- Social service professionals wanting a step-by-step treatment pattern
- Health care providers wanting to offer an additional resource to their patients
- Family and friends of victims

"A wonderful handbook to gently, yet firmly, help victims of domestic violence climb out of their situation."
—KC Eynatten, Director, Corporate Alliance to End Partner Violence

"This book saved my life. It was the key that opened the door to safety and well-being for me and my children." —E.L. (survivor)

"Particularly effective with women in shelters—as individuals or groups—to begin the work of recovery."
—Pat Paluzzi, CNM, MPH, Sr. Technical Advisor, Amer. Coll. of Nurse-Midwives

This is a well-developed alternative to the Cycle of Abuse. It includes a gentle, positive style, checkpoints and action steps, survivors' stories, success tips, Get Safe and Stay Safe plans, and coaching in empowerment and self-esteem

It's Not Okay Anymore

Your Personal Guide to Ending Abuse, Taking Charge, and Loving Yourself

"Fear is a woman's worst enemy. Fear serves to paralyze women, holds us in place, saps our energy and attention from important work, and limits our creativity and imagination. Fear keeps us close to home. It silences us. And if we wait until we are unafraid, or fixed, or analyzed, we may have waited too long."

Harriet Goldhor-Lerner

It's Not Okay Anymore

Your Personal Guide to Ending Abuse, Taking Charge, and Loving Yourself.

by Greg Enns and Jan Black

New Harbinger Publications

New Harbinger Publications
It's Not Okay Anymore! Your Personal Guide to Ending Abuse, Taking Charge, and Loving Yourself

Featuring "The Cycle of Personal Responsibility"
Domestic Violence Services, Pendleton, Oregon.
Contributors: Dr. Jerry Canning, Kathleen Cary, R.N., Carol Funk, M.S., Teresa Wilhelmi, Kricket Nicholson, Stacy Pierce.

Published for the trade by New Harbinger Publications
5674 Shattuck Avenue, Oakland, CA 94609

Special sales and marketing by Hannibal House, Inc.
1320 Edgewater NW, Ste B10
Salem, OR 97604

Distributed in U.S.A. by Publishers Group West; in Canada by Raincoast Books; in Great Britain by Airlift Book Company, Ltd.; in South Africa by Real Books, Ltd.; in Australia by Boobook; in New Zealand by Tandem Press.

Library of Congress Catalog Card Number: 96-71155
ISBN 1-57224-066-0 paperback

Printed in Canada on recycled paper.

10 9 8 7 6 5 4 3 2 1

To those who have broken free of abuse, those wanting to, and those who lead them.

FOR YOUR SAFETY

This book is intended to personalize your walk through the process of ending abuse. We encourage you to keep it in a private, safe place - away from your abuser. We want you to be safe!

PUBLISHER'S NOTE

For purposes of readability only, the editors have chosen to direct the language of this book to women, since over 90% of reported partner abuse is against women by men. They wish readers to know this decision is due to a limitation of language, not of heart, toward the growing number of men being abused by women or toward those experiencing abuse in same sex relationships.

AUTHORS' ACKNOWLEDGMENTS

We wish to thank all of those who have contributed directly and indirectly to the production of this book. Specifically, we are grateful to the team at LifeTrack Strategies for Living for their insights and edits, to Kricket Nicholson and Stacy Pierce for creating the Cycle of Personal Responsibility and for their belief in the entire project, to the staff and board of Domestic Violence Services, to survivors of domestic abuse who have said, "It's not okay anymore," such as those pictured in this book, and to the community of domestic violence prevention for their courage, skill, and persistence.

NOTE: The courageous women pictured on the title pages of this book are survivors of domestic violence. The date under each name is the day they decided "It's not okay anymore."

Dear Reader, 

Your life belongs to you. It is yours. You get to make choices for it. Choices that satisfy you, help others, make you feel good, let you express who you are inside, and make a difference. You get to decide what to learn, who to love, where to work, what to play, who to be with, what colors to wear, what styles you like, how to arrange your livingroom, what kind of parent, friend, lover you will be, what authors to read, what movies to enjoy, and what Saturday mornings will be like for you. Your life belongs to you, unless you give it away. Then someone else will make these choices for you and you will live with a knot in your gut that begs you to take your life back again.

Everyone who has worked on this book knows that feeling in some way. Some of us have been beaten by a partner who claimed to love us. Some of us have been emotionally or mentally abused. Others of us have been addicted to drugs, alcohol, food, work, or pleasing people. We know what it is like to be in a mess we think we can't get out of. But we did get out of it and we are writing this to tell you that you can, too.

Whether your mess is topped by getting your face smashed into the floor by your partner or your soul slashed with cutting words, the situation is reversible. You can get your life back. You can end the beatings. You can change the pattern. You can overcome the lies that tell you you are ugly, feeble, stupid, worthless, helpless, and destined to fail.

In our jobs as life coaches, we help people live the kind of lives they want. In this book, we will coach you through each step of ending abuse, taking charge of your life, and loving yourself. There isn't a magic formula, but there is magic in saying "yes" to the process.

Greg Enns and Jan Black

Coaches' Chalk Talk

Before we go any further, we would like you to know these things:

1. The incidence of violence and homicide increases when victims leave or are planning to leave their abusers. It is imperative, therefore, that you work closely with helping professionals as you make your choices for safety at home, at work, for your children, if any, at school, for legal issues, protective measures, and custody issues.

2. The publisher and authors share a zero tolerance for violence and other forms of abuse.

3. You are not to blame for your abuse, nor are you responsible to try to change your abuser.

4. You cannot predict or control your abuser, nor is it safe to try.

5. We honor your right to leave a hurtful relationship or stay.

6. You are worthy of respect and safety.

7. This book is your personal coaching guide out of abuse. For a more thorough study of ending abuse or any other topic we present, we strongly urge you to use the resources in "Part Four: Other Helps."

8. You can read and apply this book in the privacy of your home, with a trusted person, or in a small group. A leader's guide is available for group use.

9. The strategies in this book are meant to help you increase your personal success. They are not meant to give you the false hope that by using them your abuser will stop hurting you. Remember, it is not your behavior that is causing the abuse; your abuser is causing it.

To help you know exactly what we mean by the terms we use in this book, we have listed them for you on the next page.

WHAT WE MEAN BY THESE TERMS

Abuse - Any behavior that results in the mistreatment of another.

Assertive - A manner of living that is both powerful and respectful.

Boundaries - Limits I set to let the good in and keep the bad out.

Cycle of Abuse - A step-by-step pattern of behavior that builds to the point of abuse.

Cycle of Personal Responsibility - A step-by-step pattern of behavior that moves a person away from abuse and into personal safety and success.

Cycle-Jumping - Moving from the cycle of abuse to the cycle of personal responsibility.

"Fire" - Any act of abuse.

Loving Myself - Doing those things that show I value myself.

Responsibility - A commitment to selecting and managing the roles, duties, and relationships that are genuinely mine.

Self-esteem - The way I think and feel about myself.

"Smoke" - Tension-building signs of increasing risks for abuse.

Success - Making good choices for my safety and well-being and those in my care.

Taking Charge - Taking responsibility for my decisions, actions, and reactions in order to lead a responsible and loving life.

Trusted People - Individuals whose words and actions are consistently respectful toward me.

Violence - Any unwanted and forceful physical contact.

Well-being - A manner of living that moves beyond surviving to thriving.

Contents

Part 1: Ending Abuse

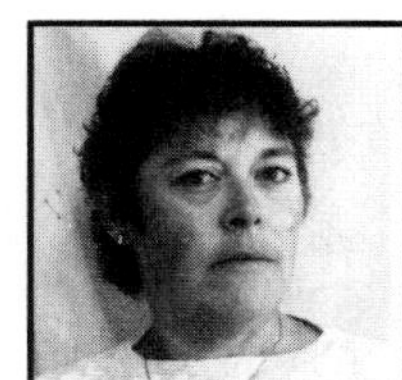

Linda

November

26,

1995

What is Abuse?

Generally speaking, abuse is any behavior that results in the mistreatment of another. There are five major kinds of abuse: physical, emotional, sexual, social, and spiritual.

To describe what we mean by "mistreatment of another," we have listed some common examples of abuse. As you read them, you may want to *place a check mark by those you have experienced in your current relationship*. To help you discover if you have a pattern of being abused, you could also *circle any abuses you have experienced in any past relationships*. If an abuse you are experiencing is not on the list, please add it to the list in the space provided.

EXAMPLES OF PHYSICAL ABUSE

☐ 1. Destroying your belongings.
☐ 2. Throwing objects at you.
☐ 3. Touching you in ways that hurt or scare you.
☐ 4. Twisting your arm, slapping, or biting you.
☐ 5. Pushing or shoving you.
☐ 6. Depriving you of food, shelter, money or clothing.
☐ 7. Threatening you with weapons.
☐ 8. Hitting, punching, or kicking you.
☐ 9. Choking or throwing you.
☐ 10. Hitting or kicking you in a series of blows.
☐ 11. Abusing you to the point you need medical treatment.
☐ 12. Breaking your bones and/or causing internal injuries.
☐ 13. Causing a miscarriage or injuries that require a therapeutic abortion.
☐ 14. Denying you medical treatment.
☐ 15. Inflicting permanent disabling and/or disfiguring injuries.
☐ ____
☐ ____
☐ ____
☐ ____
☐ ____

EXAMPLES OF EMOTIONAL ABUSE

- ☐ 1. Taunting you in the name of "fun."
- ☐ 2. Ignoring you and/or your feelings.
- ☐ 3. Insulting you repeatedly.
- ☐ 4. Yelling at you.
- ☐ 5. Telling you you will fail.
- ☐ 6. Blaming you for his faults.
- ☐ 7. Threatening you with violence or retaliation.
- ☐ 8. Threatening to hurt your pets.
- ☐ 9. Threatening to abuse the children and/or get custody of them.
- ☐ 10. Telling you you must stay because you can't make it alone.
- ☐ 11. Accusing you of being violent when you protect yourself in any way.
- ☐ 12. Labeling you as crazy, stupid, bitch, ugly, or a whore.
- ☐ 13. Blaming you for things that go wrong.
- ☐ 14. Holding back approval as a form of punishment.
- ☐ ____
- ☐ ____

EXAMPLES OF SOCIAL ABUSE

- ☐ 1. Insulting you publicly.
- ☐ 2. Controlling your use of money.
- ☐ 3. Putting down your abilities as a wife, mother, lover, or worker.
- ☐ 4. Checking up on you.
- ☐ 5. Taping conversations.
- ☐ 6. Following you from place to place - stalking.
- ☐ 7. Demanding all of your attention and resenting any focus on others.
- ☐ 8. Making a public display of destroying property.
- ☐ 9. Threatening to hurt your extended family and friends.
- ☐ 10. Isolating you from friends or activities.
- ☐ 11. Spending paychecks without meeting obligations.
- ☐ ____
- ☐ ____

EXAMPLES OF SEXUAL ABUSE

- ☐ 1. Talking about you or others as sexual objects.
- ☐ 2. Forcing you to have sex, including sex after a beating.
- ☐ 3. Criticizing your sexual performance.
- ☐ 4. Withholding affection to punish you.
- ☐ 5. Accusing you of looking at, talking to, or having sex with another.
- ☐ 6. Forcing you to engage in sexual activities that are uncomfortable for you.
- ☐ 7. Inflicting harm or mutilation to your genitals.
- ☐ 8. Choking or slapping you during sex.
- ☐ ______________________________
- ☐ ______________________________

EXAMPLES OF SPIRITUAL ABUSE

- ☐ 1. Discounting your sense of right and wrong.
- ☐ 2. Denying, minimizing, or ridiculing your spiritual beliefs.
- ☐ 3. Denying your value as a person with legitimate wants and likes.
- ☐ 4. Questioning your motives for just about everything.
- ☐ 5. Questioning your sense of reality.
- ☐ 6. Refusing to allow you access to worship communities or support groups.
- ☐ ______________________________
- ☐ ______________________________

CHECKPOINT
Are you being abused?
Yes ☐ No ☐

WHO IS INVOLVED IN ABUSE?

Abuse is a downward spiral that involves millions of people each year. A worldwide problem, abusers and victims come from every class, gender, age, faith, and race. While not everyone alive is a victim or an abuser, everyone alive is affected by abuse in some way.

Abuse is about control and selfish power. It is about one person doing harm to another in order to get his way or make a point. Like bullies in a schoolyard, abusers pick on people they can control. In most cases in our country, this means women and children. However, more and more cases of abuse are being reported by people of both sexes and of all ages.

ABUSER AND VICTIM PROFILES

It is unwise and inaccurate to lump all victims or all abusers into a single profile. Therefore, we choose to loosely describe them, knowing from experience that no single profile fits everyone.

Abusers:

- Come from all races, religions, walks of life and income levels.
- May appear to be non-abusers.
- Often, but not always, come from abusive homes.
- Often limit abuse to the privacy of home.
- Often show remorse after abusing and may or may not intend to do it again.
- May misinterpret religious doctrine in order to justify abuse.
- Can be manipulators and liars.
- May or may not move from emotional abuse to physical abuse and even murder.
- Often suffer from low self-esteem
- Often compensate for a sense of powerlessness by overpowering others.
- Often are impulsive and become easily frustrated.

Victims:

- Come from all races, religions, walks of life and income levels.
- May or may not have come from abusive homes.

- Often believe they cause and/or deserve the abuse.
- May have been blind-sided by an abuser who appeared calm and controlled while dating.
- Often hesitate to tell others about the abuse.
- Usually wait too long before getting help.
- Can often be convinced by their abusers that abuse isn't abuse.
- Usually suffer from low self-esteem.
- Usually stay in abusive relationships because they feel trapped economically and socially.

Some victims, even women who are successful in other parts of their lives, come to believe that "abuse is my destiny and the best that I can hope for." Abuse is not a destiny. Like survivors around the world, you can change your situation now. Your destiny is in your hands, not your partner's. Your life will change when you change it.

On the next page, we will look at one victim's story.

CHECKPOINT
Do you believe you can change your life?
Yes No

Stacy Pierce's Story

Like so many others, Stacy's self-esteem was low as a child. When her future husband walked into her life and said "I love you," she was starved for love and married him four weeks later. Eight years of every kind of abuse followed the wedding.

Stacy stuck it out until her husband aimed his abuse at their two-year old son. She planned her getaway for a time when her husband was away from the house.

Stacy refused to go back, even though the abuse and harassment continued after the separation. Through what she believes was divine intervention, she got a job at Domestic Violence Services (DVS) in Pendleton, Oregon, working with other victims.

Now, five years later, Stacy is in a healthy, loving relationship with a man who respects her and nurtures her and her two sons. She is Administrative Assistant and Victim Advocate at DVS and also facilitates the Women's Support Group there.

Stacy is co-creator of the Cycle of Personal Responsibility, featured later in this book. "It has been the missing link we have needed to help women out of abuse," says Stacy. "Now we do more than help them become aware of their victimization, we teach them to use the Cycle of Personal Responsibility to move out of the role of victims and into the role of happy, healthy, successful people."

We will look at Stacy's story more closely and chart it on page 22.

The Cycle of Abuse

The pattern of abuse is like a downward spiral that goes round and round in a predictable way. It always takes you down, and, if you have children, it takes them down, too.

We call this cycle the "Cycle of Abuse." The cycle of abuse is pictured and described below and on the following page. People who have studied violence and abuse have found these stages to be common in abusive relationships. If you are being abused, your pattern may not *exactly* match the cycle of abuse, but for the most part, you probably fit into it.

The stages of the Cycle of Abuse are:

ABUSE OCCURS

1. EXCUSES - My partner and/or I rationalize the abuse. (This is a common defense mechanism for victims.) He may tell me he didn't mean to do it or he couldn't help himself, that I've got to try harder to love him better and do what he wants, or that if I was just more perfect he wouldn't have to get so upset.

2. HONEYMOON - Things seem great. My partner and I apologize and make promises. I may get roses or a dinner out or new lingerie. We may have stars in our eyes and I may tell myself the abuse is over.

3. ROUTINE - We return to the routine of our lives, with its normal ups and downs.

4. TENSION - Tension is building. I can tell things are starting to upset him and I start "walking on eggshells" to avoid triggering abuse.

5. TRIGGER - Something sets off the abuser. I'm late getting home or I forget to fill the gas tank or the laundry isn't folded or I was too nice to the grocery clerk.

ABUSE OCCURS - It happens again. I move back into excuse-making and the cycle continues.

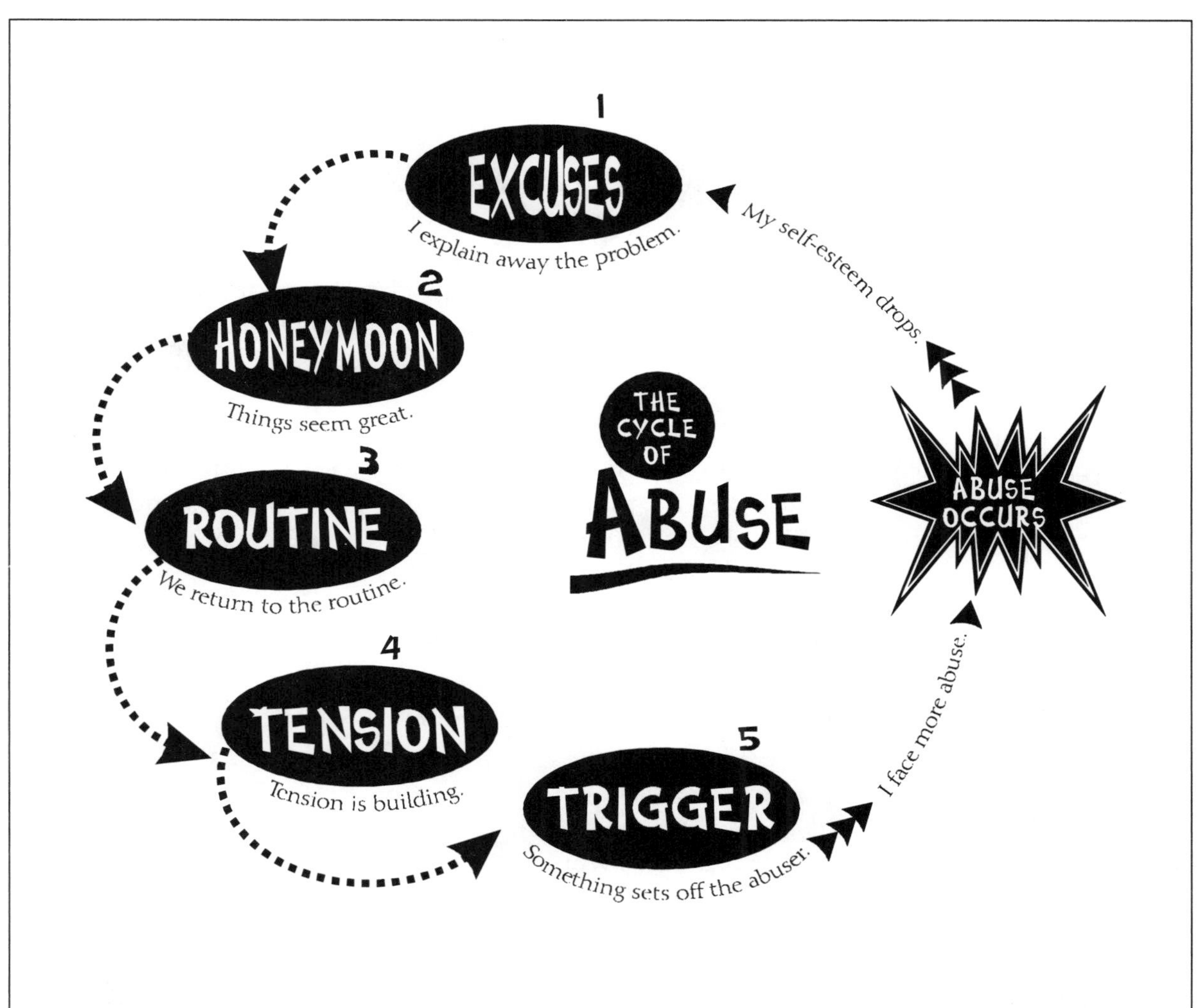
1
EXCUSES
I explain away the problem.
2
HONEYMOON
Things seem great.
3
ROUTINE
We return to the routine.
4
TENSION
Tension is building.
5
TRIGGER
Something sets off the abuser.
I face more abuse.
ABUSE OCCURS
My self-esteem drops.
THE CYCLE OF ABUSE

How the Cycle Works in Real Life

Using Stacy's story on page 19 as a starting point, let's chart her pattern of abuse on the Cycle of Abuse. First, here are more details about Stacy's life during the time of her abuse:

"We lived on a meager fixed income. My husband was on disability following a back injury, and I was only allowed to work until the hours, or job, or boss didn't suit him. When I was not working, I was not allowed to leave the house without permission. I spent my days doing housework and laundry. My wages and the disability check were deposited directly into the bank. My husband would go to the bank and take what he needed to support his habits, and I got what was left to pay bills.

"There was never enough money for all the bills, so I would choose a different payment to miss each month. He would leave the house at 9 AM to pick up the mail and not return until about 4 PM each day. When the late notice from the bill I hadn't paid the month before arrived in the mail, he would come home and beat me. There were other, often more severe, beatings between late notices, but the 'bill beatings' were chartable."

Charted on the Cycle of Abuse, Stacy's story would look like this:

ABUSE OCCURS: Physical and verbal beatings are triggered by a late notice.

1. Excuses

Stacy survives by telling herself her husband wouldn't hit her if she were a better money manager. This matches his claim that he is only trying to help her learn to take better care of their money.

2. Honeymoon

He says he loves her and asks her to forgive him. He takes her out to dinner, but the servers and food are never good enough. (Note: He is already setting her up for the next abuse because later he will blame her for having to spend money they don't have on dinner out.)

3. ROUTINE

Things get comfortable and agreeable (although now she sees how uncomfortable the routine really was).

4. TENSION

The past-due notice is coming any day now.

5. TRIGGER

The past-due notice arrives.

ABUSE OCCURS: Stacy is beaten again for being a "poor money manager."

This cycle continued until Stacy said "It's not okay anymore." We will look at Stacy's break into freedom in "Part Two: Taking Charge."

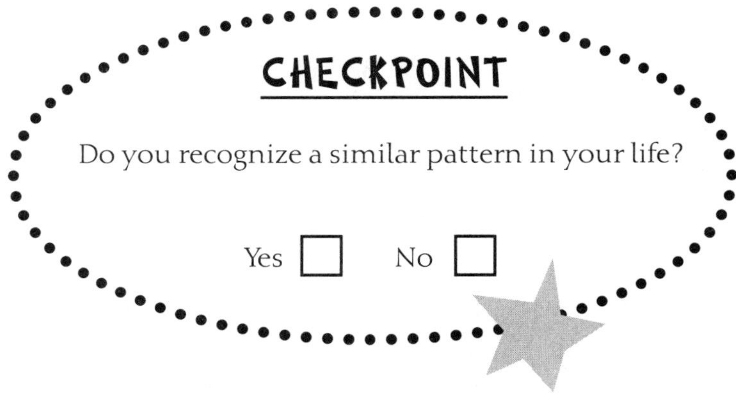

CHECKPOINT
Do you recognize a similar pattern in your life?
Yes
No

How Did I Get Here?

More than one victim has sat in a heap on the floor in tears and asked the question, "How did I get here?" The answers vary, but often victims share certain risk factors such as those listed below. Mark any that are true of you.

☐ 1. As a child growing up I was directly or indirectly exposed to violence or abuse.
☐ 2. When I think about my childhood I feel sadness, disappointment, and/or despair.
☐ 3. I grew up in a home with parents who were addicts or alcoholics.
☐ 4. I have suffered from low self-esteem since childhood.
☐ 5. I tend to try to figure things out on my own because I don't like to bother people.
☐ 6. I focus on the positives in my life and have learned to ignore negatives, like abuse.
☐ 7. I have trouble making long-term commitments in my personal and professional relationships.
☐ 8. Since childhood, I have been deeply and painfully involved with people, causes and compulsions that threaten my health and safety.
☐ 9. I have trouble making decisions that are good for me.
☐ 10. I married or left home to get away from a bad family situation.
☐ 11. I stay in a bad relationship because I am afraid to leave.
☐ 12. I don't feel like I have power or control to make good choices.
☐ 13. I don't think I deserve anything better than what I have.
☐ 14. I have had no experience with abuse and was not familiar with the danger signs.

The answer to "How did I get here?" is important, but the more important question is "What shall I do now?"

What Shall I Do Now?

Safety first! Before going any further in your effort to end abuse, we recommend you prepare the following "Get Safe Plan." It will organize your escape from abuse, should you need it. This is a favor you do for yourself and your children.

Please do not minimize your abuse or assume you do not need a Get Safe Plan if you are not suffering bodily harm. Domestic violence professionals know that a hit on the mind can carry the same punch as a hit in the face. Both leave lasting scars, and to be safe, both require a Get Safe Plan. It is a matter of hoping for the best but planning for the worst.

Depending on the nature of your abuse, your Get Safe Plan may be as complex as an escape to another state with a new identity or as simple as going to the next room and closing the door.

The Get Safe Plan is much like an escape plan you make in case of a fire. It describes precisely what to do when you see the "smoke" of tension building or the "fire" of an act of abuse. The plan can include trusted people in your life, and we suggest you give a completed copy of your plan to them. Their job is to support you and your efforts. Your job is to accept responsibility for your safety, work your plan, and love yourself.

EXAMPLES OF "SMOKE"
Tension-building signs that abuse may come.

Batterer's Behavior

- Missing a counseling appointment
- Irritability
- Depression
- Denial of behavior
- Excuses for behavior
- Accusations

Victim's Behavior

- Missing a counseling appointment
- Anger (repressed)
- Fear
- Knots in the stomach
- Walking on eggshells
- Over-responsible behavior

(Batterer's Behavior, con't.)

- Blaming others
- Self-pity
- Explaining or justifying
- Dropping out of support groups and other activities
- Breaking promises

(Victim's Behavior, con't.)

- Covering up
- Anxiety
- Enabling
- Feelings of guilt-shame
- Minimizing crisis

EXAMPLES OF FIRE

Any act of abusive or violent behavior.

Get Safe Plan

Important! Please keep this plan in a safe and private place, away from your abuser. Also, do not refer to this plan with anyone who is not a part of it, or at least a strong advocate for your safety. It is normal to feel afraid when completing and carrying out a safety plan, since the risk of abuse is often greater at this time. This is why it is important for you to carefully *complete this safety plan as well as others related to legal and protective concerns that may be recommended to you by the professional helping agencies listed in Part Four.*

This GET SAFE PLAN is designed for:
Name ______________________________ Phone ________________
Address ______________________________ City __________ State______

WHO CAN I CALL?

Counselor/support group contact: ____________________ Phone ____________
Recovery partner/peer helper: ____________________ Phone ____________
Shelter contact/crisis services: ____________________ Phone ____________
Doctor/health care provider: ____________________ Phone ____________
______________________________ Phone ____________
______________________________ Phone ____________

WHERE CAN I GO TO BE SAFE?

Practice how to get out safely. What doors, windows, elevator, stairwells, or fire escapes would you use? Also, practice how you are going to get to the safe places listed below.

Safe Place #1: ______________________________ Phone: __________
Address: ____________________________ Contact Person: ____________

Safe Place #2: ______________________________ Phone: __________
Address: ____________________________ Contact Person: ____________

Safe Place #3: ______________________________ Phone: __________
Address: ____________________________ Contact Person: ____________

OTHER THINGS I NEED IN ORDER TO BE SAFE

(If possible, put these items in one place so they can be grabbed quickly.)

- [ ] 1. Money (enough for cab fare to any of your safe places)
- [ ] 2. Prescriptions and medications (for yourself and your children)
- [ ] 3. Clothing (an overnight bag packed for yourself and children)
- [ ] 4. Other items:

- Get Safe Plan
- This book
- Driver's License
- Birth Certificates
- Passports
- Bank books
- Credit cards
- Insurance card
- Health records
- Medical, police reports
- Pay stubs
- Address book
- Journal
- Car and house keys
- Social Security cards
- Welfare identification card
- Green card
- Children's favorite toys/blankets
- Items of sentimental value
- Marriage license
- Photos of any of your injuries
- Other:________________________

You may wish to pack a bag in advance and leave it with a friend or neighbor. Also, it may be wise to hide an extra set of keys to the house and car.

Stay Safe Goals

Staying safe is as important as getting safe. The Stay Safe Goals listed below will strengthen you in areas that could sabotage your efforts at abuse-free living. We suggest you begin work on these goals immediately, whether you remain in your relationship or leave it. They will improve your life and jump-start your well-being.

ECONOMIC GOALS

Economic Goal #1. A safe place to live.

▯ A safe place for me to live is ____

____

▯ If "home" is your answer, under what condition is home a "safe" place? ____________

____

____

____

____

Economic Goal #2. A source of income.

▯ I have an adequate and stable source of income. Yes/No

▯ If "no," my task is to identify an assessment and training center that can help me prepare for, and find, a job that I can enjoy doing and do well.

Employment placement service: ______________________ Phone :____________

Training center: (Ex: Jobs Council, Job Corps, Community College):

____ Phone :____________

____ Phone: ____________

____ Phone: ____________

Economic Goal #3. Childcare arrangements, if necessary.

- [ ] A safe and healthy place for my child(ren) to be cared for: ____________________
- [ ] My FREE childcare options include: ____________________
- [ ] Emergency childcare options include: ____________________
- [ ] Written instructions for care of children, especially if child has medical needs, prescriptions, etc.: ____________________

____

____

____

____

Economic Goal #4. Transportation.

- [ ] I have ready access to safe transportation.
- [ ] I have my own car (in good working condition).
- [ ] I have bus fare and know the bus schedule in my area.
- [ ] I have taxi fare put aside for emergencies.
- [ ] Other transportation readily available: ____________________

____

____

RELATIONSHIP GOALS

You have many resources to help you develop your relationship skills. In addition to books, videos, cassettes, and some television programming, you can receive help from your doctor or nurse, most domestic violence shelters, community colleges, YWCA's, and counseling centers. Check to see if your employer has an employee assistance program. If these groups cannot help you themselves, they may know where to send you.

Relationship Goal #1. Self-nurturing Skills

☐ I know how to effectively communicate my affection and respect for those I care about (including myself).

If this statement is not true for me, then my plan to develop this skill is to: (Example: Select a book from the Book List in Part Four, under "Loving Yourself." Begin using the suggestions.) ________________________

____

____

Relationship Goal #2. Parenting Skills

☐ I know how to give my children consistent love and attention, see that they receive the guidance they need, show them appropriate behaviors by the way I act (including not hitting them), be consistent about rules and discipline, limit exposure to violence, and teach them ways to avoid becoming victims of abuse.

If this statement is not true for you, then your plan to develop this skill is to: (Example: Attend local parenting classes, support groups, read books on parenting, watch parenting videos.) ________________________

____

____

Relationship Goal #3. Refusal Skills

▯ I know how to say "no" to people, places, and things that violate my set personal limits (boundaries).

If this statement is not true for me, my plan to develop this skill is to: (Example: Complete the action steps in the "Boundaries" section of this book.) ____________________

____

____

Relationship Goal #4. Assertiveness Skills

▯ I know how to get my needs and reasonable wants met without becoming dishonestly compliant (saying "yes" when I think and feel "no"), or becoming hostile or aggressive.

If this statement is not true for me, then my plan to develop this skill is to: (Example: Rent a video at the library, practice with a trusted friend.) ____________________

____

____

Relationship Goal #5. Conflict Resolving Skills

▯ I know how to settle disagreements and fights in a positive way.

*If this statement is not true for you, then your plan to develop this skill is to: (Example: Enroll in a class on conflict resolution at the YWCA.)*____________________

____

____

"You can do it."

Voices of survivors around the world.

Ending Abuse Action Steps

In Part One we have focused on the beginning stages of ending abuse. The following action steps summarize this section and can help you apply what you have learned to your life even further:

- ☐ 1. From the examples of abuse on pages 14 through 16, compile a list of those you have experienced, or mark them on the checklist.
- ☐ 2. Chart your story of abuse on the Cycle of Abuse, as Stacy did.
- ☐ 3. Think through the risk factors that set you up for an abusive relationship. If those risk factors are still in your life, make a choice to change them.
- ☐ 4. Complete your Get Safe Plan. *(Please do this first!)*
- ☐ 5. Start work on one of your goals from your Stay Safe Goals sheet.

CHECKPOINT
Are you ready to say,
"It's not okay anymore?"
Yes ☐ No ☐

A Voice from the ER

Dear "Sarah"
Please forgive me. It was hectic the night you came to the Emergency Room. I was overwhelmed. The haunted look in your eyes as you told me how you had broken your arm was a sure clue, but in my hurried pace I brushed aside the intuitive sense. My brisk manner and matter-of-fact examination muted your already silent plea for help. I am so sorry. I learned so much from you. I learned to listen to the silence. I hope you have gotten the support you need.

Dear "Helen"
Thank you for your persistence in reaching out for help. When you came to the ER the first time, I took care of you. You told me the cut on your forehead was "from a fall." The next time, you had two broken ribs. This time you had "fallen against a chair." When I wheeled you out to the waiting room, you finally told me that your boyfriend had punched you because you had "worn the wrong suit to an office party." Thank you for trusting me to help you. But more than that, I applaud you for proclaiming that day as the day you decided to get safe because you saw yourself as worthwhile.

Kathleen Cary, R.N.

Part 2: Taking Charge

Sylvia

July

5,

1995

Taking Charge

In Part One of this book, we focused on the initial steps in ending your abuse. Now we turn our focus to "Taking Charge." Deciding to end abuse is the first step, taking charge of your life is the second.

MOVING INTO YOUR SUCCESS ZONE!

"Taking charge" means many things to many people. To us, it means taking charge of your decisions, actions, and reactions in order to lead a responsible and loving life. To those who have been beaten down physically, emotionally, and spiritually, "taking charge" may mean taking power and control in order to get even with their abusers. While this attitude is understandable, it is not the effective answer if you want to move into true personal success.

The effective attitude, or motive, behind taking charge is not to get even but to get free.

In reality, you have at least three choices when it comes to taking charge:

1. Become aggressive and over-controlling, like your abuser(s).
2. Become passive and under-controlling, accepting anything that comes along.
3. Become assertively responsible and self-controlled.

Choice #3 is where success will happen. By "success," we mean making good choices for your safety and well-being and those in your care.

The three choices listed on the previous page can be pictured like this:

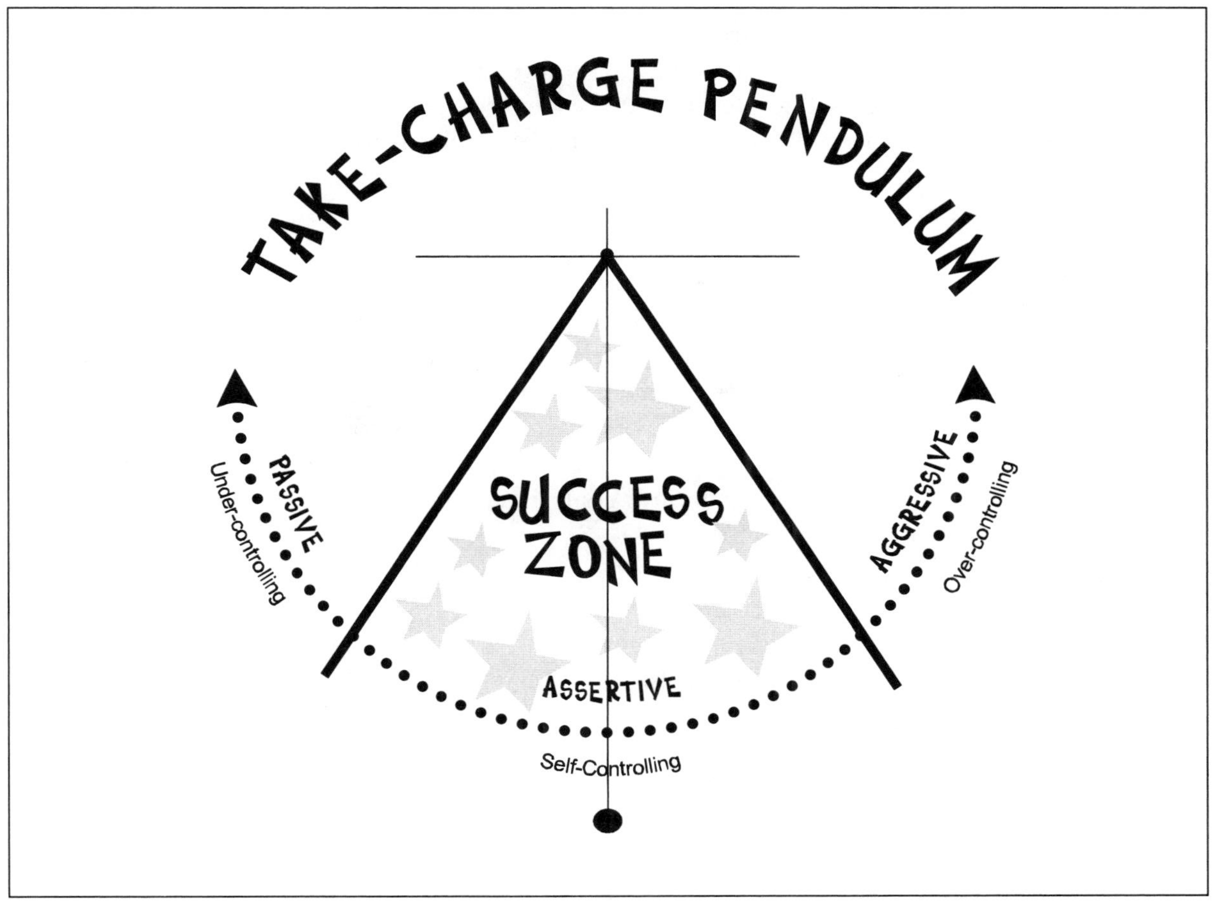

"Don't waste your power on getting even."
G.E.

The Take-Charge Tool: The Cycle of Personal Responsibility

We are very pleased to present an important take-charge, get-free tool called the Cycle of Personal Responsibility (COPR). The COPR was created by survivors of domestic violence in the spring of 1995. Kricket Nicholson, Executive Director of Domestic Violence Services of Pendleton, Oregon, and Stacy Pierce, whom you met earlier in this book, wanted to offer the women at the shelter a step-by-step alternative to the cycle of abuse. They were frustrated over the damaging patterns that trapped abused people, and so the cycle was born on a piece of scratch paper one afternoon in March.

Even in its raw, undeveloped form, the new alternative brought hope to the women at the shelter and in support groups. It gave them a path out of abuse. In the very first week it was presented, three women got jobs. Since then, many others have stepped out of abuse and into successful responsibility for their own lives. Those who have adopted the cycle find it useful for all decision-making, and parents are pleased with the way it is helping their children learn to accomplish tasks and goals. We have included some of their success stories at the end of this section.

The Cycle of Personal Responsibility includes these steps:

1. Awareness - I become aware of the problem.
2. Options - I check out my options.
3. Choice - I choose an option.
4. Plan - I make a plan.
5. Do It! - I carry out the plan.

These steps are pictured and described on the following pages.

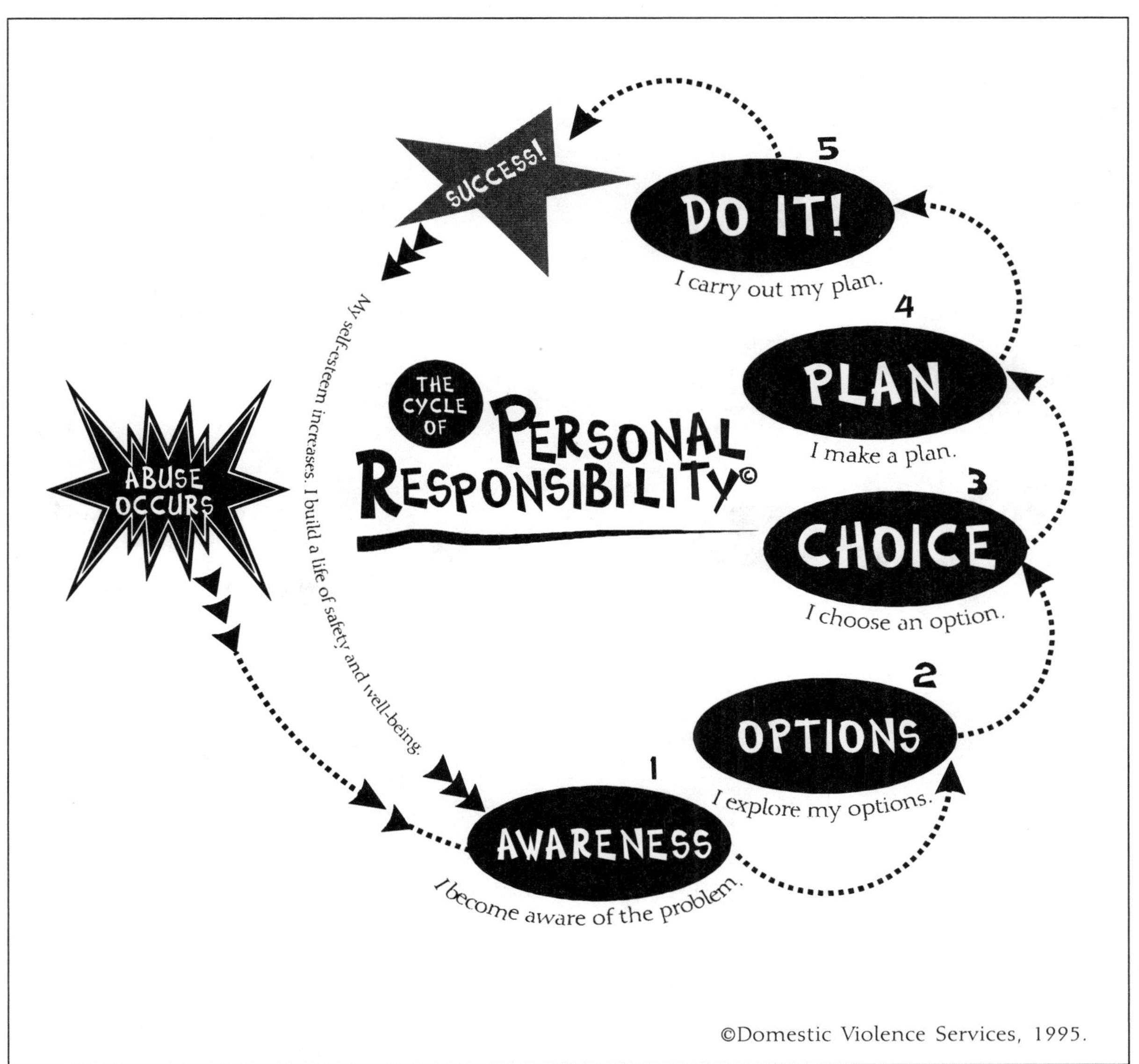

THE CYCLE OF PERSONAL RESPONSIBILITY©
ABUSE OCCURS
1
AWARENESS
I become aware of the problem.
2
OPTIONS
I explore my options.
3
CHOICE
I choose an option.
4
PLAN
I make a plan.
5
DO IT!
I carry out my plan.
SUCCESS!
My self-esteem increases. I build a life of safety and well-being.

The Cycles Compared

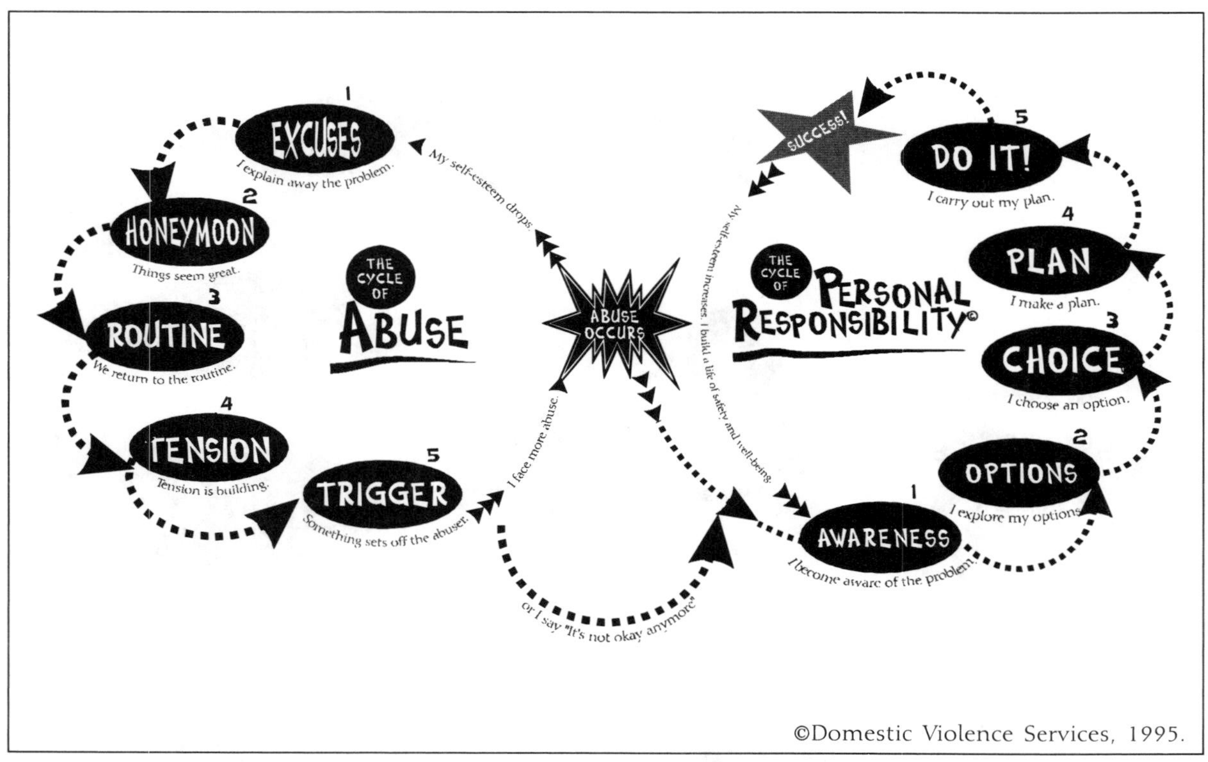

The Cycle of Abuse
1 Excuses
I explain away the problem.
2 Honeymoon
Things seem great.
3 Routine
We return to the routine.
4 Tension
Tension is building.
5 Trigger
Something sets off the abuser.
I face more abuse.
My self-esteem drops.
Abuse occurs
or I say "It's not okay anymore"
The Cycle of Personal Responsibility©
1 Awareness
I become aware of the problem.
2 Options
I explore my options.
3 Choice
I choose an option.
4 Plan
I make a plan.
5 Do it!
I carry out my plan.
Success!
My self-esteem increases. I build a life of safety and well-being.
©Domestic Violence Services, 1995.

HOW THE COPR WORKS IN A REAL-LIFE STORY

In Part One, you saw how Stacy's abuse story looked on the Cycle of Abuse. Now we will see how her take-charge story fits onto the steps of the Cycle of Personal Responsibility (COPR).

Stacy's story on the COPR:

1. AWARENESS

A Saturday in March, 1989. My husband verbally abuses my 2-year old son. Later that day my husband's hands are around my neck. My son is calling me and I can't get to him. My awareness is that I want my kids safe.

2. OPTIONS

I sort through my options. I can stay or leave.

3. CHOICE

I choose to leave.

4. PLAN

I will leave on Monday when my husband goes to get the mail.

5. DO IT!

I leave in the morning.

Two weeks later, I agree to meet my husband in the park. He is late and I am angry. He threatens to take the kids to Hawaii where I will never see them again. I get the kids back in my car and while I am trying to leave, my husband breaks my nose.

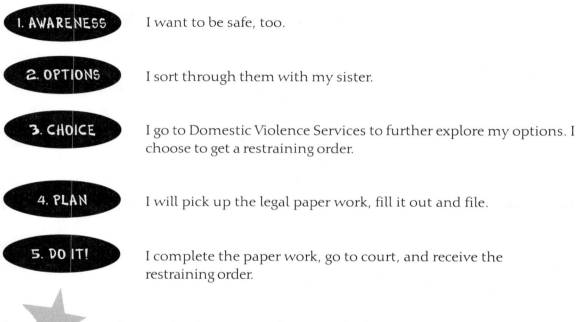

1. AWARENESS I want to be safe, too.

2. OPTIONS I sort through them with my sister.

3. CHOICE I go to Domestic Violence Services to further explore my options. I choose to get a restraining order.

4. PLAN I will pick up the legal paper work, fill it out and file.

5. DO IT! I complete the paper work, go to court, and receive the restraining order.

Success - I am no longer afraid in my own home and I choose not to believe the threats my husband makes about taking the children away.

"Each time I go full cycle in my COPR, I have success. For me success has been many things: safety, emotional wellness, two wonderful children, a healthy significant relationship, money, power and control over myself, and, most important, self-love."

Notice how the COPR can be used again and again as problems and challenges arise. To see how you can apply the COPR to your situation, let's look closely at each step and watch a plan unfold.

Step One: Awareness

The first step of the Cycle of Personal Responsibility is "Awareness." In this step, you become aware you have a problem. Many women are battered and abused for a period of time before they become aware that they aren't at fault, that they won't take it anymore, and that they can do something about it. When awareness presents itself to us, we are forced to pay attention and to make a choice.

COMMON BLOCKS TO AWARENESS

It may be helpful for you to see what often blocks awareness. Look at this list and ask yourself if any similar blocks have been, or are, present in your life:

1. I excuse or tolerate the abuse because the kids need a father.
2. My partner says something like, "Of course I love you. If I didn't, I'd leave."
3. My partner has convinced me that no one else would want me.
4. My partner minimizes his behavior, saying things like "I was teaching you a lesson for your own good."
5. Abuse seems normal to me because I grew up in an abusive home.
6. My partner refers to the abuse as "just an accident."
7. I believe I deserve "it" because I don't know how to manage money, or I didn't get dinner made on time, or I'm a nag, or stupid, or lazy, or too smart for my own good, or any number of other excuses.
8. I believe my partner will stop. I keep believing it won't happen again.
9. I'm embarrassed by the abuse.

WORKING THE COPR WITH "KIM"

To help us work through the COPR, we will focus on "Kim," a woman we have created to represent victims in general. Let's say that as a result of being slapped this morning, Kim has come to the awareness that she is in danger.

Kim's Awareness: I am in danger.

WHAT IS YOUR AWARENESS?

Where are you in the process of awareness? Mark the statement that is closest to your true place of awareness at this moment. Place a date next to your response for future reference.

- ☐ 1. I have come to full awareness that I am being abused and things are out of control. I am ready to take the next step.

- ☐ 2. I have come to full awareness that I am being abused and that things are out of control. I am frightened and don't know what to do next.

- ☐ 3. I think I am being abused but am confused about it.

- ☐ 4. I suspect I am being abused but feel helpless to change it.

- ☐ 5. I don't know if what I am experiencing is abuse, I just know I don't like what's happening.

- ☐ 6. Other: ______________________________

____

____

"In my experience, we do not change until we have some kind of awakening to the fact we are going to lose something we are not prepared to live without if we do not change."

Ernie Larsen

Step Two: Options

The second step of the COPR is "Options." In this step, you list possible solutions to your problem. When you are caught in a bad situation, it can feel like you don't have any options, but you do.

Here are some options open to Kim, and to you:

KIM'S OPTIONS

1. Leave the place where the abuse is happening.
2. Contact a domestic violence shelter for assistance.
3. Get into a support group, possibly through the domestic violence shelter.
4. Work through this book to learn more about getting safe and staying safe.
5. Call 911 - get police assistance.
6. Identify other safe people and safe places.

YOUR OPTIONS

According to your answer on page 44 about your own awareness, what options are possible for you?

____

____

____

____

____

____

____

____

____

____

____

____

____

If the abuse you are experiencing is not physical, the internal damage is still violent. Your options list, however, may be different than Kim's, depending on your situation. For example, in addition to leaving the place where the abuse is happening, your options might include things like:

- [ ] 1. Attend a support group.
- [ ] 2. See a counselor.
- [ ] 3. Take a class for assertiveness training (to learn how to say "no" effectively).
- [ ] 4. Say "no" to abuse in a planned way.
- [ ] 5. Go to another room, away from the abuse.
- [ ] 6. Go for a walk or a drive.
- [ ] 7. Call a friend for support.

Step Three: Choice

The third step of the COPR is "Choice." In this step, you choose one or more of the options you listed in Step Two. Let's see how the process works by watching Kim make her choices. While the options Kim selected are good ones, they may not be the ones you would choose for yourself.

KIM'S CHOICES

Here are Kim's options from Step Two:

1. Leave the place where the abuse is happening.
2. Contact a domestic violence shelter for assistance.
3. Get into a support group, possibly through the domestic violence shelter.
4. Work through this book to learn more about getting safe and staying safe.
5. Call 911 - get police assistance.
6. Identify other safe people and safe places.
7. Stay in the relationship, hoping things will get better.

Kim chose the first two options. She decided to:

(1) leave the place where the abuse was happening, and

(2) contact a domestic violence shelter for assistance.

Remember: None of us makes the perfect choice every time. "Perfect" is not the important thing; making a choice away from abuse is what is important.

YOUR CHOICES

From your options list on page 45, which one(s) would you choose?

HAVING DOUBTS

It is common to doubt your choices at a time like this and ask yourself questions such as those listed on the next page. We suggest you prepare yourself for these doubts by answering your questions before you ask them. We have helped you get started on this by listing actual answers from survivors. You may adopt their answers or write your own. The important thing is to be prepared within yourself to withstand your doubts.

COMMON SELF-DOUBTING QUESTIONS DURING CHOICEMAKING

1. What if I fail?
    - I will try another choice on my "Options" list.
    - No one is perfect.
    - This is a process that takes practice.
    - There is no failure in trying.
    - There are people to help me make another choice.

2. What if my choice doesn't work?
    - Then I will try another approach.
    - A bad reaction doesn't mean the choice was bad. It just means the choice didn't work this time.

3. What if he finds out and things get worse?
    - I need to have my safety plan in place and follow it.

4. What if I don't have what it takes to follow through?
    - I am not alone.
    - What I don't know I can find out from others. No one knows everything.
    - I do have what it takes.

5. What if I find out things weren't so bad after all?
    - Abuse is always bad.
    - I can have a better life.
    - I will not settle for a not-so-bad life.

What other questions do you think your doubts will ask? Write the questions and your answers in this space.

"Courage can be just as infectious as fear."

Alice Miller

Step Four: Plan

The fourth step of the COPR is "Plan." In this step, you make a plan based on your choices from Step 3. In our example, Kim made these choices:

1. Leave the place where the abuse is happening.
2. Contact a local domestic violence shelter.

MAKING A PLAN

To make a plan, ask this question for each choice you make: "What must be done for this choice to happen?" Your answers become your plan's action steps.

KIM'S PLAN

In Kim's case, she asked "What must be done in order for me to leave the place where the abuse is happening?" Her answers were:

1. I must identify a safe way to exit the building.
2. I must locate any people or items needed to get help in leaving (See "Get Safe Plan," page 27).
3. I must anticipate a safe time to leave.

Important note: This is an ideal plan. However, you may need to leave before these action steps are organized and completed. Your safety and the safety of your children, if you have them, is more important than following each step of your plan.

To complete her plan, Kim next asked: "What must be done for me to contact a local domestic violence shelter?" Her answers were:

1. I must locate a shelter or similar safe place in my area.
2. I must get to a safe phone as soon as possible.
3. I must know or be able to get the phone number and address of the shelter.

YOUR PLAN

Using your choices from Step Three, answer the question "What must be done for this choice to happen?"

List your answers in the form of a plan, as above:

Step Five: Do It!

The fifth step of the COPR is "Do It!" In this step, you follow your plan from Step Four. Kim's plan looked like this:

1. Leave the place where the abuse is happening.
   - Identify a safe way to exit the building.
   - Locate any people or items needed to get help in leaving.
   - Anticipate a safe time to leave.

2. Contact a local domestic violence shelter.
   - Get to a safe phone to call the shelter.
   - Call the shelter.

KIM'S "DO IT!" STEP

Let's watch Kim carry out her plan. At the right time, she:

- Quietly collects the kids, keys, cash, medications, this book, her safety plan, etc.
- Moves quickly and quietly toward the safe exit.
- Leaves.
- Walks or drives to a safe location where there is a telephone.
- Calls the shelter for assistance.
- Follows their instructions for the next step in staying safe.

If Kim's plan gets blocked, she will get out any way she can. Many survivors suggest having an alternative plan in place in case the first plan doesn't work out. This is good advice. Flexibility is important when making plans and carrying them out.

In our example, Kim has now moved to safety and has declared by her actions that "It's not okay anymore." She has completed each step of the Cycle of Personal Responsibility.

You may find, as many people have, that you "jump cycles" a few times before working your way clear through the Cycle of Personal Responsibility. We will explain cycle-jumping later in this section.

For now, stop a moment and let yourself imagine that you have just completed Kim's plan. Feel it in your mind and spirit. Note the many emotions running through you. Just as you have imagined Kim carrying out her plan, someone somewhere is really doing it right now. Wish her well.

YOUR "DO IT!" STEP

In your mind, walk through your own plan from Step Four. We encourage you to write it down as if it were happening now, as we did for Kim.

____

____

____

____

____

____

____

____

____

Step Five is the final step of the COPR, but it is not the end of the freedom story. There are two more exciting results of taking charge of your life: Success and Self-Esteem.

"When I dare to be powerful, to use my strength in the service of my vision, then it becomes less important whether or not I am afraid."

Andre' Lorde

Success and Self-Esteem

What is success? In terms of the Cycle of Personal Responsibility, success is any movement toward safety and well-being. *Any movement*. It is not necessary to always complete the cycle in order to be successful. Setting yourself free is a process full of tiny success steps. Success, no matter what its size, makes you hungry for more. It drives you to do it again and again, creating a force that carries you to more success and higher self-esteem.

WHAT IS SELF-ESTEEM?

Self-esteem is what you think and how you feel about yourself. High self-esteem means you think well of yourself. Low self-esteem means you think poorly of yourself.

HOW DO SUCCESS AND SELF-ESTEEM WORK TOGETHER?

Success and self-esteem feed each other. Success increases your self-esteem and self-esteem leads you to more and more success. By taking charge of your life, you step onto the upward path of personal fulfillment.

HOW IS SELF-ESTEEM DEVELOPED?

Your self-esteem is developed by your impressions of yourself based on your successes, failures, and other people's opinions, comments, and actions toward you. This is why words and actions toward children are so important - they form their early identity. In a perfect world, we would each think well of ourselves. In the real world, most of us struggle to believe we are valuable.

The following messages are typical of those that build or lower self-esteem. Mark the messages in either column that resemble those you have adopted about yourself.

<u>Messages that Build Self-esteem</u>

- ☐ 1. You are gifted and capable.
- ☐ 2. You are desirable.
- ☐ 3. I'm lucky to have you in my life.
- ☐ 4. You are bright, attractive, sensible, valuable, powerful, a winner.

<u>Messages that Lower Self-esteem</u>

- ☐ 1. You'll never amount to anything.
- ☐ 2. Nobody would ever want you.
- ☐ 3. You are lucky to have me.
- ☐ 4. You are stupid, ugly, brainless, worthless, a loser, good-for-nothing.

(Messages that build self-esteem, con't.)

☐ 5. You are able to be a great wife (mother, student, person).

☐ 6. I'm here to help you.

☐ 7. You're no bother.

Add others:

____

(Messages that lower self-esteem, con't.)

☐ 5. You're an awful wife (mother, student, person).

☐ 6. You're on your own.

☐ 7. You drive me nuts.

Add others:

____

Some people with high self-esteem enter abusive relationships unknowingly. Either they have not seen or recognized the signs of abuse or they believe love and a positive attitude will overcome the abuse. However, high self-esteem and abuse cannot live together for long. Either the victim will end the abuse or the esteem will drop.

When your self-esteem is low, it is common to feel worthless, hopeless, stupid, overwhelmingly guilty and/or ashamed. These feelings can make it very difficult to muster the courage to take charge of your life and move away from abuse. But you are no stranger to difficulties. You already are a person of courage. Now you can apply that courage to your own life in new ways. Life is hard, but life is best when you take charge of it.

RE-BUILDING SELF-ESTEEM

When you say "yes" to taking charge of your life, you begin re-building your self-esteem. Gradually, or in some cases quickly, you reverse the downward spiral of abuse and learn to act responsibly for your own good and the good of others. You unpack and discard the lies that keep you hopeless, and you pack in the truth that sets you free.

For example, Kim believed she was to blame for her abuse. Her "truth" was not reality. The actual truth was that Kim was in a relationship with an abuser who would make a reason to hit her. She had the power to end it.

High self-esteem is built on truth and accomplishment. The following truth statements will help you begin speaking truth to yourself. Read each one slowly, pausing briefly to think it through. Select those that seem to help you the most and use them often to remind yourself of your value.

TRUTH STATEMENTS TO BUILD YOUR SELF-ESTEEM

- [ ] 1. I am good enough.
- [ ] 2. I can trust myself to make good choices.
- [ ] 3. I have the right to be here.
- [ ] 4. I am a unique and special person.
- [ ] 5. It's okay to make mistakes.
- [ ] 6. I don't have to be perfect.
- [ ] 7. I deserve to be happy.
- [ ] 8. I can disagree and it's okay.
- [ ] 9. I can express my true feelings.
- [ ] 10. I am a valuable person just as I am.
- [ ] 11. I have a wide range of talents, skills and abilities.
- [ ] 12. I am an attractive and likeable human being.
- [ ] 13. I can choose to see the best in my situation.
- [ ] 14. There are healthy-minded people waiting to love me.
- [ ] 15. I am a powerful and capable person.
- [ ] 16. I have lived through a lot and I can make my life better.
- [ ] 17. Success comes in small steps and I am able to take them, one at a time.

ACCOMPLISHMENT AND SELF-ESTEEM

An accomplishment is simply doing something positive and satisfying. You are accomplishing something positive by reading this book, completing the exercises, and by every act you take to nurture yourself and those around you. Nurture includes everything from stopping to drink a cup of tea while listening to a soothing CD, to lovingly brushing your child's hair, to making and keeping a doctor's appointment.

Each accomplishment is a brick you place in the foundation of your self-esteem. What will you accomplish today?

Success Tips!

Here are three more skills that will increase your success and self-esteem. You can begin using them right away. Like any new skill, it will take time to get it right. Remember, perfection isn't required for success, determination is.

SUCCESS TIP #1: CYCLE-JUMPING

Cycle-Jumping is the art of jumping out of the cycle of abuse each time you realize you are in it. At any point in the cycle of abuse, you can jump to the Cycle of Personal Responsibility. Here is how cycle-jumping works:

Let's say you are successfully working the COPR when your partner comes home in a rage, kicks the dog across the room, pushes your son aside, and verbally assaults you. His abusive actions are the "Fire!" we talked about in Part One. You are caught off-guard. Instead of activating your Get Safe Plan, you choose to endure the abuse. That night, he apologizes and promises to get help. You become aware that you have entered the "honeymoon" stage on the cycle of abuse. You say to yourself, "I've been here before. It feels good now, but based on past experience, I can predict what's coming and I don't want it."

At this point you jump cycles over to the COPR. By recognizing the stage you were in on the cycle of abuse, you have already passed "awareness" on the COPR and are now at "Options." You think through your options, make your choice, create a plan, and do it.

Here is another example of cycle-jumping:
You become aware that you have left the COPR and are on the cycle of abuse somewhere between "tension" and "trigger." Abuse could happen at any time. Let's say your partner's abuse is triggered by jealousy. He has been ridiculing women he sees flirting on television and you know he will be looking for a reason to accuse you of flirting, too, and even worse. On this day, he is waiting in the car for you after work. On your way out of the office, a male co-worker stops you to ask a work-related question. From experience, you sense seeing this encounter could trigger your partner into abusing you. You weigh your options and quickly make a plan. You walk to the car but you do not get in it. You greet your partner and engage him in conversation to sense his mood. You sense he has been triggered

by seeing you speak with your associate, and you walk back into the building and carry out Get Safe measures you have already prepared.

No one should have to live like this, yet many victims do. If you choose to stay in the relationship, do what you can to protect yourself. Learn the COPR, and when you enter the cycle of abuse, jump cycles and take charge at the earliest moment.

Abuse is familiar territory for a victim; taking charge of life is not. Gradually, as you change your pattern, taking charge will become your familiar response. During the transition, cycle-jumping will be an important success skill you will want to adopt.

SUCCESS TIP #2: TAKE-CHARGE WORDS

Take-charge words are simply words that state your feelings and choices in clear ways. Clarity is important because abusers like to pick apart how you say things in order to keep the focus off of their actions.

Adjusting your talking pattern, therefore, can help protect you and speed your freedom from abuse. These tips can also increase your success in other parts of your life.

While we don't suggest putting off your escape from abuse until you have mastered the right words, we do want you to be aware of the power of the words you use. We also want to make it clear that you do not owe your abuser well-spoken words. This success tip is for *your* protection and empowerment.

We have asked communications expert, Dr. Jerry Canning, to comment on this and give us examples of effective and ineffective talking patterns:

TAKE-CHARGE TALKING PATTERNS

"You want your words to work for you, not against you. Here are three examples of both:

1. UNCERTAIN VS. CONFIDENT

Uncertain Language - INEFFECTIVE

'I kind of think maybe seeing a counselor or someone might be a good idea. Do you think maybe it would?'

Confident Language - EFFECTIVE

'I am going to see a counselor. Will you come, too?'

Tip: Even when using confident words, your feelings may be uncertain. Comment on that directly. 'I know my voice is trembling, but I mean what I say.'

2. NON-SPECIFIC VS. SPECIFIC

Non-specific Language - INEFFECTIVE

'I won't stand for being beaten up again like you did the other day.'

Specific Language - EFFECTIVE

'I won't stand for another slap like the one you gave me the other day.'

Tip: You want the other person to 'let in' what you say rather than start an argument about an exaggeration, so be accurate in what you call it.

3. PERSON-FOCUSED VS. BEHAVIOR-FOCUSED

Person-Focused Language - INEFFECTIVE

'I won't put up with your thoughtlessness and insensitivity any more.'

Behavior-Focused Language - EFFECTIVE

'I won't put up with your put-downs in front of other people any longer.'

Tip: While your abuser is thoughtless and insensitive, you want him to focus on his unacceptable behavior.

Part of taking charge of your life, then, means taking charge of your words. These confident, specific and act-centered talking patterns will increase your chances of getting results, keeping side issues out of the discussion, and maintaining control of the conversation."

SUCCESS TIP #3: KNOWING YOUR MIND'S STRENGTHS

Another way to increase your self-esteem and success is to know the way your mind is wired. We have asked Learning Styles expert Carol Funk to speak with you about it:

You have many strengths, and you can use those strengths to be a successful person. Even if at this moment you don't feel strong, you are.

You were born with these built-in strengths. Scientists have proven that each human mind is pre-wired for a certain style of thinking, or learning. When you use this pre-wired style, you are using your natural strength. This is called your learning style. If you and I could sit and talk, perhaps over coffee or a glass of soda, we would quickly discover what your learning strengths are and how they can help you live free of abuse and self-hatred. You would learn that your brain has very specific ways of receiving and processing information. Your "style" effects such things as remembering details from a book, how you summarize the news, how you give directions, how you organize your life, and how you interact with people. When you discover your learning style strengths, you can begin to put these strengths to work for you in your world.

Since we are not sitting somewhere talking, but rather you are reading my message on this page, please remember this: like every human being, you have the built-in strength to live a powerful and effective life. I have watched many people move quickly and confidently into claiming their strengths after discovering their learning style. You can, too. You have a choice to make, and I hope you will say "yes" to the person you are inside."

Note: If you want more information about learning styles, we suggest you contact your local school district or library.

Success Stories

LEE

After 11 years I broke away from an abusive husband. I was on my own with four kids for a year, then he coerced me into coming back. I suffered more violent abuse for five more years. He nearly strangled me to death, then wanted sex. That was it for me. I left again and stayed away this time. Today I work with other battered women, supporting them in their journey of positive changes. I have also been in a non-abusive relationship for 14 years now.

MARVELLA

Married to an abusive man for 12 years and visually challenged, I felt trapped and isolated. I heard a program on the radio about Domestic Violence Services. I hoped they could help, so I called them. After some time in the shelter, my son and I now have our own apartment and are doing very well. It feels good to be happy and free again. I still attend the support group at DVS and continue to learn and support others. I use the COPR in my life daily.

SYLVIA

I wasn't allowed to work or spend money on myself. My oldest child was beginning to treat me the same way his father did. After calling a domestic violence crisis line, I went into shelter, attended support groups and learned so much. My husband asked me to come back and I did return, but now we are playing by different rules. Things have changed. I even bought myself a ring and a bracelet, the first gifts I ever bought for myself.

LYNN

After only a few months of marriage the abuse started. I knew I didn't want to live that way so I got help from a domestic violence program. I attended support groups and learned a lot about myself and how to use the COPR in my everyday life. I now own my own beauty shop and am much better off alone than with an abusive partner. I just want others to know there are other choices - the COPR helps you to see the choices and gives you the steps to get to those choices.

AMY

Although I broke away, my abuser continued to stalk me. He always found me. My children and I lived in terror. We had been in many shelters and I was becoming convinced that I was crazy. Finally, a shelter in a little rural town offered us love, support, acceptance, and a tool called the Cycle of Personal Responsibility. I have used the COPR to rebuild my life and my self-esteem. I continue using it to progress from a life of chaos and fear to a new life of hope for the future for me and my children. Today I know how to make good choices and I know how freedom feels - wonderful! Today I feel, at last, like I finally have a life!

Amy

February

7,

1995

The Story of Kricket Nicholson

Survivor of Partner Violence and Executive Director of Domestic Violence Services, Pendleton, Oregon, and Co-creator of the Cycle of Personal Responsibility

The night Kricket Nicholson tried to run over her boyfriend was the night the light went on in her head. She was in trouble. Now, years later and healed from the distorted thinking and harmful patterns that kept her in damaging relationships, she leads other women out of their cycle of violence. Here is her story:

"I grew up thinking that marriages were disposable. If the guy didn't work out, you got rid of him. In the years leading up to marriage, I went through several relationships with boys and at 18 I entered The Salvation Army's White Shield Home for Unwed Mothers. It was the first time I felt accepted by other girls and the first time I didn't feel alone.

"Later, I married a workaholic. We lived in the country and started accepting foster kids, the difficult kind that needed country air. The challenges of parenting my own children plus the foster kids led me to become a student of parenting. I read all the self-help books I could find on the subject.

"In reading about what kids need, I saw what I hadn't received as a child. My eyes were opened to new ways of looking at life. I eagerly grabbed the tools I was learning and practiced using them. I joined a support group and saw that I was not the only depressed housewife. The group gave me the same acceptance I had felt at the White Shield Home.

"I was excited about my growth but was aware of the hopelessness of our marriage. I took the kids and left, believing life would be better. It was, for awhile, and then my sense of worthlessness led me to drugs and men. Jarred back to reality one day when I was too high to pay attention to my kids, I stopped, got help from the Salvation Army, and remarried my ex-husband. It didn't work.

"My next relationship was my last destructive one before turning the corner on well-being. It ended the night I determined to either commit suicide or murder. A curb kept my car from hitting the man I was fighting with. While circling the parking lot to avoid the curb, I 'came to' and got help.

"I joined Al-Anon, learned to let go, and came to terms with who I was and what I could be. I got healthier and learned about relationships, then became a caseworker for ten years for The Salvation Army. I learned how to communicate and relaxed about trying to measure up. I discovered my strengths and enjoyed self-acceptance for the first time.

"In 1992, I met and married a man whose self-esteem and love for himself, me and my daughters matched my own. We enjoy a healthy, growing relationship."

Taking Charge Action Steps

In Part Two we have explored the Cycle of Personal Responsibility and outlined the success and self-esteem the cycle can produce in your life. The following action steps summarize this section and can help you apply what you have learned to your life even further:

1. Determine where you are on the "success zone" on page 37. If you are out of the "zone," use the COPR to create a plan that will move you inside the success zone.
2. Practice using the COPR in daily decision-making.
3. Read Stacy's story on the COPR. Write your intended story next to hers.
4. Develop a sense of where you are on either cycle at a given moment and practice cycle-jumping if you enter the cycle of abuse.
5. If you have not completed the steps to the cycle on paper, please do so.
6. Mark your responses to the checklists included in this section.
7. Select the truth statements you most need in your life. Repeat them often.
8. Practice take-charge words with a friend, then begin using them with your abuser.

Part 3: Loving Yourself

Marvella

August

17,

1995

Loving Yourself and Well-Being

Some victims break free of abuse but never break into loving themselves. In fact, loving yourself is an art that many people ignore. We want more for you. Life without abuse is wonderful, but abuse-free living *with* self-love is fabulous!

The idea of loving yourself can sound self-centered or even selfish. It isn't. The kind of self-love we are describing is being good to yourself in ways that bring light and life to you and to those around you.

Loving yourself and well-being are closely linked to each other. In fact, loving yourself is a part of well-being. They don't happen in a day, but the decision to say "yes" to learning to love yourself and to living a life of well-being can happen in a moment. Even this moment.

What is well-being? It is a process, a life-long journey with big rewards. It is a state of thriving in your mind, body and spirit. Thriving is way beyond surviving. It is living fully. Well-being gives you balance through life's ups and downs, celebrations and devastations. It enables you to honor yourself and others by speaking and living out the truth. It is an integrity in your spiritual core that radiates out into your body, mind, world, work, play, finances and relationships.

Well-being requires you to give love to yourself and receive it from others. It is impossible to do this without valuing yourself. When you value yourself, your central belief becomes "I can live a safe and loving life." However, when you give yourself over to shame, guilt, and self-defeat, your central belief becomes "this notion of well-being is just one more sweet dream that won't be a part of my nightmarish life."

(STOP. As you read this last sentence, did you agree that good things aren't for you? If you did, *please hear us as your coaches*, you are valuable, you are precious, and if you are willing, well-being can be yours, one day at a time.)

You arrived in this world with built-in value and it is still there inside you. Still strong. Still beautiful. Still waiting to be believed and applied. Built-in value is like an internal bank account with your name on it. It is yours and nothing you do can empty it. It is there because you are human.

What do you believe about yourself and your destiny? The following Self-Beliefs Checklist will help you find out. In order to unleash love in your life, you must begin clearing it of the false, self-limiting beliefs that hold you back. Some of the most common, and the ones that lead to almost all of our unhappiness, are listed below. In front of each of the following beliefs, circle a "T" for those you believe are TRUE for you, an "F" for those you believe are NOT TRUE for you, and an "M" for those that MAY be true for you today.

SELF-BELIEFS CHECKLIST

I believe:

T F M I can only achieve a limited amount of success.

T F M I am bad, inadequate, unlovable, or unworthy.

T F M Other people make me feel and act the way I do.

T F M I am powerless to change my feelings.

T F M I am powerless to change my life.

T F M I am responsible for people's feelings. (Example: It is up to me to make them happy and when they aren't, it's up to me to fix it.)

T F M Money, love, alcohol and other drugs, clothes, approval, sex, a great body and/or control over others will make me happy.

T F M Anger, pouting, or the silent treatment will get me what I want.

T F M The more others do what I want the happier I will be.

T F M Pain is my destiny and joy and peace are not mine to have.

T F M It is too late to take charge of my life.

T F M I am unable to make positive and lasting changes.

SIGNS AND EFFECTS OF LOVE AND UNLOVE

Like the Self-Beliefs Checklist, the following lists will help you measure where you are in loving yourself and in well-being. By marking the items in each list that are true in your own life, a personal profile will emerge. Use it as a guide in making choices for your growth.

SIGNS OF NOT LOVING YOURSELF

It is likely that you are a person who does not love yourself if:

- ☐ 1. You allow others to define who you are.
- ☐ 2. You don't know yourself very well.
- ☐ 3. You are unclear about what you want.
- ☐ 4. You are satisfied if you are just surviving.
- ☐ 5. You allow his promises to change to keep you in an unhealthy relationship.
- ☐ 6. You are unaware of your own feelings.
- ☐ 7. You have a high level of anxiety.
- ☐ 8. You are often victimized.
- ☐ 9. You suffer a lot of stress-related illnesses (such as stomachaches, headaches, ulcers, hives, colitis, panic attacks).
- ☐ 10. You don't have guilt-free fun.
- ☐ 11. You have difficulty with close relationships.
- ☐ 12. You have trouble accepting gifts and compliments.
- ☐ 13. You have trouble giving gifts with no "strings" attached.
- ☐ 14. You sabotage your own progress and success.
- ☐ 15. You often feel hopeless and helpless.
- ☐ 16. You feel guilty when you stand up for yourself or act assertively.
- ☐ 17. You tend to be overly responsible or are very irresponsible.
- ☐ 18. You tend to give in to others instead of taking care of yourself.
- ☐ 19. You don't feel loved, accepted, capable or worthwhile.
- ☐ 20. You feel like you don't belong.
- ☐ 21. You have trouble communicating about yourself.
- ☐ 22. You tend to stay in relationships that are harmful.

The Effects of Not Loving Yourself

The following statements are often true of people who struggle with loving themselves. Mark those that are true of you.

When you don't love yourself:

- ☐ 1. You accept anything that is dished out, tolerating neglect and abuse.
- ☐ 2. You become easily discouraged.
- ☐ 3. You resist or reject positive people, places and things.
- ☐ 4. You have difficulty forgiving yourself and others.
- ☐ 5. You give in at the expense of your own good.
- ☐ 6. You lack confidence, especially in making decisions.
- ☐ 7. You are often afraid and confused.
- ☐ 8. You live a chaotic life from one crisis to the next.
- ☐ 9. You are driven by the need to be perfect.
- ☐ 10. You believe you don't have rights.
- ☐ 11. You indulge in escapism (fantasy, addictions, compulsions).
- ☐ 12. You don't have clearly defined boundaries and you become entangled with your partners' needs and emotions.
- ☐ 13. You become critical of others and yourself.
- ☐ 14. You confuse love with pity or other intense feelings.
- ☐ 15. You fear opening up and being real with others.
- ☐ 16. You miss out on opportunities to be truly loved.

Signs of Loving Yourself

It is likely that you are a person who loves yourself if:

- ☐ 1. You ask for or find healthy ways to get what you need.
- ☐ 2. You become satisfied only when thriving (not just surviving).
- ☐ 3. You have a strong identity and usually approve of yourself.
- ☐ 4. You love people who also love themselves.
- ☐ 5. You relate only to a partner with whom love is given and received.
- ☐ 6. You let yourself feel anger then find healthy ways to resolve it.
- ☐ 7. You mostly feel secure and clear.
- ☐ 8. You know that you always have choices and the power to choose.
- ☐ 9. You recognize when you are happy and unhappy.
- ☐ 10. You consider alternative behavior and possible consequences before you act.
- ☐ 11. You feel comfortable with most people and authority figures.
- ☐ 12. You take healthy risks to continue to grow personally.
- ☐ 13. You accept and forgive yourself when you make a mistake.
- ☐ 14. You feel free to express any emotion (without hurting self/others).
- ☐ 15. You find satisfying ways to express your creativity.
- ☐ 16. You accept consequences and learn lessons from them.
- ☐ 17. You have confidence in your ability to learn.
- ☐ 18. You take time to become rested and renewed.
- ☐ 19. You honor and nurture your spiritual growth.
- ☐ 20. You have regular medical/dental check ups.
- ☐ 21. You practice a regular exercise program.
- ☐ 22. You maintain a sensible diet.

The Effects of Loving Yourself

The following statements are often true of people who love themselves. Mark those that are true of you.

When you love yourself:

- ☐ 1. You open yourself up to creativity.
- ☐ 2. You deal positively with anger, resentment, and fear.
- ☐ 3. You move to greater peace within yourself and with others.
- ☐ 4. You become a confident person determined to succeed.
- ☐ 5. You respect yourself and others by honoring healthy boundaries.
- ☐ 6. You have hope based on reality.
- ☐ 7. You are willing to take risks that help you grow.
- ☐ 8. You become aware that you are capable of enjoying life and making it better and better.
- ☐ 9. You become more honest with yourself and others.
- ☐ 10. You open yourself up to love.
- ☐ 11. You change your focus from what is wrong about you to what is right about you.
- ☐ 12. You take responsibility for yourself.
- ☐ 13. You claim your value and potential.
- ☐ 14. You become more humble, joyful, generous, peaceful, assured, free, harmonious, and healthful.

CHECKPOINT
Are you satisfied with how you love yourself?
Yes ☐ No ☐

Loving Yourself By Setting Boundaries

One of the keys to loving yourself is setting healthy limits, or boundaries, around your life. Boundaries are a part of all healthy and respectful relationships, so it is vital that you become skilled at forming yours. Abuse is always a violation of boundaries. Weak boundaries, then, can put you in real danger.

WHAT IS A BOUNDARY?

A boundary is a clear line between what is you and what is not you, between what is your responsibility and what is not, between what you will tolerate and what you won't, and between what you have control over and what you don't.

A boundary can be compared to a fence you build around yourself with a gate and key that you control. As the one in charge of your life, it is up to you to let what is good for you come through the gate and to keep what is bad for you outside the gate. Let the good in and keep the bad out.

BOUNDARIES OR WALLS?

What is the difference between boundaries and walls? Boundaries protect; walls imprison.

When children and adults are caught in abusive relationships, they are left with deep wounds of fear and distrust. Unless victims get help in healing these wounds, the soreness will remain. To protect themselves from getting hurt even more, victims often build walls around their wounded selves. These walls become private prisons of disappointment, survival, and fear. They may keep certain threatening people, places, and things out, but the painful memories and fears remain inside.

Walls aren't easily removed. Boundaries, on the other hand, are flexible. We like to compare boundaries with Gortex fabric. It keeps the rain from soaking through to the skin of the person wearing it, but it also lets excess heat escape from the body so that the person remains dry and comfortable. The fabric "breathes." In the same way, a healthy boundary system lets you breathe. It protects you from harsh elements yet allows you to pursue life without unnecessary discomfort.

SETTING BOUNDARIES

Since you are in charge of your life and have the responsibility to lovingly protect yourself from things that would limit or harm you, we suggest you work toward setting boundaries around your:

- Body
- Values
- Attitudes
- Beliefs
- Feelings
- Desires
- Thoughts
- Behavior
- Talents
- Time
- Choices
- Relationships
- Opinions
- Children
- Work
- Giving
- Creativity
- Love and care of self

COMMON QUESTIONS ABOUT BOUNDARIES

Since this book is a guide and not a lengthy text, we encourage you to read the books on boundaries we have listed in "Part Four: Other Helps." You may also want to seek the help of a coach, counselor or other trained professional as you continue forming new boundaries.

To get you started, here are short answers to common boundary questions:

1. How do I know what a good boundary looks like?

   A good boundary enables you to feel safe and encourages your personal growth. It sets you free to do what is best.

2. Won't boundaries upset people?

   Sometimes others will react to new standards/boundaries. Any change can be unsettling to them. However, treating yourself with respect is never wrong or bad.

3. Is setting boundaries a selfish thing to do?

Good boundaries serve others as well as yourself. They take the guesswork out of relationships, and save your energy and commitment for people and activities you most love.

4. If someone wants something of me, don't I have to cooperate?

No. You can exercise your power to choose to accept only those "invitations" that are respectful and safe.

5. Can I have boundaries and still be a nice person?

Yes! In fact, you will be a "nicer" person as you set responsible boundaries. If you don't, much of your time will be spent on resentment and regrets.

6. Could setting boundaries cause the abuse to get worse?

Setting boundaries doesn't ever make the abuse get worse. However, saying "no" to a controlling person can trigger a negative reaction. (Note: This is another reason to complete your Get Safe Plan before you boldly announce a new boundary.)

7. What is the biggest benefit of boundaries?

Freedom! Freedom to end abuse, take charge and love yourself.

8. Who can I let through my boundary gate?

Anyone you choose. Say "welcome" to healthy, respectful people, and "keep out" to hurtful people.

Boundaries allow you to "let in" people and activities that support your growth and good. "Safe" people will be those who draw you closer to who you were meant to be spiritually, emotionally, mentally, and physically. They will encourage you to be your most loving, growing self.

PRACTICING BOUNDARIES

You may already have begun setting healthy boundaries in your life, or maybe this is the first time you have ever heard of boundaries. Either way, the list below can be used to set up or strengthen your boundary system. Use the list in a way that is comfortable to you. Select items randomly, or follow them in order.

1. Watch yourself for a week to see what you think, do, and feel when people ask more of you than you want to give them.
2. Pay attention to your body's stress knots and notice when they get tight. Record those times. Are poor boundaries the cause? Did you say "yes" when you wanted to say "no"?
3. Observe other people who seem to be self-controlled and enjoy healthy relationships. Where do you see them setting respectful limits? If you are comfortable with the idea, ask them about it. Many successful people have had to learn about boundaries the hard way and are a great source of help.
4. List the relationships and activities in your life that harm you, upset you, limit you, discourage you, and scare you. Begin thinking about how setting healthy boundaries will relieve you of these burdens and fears.
5. List the relationships and activities in your life that please you, calm you, unleash you, encourage you, and inspire you. Begin thinking about how boundaries would enable this list to grow.
6. Read a book or article about boundaries.
7. Practice saying "no" without feeling like you have to give an excuse or justify your decision.

CHECKPOINT
Are you ready to begin or strengthen your boundary building?
Yes ☐ No ☐

Loving Yourself by Recognizing a Healthy Couple Relationship

While we are exploring the keys to loving yourself, we want to stop for a moment and look at the qualities of a healthy relationship. This checklist will help you measure your present relationship and any future relationships you may have. No relationship is perfect, but a healthy relationship includes growth in these areas.

A healthy couple will:

- ☐ 1. Tolerate individual differences.
- ☐ 2. Accept responsibility for one's own thoughts, feelings, and behavior.
- ☐ 3. Experience a give and take relationship.
- ☐ 4. Have realistic values and expectations.
- ☐ 5. Exchange caring behaviors.
- ☐ 6. Want to know his/her partner and be known.
- ☐ 7. Communicate effectively.
- ☐ 8. Enjoy freedom to express all emotions.
- ☐ 9. Spend time together.
- ☐ 10. Maintain separate identities.
- ☐ 11. Make sure both partners'needs are being met in a balanced way.
- ☐ 12. Share in decision-making.
- ☐ 13. Celebrate their partnership.

Mark the qualities that are present in your current relationship.

LOVING YOURSELF BY EXPRESSING YOUR CREATIVITY

Creativity and loving yourself seem to go together. Many people report that as they begin showing love to themselves, their creativity increases. Others say that as they become more creative, they love themselves more.

Creativity is the in-born ability to express who you most are in ways that are most you. Teresa Wilhelmi is an expert on creativity with this special message for you:

"There is a Turkish proverb that says 'no matter how far you have gone on a wrong road, turn back.' You can turn back from the road of abuse and reclaim your true self. I want to encourage you by saying what I believe with all my heart to be true: Every person, including you, is unique, talented, and has the ability to be highly creative. In my work, I see creative transformation happening all around me in the lives of people who once believed they were uncreative, or doomed to a stale, unfulfilling life.

Inside your brain, you have what it takes to come alive creatively. Like everyone, your brain has both a right and left mode and a way to access them. The right mode is your creative side. As you learn to activate it, you can fill in the blanks of your deep passions.

Abuse often shuts down a person's creative expression and can leave her spirit lifeless. I want to suggest two ways to breathe life back into your creative self.

EXPERIENCE NEW THINGS

First, make choices to experience new things. I have listed some for you, but the possibilities are endless. The smallest effort in trying something new brings tremendous results. Day after day, these tiny steps will increase your sense of taking charge of your life and stimulate your right brain mode. This will lead to more and more creative expression. You will be amazed.

New things to try:

- Read a book instead of talking on the phone or watching television.
- Go into a store you've never visited before.
- Try on an outfit beyond your usual style, even if you don't plan to buy a thing.
- Rearrange a drawer, or cupboard, or room in a way that makes sense to you.
- Take a new way home.
- Ride a bike or put on some skates.
- Play Monopoly and really try to win.
- Put something new, like a pansy, on your salad.
- Wash your curtains and starch them.
- Listen to a new radio station.
- Call in to a talk show or mail a letter to a columnist.
- Frame a greeting card you love.
- Start collecting something regardless of what anyone else thinks of it.
- State your opinion on a social or political issue.

FOCUS ON WHAT IS TRUE ABOUT YOU

Second, I want you to frame these words in your mind and, if it is safe, put them on cards where you can see them throughout the day:

YOU GET WHAT YOU FOCUS ON

I am asking you to frame these words because your biggest challenge will be to focus on the alive, creative person you really are and discard the lies that are disguising the real you.

If you don't feel happy with who you are, it means the real you is hidden. You have lost yourself somewhere, probably by believing lies about yourself. When you lose yourself, you can be drawn to unhealthy people who will control you. They invent your life for you, and you won't like the results because they won't match the life you were invented for.

Each of us must sort out what is true and not true about who we really are. This is a lifelong process, but each step energizes us to continue. I suggest you look at your life as if it were a Treasure Chest. Your goal is to fill the Treasure Chest with what is authentically you and remove from your life what is not.

The following activity is a beautiful and effective way to begin focusing on who you were made to be:

1. Find a box to represent the Treasure Chest of your life. It can be as fancy or as simple as you like.

2. Make or buy small pieces of paper, such as index cards, in four colors.

   - On color #1: Write the negative things you have believed to be true about yourself because you or someone else has said it is true. For example: 'I seem to stir up trouble wherever I go.'

   - On color #2: Write things that are true about you but that you don't like. For example: 'I put myself down to others.'

   - On color #3: Write positive things about yourself you know to be true or that others have said about you. For example: 'I know how to get things done.'

   - On color #4: Write what you want to be true of you that hasn't already been put in the box. For example: 'I am a woman who overcame abuse and learned to love herself and others.'

3. Put all of the cards in the box. Shake it up. Look at them mixed together and tell your self, 'This is my life right now. I need to sort out the truth from the lies.'

4. Sort out the truth from the lies by removing each card that doesn't match the person you believe you are or can be. Leave the cards you believe are really true of you. Add others as you think of them. As you make these choices, you are re-inventing yourself. You are claiming who you believe yourself to be at your deepest part.

5. Focus each day on at least one card from your Treasure Chest. Say, 'This is me and I am learning to show it.'

6. As time goes by, continue adding items to your Treasure Chest such as colors, fabrics, ideas, styles, commentaries, quotes, and your own thoughts.

Learn to treasure yourself. Keep other people's garbage out of your box. It's your turn to come alive! "

Here's to your life!

Loving Yourself Milepost

One day I was driving down an empty country road. There were no other cars, no barns spotting the fields, no groves of trees up ahead, and no landmarks to tell me I was getting anywhere. My mind shifted to other things until a huge cloud of steam started pouring from my car's engine. I pulled to the edge of the road and got out of my car, knowing I was in trouble. I needed help but no cars were coming in either direction, and a gas station was miles away. This was a bad situation, not at all what I had planned.

I was glad I had a cell phone. When I called the towing service, the dispatcher asked me to tell her what milepost I was near on the highway. In order to get help, I had to know where I was. The same is true in life.

Like the country road I took that day, abuse can be a lonely and isolated journey. Like the engine of my car, things can blow up and we get stuck. To get help, we must know where we are. We must look at the situation, study our options, choose the one that is best at the time, make a plan, then do it.

YOUR MILEPOST

To mark an important moment, event, or decision, sometimes people plant their own "milepost." For example, the women whose pictures are on the title pages of this book put a stake in their life's road by saying "As of today, abuse is not okay anymore." It marked the day they began the process of freedom. We could call it their "Loving Yourself Birthday."

You may want to follow their example if you, too, have come to that place of decision. We invite you to join the women in this book, and the others around the world, who celebrate their decision to end abuse, take charge and love themselves. Plant your milestone, then move on down the road of respect, love, and safety.

WAYS TO MARK YOUR MILEPOST

It is enough to know in your own mind that you have come to the place of "It's not okay anymore." It can also be encouraging to create a symbol to remind yourself that you have reached this decision. It is a quiet message from your loving self to your courageous self.

Here are some examples of what others have done to celebrate their "Loving Yourself Birthdays":

- Pounded a stake or other "monument" in the ground somewhere in their yard.
- Planted a flower or a tree.
- Served themselves a quiet cup of tea in a favorite cup.
- Wrote a letter to the world announcing their decision to be free, then addressed it to "The World," didn't put a return address on it, and slipped it in a distant mailbox.
- Bought something new to look at, or touch, or smell, or listen to that reminded them of their decision to be free.
- Went for a drive and took a picture of an inspiring scene to represent their future.
- Bought a book of poetry or wrote a poem of their own.
- Wrote a letter of thanks to someone who has helped them to this point.
- Took a deep breath and smiled at themselves in the mirror. (A good thing to do everyday.)

What will you do? Write it here, if you wish. Or, write to us at the address listed in the front of the book. We will celebrate with you and add your milepost to our list.

IF YOU ARE NOT READY YET

If you have not come to the place of saying "enough," a world of survivors respects the place where you are. They are cheering you on and calling you forward into freedom and love. At the same time, survivors are frightened for you, sad that you are being abused, and frustrated over their helplessness to end it. If you could hear them speak to you, this would be their message:

- Please get safe now.
- We are here to help you.
- Life on this side of abuse is better. Join us.
- We are afraid for you and your kids.
- You can still be working on yourself even if you're not ready to get out.

Where are you on the road? What mileposts have you passed? (For Example: I admitted I am abused, set a new boundary, completed my Get Safe Plan.) ______________________________

____

____

Where are you in either cycle today? I am in the cycle of ____________________at Step ____.
Date: _______________

NO MATTER WHERE YOU ARE

No matter where you are on the road, today - like everyday - is a good time to stop and do something for your personal well-being. Make a good choice, make a choice for change. Eat better, take a walk, enjoy silence with your eyes closed for ten minutes, start reading a classic, refine a piece of your action plan. Do something today for you, for your future. Only you can make it happen.

Some people like to record the good choices they make for themselves. It seems to strengthen them and help them keep at it. You may want to do the same. On these lines, write the choices you make and the date, along with any other notes you wish:

____

____

In Part Three, we have examined what it means to love yourself and move into the process of well-being. We have come to the end of this guide, but not the end of your journey into abuse-free living. The following action steps summarize this section and can help you apply what you have learned to your life even further.

1. Use the checklists in this section as a personal development guide. Move from item to item in your process of building self-love and esteem.
2. Complete the boundary exercises. Practice setting limits.
3. Complete the creativity exercises. Keep filling your Treasure Chest with who you are.
4. Celebrate your effort in reading this book and thinking through your situation.
5. Become a student of abuse-free living.
6. Plant a milepost that celebrates you.

Be patient with yourself. As Kricket Nicholson often quotes, "This is about progress, not perfection.

A Word from Your Coaches

"Home is that sacred space - external or internal - where we don't have to be afraid; where we are confident of hospitality and love".

Brennan Manning

This quote by Brennan Manning reminds us that homes were meant to be safe and welcoming. We want that for you. But that's not all. We want the home inside you to be free of damaging fear and full of confidence, as well.

We have come alongside you in your place of fear and uncertainty to encourage you, give you tools, and show you a new path to personal responsibility and freedom. By this point in the book, some of you will have already begun saying "no" to abuse. Others of you will see this liberating journey as too risky for now. Either way, your value is in place and our respect for you and your courage is constant.

In your home and in your heart, we wish you love and safety.

Greg and Jan

All of your experiences - including the
painful and shameful ones - have value when
you begin using them as tools for growth."

Susan L. Taylor

Part 4: Other Helps

Lee

September

9,

1978

Book List

ENDING ABUSE

Brinegar, Jerry. *Breaking Free*. Minneapolis: CompCare Publishing, 1992.

Levy, Barrie. *In Love and In Danger*. Seattle: Seal Press, 1993.

Walker, Lenore. *The Battered Wife Syndrome*. New York: Springer, 1984.

TAKING CHARGE

Bolton, Richard. *People Skills: How to Assert Yourself, Listen to Others, and Resolve Conflicts.* Englewood Cliffs, NJ: Prentice-Hall, 1985.

Cloud, Henry, and John Townsend. *Boundaries.* Grand Rapids: Zondervan Publishing House, 1992.

Forward, Dr. Susan. *Men Who Hate Women & The Women Who Love Them*. New York: Bantam Books, 1986.

Lerner, Rokelle. *Living In The Comfort Zone*. Deerfield Beach, Fla: Health Communications, Inc., 1995.

Norwood, Robin. *Women Who Love Too Much.* New York: Pocket Books, A Division of Simon & Schuster, Inc., 1985.

Paul, Jordon and Margaret. *Do I Have To Give Up Me to be Loved By You?* Minneapolis: CompCare Publishers, 1989.

Russianoff, Penelope Ph.D., *Why Do I Think I Am Nothing Without A Man?* New York: Bantam Books, 1982.

LOVING YOURSELF

Ban Breathnack, Sarah. *Simple Abundance, A Daybook of Comfort and Joy*. New York: Warner Books, 1995.

Hendricks, Gay and Kathlyn Hendricks. *Conscious Loving*. New York: Bantam Books, 1990.

Louden, Jennifer. *The Woman's Comfort Book, A Self-Nurturing Guide for Restoring Balance In Your Life.* New York: Harper-San Francisco, 1992.

Peck, M. Scott, *The Road Less Traveled*. New York: Simon & Schuster, 1980.

Taylor, Susan L. *In The Spirit, The Inspirational Writings of Susan L. Taylor.* Editor In Chief of Essence Magazine. New York: Harper-Perennial, 1993.

Agencies

In addition to counseling centers, religious groups, and employee assistance programs, there are many agencies in your area and nationally that are prepared to help you, such as:

- Childhelp, USA, 6463 Independence Ave., Woodland Hills, CA 91367
- County Community Health Departments (Government Pages in Phone Book)
- District Attorney's Office, Domestic Violence Task Force (a growing number of DA's offices are creating services for victims, particularly in guiding them through the judicial system)
- Local Women's Domestic Violence Shelter (Yellow Pages under "Shelters" or blue pages under "abuse" or "assault")
- National 24-hour Hotline Number: 1-800-799-SAFE (7233), 1-800-787-3224 (TDD)
- National Resource Center on Domestic Violence
  6400 Flank Dr. Ste. 1300, Harrisburg PA 17112-2778
  1-800-537-2238
- Project: Protect
  1-800-507-2560
- The Salvation Army (White Pages)
- Your doctor, pediatrician, nurse, mid-wife
- YWCA (White Pages)

About the Authors

GREG ENNS has been actively counseling victims and abusers for the past 20 years. He is the founder of Northside Counseling Associates, Salem, Oregon, and was its lead therapist until making a career shift to become a life coach.

Greg's knowledge, passion, and gentle spirit have enabled him to succeed in both human and organizational development as a counselor, human services administrator, and management consultant.

Greg has a Bachelor of Science degree from George Fox College in Newberg, Oregon, a Master of Arts degree from Ashland University in Ashland, Ohio, and certification as an addictions counselor from Oregon Health Sciences University, Alcohol Treatment and Training Clinic in Portland, Oregon.

Greg lives in Salem, Oregon, with his wife and two children.

JAN BLACK is a writer and producer who has focused most of her career on life-empowering projects for children and adults. She is author of Character Foundation Curriculum, a fourteen-book series on character development for children.

Jan currently leads a collaborative team of professionals living out their commitment to educate and equip people to reach their goals and express their individuality.

Jan lives in Salem, Oregon, with her husband. Her grown children and their families live nearby.

Other New Harbinger Self-Help Titles

PMS: Women Tell Women How to Control Premenstrual Syndrome, $13.95
Five Weeks to Healing Stress: The Wellness Option, $17.95
Choosing to Live: How to Defeat Suicide Through Cognitive Therapy, $12.95
Why Children Misbehave and What to Do About It, $14.95
Illuminating the Heart, $13.95
When Anger Hurts Your Kids, $12.95
The Addiction Workbook, $17.95
The Mother's Survival Guide to Recovery, $12.95
The Chronic Pain Control Workbook, Second Edition, $17.95
Fibromyalgia & Chronic Myofacial Pain Syndrome, $19.95
Diagnosis and Treatment of Sociopaths, $44.95
Flying Without Fear, $12.95
Kid Cooperation: How to Stop Yelling, Nagging & Pleading and Get Kids to Cooperate, $12.95
The Stop Smoking Workbook: Your Guide to Healthy Quitting, $17.95
Conquering Carpal Tunnel Syndrome and Other Repetitive Strain Injuries, $17.95
The Tao of Conversation, $12.95
Wellness at Work: Building Resilience for Job Stress, $17.95
What Your Doctor Can't Tell You About Cosmetic Surgery, $13.95
An End of Panic: Breakthrough Techniques for Overcoming Panic Disorder, $17.95
On the Clients Path: A Manual for the Practice of Solution-Focused Therapy, $39.95
Living Without Procrastination: How to Stop Postponing Your Life, $12.95
Goodbye Mother, Hello Woman: Reweaving the Daughter Mother Relationship, $14.95
Letting Go of Anger: The 10 Most Common Anger Styles and What to Do About Them, $12.95
Messages: The Communication Skills Workbook, Second Edition, $13.95
Coping With Chronic Fatigue Syndrome: Nine Things You Can Do, $12.95
The Anxiety & Phobia Workbook, Second Edition, $17.95
Thueson's Guide to Over-The Counter Drugs, $13.95
Natural Women's Health: A Guide to Healthy Living for Women of Any Age, $13.95
I'd Rather Be Married: Finding Your Future Spouse, $13.95
The Relaxation & Stress Reduction Workbook, Fourth Edition, $17.95
Living Without Depression & Manic Depression: A Workbook for Maintaining Mood Stability, $17.95
Belonging: A Guide to Overcoming Loneliness, $13.95
Coping With Schizophrenia: A Guide For Families, $13.95
Visualization for Change, Second Edition, $13.95
Postpartum Survival Guide, $13.95
Angry All The Time: An Emergency Guide to Anger Control, $12.95
Couple Skills: Making Your Relationship Work, $13.95
Handbook of Clinical Psychopharmacology for Therapists, $39.95
The Warrior's Journey Home: Healing Men, Healing the Planet, $13.95
Weight Loss Through Persistence, $13.95
Post-Traumatic Stress Disorder: A Complete Treatment Guide, $39.95
Stepfamily Realities: How to Overcome Difficulties and Have a Happy Family, $13.95
Leaving the Fold: A Guide for Former Fundamentalists and Others Leaving Their Religion, $13.95
Father-Son Healing: An Adult Son's Guide, $12.95
The Chemotherapy Survival Guide, $11.95
Your Family/Your Self: How to Analyze Your Family System, $12.95
Being a Man: A Guide to the New Masculinity, $12.95
The Deadly Diet, Second Edition: Recovering from Anorexia & Bulimia, $13.95
Last Touch: Preparing for a Parent's Death, $11.95
Consuming Passions: Help for Compulsive Shoppers, $11.95
Self-Esteem, Second Edition, $13.95
I Can't Get Over It, A Handbook for Trauma Survivors, Second Edition,$15.95
Concerned Intervention, When Your Loved One Won't Quit Alcohol or Drugs, $11.95
Dying of Embarrassment: Help for Social Anxiety and Social Phobia, $12.95
The Depression Workbook: Living With Depression and Manic Depression, $17.95
The Marriage Bed: Renewing Love, Friendship, Trust, and Romance, $11.95
Focal Group Psychotherapy: For Mental Health Professionals, $44.95
Prisoners of Belief: Exposing & Changing Beliefs that Control Your Life, $12.95
Men & Grief: A Guide for Men Surviving the Death of a Loved One, $13.95
When the Bough Breaks: A Helping Guide for Parents of Sexually Abused Children, $11.95
Love Addiction: A Guide to Emotional Independence, $12.95
When Once Is Not Enough: Help for Obsessive Compulsives, $13.95
The Three Minute Meditator, Third Edition, $12.95
Getting to Sleep, $12.95

Call toll free, 1-800-748-6273, to order. Have your Visa or Mastercard number ready. Or send a check for the titles you want to New Harbinger Publications, Inc., 5674 Shattuck Ave., Oakland, CA 94609. Include $3.80 for the first book and 75¢ for each additional book, to cover shipping and handling. (California residents please include appropriate sales tax.) Allow four to six weeks for delivery.

Prices subject to change without notice.

RAND BISHOP

The Absolute Essentials of Songwriting Success

From Song Dog to Top Dog: Making It in the Music Business

Alfred Music Publishing Co., Inc.
P.O. Box 10003
Van Nuys, CA 91410-0003
alfred.com

ISBN-10: 0-7390-7191-2
ISBN-13: 978-0-7390-7191-5

Cover photos
Background texture © iStockphoto.com / mammuth
Keyboard by Evan Wilcox
ADK TT microphone by ADK Microphones www.ADKMIC.com • Photo by Greg Blaisdell at www.ProAudioToys.com
Guitar courtesy Daisy Rock Guitars
Rand Bishop © Krista Lee Photography / Brooke

Contents printed on environmentally responsible paper.

Library of Congress Cataloging-in-Publication Data

Bishop, Rand, 1949-
The absolute essentials of songwriting success : from song dog to top dog / by Rand Bishop.
p. cm.
ISBN-13: 978-0-7390-7191-5
ISBN-10: 0-7390-7191-2
1. Popular music--Writing and publishing. I. Title.
MT67.B46 2010
782.42'13--dc22

2010029999

CONTENTS

PREFACE
Are You a Song Dog?

On occasion, I've referred to myself as an "old Song Dog." This casual tag seems an appropriate and consciously self-effacing way to describe my own stubborn, dogged determination to keep on "makin' stuff up." As I *am* growing somewhat long in the tooth, the "old" part of this personal appellation should not require any explanation. Perhaps, however, I should clarify the canine part of this reference. You see, over my 60 years, I've developed a soft spot in my ticker for those charming, eager, slobbery, four-legged creatures. I've now come to realize that the native characteristics summed up in the two, brief syllables of "Song Dog" are, for the most part, very admirable ones. there's a very, *very* good chance you'll recognize more than a few of the idiosyncrasies I'm about to describe in yourself.

Some decades ago, when I was first dating my wife, Stacey, one of her closest friends was Laura Kaye, a small, raspy-voiced armchair-philosopher. At one potluck holiday or another, Laura was observing whatever dog happened to be on campus at the time; let's just assume it was Frosty, an ever-smiling, bushy snowball of a Samoyed. As our guests arrived, Stacey instructed each of them to put their dishes with the others on the dining room table. Frosty just sat there, head cocked to the side, tongue hanging out, observing with rapt attention. As each new offering met the table, the pooch's eyes would not stop there, but would follow gravity's path to a spot on the floor, directly below where the plate or tray had been placed. *At some point,* the dog must have been figuring, *one of those scrumptious concoctions is sure to drop right through and hit the hardwood.* Frosty stared. Frosty drooled. Frosty was poised and ready to claim that envisioned prize as her own holiday treat.

Seeing Frosty repeat this laughably absurd behavior time after time, Laura summed up the personality of a dog in two succinct words: "Always hopeful," she said. I laughed, understanding the spot-on wisdom in this woman's well chosen description. It's absolutely true that dogs never abandon the expectation that some morsel will fall to their level for a quick snatch-up. Never mind that a table is impermeable, and there is little chance that anything—even the smallest tidbit—would pierce its surface and float to the earth. But dreamy optimism endures eternally in the canine heart.

Doesn't that quality match the natural demeanor of almost every songwriter? (Well, at least we invariably start out that way.) The odds against any one of our songs achieving mass public acceptance are nearly as great as a sweet potato pie slipping through a solid pine farm table. However, this rude reality doesn't keep us from our quest to compose that elusive hit song. We keep on rearranging the notes on the scale and manipulating the mother tongue, always visualizing our latest made-up masterpiece somehow squeaking past the gatekeepers, receiving unprecedented endorsement from the "No People," circumventing the morass of music-biz politics, and stealing its way into the studio, onto the airwaves, and finally imprinting millions of music-loving hearts. Songwriters are, and must remain, as Laura Kaye once said of that smiling Samoyed, "always hopeful."

Song Dogs and their canine counterparts are very much alike in many more ways. Here are just a few.

My little beagle, Millie, is a somewhat more assertive mongrel than was Frosty. Despite my constant chastising, Millie gets up on her hind legs and jumps, anteater-tongue darting out a full six inches, to steal any scrap within her reach. She'll chew up whatever she latches onto and swallow, before she's even sure it's edible. Once (I kid you not) she actually ate a clod of concrete. Workers were pouring a walkway in our backyard, and the wheelbarrow sloshed some drops of wet mix, which hardened into cement nuggets in the grass. The next morning, the puppy glommed a little ball of that crunchy stuff, chewed it up as quickly as she could, and gulped it down. Amazing! Perhaps cement makes for good fiber. When Millie spies a squirrel scooting up a tree or across a telephone wire, she nearly strangles herself, straining at the leash, eager for the opportunity to give chase. Not only is it highly doubtful that I would ever free her to gratify her hard-wired instinct for the hunt, I'll bet you dimes to donuts that little pup has failed to thoroughly consider the challenge of climbing a tree. Her lack of planning and preparation doesn't stop Millie's fervent passion for the idea that she might someday get "up close and personal" with one of those grey-furred, bushy-tailed rodents.

Being proactive, like my little beagle, is a quality many songwriters share as well. We'll sniff out any and all opportunities to play our songs for anybody and everybody we think might help us get closer to our goals, regardless of how improbable it may be that our work will find success. Too often, like Millie, we lack discretion in this regard, investing misguided faith and way too much energy in snipe hunt after wild goose chase. Too many of us tend—out of pure exuberance—to let the horse out of the barn prematurely, before we've made sure to get the feedback and do the rewriting necessary to polish off a solidly composed song.

Like our canine counterparts, most of us Song Dogs are loyal to our friends and fiercely dedicated to those who feed us. In the heyday of the mid '90s, having just scored a prestigious release with Tim McGraw, I remarked—stupidly—that I had no interest in a Toby Keith cut. Having worked with some of rock's greatest singers, the big Oklahoman's wide, country vibrato and sliding-through-the-notes baritone kind of grated on my ears. It's amazing how much better his voice began sounding six years later—when he chose to record one of my songs. And since having a five-week Number One with him, I worship the guy. That vibrato put a lotta groceries on the Bishop table, not to mention giving my family the means to provide the roof over the dining room in which that table sits. Since then, a couple of my cowriters have got in a dig at my former feelings about Keith by asking, "What other singers don't you like? Let's pitch this song to them." (By the way, since my initial testimony of ignorance, TK has proven himself to be an admirable marketing genius and one of the most genuine and dynamic recording artists of the last two decades. Come to think of it, Toby even named his record label Show Dog. Hmm, interesting.)

> Joke: Who loves you more, your dog or your spouse?
> Stuff 'em both in the trunk of your car for an hour or two.
> When you let 'em out, who's happy to see you?

Like songwriters, dogs do exhibit anger. Some, more than others. Many will ferociously defend their territory, their pack, and their master. A dog can get violently possessive when it comes to one particular toy or insanely jealous over affection handed out to another household pet. (The easiest way to get one particularly possessive dog of mine to come was to say something in a sweet voice to the cat.)

On the negative side, dogs are capable of potentially self-destructive and risky behavior due to hardwired, primitive urges and animal angst. Chaka Kahn, my beloved chow/golden retriever mix, once snatched a roast chicken from the kitchen chopping block and greedily gobbled up the whole thing—bones and all. A single, splintered, chicken bone has been known to choke a dog to death. Chaka didn't leave a single splinter behind. Fortunately for the dog, the delectable fowl she couldn't resist didn't take her life. (Unfortunately, only a few years later, much to the grief of her forlorn master, mast cell cancer did.)

Like my dog, some songwriters actually make a policy of theft. In fact, a couple of my songs have been plagiarized. One successful writer/producer borrowed the title and its seven-note melody verbatim from one of my most-pitched songs and used the exact words and music as the basis for an entirely new song—with the *same title*. When I pointed out the similarity, he denied my insinuation, even though it was common knowledge that he had heard my song numerous times. I was, however, able to nip that burglary in the bud by threatening a lawsuit. It's a shame to have to go to that extent, but we have to protect our territory, don't we, Song Dogs?

Dogs are purposefully bred to certain behaviors for specific functions, whether it be hunting, herding, guarding, or companionship. In that same way, a goodly number of Song Dogs have their own native proclivities. Some find it difficult keep away from long, liquid lunches at the local taproom. There, they empty their pockets—and, eventually, their bank accounts—to pony up daily bar tabs and reduce their once-nimble minds to mush by the time sunset creeps around. Those are the shards of chicken bone that can choke off what once looked like a very promising songwriting career. I was once privy to a drunken, obscene, rant of a phone message. A songwriter was screaming at his own publisher because Warner Brothers Records had dropped his song from a Faith Hill album at the 11th hour. How in the world any writer, regardless of his blood-alcohol level, could possibly suspect that his own publisher—who had nurtured the song, signed those monthly advance checks, financed the demo session, pitched the song, and scored the cut—would intentionally sabotage what was surely a mutual success for both writer and publisher is beyond me. Song Dogs comprise a rare breed. Of that I am certain. Obviously, after that tirade, the publisher was reluctant to re-up the offending writer's contract when his next option period rolled around.

It may go without saying that these particular negative dog-family traits are not to be admired or emulated by anyone—tunesmith, tailor or Indian Chief. However, I know from decades of experience that many creative souls (I'll be the first to raise my hand) are fully capable of burning a bridge by uttering a poorly chosen word, offering an untimely snub, or taking an inflexible stance, motivated purely by pride, resentment or ego—not to mention ignorance. We're passionate people with fragile Ids. Now and again, we're going to offend somebody. It goes with the territory. Obviously, however, we should be continually striving to learn how not to repeat these kinds of self-destructive patterns, and thus give new relationships an opportunity to become more fruitful ones than those we've unintentionally ripped to shreds in the past. Most of us prefer the biscuit to the stick. Hopefully there will be a chance to sit, stay, fetch, roll over, (hopefully not play dead) and finally be rewarded with that tasty cookie of success next time around.

While, to one degree or another, we all share similar characteristics, each of us comes with unique quirks as well. Some dogs are dominant due to that well known "alpha" nature. Some alpha dogs are more aggressive than others and can even be threatening and dangerous. Rumor had it that a very successful, award-winning songwriter would stand at the door of his publisher's office to intercept the song pluggers on their way out to their pitch appointments. His intent was to nix pitches for other writers at the company, while substituting his own titles onto the pluggers' pitch lists. That, my friends, is your classic, alpha Song Dog. More than a few dogs have been kicked around (either by humans or by other dogs) and have thus become submissive, passive pups, otherwise known as the "omega." Just like in packs of dogs, there is a pecking order amongst songwriters, one governed first by achievement level, then by the company one keeps, and lastly by overt bravado and/or some aura of mystique. This cast system gives the various cliques of the songwriting community a certain tribal quality.

One Thanksgiving, the late Chaka Kahn (my dog, not the singer) gave my octogenarian mother-in-law a pretty severe bite on her arm. I don't know if any pissed-off song scribe has resorted to pulling a Mike Tyson on an industry acquaintance's extremity. It might have happened. I just haven't heard about it. Anyway, biting—whether it be your peer, your publisher, or your spouse's mother—is definitely not advisable.

If, like me, you are a Song Dog, strive to take advantage of your most appealing canine qualities. Be a good dog, not a bad dog: eager, optimistic, friendly, kind, generous, playful, affectionate, loyal, and protective of your partners and your masters. Avoid as much as possible the temptations and pitfalls of impulsive or compulsive behavior. If you possess a natural alpha nature, try to keep your dominant and/or aggressive tendencies in check. If you're an omega, work to overcome your subservient meekness, as it will do little to serve you in your quest for success. Recognize and be aware of your own native tendencies. Optimize the positive and minimize the negative.

> And, above all, like your doggie brothers and sisters, ALWAYS BE HOPEFUL!

Within these pages, it is my intent to help you make the transition from Song Dog to Top Dog. This will be made possible because committing yourself to following these hard-won nuggets of advice will enable more and more morsels to magically drop for you to gobble up. In the meantime, be content with being part of the game. And, always be grateful for any crumb that lies within reach.

INTRODUCTION

"How do I get my songs heard?"

It's like a mantra chanted ad naseum by some shadowy cult. Nearly every day, a member of that secret society approaches me and asks that same question, word for word. I may be at church, conducting a workshop, at a birthday party, or winging on an airplane at 30,000 feet; it doesn't matter. After it becomes known that I've had some songwriting success through the years, someone with similar ambitions invariably wants to know, "How do I get my songs heard?"

Sometimes I can see 'em coming from way across the room. You know, those "creative" types, clad in thrift-store chic, a "slept-in" T-shirt, or retro-hippie garb; either young, with a yellow brick road laid out ahead of them and stars twinkling in their eyes, or seasoned, with the bitter, defeated glower that comes from weathering heart-crushing disappointment after soul-withering disillusionment. Then again, sometimes it turns out to be the most unlikely person in the room.

There I was, attending a networking luncheon in Murfreesboro, Tennessee. The facilitator kicked off the mixer in traditional fashion, by asking everyone to introduce himself or herself, with a brief explanation as to why each of us had chosen to spend a long lunch hour in that room. I stood up and said simply, "I'm Rand Bishop. I'm a songwriter, a music producer, and an author. I'm here because I'm interested in Ken's coaching program." Then I sat back down.

Our friendly host, Ken Murray, who had gathered this group together to promote his coaching business, urged me to elaborate. "Rand's had songs recorded by a whole bunch of big stars. Could you tell the group who all has recorded your songs, Rand?"

His question provided permission to talk about my favorite subject: me. So I willingly boasted my nutshell discography, listing some career highlights: recording artist for Elektra, A&M, MCA, and Epic through the 1970s and early '80s; cuts by Heart, Cheap Trick, Beach Boys, Tim McGraw, Indigo Girls, Vanilla Fudge; Grammy nomination, BMI Awards. "My List," a five-week Number One for Toby Keith, country radio's most played song of 2002. I mentioned the book I'd just published, *Makin' Stuff Up, secrets of song-craft and survival in the music-biz* (Nashville: Weightless Cargo Press, 2008), and my song-craft coaching Website, MakinStuffUp.net.

I assumed I was setting myself up for that question I hear everywhere I go, especially in the greater Nashville area. But, as the rest of the group rose one by one to introduce *them*selves, I began to realize that I had little in common with any of these folks. Officers from three banks each claimed their outfit was the best in Rutherford County. Real Estate brokers touted their personal touch and creative approach. Network marketers did their 30-second pitches. A cherubic chiropractor offered a free session. No one, it seemed, was in any way associated with the creative world. In fact, the most artistic person there was a woman who had a custom cookie-baking business. "I can put your business card on a cookie," she announced. (How an edible calling card could boost business, I'll never know. Maybe her confections had an exceptionally long-lingering aftertaste.)

Still, surprisingly enough, when the box lunches were consumed and the presentation was over, several other networkers approached me. I was engaged in a conversation with a charming, mature gentleman (he was 70, if he was a day). This seasoned fellow shared the surprising fact that he had been in an L.A. rock band in the mid '60s, gigging on the infamous Sunset Strip. He wanted to know if by chance I'd ever encountered any of the colorful characters from his long-ago musical past. Suddenly, we were rudely interrupted in mid discourse. An overly aggressive young woman brazenly barged between my new friend and me, introducing herself by boldly extending her hand in my direction. The woman told me about her shy, reclusive, sensitive songwriter of a husband. From her assertiveness, it seemed clear to me who wore the pants in *that* household. "What can my husband do," she demanded, with a slight tone of desperation in her voice, "to get his songs heard?" I told her about NSAI (Nashville Songwriters Association International) and the opportunities that incredible organization provides for members to play their songs for industry pros. I suggested that she buy my book for her husband and that she urge him to join my Website to get constructive, professional feedback on his songs. She didn't buy a book, but walked away wearing a sour expression, probably disappointed that I hadn't offered to set her poor spouse up with a major music publisher, or better yet, a record company president.

The next person to approach me was surely the most unlikely person in the room. Three-piece suit, buzz-cut hair, deep-Southern accent dripping with grits and gravy. Earlier, this guy had identified himself as the chief officer of a local banking institution. Mr. Three-Piece Suit proceeded to tell me about his ProTools studio and informed me that his true passion was songwriting. He at least invested a copy of my book. As I was signing it for him, he asked (you guessed it), "How do I get my songs heard?" It's a reasonable question, for sure. As logical as this query may seem, though, it's an incomplete one, one that stems from frustration, from feeling disenfranchised, ostracized, locked out of the inner circle of songwriting success. There is really no satisfactory answer to this question because it's really the *wrong* question.

Since that afternoon, I've pondered this proposition and decided that the only way for me to respond is in rhetorical fashion: Who do you want to hear your songs? Publishers? A&R people? Recording artists? Bus drivers, road managers, guitar players, personal trainers, personal chefs, gardeners to the stars?

Finally, and far more importantly, *What do you expect to happen* after *they listen?*

If your desire is to play your songs for a music publisher, what kind of response are you looking for? Would you want that publisher to fall in love with one of your songs and offer you a single song contract? If so, what would you expect to happen then? Maybe that publisher would demo the song and start pitching it? Maybe he might get "a hold" on it? (Meaning that an artist, a producer, manager, or record company exec might want you to hold off playing the song for anyone else until a final decision is made.) Or, pie-in-the-sky, maybe he'd even get you a cut by a major recording star. And then, that cut might even be chosen as a single. You'd marvel pridefully as your song rockets to the top of the charts. You'd reap hundreds of thousands of dollars, garner multiple awards, and gain global recognition for your tunesmithing genius. Finally, you'd have your golden ticket into the inner-circle of songwriting royalty.

Do you realize how incredibly improbable that scenario is? Why bother to write songs? Just buy a lottery ticket. It would be *far* less time consuming, and at least you'd get your disappointment over within a week's time, instead of the months, if not years, it would take to write, demo, and dispatch your tune to trek through the jungle of the music-business, while you pray fervently that your baby circumvents the quicksand traps and evades the blood-thirsty carnivores waiting behind every tree, all the while hoping, hoping, hoping that your song emerges heroically as a big hit.

"How do I get my songs heard?" Heard by whom? And what do you expect from getting them heard?

After being barraged by that pervasive question at least a thousand times—the inquiry that seems to be nagging nearly every ambitious song scribe—I've come to realize that a lot of burgeoning writers are not approaching their writing ambitions with the right strategy; or, more accurately, they really have *no strategy at all.*

Here's the truth: *Getting your songs heard is not your goal!* Your goal is getting your songs cut, released, on the radio, and on the charts!

So, how do you go about accomplishing *that* seemingly impossible task in a strategic way? That's the real question isn't it? That's exactly what this book is all about. The essays and interviews herein are for the purpose of ensuring that your inspirations, your creative children, your sparks of genius have the best opportunity to find their optimal exposure and therefore gain a better chance at achieving recognition. These pages comprise *The Absolute Essentials of Songwriting Success.*

Warning: This is not the equivalent of a "five-minute workout to perfect abs." There are no shortcuts to creating songwriting success. However, if you have any talent at all and you dedicate yourself to the tenants revealed here, I absolutely guarantee that you *will* (best case scenario, months from now; more realistically, some years, and possibly decades down the road), *eventually* have *some* level of success as a songwriter. I mean this sincerely, because here's where I'm coming from: I hope every one of you songwriters out there finds the thrill of receiving a phone call informing you that your song just hit Number One. I want every one of you to know what it feels like to tear open an envelope containing a huge royalty check made out to you. I want every one of you to experience the elation of standing in a packed arena while thousands of fans sing every word of *your* song.

I had reached my 50s, with more than 30 years in this business and more than 150 cuts by some incredible and iconic artists, before I finally knew the exhilaration of what I just described. So, I hope you understand that perseverance—and not a small amount of serendipity—is critical to achieving this very elusive plateau. But, you *do* want to be ready when the opportunity arrives, don't you? And you *do* want to know that you're taking every positive action you can possibly take to make it happen, don't you? I thought so.

What follows is some earnest and sound advice from an old warrior who's been there and done it, interspersed with some interviews, stories, and quotes from some other incredibly talented and generous folks, who've also seen the view from the top of the mountain.

Are you ready? Me, too.

PART ONE:

LEARNING THE CRAFT

CHAPTER 1
Song Craft

"Inspiration is great, but craft will save your ass."
—Janis Ian

I have a great idea. Let's start at the beginning, from the get-go.

It makes perfect sense to me that every burgeoning songwriter should commence the quest for success in the same way: by sharpening his or her tools and learning how to wield them with discretion and skill. I've actually covered the process of constructing a solidly written pop song in my previous book, *Makin' Stuff Up, secrets of song-craft and survival in the music-biz.* On those pages, I elaborate on the cowriting experience, while walking the reader through the choices every writer faces in navigating the deceptive labyrinth that leads to a bulletproof, competitive pop song. I won't be repeating that information here. I would, however, like to discuss in some detail about what songwriting is, from my own personal experience and perspective.

In your author's opinion, pop songwriting is a craft and most definitely *not* an art.

Admittedly, more than a select few, genius, contemporary melodists and lyricists have lifted certain songs to the heights of artistic expression. Jimmy Webb, Joni Mitchell, Bob Dylan, Paul Simon, Peter Gabriel, Stevie Wonder, Marvin Gaye, Neil Young, David Foster, Bacharach and David, Lennon and McCartney, Ray Davies, Pete Townshend, Kurt Cobain, Eminem, Kate Bush, Shawn Colvin, and many others have occasionally lifted the form of the popular song to a level that could be recognized as art. That list, I'm sure, could go on for pages. What is or isn't art is a matter of opinion—mine being no more credible or authoritative than yours. However, in and of itself, writing a structurally sound pop song, with enough integrity to compete in the marketplace, is something most anyone can learn how to do—well, at least anyone who possesses the following four basic qualities: a modicum of talent; a powerful impulse to write; the stick-to-it-iveness to conceive, construct, and re-work song after song, day after day; and, last but certainly not least, thick enough skin to survive the inevitable road blocks, poison darts, and disparaging responses that lurk along the jungle path ahead.

As Jimmy Webb so astutely instructs in his superb songwriting manifesto, *Tunesmith: Inside the Art of Songwriting* (New York: Hyperion, 1999), "We've chosen a profession in which, best case scenario, 90% of our work will be completely ignored." He's talking "best case scenario," my friends. That's a Jimmy Webb level of success, a man who has penned some of the most popular and lucrative copyrights of the last half-century. That is precisely why you have to be driven, compulsive, and love, love, love expressing yourself in song. Otherwise, you might as well be rolling dice in Vegas.

As I'm sure you realize by now, we songwriters don't commonly collect an hourly fee for our labor. The prize we're shooting for far surpasses minimum wage—or even a living one—by light years. So, we accept the gamble of freely investing our time, talent, and resources in the hopes that there will be a big payoff somewhere in the not too distant future. Actually, we're working for commission only, meaning that, until our music creates commerce in the marketplace, we will not be enjoying income from it. Hastening the moment when that begins to happen is exactly what having a strategy for success is all about, and, therefore, the very point of the book you hold in your hand. You see, in almost any other business, there is a direct correlation between the effort you put forth and the reward you can expect to receive. Flipping fast-food burgers or folding T-shirts at the mall will yield you a check reflecting the time between your clocking in and your clocking out. Your everyday, commissioned sales associate can usually gauge on average how many cold calls it will take to get an appointment, and how many of those appointments will yield a sale.

Not so with songwriting. In fact, you could write the most skillfully crafted, moving, poignant, clever, humorous, and/or danceable songs ever conceived, and produce state-of-the-art demos that leap out of the speakers, and there's absolutely no guarantee you'll ever make a single nickel for your entire life's output. So, my fine, furry friends, you'd better love to write because the joy and fulfillment you get from makin' stuff up is the *only* compensation you can actually count on.

Enough said about the long odds against any one songwriter's or any one song's success. As I recall, we were talking about the first step in increasing those odds: developing song craft. Keeping that key word "craft" in mind, let's just say that you've decided instead to become a furniture maker. More specifically, you have an undeniable hankering to create a fabulous line of chairs.

Recognizable

What would you want to accomplish in creating your first chair? Goal number one, I assume, would be to create something that was recognizable *as* a chair. Otherwise, it would be unlikely that anybody would be inclined to place their butt in it, that being the function and purpose of said piece of furniture. It may seem obvious, but creating something that is identifiable as a pop *song* should be priority numero uno for each and every tunesmith. And, how do we accomplish that goal? We do that by adhering to a somewhat traditional structure.

I've already described the character of a Song Dog. Now I'm about to take another leap and bring felines into my story, or at least one particular cat. Enter the ghost of the late, great Oliver. (I use the word "great" purposefully because Ollie was a big, big boy, a 25-pound, orange-tabby love machine.) This belly-draggin' lump demonstrated a curious behavior that often had me scratching my grey hairs. Suffering from urinary tract issues that restricted him to a low-protein diet, Oliver was never served canned food in his entire life. However, when anyone in the house fired up the electric can opener to crack the lid off some garbanzo beans, Ollie heard that motor from wherever he was (curled up sleeping, no doubt) and he came running. It was amazing how fast that portly fellow could move when he had the motivation! Here's the really amazing thing: Somehow, in some cortex or quadrant of his little cat brain, Oliver must have surmised, "electric can opener equals food." He had not learned this from actual experience. This automatic, involuntary response reflected an instinct that must have come from either an in utero recollection *or* from some genetic code passed down from one kitty generation to the next.

"So, what do cats have to do with pop songwriting?" Your author will now dare to compare that electric appliance and the can of chick peas it is opening to that mysterious, creative concoction we know as the pop song, which has a proven recipe passed down through the eons, mixing together the odd ingredients of music, poetry, and rhythm in a two-and-a-half to four-and-a-half minute sound snack. The result is a munchy treat we writers always hope is nourishing and, at the same time, irresistible. You see, when it comes to songs, I think Homo Sapiens are very much like our ravenous feline friend, Oliver. When we hear the melody and lyrics of a pop composition for the first time, we automatically listen with certain specific expectations. In other words, the way we perceive popular music is actually programmed into us: by our environment and our experience, yes; but also, believe it or not, within the very strands of our DNA.

"What exactly do you mean by this bold statement, Mr. Smartypants?" you might be asking. I'll answer that question hypothetically. Let's just imagine you're driving to work. It's raining, traffic is slow, maybe you're in danger of being late. Just then, a new song comes on the radio and grabs you by the ears. What do you expect to hear? First, you're accustomed to some sort of seductive intro that lasts between 10 and 20 seconds. Then you anticipate a verse that presumably invites you into the story by introducing characters and/or a situation, offering some clues as to what this ditty—or masterpiece—is about. You presume this first verse, which usually lasts between 30 and 40 seconds, is building toward a chorus or refrain that will sum up the themes of the song and will present you with the most dynamic, emotionally satisfying, repetitive, and therefore memorable part of the piece. On from there, you anticipate that this song will likely return to a second verse section to flesh out the story. That second verse, in turn, will culminate in another chorus or refrain. By then, you probably remember enough from the first chorus that you find yourself doing some mindless singing along.

After chorus two, the song will probably take a slight left turn and travel off into a heretofore unrevealed musical and/or lyrical landscape. This section is called the bridge. After crossing that bridge, you can pretty much be sure that the upcoming, culminating chorus or refrain will cap off the tune in such a way that its most unforgettable phrases will take root in your head, repeating themselves over and over—for hours, if not days, to come.

Pop songs that take this basic form have been around for centuries. Take "Greensleeves" for instance, a broadside ballad that emerged in the sixteenth century. (Legend has credited this song's authorship to Henry VIII. Some have claimed the hot-to-trot potentate penned "Alas, my love, you do me wrong to cast me off so discourteously" as he pined away for that hard-to-get vixen, Anne Boleyn.) The "verse/chorus/verse/chorus" shape of "Greensleeves" has endured intact to this day. That's not to say pop song structure hasn't wandered down some side roads since that time; but, for the most part, we've come to rely on certain covenants between the songwriter and the listener. The ultimate result of those centuries of conditioning is that, when we listen to pop music today, we are very much like that chubby lunch mouth, Oliver. The motor of the can opener kicks into gear (in the form of that tantalizing intro), our mouths water, our digestive juices begin to churn, and we fully expect to be fed something yummy. It's in our genes—passed down from generation to generation, since the bloomin' sixteenth century, or earlier—and these same expectations are reinforced in the music we hear every day of our lives. We are actually born knowing what a solidly structured pop song is and, when we crank up the iPod, that's what we're prepared to hear.

Now you're probably saying to yourself, "This Rand dude is all about formula." How dare you even think such a thing! (We hardly know one another and we're already having our first argument.) Okay, I'm taking a deep breath and a step back. In my defense, I'm so *not* about formula. In fact, nothing could be further from the truth. However (you knew a big "but" was coming, didn't you), as crafters of song, it's to our advantage to be continually mindful of the reasonable expectations of our audience. While we're continually striving to find new words and fresh melodies, more creative ways to unravel those same, time-honored plots and express those same, basic emotions, it bodes well for us to also keep our work accessible, by placing it in a familiar frame.

So, within the inherent limitations of the materials available (all the words in the dictionary, those 12 chromatic tones, and a plethora of tempos, time signatures, grooves and dynamics), every time we sit down to write a song, we set out to construct something familiar—and yet unique. Thus, the songwriter's first goal is exactly the same as that of the furniture maker: to craft a piece that is recognizable as what it is.

Aesthetically Appealing

Now, back to furniture making. After designing a piece that, upon first look, is obviously a chair, your second goal would be to design something aesthetically appealing enough so that folks will hanker to place it in their home or office. In a showroom, amongst a hundred others, your creation should stand out in such a way that a discerning consumer will be able to imagine it enhancing a certain room's decor. Likewise, the songwriter intends to pen a song of rare beauty, or genuine humor, imbibed with some quality or set of qualities that will impact the listener with a universally resonate, sincere, emotional wallop. In other words, every time out, we try to write a song attractive enough that people will be willing to invest in it and take it home with them.

Comfortable

Thirdly, as a furniture maker, you'd probably be concerned about building a comfortable chair because you don't want people to place their derrieres in it just once. You want them to sit in your chair over and over again. "A chair is still a chair," Hal David so brilliantly wrote, "even when no one is sitting there." Likewise, a song is still a song, even when no one is listening to it. You and I both have plenty of those labored-over, wannabe hits stowed away in boxes, collecting dust, unheard by the masses we're hoping to connect with. If a song is not listened to and adored time and time again, it can't carry out its mission. By the same token, if, for some reason, a chair fails to offer comfort to those who plop their bottoms in it, it is unlikely that piece of furniture will remain part of the décor for long. It's liable to be moved out on the lawn and tagged for the next yard sale. Point being: The function of any piece of furniture is equally as important as its form. In the same way, a songwriter would be wise to construct a song that sits within a cozy modality, a seductive ambience, and/or an irresistible rhythm.

There are a thousand kinds of chairs: playful, artistic, or strictly functional; armed chairs, straight-backed, office chairs on wheels, recliners, patio chairs, you name it. A song, too, can be an inviting place to rest and reflect, or it can produce fireworks of inspiration and encouragement. A song can offer solace and empathy, or it can give the listener a well-needed laugh. Whatever the demeanor of any particular song, it should fit like a glove; not necessarily one-size-fits-all, but at least warm and fuzzy enough that a good number of hands and fingers will slip right in and want to linger awhile. (Okay, I think I've used enough metaphors now.)

Practical, Durable

Finally, you want your chair to be practical and durable, so it will last for generations. The materials and components you use should have strength enough to stand the test of time and be pieced together carefully and skillfully, with the pride of a true craftsman. Like a classic, leather arm chair, songs that endure are usually deceivingly simple in design, constructed solidly, using timeless elements, and they keep the listener's interest from beginning to end, by offering specific details, continually providing new lyrical and melodic information, while upping the emotional ante.

To sum up: a well designed chair (and therefore a solid pop song) should possess the following qualities:

1. Recognizable
2. Aesthetically appealing
3. Comfortable
4. Practical and durable

You begin your journey to songwriting success by making this total commitment: From this moment, you will always strive to give your every creation these four qualities of craftsmanship. Anything less is unacceptable. Anything less should not satisfy or fulfill you. Nothing else should be more important to you as a songwriter than to create piece after piece after piece, day after day after day that, on the closest inspection, get high marks in each of these categories. When placed in the vast showroom of Songs R Us or Song Barn, any original composition not inhabiting these four qualities will more than likely fade away into its own indistinctness. Quite honestly, it might not even find its way to the floor. If you really want your songs to have a chance to succeed, they need to make it to the showroom. To accomplish that, before you do anything else, you begin by developing your craft.

Observing the Masters at Work

Now that you know the exact qualities you'll be striving for in creating your exquisite line of chairs, how might you go about gaining the craft necessary to accomplish your mission? Well, first you would be well served to take a long, hard look at every chair you could find. You would study the design and construction of each one, taking note of what parts and materials were utilized. Finally, you would evaluate critically, observing what concepts and components worked and where other, better choices might have been made. Then, you would be wise to seek out a master chair maker, generous enough to allow you to observe how he goes about his craft, to give you advice, show you the essential tools of the trade, how to use them, and even share some tales from his lifetime of experience. Aha!

For song crafters, step one is as easy as it is fun. Simply sit down and make a list of your favorite songs, going back as far as you can remember. My memory immediately recalls a 45 RPM record of "Bibbidi, Bobbidi, Boo" on the Buena Vista label, with a picture of that magical Disneyland castle from *Sleeping Beauty* on it. While a nonsensical children's ditty might not seem exemplary, every song that ever attracted my ears and captured my imagination tells me something important about why some songs had more appeal than others, why some songs succeed, why some songs fall short, and how I can go about constructing valid, complete, and competitive compositions, i.e. songs that contain qualities one through four, enumerated above.

Here are some hits from my childhood that stream through my consciousness: "Hot Diggity, Dog Diggity" by Perry Como; "Wake Up Little Susie" by the Everly Brothers; "Don't Be Cruel" by Elvis Presley; "Summertime Blues" by Eddie Cochran; "Oh, Donna" by Ritchie Valens; "Travelin' Man" by Ricky Nelson; "Sherry Baby" by the Four Seasons (the first real rock and roll record I ever owned); "God Only Knows" by the Beach Boys; "Wild Thing" by The Troggs; "You Really Got Me" by The Kinks; "Laugh, Laugh" by the Beau Brummels; "Paperback Writer" by The Beatles; "Like A Rolling Stone" by Bob Dylan; "It's All Over Now" by the Rolling Stones; "You've Lost That Lovin' Feelin'" by the Righteous Brothers. Believe me, I could go on all day, listing hundreds of titles, but you get my drift.

Return to your most beloved songs from yesteryear, paying particular attention to the faves from your pre-teen and pimply, teenaged days. Why put extra emphasis on the songs from that era? Because that was the time when you were part of the most active record-buying public, meaning that you probably went out and purchased music regularly, habitually. As long as recorded music has been available, the youth market has been the life's blood, the core demographic that motors the music business. Even more importantly, your pre-teen and teen years represent the period when you responded to music much more emotionally, without intellectualizing about it.

> This is one of my themes, kids (So get used to it!):
>
> Songs are emotional things.

The first way that songs appeal to us is through our emotions. However, now that you're older, presumably wiser, and seeking to be craftier, I advise you to listen to those old faves with new ears. Remember how they affected you then and, at the same time, listen critically now. What initially caught your attention? Was it the groove, the ambience/atmosphere, the texture or modality, a soaring or exceptionally catchy fragment of melody? Was it a particular lyrical phrase, a relatable character or group of characters, or perhaps the storyline that grabbed you? Maybe it was the overall concept of the song or the situation in which the singer finds himself or herself. Or it could have been the point of view, the attitude being represented.

"Wake Up, Little Susie" had a spunky quality, those tight, fraternal harmonies, and the song described a specific situation that every teen-aged boy since the Victorian era has dreaded: bringing a girl home late from a date. "Summertime Blues" had that rebellious attitude, lyrics that spoke directly to a generation of teens, not to mention that pumping acoustic guitar chord pattern and snarling vocal. The caveman, out-of-tune primitiveness of the sexually suggestive "Wild Thing" made my desires sing. "Paperback Writer" had that layered, youthful vocal blend, an incredible guitar riff, and undeniable vigor, along with a storyline and characters worthy of pulp fiction. I was already enamored of the awesome emotional power of "You've Lost That Lovin' Feelin'," the yin and yang of those two soulful voices and the grandeur of Phil Spector's wall of sound. Then, in the spring of my sophomore year of high school, I was dancing in the tight embrace of my girlfriend, Randall Lechner, to the strains of those very righteous harmonies (yes, we were Randy and Randi; cute, I know). The tears that streaked my girlfriend's cheeks told the tale. That song became *our* song as we broke up that night. Some songs from the past, as I'm sure you well know, are tied strongly to unforgettable and formative experiences.

So, looking back over your own list, more than likely you'll discover that it was a combination of several qualities that led your personal favorites to having a particularly powerful emotional impact on you. Study and take note of these attributes, so that you can have a point of reference the next time you sit down to write. If you discern why those certain, important songs appealed to you, it will give you more ammunition with which to go about penning songs that will appeal to others.

Please note: I am *not* advising you to plagiarize anything from a classic song. I'm merely suggesting that you seek to understand where the real appeal is in each song on your list of faves. Then, while you're writing, you can try to build some of those same, appealing qualities into your own compositions.

For instance, while listening to The Kinks' debut hit, "You Really Got Me," maybe you'll recall that what first grabbed you was Ray Davies' brilliant line, "You got me so I can't sleep at night." Ask yourself the question: *What is it about that particular lyric that struck me at gut level?* That's not hard to figure out, is it? What teenager can't imagine tossing and turning, alone in a single bed, lonesome, alienated, and obsessed by some elusive someone to whom he or she feels irresistibly attracted? So, that phrase is ultimately effective because it captures a universal emotion by painting a specific and easily relatable scene. Bingo! So, if you were to be writing a song of agitated, youthful longing, that line might serve as your template. Then, you could seek to describe another situation as clearly as Davies did, with equal emotional impact. If you succeed at that, you have a good chance of appealing to that same gut level in a whole new generation of music lovers. On the musical side, listen to the shape of a melody you've always loved; not the actual notes, but the way they ascend and descend, where they stretch out, and where they speak with brevity. Listen for the texture and modality of a favorite song, how the melody fits into the chords and how those chords are voiced. Find chord progressions that intrigue you; then modify them, changing their order, adding, subtracting or substituting.

The fact is this: No pop song is absolutely original. Every new composition is derived in some way from a previous one. More likely, each new piece is actually a hybrid of several ancestors, just like every new baby born carries family traits from both parents and all the generations that went before.

Make your list now, and keep adding to it as you recall more of those personal songs. Listen to those songs again with newly educated ears, recalling the impact those words and melodies had on you back in the day. Do some forensics work. Observe the techniques the songwriters utilized to weave an effective lyric together with a memorable melody. The knowledge you acquire from this process will arm you to take your own creative intuitions and fashion them into better, more accessible songs, with more universal appeal.

CHAPTER 2
Coaching

You want to know what really curdles my cheese? Okay, brace yourself, because you're probably not going like this: You do!

Well, maybe I'm being a little unfair, presuming that you—the person so graciously taking the time to absorb the priceless career advice I've culled and compiled from decades of trial by fire—are the kind of songwriter who gets my goat. Let's back up a second, so that I can re-address my pet peeve in the form of a question: Why is it that so many songwriters are so very reluctant to accept instruction, constructive criticism, and/or coaching? Why, for the vast majority of tunesmiths, is advice on craft so unwelcome? (Especially when that advice and/or coaching comes at any expense at all to the songwriter.)

If you had a bug up your bum to improve your golf swing or your tennis serve, learn some more challenging yoga poses, become a graceful tango dancer, refine your culinary skills, lay down a professional-looking tile floor in your kitchen, or even master some new guitar-picking techniques, you probably wouldn't think twice about seeking out a qualified instructor or coach. Admit it. You wouldn't have a single, solitary qualm about signing up for a class or, at the very least, picking up a book to give you some expert insight. Classes, personal instruction, and books on craft can amount to fairly substantial investments in cash and time.

Research by music-industry book guru, Mike Lawson, reveals that a book on mixing in ProTools or a recording engineer's guide to microphone placement written by an admitted tech-geek, with scant literary skills, has the potential of selling 100,000 copies or *more*. A successful book on song craft, authored by a life-long wordsmith, with excellent command of the English language and decades of experience manipulating it, will sell a third of that—*max*. For too many song scribes, it seems, there is something precious, something mystical, something untouchable about songwriting. I'm sure you know the type: writers who refuse to make time every day to apply their talent, writers who prefer to go about their writing careers passively, just waiting for inspiration to strike. When the muse does drop by for her occasional visit, these chosen ones believe their first instinct must have been beamed in from heaven above. *Can't mess with that stuff. No, no, no!* No constructive feedback, no well-intended critique, no amount of rewriting could possibly improve those intuitively captured notes and words. In fact, those folks believe that outside opinions can only serve to sully the sacred script, muddle that magical melody, or contaminate those celestial chord changes. This, my friends, in my less than humble opinion, is B.S.

If you think you're in touch with a divine muse, you're absolutely right. However, I hope it doesn't burst your bubble when I tell you that every other writer is also in touch with that same source. It's a very rare phenomenon when a song arrives from the dreamy netherworld fully formed and absolutely perfect in every way. It happens, yes, but, 99.9 percent of the time, solid, polished, first-rate writing requires conscientious craftsmanship. Like any inspired, useful, functional invention, most songs need lots of experimentation, some beta testing, more than a bit of tearing apart, reworking, reworking, and reworking until they really function well.

Danny Arena of the excellent, songwriting education site SongU.com says, "There is a misconception among some songwriters that writing comes solely from inspiration. Yet, I have never spoken to a professional songwriter in any genre who has told me they feel that way." The key word here is "professional." Do you want to become a professional writer, meaning you actually intend to make a living at it? Then, get with the program, bite down hard on the bullet, and admit that what flows so effortlessly from your fingertips and rolls off your tongue is not perfection. Use those wonderful inspirations, yes! Then, apply yourself to learning the craft of songwriting, or you will be forever complaining about how you're not finding success, or, more accurately, that success is not finding *you*.

Tom Snow, composer of numerous huge hit copyrights over the last 40 years, says, "The most important thing for any songwriter is just to really learn your craft and never fall in love with your material—because the most important part of writing is rewriting."

If you keep the creative spigot open, listen to the wind, pay attention to the ramblings of your subconscious, and travel through life with an open heart, you will find yourself inspired. What really matters is what you *do* with your inspiration. How you apply, assemble, and reassemble your gut instincts will make the difference between remaining a dilettante and growing into a real professional. To accomplish this growth, most every writer can use some help in the form of instruction, constructive feedback, and coaching. Get over yourself! Swallow your silly pride. Yes, your work is precious, but it's not so precious that it can't be made better through interaction; that it can't be improved by helpful, educated evaluation and unbiased input; that it can't be elevated to its highest potential through accepting and incorporating experienced, constructive suggestions. The purpose of the song is to communicate. If it falls short in any way in getting your intended point across, then you have more work to do. If it bears any explanation at all, it's not the fault of the listener. It is the writer's job to sharpen and clarify the language, to hit the message home. It is the composer's responsibility to marry those words to the perfect melody—one that is as natural and singable as it is unforgettable.

The Apprentice

The apprentice learns by sitting at the feet of the master, by observing and emulating time-honored techniques. Only after absorbing the basics, learning the traditions of the trade, can the apprentice expect to spread his own wings and take a solo flight. Even a circus clown doesn't just skip into the center ring and start falling down. First, he trains in juggling, tumbling, and walking the wire. He studies mime and dance. Only after mastering the fundamentals can he confidently move on to the divine work of clowning.

So, now that you've been sufficiently chastised for a negative trait you may or may not have, let's take a look at your alternatives. Where could you possibly seek out the expertise, the objective and professional feedback, the personalized coaching that could make all the difference in the development of your craft? Here is a brief list of the types of resources available to you, each of which I'll cover in more detail:

- Songwriting classes
- Books
- Workshops, seminars
- Organizations
- Online evaluations

Classes

Songwriting classes are offered in a number of colleges and universities, by some performance rights organizations (PROs), by various songwriting organizations, and certainly conducted privately and in groups in the offices and living rooms of individuals.

Books

Books on song craft are plentiful. I have no qualms whatsoever about recommending my own *Makin' Stuff Up*. Not only does this tome walk the reader through the process of creating a solidly structured pop song—covering every step of the way, from concept to demo—every other chapter tells a true tale culled from an old Song Dog's journey from fledgling to journeyman and on to becoming a bona fide hit writer. Not only will those autobiographical chapters instruct you about the numerous, treacherous pitfalls along the path to Hitsville, you will also get vivid insights into what you might do to avoid them. Other than my book, I love Jimmy Webb's brilliantly worded *Tunesmith*. Although I don't agree with every theory the pop genius purports (especially his insistence on hard rhymes), the book is beautifully authored by a man with undeniable credentials. For lyric writing, nothing beats Pat Pattison's *Writing Better Lyrics* (Cincinnati: Writer's Digest Books, 1995). There are a plethora of books on lyric writing; I'm sure many of those titles are very instructive as well. As an overall text, John Braheny's *The Craft and Business of Songwriting,* 3rd edition (Cincinnati: F+W Publications, 2007) is considered by many to be a songwriter's Bible.

I encourage you to read books on songwriting. Your learning process should never stop. I need to add that you will learn more by digging in and doing it every day than you will by reading about it.

Workshops

Workshops and seminars are sponsored and/or conducted by PROs and songwriting organizations, colleges and trade schools, networking groups, and individual teachers, like myself. BMI's national headquarters in Nashville offers a monthly workshop with Jason Blume. Nashville Songwriters Association International (NSAI) has song-evaluation workshops on a regular basis at its Nashville office and hosted by its regional chapters. NSAI also offers Spring Training, which is a weekend seminar with panels and workshops in conjunction with its Tin Pan South songwriters' festival, and Songposium, a week-long intensive in Nashville, where songwriters can attend lectures and classes conducted by pro instructors. Tennessee Songwriters Association International (TSAI) has regular meetings for its membership where invited authors and teachers share their expertise. Like NSAI, TSAI offers its membership professional song-critiquing and pitch sessions featuring top publishers and producers. The West Coast Songwriters Association (formerly the Northern California Songwriters Association) has an annual conference in the Bay Area, where attendees can play songs for publishers and producers, receive on-the-spot evaluations and get the chance to actually get a song published or even eventually score a cut. Since 1996, the Durango Songwriters Expo has conducted similar educational and business-opportunity songwriter get-togethers around the country. The Folk Alliance stages its annual event in Memphis, featuring industry panels, classes, and performances by acoustic-based writers of all success levels. A quick Internet search will clue you in to events similar to these in your area.

One incredible resource for independent songwriters and recording artists is the Independent A&R juggernaut, TAXI. Not only does TAXI provide its members year-round, up-to-date pitch tips and access to industry decision makers, it offers educational opportunities as well, through its giant Road Rally event in Los Angeles every fall. TAXI membership is not cheap. However, this organization has a proven track record of helping unpublished songwriters and unsigned artists find legitimate, money-making and résumé-building outlets for their songs and recordings.

SongsAlive! was founded in 1997 in Sidney, Australia, by singer/songwriters Gilli Moon and Roxanne Keily. Under the continued, high-energy leadership of these two female dynamos, this organization has grown into an international force with 20 chapters around the world. Run by songwriter volunteers to serve songwriters, SongsAlive! offers its members monthly songwriting critique workshops with top pros sharing their career experience and giving constructive feedback. Chapters also host performance showcases and writer nights.

So, if you don't have a songwriting coach, or don't have access to classes or seminars in your town, do some research, ask around, Google your fingers off. And, no matter how isolated you may be, there are some great online resources that will give you a sense of being part of the international songwriting community: Songstuff.com, JPFolks.com (stands for Just Plain Folks), Musesmuse.com, and SongwritersRUs.com are some of the sites where you can interact, discuss your craft, and shoot the industry bull with brothers and sisters from all over the world. Use caution on these forums though, because a good number of the writers taking part will tend toward striking a stance for complete creative independence from convention, while they simultaneously moan that the mainstream of the business won't give them a break. In the early 1990s, I remember attending a music-business panel in Los Angeles. Renegade singer/songwriter Shelby Lynne was on the dais. "I don't make records for radio," Lynne declared, defiantly. Then, in her very next breath, she complained vociferously that radio wouldn't play her records. A lot of this kind of kvetching happens on these message boards. If a songwriter won't accept feedback that can make his work more accessible, he certainly has no right to protest when his songs fail to communicate with the masses. As tempting as it may be sometimes, you definitely don't want to slip into that kind of self-defeating, negative posture. This business is tough enough already, without you getting yourself in a lather over its most painful realities. You can vent every now and then, just don't make a habit of it.

Organizations

Every aspiring songwriter should join NSAI. This organization offers the most comprehensive, ongoing education and strident advocacy for songwriters and deserves your support. The Songwriters Guild also sponsors excellent classes. My dear friend, Phil Swann, teaches under the Guild banner in L.A. The Guild also gives its members good, informed legal advice and support and is a strong advocate for songwriter rights. The West Coast Songwriters Association, under the leadership of Ian Crombie, is a fantastic group. WCSA has some great success stories, including the brilliant Sara Bareilles. As I've mentioned, TAXI can be very effective, not only in its independent A&R services, but as an educational resource. TSAI is terrific, too, offering on-going education and access to top industry professionals.

There are numerous songwriting groups around the country. Perhaps there is one meeting in your area. We learn our craft not only from applying our talents and getting coaching, but also by observing our peers. Getting actively involved in an effective organization can help accelerate your learning as well as put you in a place to begin building the most important relationships of your career: your peer network. (Much more about that in Part Four of this book.)

Online Song Evaluations and Coaching

For online coaching and classes, SongU.com offers the most extensive program. Founded by Danny Arena and Sara Light, along with Web wizard Martin Bell, SongU is endorsed by ASCAP, the Songwriters Guild, and Songwriters Association of Canada. Arena and Light have assembled a capable and experienced "faculty" and put together an impressive, well-organized curriculum. Other excellent resources for online song evaluations are jasonblume.com, barbaracloyd.com, robinfrederick.com, and Pete and Pat Luboff's WriteSongs.com. At this writing, my Website, makinstuffup.net, is still small enough so that my members can be assured that I will be their personal songwriting coach. My evaluations are graded on a point scale. Every important decision in the writing process is rated separately, so the writer will know what he or she might address in a rewrite. I also inform the writer where they are succeeding in a composition, and precisely where a work in progress could use improvement. Often, I'll even suggest a specific alternative to a lyric, a structural issue, or a melodic passage. I believe that makinstuffup.net is the only site offering rewrite evaluations at a discount. You can see some testimonials from the makinstuffup.net membership at www.makinstuffup.net/news.php.

Songwriting Contests

I will not get into a protracted discussion about the virtue of the myriad songwriting contests conducted around the world every single year. In fact, I'm innately skeptical about how much you can learn or how much your career can benefit from entering—or even being acknowledged by—any given competition. Unless a contest actually guarantees some kind of genuine, high-level industry attention to its winning songs, pitting one composition against another is a dubious exercise that invariably involves way too much subjective judgment. Any organization that has as its main objective to give an award, or to produce an awards show—whether it be a locally sponsored contest or the Grammy Awards—is suspect in my book.

First, consider the fact that every entrant to a songwriting competition has to pony up a fee. Certainly, staging a contest can be a great way for an organization to raise much-needed capital, without hiking membership dues. However, the first line of screeners are invariably volunteers, and often amateur songwriters themselves, each of whom harbors his or her own taste preferences in writing styles and genres of music, so it becomes a very random roll of the dice as to which songs even get past the first level of competition. Unless the contest includes responding to each entree with a detailed evaluation that offers its writer(s) constructive feedback, I don't know how entering a contest can help writers improve their craft. There is no question that winning a contest, or even getting an honorable mention, could be a very real confidence booster, and heaven knows we all need some of that. Even then, however, winning or placing has to be taken with a certain grain of salt, knowing how random the screening process is. Contests are too much a matter of the judges' individual preferences and not enough a true evaluation of the quality of the song craft. I've seen quite a few writer discographies claiming awards from songwriting competitions but lacking any significant cuts or chart successes. After all, isn't that our real goal—seeing our songs on the charts?

CHAPTER 3
PROFILES IN MENTORSHIP

When I started scrawling ditties, there was nowhere for me to go to learn how to write a pop song or to get tips on how to improve my craft. Seven years of classical-piano lessons gave me some rudiments in music theory, and my brief stint as a folk-singer taught me some things about chord progressions and song structure. Other than that, all I could do was listen to the radio, peruse my record collection, and attempt to emulate the pop songs I admired. The first templates I used were those primitive, riffy, pop/rockers by The Kinks and The Troggs. I also retained a strong imprint from the vibrant rock singer/songwriters of my childhood, pompadoured guitar slingers, like Eddie Cochran and Ritchie Valens.

That is exactly how my heroes learned about songwriting, too. Dylan shamelessly followed in the footsteps of Woody Guthrie. Lennon and McCartney paid homage to Boudleaux and Felice Bryant, Otis Blackwell, as well as the spectacled Texan, Buddy Holly. The great, American hit writers of the Brill Building (Mann and Weil, Goffin and King, Ellie Greenwich, Jeff Barry, and Neil Diamond) derived their basics from classic New York, Tin Pan Alley tunesmiths, like Hoagy Carmichael and Irving Berlin. Mike Lieber and Jerry Stoller leaned on blues pioneers, such as Willie Dixon, Sonny Terry, and Brownie McGhee. Phil Spector took 1950s doo-wop and made it symphonic.

But, for this overly ambitious, teenaged wannabe in 1965, there were no classes to attend, no books to read, no workshops to sign up for, and no World Wide Web to surf. The fledgling songwriters of my youth were completely on our own. Amazingly enough, however, some of the finest songs of the pop era came out of those fertile seasons of naïve, intuitive composition, when every kid with a cheap guitar and a Mel Bay chord book was making up songs.

Today, self-appointed song-craft experts abound, and a good many of them seem to be sharing their theories and techniques via YouTube. I recently spent a mind-boggling afternoon clicking on a bunch of these homemade instructional videos. Here's my conclusion: I fail to understand what gives most of these people the credibility to teach, why the vast majority of these lessons were posted in the first place, and especially why some of these intolerably boring and banal lectures have attracted tens of thousands of hits. The desperate narcissism that must inspire a young lady to shoot a video in her bedroom in Ireland to explain how she came up with a three-chord pattern and four lines of fairly average melody and lyrics is beyond me. The veracity of some unaccomplished fellow, who presumes to expound the secrets of composing a completely generic piece of drivel, wielding a Magic Marker across a piece of poster board taped to his piano keys is, well, simultaneously amusing and infuriating.

What makes these videos even more dangerous is they are captioned with such titles as, "How To Write A Song," "Songwriting Made Easy," and "Simple Songwriting Techniques." As soon as somebody implies that songwriting is simple or that finding success as a songwriter is a piece of cake, run away—*fast!* It is true that—if you're blessed with certain, basic talents, have a strong desire to write, possess the pluck to apply yourself, and have developed enough spine to ignore the word "No" every day for the rest of your life—you have everything it takes to become a successful songwriter. However, the many choices that go into crafting a great song are not by any stretch of the imagination easy, the process requires the patience of Mother Theresa and the stamina of Superman. In addition, the life of a writer is often fraught with unpredictability and frustration. Just because a pretty blond in front of a white board informs you that, in five minutes you, too, can dash off a song worthy of broadcast on the airwaves, doesn't mean it's fact or that it's likely to happen. If that were so, then each and every one of those 10,000-plus eager, potential hit makers who've viewed her video would already have a chart-buster of their own, wouldn't they?

Fortunately, in this day and age, there *are* credible song-craft education resources from which to draw and some proven teachers. Please use discretion when it comes to whom you trust to help you along. That advice begs the question: What exactly are the qualities and qualifications you might be looking for in a song-craft mentor? For instance: Does this person need to have an impressive track record as a songwriter? Not necessarily, but extensive experience with the songwriting process, a complete mastery of the vernacular, and a comprehensive knowledge of pop-song history are all essentials. Outside of those more academic prerequisites, it really comes down to style, emphasis, and personality, along with accessibility, logistics, and (of course) expense.

Like me, I'm sure you have fond memories of those rare schoolteachers, neighborhood music instructors, or sports coaches who helped bring out your highest intuitions, encouraged your natural talents, and ultimately influenced your life for the better. There are other teachers, coaches, and mentors you may have despised (for good reason), while the mediocre rest have probably faded into a haze of anonymity. Finding a songwriting mentor worthy of your trust, who has your best interests in mind, and is capable of communicating honestly, constructively, and with compassion is a rare thing. You're looking for a coach/instructor with whom you have chemistry, whose teaching methods resonate with you, and who has the potential of providing the best boost to your writing style and craft. Only when you find the right mentor or mentors will you completely understand the value of coaching and instruction. Only when you take down your guard, swallow your pride and learn to listen and apply time-worn advice, proven techniques, and constructive criticism will you be able to raise your work to its greatest potential. Every songwriter, professional or amateur, veteran or rookie, can benefit from coaching and feedback.

I love this quote, from highly regarded songwriter and tunesmithing coach, Robin Frederick:

"Song-craft tools exist because, over hundreds of years, songwriters have found that they help listeners to understand, experience, and remember the emotional message at the heart of our songs."

Does that make sense to you? You're inspired to communicate an emotional message with words, music, and rhythm. Some fragments of melody and a few rhymes pop into your head. You're on the ball enough to capture those bits and pieces on tape. You apply yourself to the hours it takes to experiment with chord changes, melodies, and structures. You scribble pages of lyrics, as you assemble this song. You think it's finished; and you think it's pretty good. Is it the best it can be? How can you possibly know? You play it for friends, maybe for Mom. Everybody seems to be impressed. But, what do they really know? You could really use a mentor, a coach to give you constructive feedback; to inform you where your work is succeeding creatively and where it may need improvement; to make the suggestions and open new doors of possibility; to dare you to be the best songwriter you can be and help you write the very best song you can write.

I've created brief profiles of some of the top people in songwriting education today. The following professionals all have the knowledge, real-time experience, and expertise to wear the mantle of "pop-songwriting educator." You may not have the means or the opportunity to work directly with any of the teachers on this high-echelon list, but these are the people who set the bar. If you're really serious about developing your craft, you will seek out somebody of this caliber.

John Braheny

John Braheny is not known as a hit songwriter. Yet, for more than three decades, this unassuming, gracious, smiling gentleman has become perhaps the most visible and credible advocate for songwriting education in the U.S. The National Academy of Songwriters called Braheny's book, *The Craft and Business of Songwriting* "...a veritable songwriter's bible. This is the definitive work on the subject of songwriting."

With Len Chandler, Braheny co-founded the Los Angeles Songwriters Showcase and Songwriters Expo, nurturing the talents of such songwriting legends as Lindsey Buckingham, Stevie Nix, Stephen Bishop, Karla Bonoff, Steve Seskin, Wendy Waldman, Warren Zevon, and the world's most successful contemporary-pop tunesmith, Diane Warren, for whom Braheny and Chandler critiqued more than 150 songs, when she was a burgeoning 15-year-old prodigy. (If that doesn't testify to the power of seeking constructive coaching, I don't know what possible could.) So, even without having penned hits of his own, John Braheny's impressive credentials add up to tremendous credibility when it comes to helping a writer learn his or her craft.

Jason Blume

Jason Blume not only lays claim to some very impressive coaching cred, but he has racked up an imposing discography of his own. Having penned songs with and for Britney Spears, Backstreet Boys, and Jesse McCartney, as well as for country artists John Berry and Collin Raye, Blume is one of the few writers to ever have songs on the Pop, R&B, and Country charts simultaneously. Blume is the author of two books: *Six Steps To Songwriting Success* (New York: Watson-Guptill Publications, 2008) and *The Business of Songwriting* (New York: Watson-Guptill Publications, 2006). At this writing, he has conducted songwriting workshops for BMI for more than ten years, taught classes at UCLA and Vanderbilt University, and continues to travel the world helping songwriters develop their talents, by speaking about songwriting and conducting workshops. Blume's Website (www.jasonblume.com) also offers online evaluations and coaching.

Pat and Pete Luboff

Pat and Pete Luboff have enjoyed some success as writers as well. Through their 40 years as a team, the Luboffs have scored cuts with Snoop Dogg, Bobby Womack, and Patti LaBelle. Together, this couple has been helping songwriters improve their craft since 1979 and have co-authored two books, *101 Songwriting Wrongs and How to Right Them* (Cincinnati: Writer's Digest Books, 2007), and *12 Steps to Building Better Songs* (Nashville: Pea Pod Music, sixth revised edition, 2009). Generous and fun, fun, fun, these two songwriting enthusiasts inspire their students and clients to do their best work with positive energy. Favorites of NSAI, Pat and Pete Luboff are ubiquitous and accessible at most any event pertaining to songwriting. Their Website is www.WriteSongs.com.

Deanna Walker

Charming, lovely Deanna Walker conducts classes for Blair School of Music in Nashville, where she is adjunct artist teacher of piano and director of the songwriting program. As a writer herself, Deanna has scored cuts with Reba McIntire, Blake Shelton, and Kenny Rogers. With a masters in music from Johns Hopkins University, Walker divides her evening classes between instruction and a live, classroom interview with a hit writer. I have been fortunate enough to be invited in for a Deanna Walker interview. It was a rare treat. Denitia Odigie, summer 2009's "Find of the Fest" at POP Montreal International Music Festival, credits Walker with giving her the courage to pursue her singer/songwriter dreams. Everyone I know who has been privileged to attend a semester under Deanna Walker's tutelage has waxed rhapsodic about the experience.

Pat Pattison

Pat Pattison is certainly one of our most academically prestigious songwriting instructors. A professor at Massachusetts's Berklee College, Pattison has three very successful songwriting books to his credit: *Writing Better Lyrics*, *Managing Lyric Structure* (Boston: Berklee Press, 1991), and *Rhyming Techniques and Strategies* (Boston: Berklee Press, 1991). Pattison teaches lyric writing through exercises to develop and strengthen the student's literary muscles; object writing being one of his most stressed techniques. Gillian Welch, Berklee class of '92, gives Pattison's classes kudos for helping her to achieve her storied success. Although Pattison doesn't claim an impressive list of cuts, his lyrics have won more than 40 awards. Pattison offers online training in addition to his Berklee classroom work.

Danny Arena and Sara Light

When it comes to sheepskins (I'm talkin' diplomas, kids, not fuzzy car-seat covers), the married team of Danny Arena and Sara Light are well positioned in the world of song-craft education. Arena's dual degrees (computer science and music) and Light's masters in English education (all from Rutgers University) fully equip these dynamos to be on the cutting edge of what Arena calls "distance education." Melody specialist Arena is an associate professor at Volunteer State College in Tennessee, a member of the Vanderbilt University faculty, and has given the keynote address for NSAI's Songposium. Arena and Light created the downloadable audio series, *The Songwriters Survival Kit*, the online songwriting campus, SongU (www.songu.com), and The Songwriters Education Resource, which provides links to essential song-craft sites and materials.

As songwriters, these two folks don't lack for credits either. Light (who had never written a song until the pair were poised to get married, when she bailed her hubby-to-be out on his wedding-song lyric) wrote John Michael Montgomery's hit, "Home To You." Arena is a Tony Award nominee for his contributions to Broadway's *Urban Cowboy, The Musical.*

Harriet Schock

Harriet Schock has a well-rounded pedigree as a hit writer, author, and recording artist, as well as a well earned reputation as one of the world's most-respected song-craft instructors. Schock's "Ain't No Way To Treat a Lady" was a Number One smash for Helen Reddy and garnered a Grammy nomination. Since that hit, Smokey Robinson, Roberta Flack, Lee Greenwood, and Johnny Mathis have recorded Schock compositions, and many of her songs have been featured in films and on TV broadcasts. She began teaching at University of Southern California, then in the early

1990s, conducted songwriting classes with legendary producer Nik Venet (Beach Boys, Lou Rawls, Glen Campbell, Linda Ronstadt). Since Venet's passing in 1998, Schock has capably and passionately carried on the work they began together. Schock is available for private, one-on-one coaching, L.A.–classroom, and correspondence courses, as well as consultation/song critiques. Schock authored the book, *Becoming Remarkable: For Songwriters and Those Who Love Song* (Nevada City, CA: Blue Dolphin Publishing, 1999).

Robin Frederick

Robin Frederick heads the A&R team at TAXI, the world's largest independent A&R company and was formerly A&R Director for Rhino Records. A songwriter with more than 500 credits, Frederick published the book, *Shortcuts to Hit Songwriting: 126 Proven Techniques for Writing Songs that Sell* (Calabasas, CA: TAXI Music Books, 2008). Frederick offers a plethora of helpful info on her Website (www.robinfrederick.com) and regularly attends the TAXI Road Rally among other music business events.

Barbara Cloyd

If anybody knows songwriters, it's Barbara Cloyd. Booking the Mecca of the performing songwriter, Nashville's Bluebird Café, for more than 20 years, and hosting the venue's vaunted Monday open-mic nights, she's met more than a few. Country diva, Lorrie Morgan, hit the Top Ten with Cloyd's "I Guess You Had To Be There," cowritten by Jon Robbin. This is a song many in Nashville consider a perfect composition. In 2001, in response to continual requests for help from developing writers, Cloyd founded a consultation service, which she named Ready for the Row. Through workshops, classes, recorded critiques, and individual sessions, Cloyd continues to assist new writers to develop their writing skills and navigate the maze of the music business. Many helpful Cloyd-authored articles on finding success on Music Row are posted on her Website (barbaracloyd.com).

Several other very worthy song-craft coaches offer services and/or educational materials for aspiring writers. Music Row hit man and CMA song-of-the-year nominee Odie Blackmon has released an excellent DVD called *The Craft of Writing Hit Songs*. CJ Watson and Don McNatt are veteran songwriting coaches. Steve Leslie is relatively new in the coaching game, but this thoughtful, talented gent comes with strong tunesmithing credentials and has much to offer to any writer truly interested in improving his or her craft. Billy Seidman offers classes through BMI's New York office. Last, but not by any means least, I offer my services as coach, author, and mentor, through my books, my Website (makinstuffup.net), via telephone and face-to-face consultations, and at conferences, workshops, seminars, and panels.

PART TWO:

THE BUSINESS

CHAPTER 4
Some History

"The first professional songwriter was Stephen Foster," Bart Herbison often commences his talk, whether he is speaking to a room filled with music business professionals or to a group of legislators. As the Executive Director of NSAI, Herbison is one of the fiercest and most effective advocates on behalf of songwriters. Herbison also feels it's important that songwriters learn a little about the stepping stones that led tunesmiths to an era when a hit song is capable of making millions. Knowing where we came from gives us perspective, helps us appreciate what we've gained so far, and motivates us to continue to fight for our rights to retain control and equity in our own work. Before Stephen Foster, Herbison explains, songwriters were never paid for their creations.

Talk about copyrights! Stephen Foster cranked 'em out, way back in the middle of the nineteenth century: "Beautiful Dreamer," "Swanee River," "Jeannie with the Light Brown Hair," "Camptown Races," and many, many more. This cat was a virtual hit machine. However, in those long-ago good old days of the mid 1800s, there was no way of recording music. Even if there had been, there would have been no machine that could play it back. The only way songs could generate income was through the sale of sheet music. Pianos were beginning to become more commonplace in the living rooms of America. So, entrepreneurial music publishers took advantage of this growing trend by mass-producing sheet music of current popular songs. Ah, the free market! Retailers who sold sheet music would often hire a piano player to play requests. If a customer were to be interested in a particular title, he or she would pull it from the rack, take the manuscript to the pianist, and ask to hear the arrangement in a spontaneous, live performance. That tune and its written rendition would be exposed to everybody in the store. And that, my friends, was how the hits of the day were made and how those hits made money.

Voila! A new industry was born, founded on popular songs and the sale of sheet music (pianos and player-piano rolls, too, for that matter). This new industry also opened up opportunities to a good number of burgeoning performers: the music business's first "demo singers," who tickled the ivories and warbled for rapt, captive audiences in those stores. Somehow, however, the songwriters who had crafted the very songs that were the foundation this new "music business" had been left out of the mix. They had not been invited to share in this booming commerce. Stephen Foster was the first hit songwriter to negotiate single song agreements with music publishers, culling cash for his original compositions. He received a whopping $100 for "Oh, Susanna." "Old Folks at Home," his biggest hit, gained him a grand total of 15 smackers. Soon thereafter, two separate

New York publishers offered Foster a new kind of deal: two cents for every copy of "Oh Susanna" they sold. Thus, the concept of mechanical royalties was born.

The problem was that although Foster was signing away duplication rights for his songs (*in perpetuity,* meaning "forever"), these slick New Yorkers refused to allow him to receive royalties for any run after the very first printing. So, although Foster's first publishing deals represented a huge breakthrough for songwriters' rights to earn residual income from their own labors and set a precedent for others to enjoy at least *some* compensation for their creative inspirations, tunesmiths still had a long slog ahead. Ever since Stephen Foster pioneered the concept of professional songwriting, those who write the songs that make the whole world sing have been struggling to hold on to ownership and control, and to earn a reasonable share of the income generated by their work. For more than 150 years, every step of the way, some entrepreneur or corporate entity has been trying to keep content creators from claiming the fruits of their own labors. At the advent of every new technological innovation, songwriters have had to fight to receive a reasonable return for the most essential contribution—the nuclear fuel rod that ignites the engine that turns the turbine of commerce—the song itself.

The first sheet-music portfolio was published in 1640 in the form of *The Whole Book of Psalms.* So, it had taken two hundred years for a songwriter to receive the first royalty payment. In the second half of the nineteenth century, creators of popular songs were finally figuring out how to make a living—and even ways to grow wealthy. They did this by taking their songs directly to the public, not waiting around for the public to come to them. The most enterprising of this new breed established one-stop shops for the creation of songs and the manufacture, sales, and distribution of those songs' sheet music. In other words, these were not only the first self-published songwriters, but also the first song pluggers. In order to maximize exposure for their product line, they would go to nightclubs and vaudeville theaters to pitch their wares to performers. Some would stand on street corners, in department stores, or arcades, singing tunes from their catalog. As these creative—and certainly assertive—fellows smartly held onto the duplication rights to their own stuff, and found the means to do it, they were also able to keep *all* the profits from the sales, not just two cents a copy. This was how the first music publishing houses were born. M. Witmark and Sons was the archetype. One Witmark brother was the writer, the other the performer. After hustling to score a handful of self-published hits, they were able to open an office in New York's Union Square, which was America's entertainment capital. Soon, the Witmarks had the resources to sign songs by other songwriters and began building a formidable lexicon of hit copyrights.

So, even back in the pioneering days of professional tunesmithing, creative types were figuring out that the most committed and effective advocate for any writer's songs is the writer himself (or *her*self, as the case might be). This remains true to this day and is a lesson anyone with designs on ever getting a tune on the pop music charts should take to heart. Regardless of your song-dog nature, alpha or omega, outgoing or reserved, ferocious or docile, the one who cares about your songs more than any other person on Earth is *you*. You cannot afford to hide away in a cave, scribbling and scratching out your inspirations, and expect success to find you. You have to be proactive, to take the initiative, to make your presence known, to develop the relationships that will give your songs a chance to achieve their greatest destiny. Like the Witmark brothers, you need to do your own version of singing on street corners, of finding talented musicians and singers to perform your tunes. Of course, you will also be well served to balance your energies between the writing (always striving, uncompromisingly, for excellence), and cultivating strategic friendships, and hawking your line of goods. If you pick up the ball every day and carry it as far as you can yourself, you will eventually find teammates to help you score.

As the nineteenth century came to a close, the music-publishing business flourished. Publishers started categorizing songs and marketing them generically: Irish songs, blues, rags, dialect songs, cakewalks, nostalgia songs, and so on. The biggest hits were popularized by the great vaudevillians of the day: George M. Cohen, Sophie Tucker, Al Jolson, and later, Eddie Cantor. Pianist/composer Scott Joplin broke out as the most successful purveyor of ragtime. In 1913, *Billboard Magazine* began featuring its first sheet music chart of the nation's most popular songs. Musical theater soon took over from vaudeville as the primary vehicle for the popular song, featuring the great pop compositions of Jerome Kern, Irving Berlin, and the Gershwin brothers. A true community of songwriters blossomed, as New York's Tin Pan Alley became the breeding ground and birthplace for the American popular song.

Then came the advent of sound recording. Movies started to talk, and music naturally jumped in to fill the silence with incredible song and dance numbers performed by Fred Astaire and Ginger Rogers, Cab Calloway novelty numbers, and breathtaking extravaganzas staged by Busby Berkely. Big bands and blues ensembles toured, breaking new hit songs and instrumentals. All the while, sneaking up stealthily to bring recorded music into every home was Edison's 1877 invention, the phonograph. Enrico Caruso started making and releasing records in 1903. The companies that eventually became Columbia, RCA, and Universal Records were formed. By the 1920s, recorded discs were selling in the millions. Music publishing and songwriting was now big business.

At first, thick, brittle, 78 RPM records played on hand-cranked turntables, amplified only by a cone-shaped bullhorn. Those primitive but miraculous contraptions gave way to electric turntables, tube amplifiers, and magnetic speakers. The 1950s popularized mono 45s and the 33⅓ RPM, long-play record album (the LP). In the '60s, monophonic recordings were eclipsed by stereo, ushering in the magic of high fidelity—hi-fi—sound. Live, direct-to-tape recordings were overtaken by multitrack. Then sound quality took a backseat to convenience with 3¾ inch-per-second, thin-tape audio cassettes. Suddenly, consumers had the means to record music themselves, either from the radio or from a friend's record album. The copying and pirating of music presented a new challenge to the industry. However, while this was a problem, the generation loss from analog copying and the time it took to duplicate sound (even at high speeds) softened the blow to the industry. Furthermore, the audiotape manufacturers were forced to make up some of the losses by charging a fee per tape sold that went into a fund to be distributed to record companies and music publishers, part of which was ostensibly passed on to artists and songwriters.

With the compact disc, analog reproduction for commercial distribution gave way to the digital format. Fragile, easily scratched or warped records were replaced by smaller, more resilient CDs. With none of that surface noise created by the contact of the needle on vinyl and with the more antiseptic, digital sound, the public acclimated its collective ears to a new audio standard. Content distributors and hardware manufacturers used shrewd marketing to connote to the public that "digital means better." Solid argument on both sides of the analog vs. digital debate notwithstanding, one fact rings true: By participating in this propaganda campaign on behalf of digital, the record companies were shooting themselves in the foot, helping set the stage for their own potential demise. When home CD burners became affordable, digital files could then be easily reassembled and copied time and time again with no loss of sound quality. The floodgates were now wide open for music piracy to become rampant. That's when the feces really hit the fan! Record companies, publishers, songwriters, and recording artists began to see some very ominous writing on the wall.

Compressed, digital audio files—the most common and popular being MP3s—looked like the final nail in the coffin. Today, a billion illegal, unpaid downloads are shared monthly. The entire music biz is struggling desperately (with what's left of its strength) not to be stuffed into that pine box and buried while it still has breath. Back in the second half of the 1970s and through the '80s, the most successful record albums, cassettes, and CDs sold upwards of 25 million to 30 million copies worldwide. Artists like Peter Frampton, Bee Gees, Fleetwood Mac, and Michael Jackson kept the industry thriving by selling mass quantities of their collections. The enormous amounts of cash generated by these few artists kept the labels investing in new talent. The mid '80s had its breakouts, too, including multiplatinum acts such as Quiet Riot, Motley Crüe, Guns and Roses, Ratt,

Poison, Winger, L.A. Guns, and Cinderella. The later '80s produced Pearl Jam, Nirvana, and the grunge movement, plus a new, bolder breed of female singer/songwriters, Alanis Morissette and Sarah McLachlan. Even in the all-CD era of the '90s, country performers like Garth Brooks, Billy Ray Cyrus, and Dixie Chicks, hip-hoppers like Lauren Hill and Eminem, pop-alternative innovators like Moby and Beck, even middle-of-the-road, adult-contemporary artists like Bonnie Raitt sold in the multi-millions.

By the beginning of the new millennium, CD-album sales began to fall off by double-digit percentages yearly. With the growing popularity of MP3 players, like Apple's ever-popular iPod, more and more consumers who were willing to pay for music were going to iTunes, Rhapsody, CD Baby, and other online music stores to purchase single tracks. Now, retail record stores have all but disappeared. Hard-copy CDs are mostly sold at large discount outlets, like Target, Best Buy, and Walmart, bookstores like Borders and Barnes and Noble, or online, through Amazon.com. So today, even the biggest-selling artists in the world struggle to break five million units in worldwide CD sales. Platinum albums become rarer as the years go by. Retail sales of music cannot support the structure of the business. A new industry template is needed if popular music itself is to survive.

So, sitting at the bottom of the food chain, songwriters find themselves a particularly endangered species because of this downward-spiral of business revenues. Digital downloading is not the only culprit in this bleak scenario. Huge radio conglomerates and their corporate-controlled radio playlists are providing fewer and fewer opportunities for the songwriter of today to get songs on the air. For performing songwriters, rising fuel prices make touring more expensive and less profitable. With high unemployment across the board, coupled with a global recession, discretionary spending is down for music and entertainment, especially those pricey concert tickets. "Yikes," you might be exclaiming, "this sure doesn't look good!"

However, do not despair, my children, for the news is not *all* bad. Hit copyrights today are capable of making far more money far faster than even the biggest smashes of prior decades. When a song hits, it *really* hits! In addition to traditional means (radio play and sales), hit songs have a plethora of ways to rake in oodles of cash: film, TV, commercials, Vegas, Broadway, ringtones, greeting cards, toys…you name it. Songs can be licensed and attached in a thousand ways, all of which can add up to millions and millions for publishers and songwriters.

And, while new technology can certainly take a lot of the blame for bringing big record labels and top recording artists to this crisis point, it has also leveled the playing field considerably, giving anybody with talent, ambition, and some basic, affordable tools an avenue to reach their audience—directly. Yes, my friends, I *am* talkin' 'bout the World Wide Web! The newest innovations also speed up every step of the process, enabling us to communicate in a borderless universe, instantaneously. I wonder if you youngsters remember a time when folks had to copy recorded music in real time, from a record to a tape, or from one tape to another tape. Back in those primitive days, if we wanted to share recorded music, we'd either have to deliver that copy by hand, or put it in the mail. It could take as much as a week for a friend or colleague on the opposite coast to hear a new mix.

Today, an audio file can be copied in seconds, attached to an email, or uploaded to a file-sharing service—via cel phone, for Pete's sake—and sent off instantly to anywhere in the world. MySpace opened up new vistas of possibility for the savvy networker/self-marketer. Now, you can be your own distributor, your own publicist, your own promotion person. Now, you can make "friends" with literally thousands of people you may never even meet face to face. The entire social-networking vernacular is curious, isn't it? "Friends," not "fans." Sure, at its heart, it's peer networking and peer marketing, which makes the term "friends" appropriate. But when an artist gets to the level of a Colbie Caillat or a Taylor Swift, a half a million devotees ain't friends; they're fans, pure and simple. Still, I'm sure it's as big a kick in the pants for some kid in Smalltown, Ohio to brag, "I'm MySpace friends with TSwift," as it is for me to say, "I'm Facebook friends with Jimmy Dale Gilmore." Nevertheless—Caillat and Swift being prime examples—stars are now made through savvy, social networking on the Net. YouTube has democratized the media as well, offering anyone with a video camera, some vision, and a lotta chutzpah the chance to attract thousands of viewers. What used to take a ton of stamp licking, poster hammering, and door knocking has been distilled down to a couple of key strokes and a click of a mouse. Wow! You now have no excuse for not laying your career groundwork, aside from being out-and-out lazy, too stupid to breathe, or stone-ass drunk 24 hours a day. (And those have never really been very good excuses, have they?)

The question regarding using all this new media is this: How do you commodify it? How does an Internet entrepreneur turn those Web-marketing skills into cold, hard cash? Well, kiddos, here's the irony: The brilliant minds behind MySpace and YouTube have done just that. You provide the content and attract all of the traffic. But, *they* sell the advertising that your traffic sees on the site. You get zipola for the performance of your song, but MySpace and YouTube rake in the cash from the ads that your listeners and viewers are forced to wade through to get to it. Somebody else *always* seems to be benefiting from the creative inspirations of songwriters. So, therein lies one of the newest battlefields for music publishers, musicians, and song scribes, as we continue our never-ending struggle to get a little sliver o' the pie: Should social networking and video sites have the right to broadcast content for free? Or, since they sell ads on the backs of the content we provide, should they be required to pay performing rights fees for the privilege? A quandary, for sure. And one that will not be settled without some shouting and hair-pulling.

If he were to time travel from a century and a half ago, I can't help but imagine what Stephen Foster would say about how the business of songwriting has evolved since he commanded all of 15 bucks for what became his most popular copyright. "You get 9.1 cents for every sale?" he might marvel. "Hit songs sell millions of copies? And you're complaining?"

"Yeah," you might respond, "but you have to get a cut first. It's a jungle out there! You were only competing with a handful of songwriters in your day. Now, there are hundreds of thousands of us, all grabbing for a bite of the same carrot."

Foster might then choose to point out the technological advantages modern songwriters now have at their fingertips: "You have the ability to reach millions of people in seconds through your magic computer box!" Then, he might make this assumption: "All you need to do now is to write a hit song and post it online for the world to hear."

"Oh, if it were only that simple," you could answer. "If it were only that simple."

CHAPTER 5
Copyright Ownership

Here are some stupid questions, to which the answer is always an obvious and emphatic *No!*

Would you call yourself a real estate agent and list your neighbor's house for sale if you didn't know how to order an appraisal, how to fill out a sales contract, how much commission to charge, and who is responsible for paying it? *No!*

Would you call yourself a contractor and dispatch a bulldozer to dig a foundation if you didn't know the first thing about pulling permits, how to read a blueprint, or what the going rate is for labor? *No, of course not!*

Here is a follow-up question for which there is no satisfactory answer: Why then do so many creative souls go into the business of songwriting without possessing an iota of information about what a copyright is, how a copyright generates income, and where that income comes from?

Maybe it's because we are so grateful to have any opportunity at all to make stuff up that we simply neglect to find out these seemingly academic, mundane, but absolutely essential things. Maybe we songwriters are so naïve that we actually think that, should we somehow stumble upon a hit, our bank balances will suddenly and automatically increase a million fold. I can't tell you how many tunesmiths I've encountered through the years who have had big chart successes, yet they were forced to spend decades chasing down money due to them, all because they neglected to join a performing rights organization; or failed to register a title; or signed a piece of paper they either didn't understand or read thoroughly. Royalties don't just arrive by way of magic, kids. Here's the reality: *You* will need to take care of some basic tasks to put your brand on your own work and claim its spoils. You will encounter players/partners/entities/organizations along the way who will be important to your success. Bottom line, before you go into business, it pays to know how that business works. In spite of how thrilled we may be to be living the creative life, that platitude is just as true for us songwriters as it is for real estate agents and contractors.

Copyright

So, let's begin by answering the first question: What is a copyright?

In essence, a copyright represents the lyrics and the melody (music) of a song. (Note that there is no mention here of chord progression, groove, or arrangement—even though those are certainly integral parts of every pop song.) Technically, the ownership of a copyright is divided into two halves. The publisher of the song gets 50 percent of the copyright income from the song. The other 50 percent of the song's copyright income is divided evenly: The author of the lyrics gets 25 percent of the song's total income; the composer of the melody also gets 25 percent of the song's copyright income. If a song has multiple publishers, lyricists, or composers, their respective shares are then divided further. If the copyright has not been assigned to a publisher or publishers, then the publisher's share of the copyright ownership is automatically assigned to the song's creator(s), the songwriter(s). In other words, by default, until you assign a copyright to a publisher, *you* are the publisher of your own work. A songwriter is not, in any way shape or form, required to have a publisher.

So, if you were to write an original song today by yourself, you would own all of the copyright, because you are lyricist, composer, and publisher. This is a copyright in its simplest form: a pie solely owned, divided into two halves, but controlled by one creative person. However, as more collaborators come into the process—and publishers, too—dividing the pie gets more intricate, and can actually become extremely complicated. Being aware of how this works could be very important to your future, as well as the future of your children, not to mention your children's children. I put that possibility in the category of good—but totally avoidable—problems to have.

Supposing, instead of flying solo, you were to cowrite a song with Donna. As you and Donna both write lyrics and melody, you guys have two options when it comes to dividing up your ownership shares. The easiest route is to divide the copyright right down the middle into two equal pieces. A couple of kids from Liverpool, John Lennon and Paul McCartney, always did it this way. Regardless of who was primarily responsible for the lion's share of the creative work, they split the credit—and the ownership—equally. "Yesterday," for instance, was a McCartney composition, but bears both writers' names. This all-for-one, one-for-all philosophy is based on the concept that over the course of time, ultimately it will all come out in the wash. The vast majority of the time here in Nashville, no matter how much or how little each credited cowriter contributes to the song, credit is divided evenly among the writers on the session. It's simpler that way, and I've heard few complaints.

Strange but True

In a three-way collaboration, a top session player I know wrote a song with an established songwriter and a star artist. Their collaboration became a hit single. A colleague was curious as to which of the writers had been responsible for what part of the composition. "Did the artist write the music?" he inquired.

"No," the session player answered, "I pretty much took care of the music."

That prompted the obvious question to follow: "Then, did he write the lyrics?"

"No, the other songwriter wrote the words," responded the session player.

"Then," the frustrated colleague persisted, "what did the artist write?"

"Well," the session player pondered, "he kinda got the groove."

Yet, without writing a word or a note of the song, the star was credited with a full third of the copyright. That's pretty much the way it works in Nashville. Whether silent or vociferous, an instigator, a perpetrator, or merely a witness, if you were in the room when the song came to be, you are credited as an equal cowriter. You don't have to be a star artist to qualify. You just have to show up at the appointed time and place. Elsewhere, particularly in other music capitals, like New York, L.A., and London, collaborators might be more inclined to negotiate more disproportionate splits, according to which writers might have offered more or less to the song's creation. I've seen these kinds of deliberations get down to the Nth degree, with collaborators haggling for hours about who came up with what exact syllables. That could result with a copyright split into such peculiar divisions as 82.3 percent to one writer, 12.8 percent to a second, and 4.9 percent for the third. There is no absolute, set creed about dividing up a copyright. What is important is that the writers do communicate and agree on the splits, preferably as soon as the song is completed. Some kind of written and signed documentation could be useful to commemorate your agreement as well. Selective Memory Disease is rampant in show biz, especially when big money comes into play.

On that note, some years ago, another friend of mine cowrote a tune with a tunesmith/buddy and brought it in its completed form to a talented singer. The singer recorded the finished song, then demanded to be credited as a third writer. (This tactic, by the way, has been common practice for decades. Does anybody really believe that Elvis Presley really sat down and cowrote "Don't Be Cruel" with Otis Blackwell?) Surely there's a ton of greed and ego demonstrated in this kind of legalized extortion. But, while many writers consider this sort of thing absolutely repugnant and completely unethical, it really amounts to a win/win for both writer and performer. This policy is, as it were, a victimless crime. Similar standard operating procedure takes place all the time in movies, television, and other entertainment businesses as well. Ever wonder how a movie can have seven producers in addition to an assortment executive and assistant producers?

Anyway, this "now three-way" collaboration shot to the top of the charts. At that point, the singer boldly proclaimed that he had actually written the song *by himself.* He had an injunction put on the copyright's income, hoping to screw the real writers out of their credits *and* their royalties. Hundreds of thousands of dollars due to the songwriters and publishers were held up in escrow, while this ugly dispute waited its turn in court. The fair shares of the song were eventually settled. However, had the writers written up and initialed a simple agreement prior to the record release, this despicable dishonesty might not have had a chance to fester. It's hard enough for songwriters to achieve success. To have something as underhanded as this take place when success finally arrives is tragic. This kind of ugly scenario is, however, avoidable.

Now, let's shake off the yuck of that horror story and get back to the subject at hand: copyright ownership. Each cowriter's share of a copyright must be matched by an exact corresponding publisher's share. In that hypothetical solo-written song, as you are responsible for 100 percent of the lyrics and music, 50 percent of that copyright's income is due to you as the sole author and composer. Correspondingly, you own a 100 percent publisher share, representing the other 50 percent of income, too (see Fig. 1).

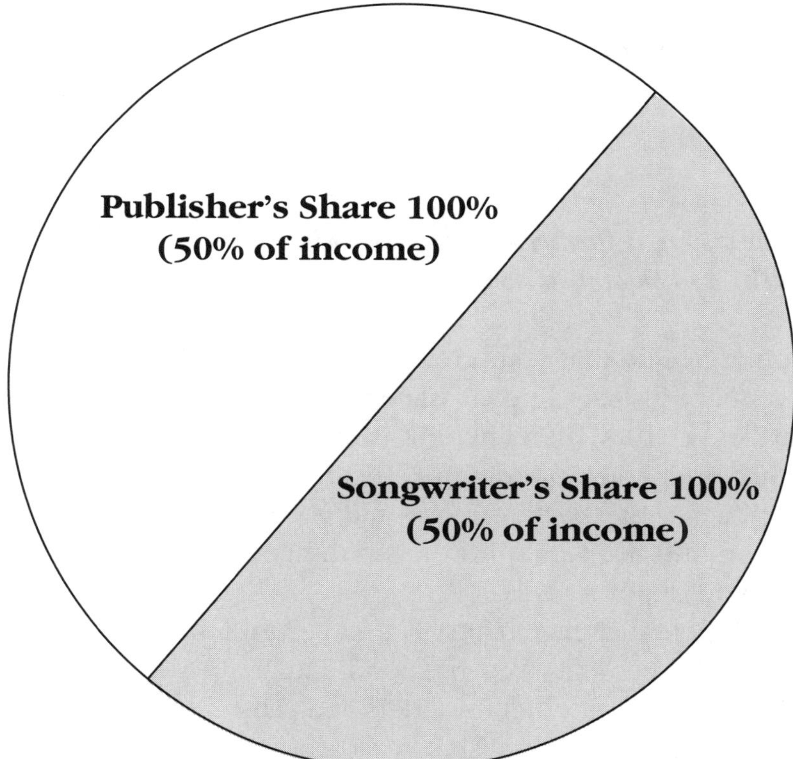

FIG. 1: Here is the basic breakdown of copyright income from a song completely composed and written by a single songwriter.

In your cowritten song, assuming that you and Donna have agreed to divide your credit equally, your writer's share would be 50 percent, representing 25 percent of the income, as would your corresponding publisher's share. That would go for Donna as well (see Fig. 2).

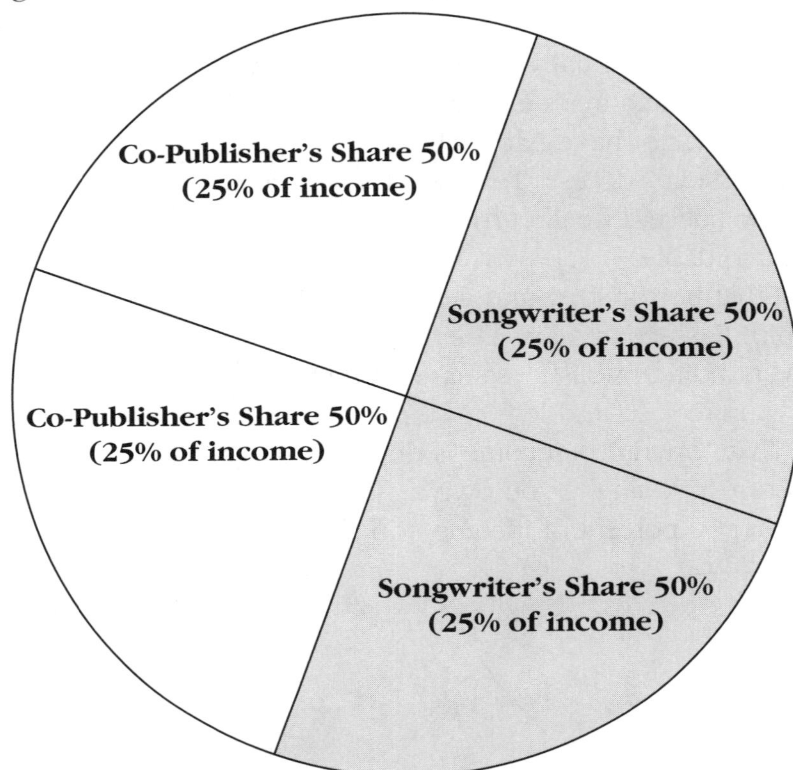

FIG. 2: The copyright income for a song is further broken down when two songwriters cowrite and copublish the song.

In the event that you and Donna decide that your creative contributions warrant a different split, you two might instead agree to slice up this pie in unequal disproportions. Regardless of how the copyright is divided among the writers, it must have an exact corresponding percentage of the publisher's share representing each writer's share. We could go on for pages examining every permutation, but that would bore even the geekiest of the geeks. And, I'm pretty sure you're not a geek.

However, there is one additional, potential eventuality that may get a little confusing. As I've stated, the publisher's share has to correspond equally with the writer's share; that should be simple enough to understand. The potentially confusing thing is this: More than one publisher could co-own that publisher's share. For instance, here's a real example from my own personal experience. After Toby Keith recorded "My List," Rob Hendon, from Toby's publishing company, Paddock Music, gave me a call. "Rand," Hendon began (the tone of his voice told me that something important was in the offing), "I really want this song to make Toby's album."

"You and me both, Rob," I agreed, whole-heartedly.

"I'm gonna work my tail off to make that happen, but there's no guarantee that it will," Hendon elaborated. "But honestly, it would make my job a whole lot easier if I had a bigger share of the copyright." Well, I knew what was coming. He wanted me to sign over my publishing rights to Paddock. Now, I was a veteran of more than three decades in the trenches, with nearly two hundred songwriting credits and some prestigious awards. In my mind, I had earned the right to retain ownership of my own publishing. However, I also knew this: A Toby Keith cut—which at that time guaranteed about three million sales—was worth a heck of a lot more than a song that was still languishing on the shelf two years after it was written. I saw the upside of what Hendon was suggesting. I could make Hendon look like a hero and, at the same time, give Keith more incentive to include the song on his album. So, instead of hanging up the phone in anger, I swallowed my pride and negotiated a deal with Hendon. At the end of the day, I signed over a copublisher's share of the song—half of my half. In exchange, Hendon gave me other conditions, including a guarantee that "My List" be released on Keith's next DreamWorks album. If the song wasn't released, Paddock's copublisher share would revert back to me.

So, when you look at the pie chart for "My List," my corresponding 50 percent publisher's share is split once again—but only on the publisher's side of the pie—in equal shares, between Keith's company and my dba publishing entity, Weightless Cargo Music. In fact, a publishing share can continue to be sold off and doled out in portions to any number of copublishers, as long as the total percentage of the publisher's share is equal to the corresponding writer's share.

This leads nicely to our next question.

What Does a Publisher Do?

As you make your way into and through the oft-times frustrating and overwhelming maze of the music business, you're liable to hear one piece of unsolicited advice repeated loudly and often, in these exact words: "Don't give away your publishing." While that credo will certainly be heartfelt, valid, and worthwhile, its exact verbiage will also be more than a little bit misleading. You see, I can't think of a single instance in which you would actually "give away" your publisher's share of a copyright. The reason I say this is that, theoretically, you should always have a reason to make the deal, an exchange of some kind, some quid pro quo that would incline you to consider surrendering your publishing share, or a portion of it. For example: I gave up half of my publisher's share of "My List," because it guaranteed the release of the song. There was no gamble for me in making that trade because had the song not been released, the entire copyright would have been returned to me. It was a definite win/win. And, the deal paid off in a big way, because the song became a huge hit and has been a cash cow for all of the partners involved. So, you couldn't really say that I "gave my publishing away." By trading a share of my publishing, I got myself a Number One, BMI-award winning, million-play song, as a writer *and* as a copublisher. So, try to get the concept of "giving away publishing" out of your head. When a publisher expresses a desire to publish a song, they should have something real to offer in return. And, the writer doesn't *give* a copyright away. The writer *assigns* it to the publisher in exchange for whatever the publisher provides the writer.

This gets down to the most essential part of what a publisher does: A publisher owns copyrights. Why does a publisher want to own copyrights? Simple. By owning a copyright, the publisher not only controls how that copyright can be used, the publisher also controls the income from its use. In order to do this, the publisher usually acquires copyrights through one of three means: putting writers under exclusive contracts; purchasing existing catalogs; or by signing individual songs.

So then, how does a music publisher create commerce? A publisher exploits its song catalog, creating as much licensing activity as possible. They do this by pitching what they consider their most commercially viable songs to artists, producers, managers, agents, record companies, films, TV shows, video game manufacturers, ring tone distributors, and any other entity that licenses music. A publisher could also develop recording projects and opportunities for staff writers, producers, and artists and set up collaborations for staff writers with recording artists and hot writers from other companies. It is important to note that a publisher doesn't *sell* songs; a publisher *licenses* songs for use. To sell the songs would defeat the very purpose of music publishing and behead the goose that lays the golden eggs. Selling songs off one and a time would, in the long run, actually put the publisher out of business.

In my naïve, fledgling days in this business, I used to think that publishers were just banks that gambled by signing certain writers and songs to exclusive contracts. That was, until I co-founded my own independent publishing venture, Writer Zone Music, LLC. While it may be true that one of the primary functions of most music publishers is to invest in talent—by paying staff writers advances against future royalties and financing demo sessions—a good music publisher does much, much more than that. A publisher provides a home for its writers and staff. There, the writers can do their creative thing and cull constructive feedback from the staff on their works in progress. There, the executives and pluggers can encourage and critique the writers' output, acquiring pride of ownership in the material. Ideally, this daily bonding produces a team atmosphere and a higher level of commitment on both sides of the desk.

My biggest surprise came, however, when I got a good look behind the curtain at the secret machinations of music publishing. Keeping the books for even the smallest publishing operation is a task of daunting proportions. A comprehensive file must be kept on each writer that tracks his or her song output, including work tapes and lyric sheets. A spread sheet must be continually updated, indicating cowriters and publishing splits for every title, plus expenses incurred for demos and how much of those expenses is recoupable from each writer's account. Copublishers have to be billed for their writers' demo expenses, and bills must be paid to copublishers for the demos they have been responsible for producing. Every staff writer's advances must be entered monthly, balanced against any royalty income, making sure that the proper percentages are credited toward recoupment. As every writer's contract is different and packed with legal nuances, the challenge of this job is nearly insurmountable. In my opinion, any publishing company that exhibits the ability to keep clean and accurate records and books is working miracles.

In addition to the confounding, record-keeping tangle, the publisher is responsible for filing copyright applications, performance rights registrations, negotiating sync licenses and collecting for them, and setting up domestic and foreign administration.

To sum up, a publisher owns copyrights, controls their use and their income. For its staff writers, a publisher often provides steady income in the form of monthly advances against royalties, demo expenses, a creative home, and constructive feedback. A publisher might also help manage its writers' careers by setting up strategic cowrites with hot writers, producers, and artists. A publisher should exploit its catalog through strategic and comprehensive pitching. Finally a publisher keeps track of every writer's song output, demo expenses, advances, and royalty income, while taking care of registrations and administrative necessities.

Recouping an Advance

Writers recoup advances and demo expenses "at their own rate." In other words, only the income share belonging to the writer will go toward paying back (recouping) the advances and recoupable expenses the writer has incurred. Supposing Donna has a traditional 50/50 publishing deal that provides her with a $20,000 per year advance. In the middle of year three of the deal—at which time she has received a total of $50,000 in advances—her publisher receives a $50,000 royalty check from Capitol Records for one of her solo-written songs. Since the publisher is due 50 percent of that $50,000, only $25,000 of that income is credited toward Donna's recoupment. She still remains $25,000 away from recouping her advances.

Publishers also recoup out-of-pocket demo expenses from money received on behalf of the writer—proportionate to the ownership of the copyright. Let's say that Donna spent $800 on a demo of a solo-written song. As she owns half of the copyright, she is responsible for half of that demo's expenses; so, $400 of those costs is recoupable from any and all income the publisher receives from her catalog. Along with advances, demo expenses tend to mount up; so, it's important for a writer to keep an eye on those demo bills and be aware of how much her publisher is spending and charging back to her for demos. Itemized charges—like musicians' cartage, piano tuning, extra engineering expenses, and so on—can add substantial recoupable expenditures to a writer's ledger, and someday could make the difference between a writer seeing royalties or not. Some major publishers require their writers to demo their songs in in-house studios. Then, they charge back an hourly fee for the studio time and engineer that is way above the rates the writer could get on the open market. And, as Donna is recouping with only half of the income received by her publisher, it may take some time for her to get her account in the black and see some royalty income.

Note that an advance is not a loan. The publisher has no right to demand that a writer repay unrecouped advances, unless that repayment is part of a negotiated termination agreement, under which the writer gets his or her copyrights back. Writer contracts usually have "audit clauses," which enable the writer to double check the company's books from time to time to make sure that accounts are square. If you ever sign a publishing deal, make sure that you have the right to audit the publisher's books at least once a year. Audits are few and far between that don't discover some income due to the writer—and, sometimes, it's a substantial sum.

CHAPTER 6
How Do Copyrights Make Money?

For several years now, I've been speaking regularly to college classes on the topic of music publishing. I am constantly amazed that, even in the top music-business schools, very little emphasis is placed on the ABCs, the rudiments, the bottom-line nitty-gritty of music publishing: the various ways that songs create income. Sure, we all want to be involved with inspired songs, hang out with hip, creative people, get cuts with big stars, hear those tunes on the radio, and see those recordings bullet up the charts and sell millions of copies. That's all good stuff, for sure. However, if you're visualizing those kinds of experiences in your future, then it is of critical importance to have a basic knowledge of just who will be compensating you for your future successes and how.

Basically, copyrights make money through licensing. With very few exceptions (buy-outs, or works for hire), songwriters and publishers do not "sell" songs. Copyrights are capable of creating enormous residual income for generations to come—the key word here being "residual." Once a song has been recorded and released, placed in a film, or integrated into a theatrical production, the royalty and licensing money it brings in for the publishers and composers can pretty much be classified as "passive income." Now, just because the hard labor is over doesn't mean this money is undeserved. The writers certainly did their bit. They began by answering a creative urge. Then, they honed their craft and survived somehow in a very risky profession. They conceived of a concept, composed and refined the music and lyrics. More than likely, they invested time, effort, talent, and resources into producing a quality demo. In addition, assuming the writers are true pros, they played a part in exposing the song to decision makers and pulled whatever political strings they could, before crossing fingers and toes and moving on to the next inspiration, for which, like all the others, there was no guarantee of remuneration.

The publishing company did its part, too, providing the writers with a creative environment and sustenance enough so that they could spend adequate time being creative and getting the song right. Maybe the publisher also offered the constructive feedback that ultimately made all the difference to the final composition. Then, after approving and financing the demo, the publisher probably helped get the song out there and closed the deal. After that, the publisher's job is not over by a long shot, because, whether or not the song makes a dime or ten million bucks, books will need to be kept, registrations and licenses will have to be completed, and statements and checks sent out. That being said, what publishers and songwriters are striving for is residual/passive income. So, as I've already mentioned, selling its copyrights would deplete a publisher's inventory of assets and, in the long run, put the company out of business. That would be the equivalent of a landlord selling his rentals off unit by unit. Sooner or later, no rent will be coming in.

Here's how it happens in simple terms: A record company, a film production house, an independent artist, a performance venue, a karaoke manufacturer, a ring-tone distributor will seek a license for the use, broadcast, duplication, and/or sale of each song. That license will spell out the terms by which the composer(s) and publisher(s) will be paid. To clarify the mysterious and murky waters of music licensing and the various entities cruising these shadowy depths, I'll attempt to describe them without resorting to tricky lawyer-speak. Hopefully, this won't make your head spin.

Mechanical Licenses

Any time a record company, independent artist, or karaoke distributor intends to sell a recording of a song, it is required to procure an agreement called a *mechanical license* from the publisher of that song. A mechanical license signed by the owner of the copyright (be it the official legal representative of the song's publisher, or at least one writer/copyright owner of an unpublished song) gives the distribution entity permission to sell recordings of the composition and spells out how much the entity will pay the publisher or writer for every copy sold, at what intervals those payments will be made, and where the statements and checks are to be mailed. A separate mechanical license is required for every new recording of a song or re-release of a previously recorded version of that song. For example: The initial mechanical license for Toby Keith's recording of "My List" on his DreamWorks CD, *Pull My Chain,* was issued to Universal Music, the parent company of DreamWorks Records. Then an independent record company requested a mechanical license to include a newly recorded production of the song on a bluegrass instrumental album. Likewise, when Universal Music re-released the original Toby Keith recording on a greatest-hits CD, and then again as part of a box set, each new product required a new mechanical license. In the case of a massive copyright, like my dear friend Amanda McBroom's "The Rose," which has been recorded hundreds of times, a separate license would have been required for every recorded version of the song.

> Note: The publishers and/or songwriters only have control over the mechanical license of first recording of a copyright. After any song has been published (i.e., broadcast over the airwaves and/or sold commercially), if a publisher does not issue a mechanical license, a distributor can get what's called a "compulsory license" to re-record and distribute that piece. So, it is of the ultimate importance, if at all possible, for a publisher to choose the most strategic and high-profile initial recording of any song, the recording that will introduce the song to the industry and the public in its most flattering light.

Strangely enough, music publishers and songwriters comprise the only U.S. industry for which federal statute dictates exactly what their products earn for each sale. This statutory rate is currently set at 9.1 cents per copy sold. So, assuming that a publisher and writer have a traditional, 50/50 publishing arrangement and a song is solo-written, the publisher would keep half (4.55 cents) from each sale and credit the remaining 4.55 cents to the writer (either to the writer's account against advances; or, if the writer has taken no advances or is already recouped, account to the writer for that amount on the next quarterly or bi-annual statement.)

Before the creative hay day of the glorious 1960s, 33⅓ RPM LPs most commonly contained ten titles. Three reasons why: industry convention; writers sticking to traditional song structures; and a vinyl record album could only hold a certain number of minutes of music in its grooves without sacrificing sound quality. Then, along came that naughty foursome from Liverpool and their infamous White Album. The Beatles registered every little song fragment in the long medley/audio collage on side two of that notorious release as a separate copyright. As a result, Capitol Records had to pay the statutory rate of the day (considerably less than it is now) on every one of those separate titles. Seeing the possibility of their profit margins diminishing due to these unprecedented royalty costs, record companies, in their own defense, came up with a contractual way to keep more pennies per album for themselves. They called it the "Controlled Composition" clause. For any artist who wrote the lion's share of his or her own material, the record companies began to insist that the artists be paid at three-quarters of the statutory rate on a maximum of ten songs. These kinds of agreements are still common in today's recording contracts, especially those signed by new artists. The controlled composition clause represents only one tiny skirmish in an ongoing, titanic struggle between the artists who write and make the music and the corporate entities that promote and distribute it. This round goes to the record companies.

Administration Rights

One all-important aspect of copyright ownership is the *right of administration* or admin. Admin rights should be spelled out clearly in every publishing contract, whether that agreement assigns copyright ownership for a single song from a writer to a publisher, or it signs a writer to an exclusive, long-term contract with a publisher. The entity (or individual) retaining contractual administration rights not only controls the use of the copyright (who can or cannot initially record the song, whether it can be attached to a movie, TV show, advertisement, video game, etc.), but its address will be the first recipient of the gross amount of the copyright's non-broadcast income. So, the very essence of music publishing is contained in right of administration: controlling not only the use of copyrights, but the income from them. Along with the right of administration comes the responsibility and obligation to divvy up the royalties, crank out statements, and account to copublishers and songwriters for their share.

When a songwriter achieves a sufficient success level and credibility to become a copublisher of his or her own material, administration rights for the songwriter's copublishing share will come into play. The publishing entity with which the songwriter negotiates a copublishing deal will invariably attempt to maintain administration over the songwriter's copublishing interests. Maintaining admin enables the partner company to not only call the shots on how any song can be used, but to hold onto the copublisher's income for the months between royalty statements. That—in the case of a hit song, or multiple hits—could amount to big bucks delayed to the copublisher, along with more liquidity and some substantial interest earnings for the administrating partner. So, admin rights are something to pay attention to. However, it makes no sense to struggle to maintain your own administration rights unless you have the expertise and wherewithal to collect royalties on your own behalf. That's where administration companies come in.

Publishing Administrators

The vast majority of publishers do not collect mechanical royalties directly from music distributors. For this service, they usually depend on administration companies. A number of administration companies specialize in collecting on behalf of music publishers. Harry Fox Agency is the U.S.'s most ubiquitous outfit. HFA represents a long list of publishers, from tiny independents to several of the largest in the business. An Internet search will reveal a number of other music publishing administrators, including Farm to Market, Bug Music, Evergreen, and The Loving Company. Some administrators are also publishers, acquiring, owning, and promoting large, lucrative publishing catalogs. Music Sales Corporation, for instance, owns hundreds of classic copyrights and master recordings, as well as G. Schirmer Music, which has the world's largest stable of contemporary classical composers on staff.

Administrators generally take a commission off the top (usually between 3 percent and 10 percent), before forwarding the balance to the publishers to be divvied up and paid toward their various writers' accounts. In the U.S., it's not absolutely necessary to use an administrator to collect mechanicals. But, as administrators generally have strong, direct relationships with distributors, along with a well developed expertise for finding every possible source of income, their collections will usually exceed what a publisher or individual writer could ever come up with on their own. Most publishers find that a good administrator more than pays for its own services, while eliminating the enormous amount of time and effort that goes into chasing down those evasive royalties. As they work purely on commission, administrators have every incentive to collect as much money as possible, as quickly as possible.

Many admin companies will take care of certain licenses and registrations, too. These services also free up a publisher's staff for more creative endeavors, allowing them to devote more time and energy to exploiting a catalog and creating more commerce, which, in turn, presumably creates more income for the administrator to collect. Ideally, in and of itself, this symbiotic relationship is an economic stimulus package for all parties involved.

Mechanical Royalty Societies

In territories outside of the U.S., songwriters, publishers, or publishing administrators cannot collect mechanical royalties from distributors directly. Foreign distributors submit publishers' and writers' royalties to a mechanical royalty society. (Mechanical royalty societies collect and redistribute mechanical royalties basically the same way performing rights organizations do for broadcast royalties. We'll be discussing PROs next.) In order for a writer, publisher, or administrator to collect from a mechanical royalty society in any foreign territory, they need to be a signatory member. Because of certain residency requirements, most U.S.–based publishers are not directly affiliated with foreign mechanical societies. For this reason, U.S. publishers have traditionally depended on foreign sub-publishers who are members of the local mechanical societies to collect on their behalf. These sub-publishers retain a co publishing share of the income (from 12.5 to 25 percent) before forwarding the remainder to the administrator, who takes its commission before sending what's left to the publisher to split with the writers.

A foreign sub-publisher might share in a U.S. publisher's income in just one country; or that same sub-publisher might oversee and collect in a certain group of countries or territory (Scandinavia or the Benelux countries, for instance). More recently, some U.S. publishers have established a minimal presence in certain foreign territories so that they could qualify to join the mechanical societies there and bypass sub-publishers altogether. Theoretically, doing that enables those publishers to earn more money faster, by eliminating a sub-publisher deducting its percentage and the time between the sub-publisher receiving and accounting for the royalties. A strong argument can be made either way as to whether it's really worth the effort and investment to maintain multiple offices and send personnel to these territories on a periodic basis. There's a lot to be said for having boots on the ground in every territory, year-round, working on behalf of your catalog. On the other hand, a motivated, active, and highly connected sub-publisher can also generate additional cuts and translations, thus generating more releases and income in its territories.

You can see how convoluted getting paid becomes and how many partners come into play, each taking a piece of the action, as the money, like evaporating molasses, slowly trickles down to the folks who actually created the songs in the first place: the poor, lowly songwriters. Sometimes it feels like we're the little orphan at the far end of the dining table. A plate of plump chicken pieces gets passed down. Every kid along the way takes a fat one for himself. Not only do we have to wait while everybody else is already enjoying a delicious meal, we are left to grab for whatever scrawny piece finally makes it the length of the table.

Performing Rights Organizations

Radio stations, TV networks, Internet content providers, concert and club venues, restaurants, Muzak providers, any business that uses music to draw an audience or to enhance the experience of its customers is required to pay for the recorded music they broadcast. The entities that collect these payments on behalf of music publishers and songwriters are called performing rights organizations (PROs). In order to receive broadcast or performance royalties, every songwriter must affiliate with a PRO. Any publisher acquiring ownership of a copyright by an affiliated songwriter must have a publishing entity affiliated with that same PRO. In the same way that a writer's share of a copyright must have an equal, corresponding publishers' share, that entire publisher's share (regardless of how many publishers split ownership) must all be affiliated with the same PRO as the writer. In the U.S., we have three different performing rights organizations from which writers can freely choose: Broadcast Music, Incorporated (BMI), The American Society of Composers, Authors, and Publishers (ASCAP), and SESAC (originally known as The Society of European Stage Authors and Composers).

Songwriters often debate the pros and cons of these three organizations, weighing one against the others. I will not be entering that discussion here.

I will, however, describe the most basic differences between them: BMI is a not-for-profit corporation, owned by broadcasters; ASCAP is a society of songwriters and publishers, owned by its membership; SESAC is a privately owned, for-profit corporation. Each PRO sets out to do basically the same job: collect as much broadcast money as possible for its publisher and writer affiliates. When anybody asks me which of these outfits is the best, I respond by advising that person to go down and meet the people at all three. Do your own hands-on research. Then, listen to your own gut. Because, in the long run, any performing rights organization is only as good as the service they provide to *you*. If you find an advocate or liaison at a PRO, someone you really like and who really seems to like you, somebody who will give you access and attention, is willing to listen to your concerns, help you solve your issues, and introduce you to people in the industry, that's the PRO for you. Settled. End of discussion. If you do not live in or near a city in which these organizations maintain an office, you would be well advised to take a trip to New York, L.A., or Nashville if only to meet with the PROs. This is not a decision to take lightly or blithely.

Reputedly, each of the U.S. PROs is stronger in different radio formats and pays higher royalties for different genres of music. That may be true. Once again, ask around. Do your research among writers with actual experience. You will definitely find writers with strong opinions and no qualms about sharing their good experiences as well as their nightmares. Keep in mind, however, that songwriters, as a breed, are chronic complainers. So, take the grousing with a grain of salt. One writer's negative experience doesn't necessarily portend the same sort of thing happening to you—especially if you have an advocate at your PRO. If, however, you hear similar anecdotes from several writers, you definitely wanna pay some attention.

Most foreign nations have only one PRO, so the songwriters and publishers in those territories don't have the choice (or the dilemma) we have in the States. In some of those countries, the PRO (which can also be called a "copyright collective" or "copyright collecting agency") does double duty, serving as the mechanical rights society, too. BMI, ASCAP, and SESAC all have reciprocal agreements with all of the foreign PROs and will automatically collect and account to affiliates for foreign performances. So, it's not necessary for a U.S.–based writer or publisher to join any foreign PROs in order to be paid for foreign broadcast income. Still, because they want to cut out another middle man and get more royalties quicker, some writers and publishers do choose to join foreign PROs anyway.

Interestingly enough, in foreign territories, a portion of every movie ticket sold is earmarked for the composers and songwriters who contribute to the score and music soundtrack, along with their publishers. This is not true stateside. Film composers, soundtrack songwriters, and their publishers are only paid by PROs in the U.S. when their movies are broadcast on television. For that purpose, the film company submits a "cue sheet" to the PROs, which is like a graph of all the music, mapped from the beginning to the end of the film, showing how many seconds of each piece from the soundtrack is being played, indicating whether it is used as score, featured, background, or "source" music (music coming from an on-screen radio, TV, juke box, etc.). From that map, the PRO divides the income from each broadcast of the film and distributes it to the writers and publishers. In this way, getting songs into or scoring feature films and/or TV shows can create residual income for decades, as movies and show reruns continue to be broadcast on the multitudes of cable channels proliferating on the tube. I still see PRO income from the first feature film to which I contributed songs, 1971's *Vanishing Point.*

PRO Registrations

After you've affiliated with the PRO of your choice, you're ready to register your songs. Registration means entering the proper information into the PRO database, so that you and your cowriters can be compensated for your broadcast performances. This is only absolutely necessary when your songs are about to released, or if you've licensed one of more songs to an upcoming movie or TV show. It's a good idea to do it anyway, because registering your compositions at the very least stakes a public claim to your copyright ownership. You can register your songs online or with a mailed-in paper form. For this purpose, it helps to know the PRO member number, Social Security number, the exact splits on the songs, the publishing company names, and PRO affiliations for you and for your cowriter(s).

In a PRO song registration, each title will be divided up into two, separate 100 percent shares. One hundred percent of one share belongs to the songwriter(s); 100 percent of the other share belongs to the publisher(s). So, regardless of how you split credit with your cowriter(s), make sure each side adds up to 100 percent; and, of course, assign a corresponding publisher's share for each writers' split. In order to collect a publishing share from your PRO, you will have to create a D.B.A. (doing business as) publishing company. A D.B.A. is just another name for yourself and is attached to your Social Security Number. You apply for your D.B.A. through your PRO. As your PRO will want to avoid any potential confusion in its royalty distribution, it will have to do a comprehensive search to discover whether there are other entities with similar names. So as to not send performance royalties to the wrong company, names that are too similar to existing publishing entities will not be cleared, so be prepared with several name choices on your application. Some PROs charge a fee for setting up a D.B.A. publisher name. Others provide this service for free. Some states require a separate bank account to deposit a check made out to a D.B.A., so do your research and find out what your local requirements are. Ultimately, as you begin to reap rewards for your songwriting toil, it will serve you well to have your bank accounts at a bank with an "entertainment division" accustomed to the arcane ways of the music business. Otherwise, when you receive that first BMI check made out to Sally Songwriter/D.B.A. Mud Puddle Music, you're liable to get some discouraging head shakes at the teller window when you try to make a deposit.

Copyright Registration

For your own protection, as you write and complete each song, it's a good idea to keep good, clean records, making sure to document each piece's date of creation (having this in a computer program is very helpful). Any paper trail, computer imprint, or other proof of authorship could help you, should any dispute arise over the originality of the copyright. However, if you apply to the Library of Congress for an official copyright for every original song you write, you will be spending a lot of unnecessary time and resources. Here's why: A copyright registration is not official until a composition is officially published, meaning that it has either been sold as a commercial product, or it has been broadcast over the airwaves. As long as you have some proof that you actually composed your songs, until they are released for sale or broadcast, there is no absolute necessity to apply for a copyright registration, nor will that registration actually protect your ownership.

CHAPTER 7
More Ways That Songs Make Money

In the previous chapter, I dropped you into the maze of songs and their income and administration. Believe or not, we're not through yet. Here are even more ways songs generate income.

Synchronization Licenses

Whenever a recorded copyright is attached to picture—as featured music (a music video, or performed by an actor or band in a movie, TV show, or ad), as background (as part of the score to a TV show, feature film, or advertisement), or as source (coming from a radio, TV, jukebox, etc., depicted in a film, TV show, or ad)—an agreement known as a synchronization, or *sync,* license is required. More accurately, two such licenses are required: one giving permission to attach the copyright (the song) to picture, the other giving permission for use of the master recording of that copyright. (A master recording is the music production, or record, which is owned either by the performing artist or the artist's record label. The master is separate from the song in that it comprises the performance of the song, not the song itself.)

Let's use a hypothetical scenario. Paramount Pictures is producing *Action Picture,* starring Vin Diesel. Publisher A owns (and has administration rights to—*very important*) a song called "Bump and Run," which was written and recorded by Loon-a-tick Flange, a hot new act on Mayhem Records. The film's music supervisor, Tara Taste, thinks "Bump and Run" just might work as the musical accompaniment to Diesel's big *Action Picture* car-chase scene. Tara instructs the film editor to "temp" "Bump and Run" into the car chase, so she can screen it for the director and producers of the movie. (Temping songs is common practice. Editors and music supervisors put songs into scenes temporarily at no cost to the filmmakers to fill the silence and/or to get a feel for how a certain song or kind of song works with the picture. In some cases, the director and producers become accustomed to a temped song and they instruct the music supervisor to pursue licenses to include that song and its recording in the final film.) The screening goes well, and it's unanimous. Everybody is on board, delighted with "Bump and Run." The Loon-a-tick Flange track is the absolute perfect vibe for Diesel's car chase. It makes the visual more exciting, the sequence more suspenseful, gives the action even more impact. Tara, the music supervisor, is as big of a behind-the-camera hero as Vin Diesel is on the film. Oh, but hold your horses, because Ms. Taste's job is far from over yet. In fact, she has a real challenge ahead of her. She has to acquire the rights to use this song and recording by negotiating the required synchronization licenses.

The music supervisor will first have to contact Publisher A to negotiate a sync license for the right to attach the copyright, "Bump and Run," to picture. Then, she will go to Mayhem Records to work out a sync license for the use of Loon-a-tick Flange's master recording of the song. (Or, she could do it the other way around. It really doesn't matter. Initially, she'll probably go to whomever she has the best personal and/or business relationship.) A scenario nearly identical to this one happens pretty much every time a recorded song is attached to a film, TV show, advertisement, or computer game.

Someone's job description (usually a music supervisor or an ad agency's music person) is to find the best available musical accompaniment for a particular scene or advertisement. To accomplish that, she will more than likely listen to a whole bunch of music online, sift through a pile of submissions, and/or cull something from her own personal library. (On some occasions, she'll even go to a favorite songwriter or artist and ask them if they'll custom write and/or produce something on spec.) Then, she'll narrow down the candidates to a short list and try one or two out by temping them to picture. After that, she'll screen the ones she feels strongest about for the director and producers. When there's a consensus among the powers that be, she will go after the sync rights for the selected song and master. Sometimes, after a song is chosen and/or licensed, the music supervisor's next task is to find the perfect artist to custom-record the song for the project. The filmmakers might choose this route because either the song was composed especially for the picture, the original recording of the song is too pricey to license, or they're looking for a completely different interpretation, a novel approach to the song. It can be as much fun to hear new versions of classic songs as it is to hear great new songs performed by classic artists. But, in my opinion, best of all is when a fresh voice and a great new song gets noticed through the perfect placement. Music supervision is a challenging, extremely creative job, requiring a lot of switching from one side of the brain to the other—one moment visualizing how a certain piece might work behind a certain scene, the next negotiating deals to fit within a finite budget.

A music supervisor is usually given a budget for the whole project. So, due to financial restrictions, creative vision is not the only criterion that determines which exact songs eventually end up in the final edit. It's not unlike trying to assemble the best athletes possible to compete in the NBA or NFL under a salary cap. Sometimes you might discover incredible players who didn't even get drafted, while other times you're bidding for free agents who will surely command maximum contracts. Some copyrights and their most recognizable recordings are far too costly. You will seldom, if ever, hear a Beatle song in a movie actually performed by the band itself. The master rights are either unavailable or sky high. Speaking of sky high, screenwriter/director Cameron Crowe wrote a scene for his brilliant film, *Almost Famous*, that he considered absolutely essential to the movie's storyline. The passage in question featured the entirety of one of the most-popular—and lengthy—rock recordings of all time, Led Zeppelin's "Stairway To Heaven." In this pivotal scene, several of the movie's main characters sit in a living room listening to the classic Zeppelin recording from start to finish. Unfortunately, after shooting and editing the scene, Crowe discovered that getting sync licenses for that song and its infamous Atlantic Records production would have cost as much as his entire music budget. *Almost Famous* is a film about musicians, incorporating music and songs from top to bottom. Those songs, in turn, presumably required dozens of sync licenses, each of which has its own cost. So, much to his chagrin, for lack of money, Crowe had to remove the "Stairway" scene from his film. By the way, you can see the scene—sans Zep of course—on the *Almost Famous* DVD outtakes. Crowe provides you with a needle drop cue so you can add "Stairway" out of your own music collection. It's really worth a gander.

As time goes on, sync licenses are becoming more and more important as a means of creating income for copyright owners and producers of recorded music. Due to the growing popularity of downloading digital files of individual songs, there has been a massive decline in sales of CD albums. Music publishers and record companies all seek alternative ways to make up for all that lost mechanical revenue. Placing songs and masters in movies, TV shows, advertising, and computer games not only generates immediate cash through sync licenses, it also increases exposure for the songs and the artists who perform them. More and more original programming is being produced for more and more television outlets. TV, films, advertising, and computer games have become equally as important as radio in breaking new artists and making songs into hits. To place a song in a featured spot on a popular show like *Grey's Anatomy* (which has a younger demographic that is more likely to respond actively to a recording heard on a TV show) can be gold for not only the artist, but the writer and publisher of the song. These titles also generate performing rights income every time they are broadcast or rerun over the airwaves and, in the case of feature films, every time a movie ticket is sold in a foreign territory.

Unlike mechanical licenses, which are governed by set, statutory rates, prices for sync licenses are completely negotiable. A sync license could sell for as little as one dollar or as much as several hundred thousand dollars. An average licensing fee falls in the low thousands. For huge, national advertising campaigns, big hit songs can often demand $250,000 to $350,000 for a single cycle's use (13 weeks). Imagine how much Bob Seger must have raked in for Chevy's "Like A Rock" ads. That campaign kept going for years. A publisher and owner of a master recording will tend to charge a major film studio top dollar for a license, while they will usually be easier on a small, independent filmmaker for a similar use of the exact same song and master. Some sync licenses for indie films are negotiated on a *step basis*. This means that there is one payment (or waver of payment) for film festival screenings, another payment if the movie is shown in theaters, another if it's released on DVD, another if it's broadcast on TV, and so on.

TV shows generally don't pay big bucks for sync licenses, if they pay anything at all. This is because songwriters and publishers are generally satisfied with the PRO income they'll be receiving from the broadcast, and record companies and artists are more than grateful to get the mass exposure the broadcast provides. Computer game manufacturers, on the other hand, are used to budgeting substantial payments to use both recognizable copyrights and custom-crafted masters because there will be no performing rights income on the back end. A sync license for a computer game is often pretty much a non-exclusive, one-time buyout. So, for games, publishers and master owners tend to drive harder bargains. One of the goldmines of the computer game world is *Guitar Hero*. Publishers and record companies demand boffo sync fees for that phenomenally successful game's use of their songs and masters because *Guitar Hero*'s entire premise depends on licensing and utilizing the most-enduring and most-recognizable hit songs.

Songwriters commonly try to negotiate their approval of sync licenses into their publishing contracts. They do this to prevent their songs from potentially being used to sell a product they don't believe in, to endorse a political candidate with whom they strongly disagree, or having their creative work associated with a film or TV show they consider somehow immoral, improper, or repugnant. So, even if a publisher has admin rights to a copyright, the songwriters might still retain veto power over what exact sync licenses can be issued for the use of a song.

Grand Rights

Another way that copyrights can generate income for songwriters and publishers is through a catch-all concept called *grand rights*. Basically, the concept of grand rights pre-dates both mechanical income and performing rights income by hundreds, if not thousands of years. Music and songs have been performed for paying audiences for centuries. Live theatrical productions that sell tickets for admission have commonly used music and lyrics as an integral part of telling stories, defining characters, and entertaining their audiences. So, it only seems fair and logical that the creators and owners of those songs should share in the income from those ticket sales. This applies to musical theater productions, operas, classical concerts, Las Vegas shows, circuses, ice shows, and the list goes on and on.

If a songwriter writes music and/or lyrics for a successful musical, either on Broadway or one produced in regional theaters (professional, community, and/or school productions), the ongoing, residual income stream from those licensed productions can be enormous. But, to accomplish that often takes years and years of development and perseverance, and all that hard work and patience needs to culminate in a good show and finally meet up with some very generous angels and kind reviewers along the way—two exceptionally rare breeds.

A pair of Manhattanites, Vern and Frank, are walking down Amsterdam Avenue. "Oh, my God!" Vern cries out, pointing up ahead. Following Vern's pointer finger, Frank sees a man falling from a tenth story window. Miraculously, what surely looks to be a fatal fall is slowed, as the fortunate fellow bounces off of an awning protruding from the fifth floor. He then resumes his fall, only to trampoline off of another awning at the second-floor level, and finally to land softly in a dumpster conveniently filled with packing peanuts. He climbs out of the dumpster, evidently unhurt, and begins gingerly brushing himself off. "Wow!" exclaims Frank. "That guy has got to be the luckiest man in New York City."

"Second luckiest," Vern corrects him.

"What do you mean?" Frank wonders out loud.

"Andrew Lloyd Webber," Vern explains. "He's the luckiest man in New York City." (These are the jokes, folks...Ba-da-boom!)

One can only imagine the grand-rights royalty income earned every single day by the composer of such massively successful Broadway shows as *Cats*, *Phantom of the Opera*, *Evita*, and *Jesus Christ Superstar.* These musicals have not only run for years on the big stages of the Great White Way and London's famed West End, they are being mounted continually by touring companies, and in regional, college, and high school theaters. For every ticket sold, for every single production of every title in his long repertoire of smashes, Lloyd Webber enjoys a percentage. Those nickels and dimes add up to an ever-growing largess that certainly must rival Scrooge McDuck's mountain of gold. The only difference being that Lloyd Webber's wealth is not a cartoon. I don't know if I'd call him lucky. But rich...there is no question about that.

You don't have to reach a Lloyd Webber level of success to make a good pile of greenbacks from theatrical grand rights. Even musicals that never get within a hundred miles from Manhattan have grown into cash cows for their visionary and perseverant creators. Shows like *Forever Plaid, Nunsense,* and *Pump Boys and Dinettes* began as modest, workshop productions. Yet, through the resources and pluck of their producers and the willingness of their creative teams to work and rework the material year after year, they eventually became solid vehicles, found their audiences, and established themselves in the liturgy of the American theater. In their best years, with touring companies and multiple regional productions, these relatively modest musicals have all generated millions in grand-rights income.

If you've been bitten with the Broadway bug and have an overwhelming compulsion to write for the musical stage, you might want to consider starting with a smaller, conceptual, ensemble musical (like the ones mentioned in the previous paragraph) and try first to get it workshopped outside of New York. If you have the fortitude and are fortunate enough to do that, you'd better not be adverse to rewriting, reworking, and refining the piece for the next production. It takes amazing stamina and enormous resources to bring a musical property to fruition, at any level. Trying to crack Broadway is like climbing Everest—blindfolded and on crutches. You'd be wise to tackle a few lesser peaks before you take on the behemoth. In fact, attempting Broadway can be so precarious as to actually be life-threatening. A number of incredibly talented and successful pop writers have devoted decades to the challenge and still remain locked out of the inner circle. Like the infamous Sir Richard Branson, these bold adventurers have yet to circumvent the globe in their hot air balloons, but they've been willing to perish by making attempt after attempt.

In 1991, I was sitting in the audience for a showcase sponsored by BMI at Los Angeles's historic Wiltern Theater. On the bill was a parade of extraordinarily talented songwriter/performers, some well-established, some still up-and-coming. Vince Gill and Boyz II Men were among the fresher faces of the day. An old acquaintance, Peter Allen, was among the legends. Back in 1976, when we were both artists under contract to A&M Records, I would frequently encounter Allen on the label lot. Ebullient and sharp-witted, he was always friendly, unpretentious, and extremely likeable. The cowriter of such standards as "I'd Rather Leave While I'm In Love" and "Don't Cry Out Loud," Allen also won a best-song Oscar for "Arthur's Theme (Best that You Can Do)." A veteran cabaret entertainer of prodigious skills, Allen went on to star in a couple of Broadway productions, before devoting his talents to writing for the stage. His musical, *Legs Diamond,* co-authored with Harvey Fierstein (no slouch on the New York theater scene himself), had a brief Broadway run in 1989.

Two years after *Legs Diamond* closed, Peter Allen was on the Wiltern stage, pale, slight, hair-receding, and doing the best he could with his tattered vocal chords. As I and several hundred other music fans applauded a solo rendition of his Olivia Newton-John hit, "I Honestly Love You," Allen grabbed his vocal mic, pushed back the piano bench, and strode to the footlights to face the house. "How many of you are writing a musical or ever intend to?" he asked, hoarsely. Shielding his eyes from the stage-light glare, Allen observed dozens of hands rising in the crowd—including my own. "Don't!" he warned. "It'll kill ya." A year later, Peter Allen succumbed to AIDS–related throat cancer. I don't know if *Legs Diamond* Broadway actually bumped off the celebrated songwriter/performer. However, Allen's remark that night on the Wiltern stage seemed to support the theory that the legendary gangster's ghost had something to do with the composer/performer's premature demise. Ironically, Peter Allen's biggest theatrical success arrived posthumously, in the form of the autobiographical musical about him called *The Boy From Oz.* Fellow Aussie, Hugh Jackman, starred on Broadway in the colorful lead role of Peter Allen.

Many other enormously gifted songwriters with amazing credits have put a ton of effort into piercing the invisible, impermeable bubble of Broadway, without breaking in. Mike Reid is one. Until he was thwarted time and time again by the stages of New York, Reid's life story told of one triumph after another. In 1969, playing football for Penn State, Reid won the Outland Trophy, as the most-outstanding collegiate defensive lineman in the country. A first-round draft choice of the Cincinnati Bengals in 1970, he became the NFL's Defensive Rookie of the Year. Several times an All Pro, he played five seasons, until knee surgery ended his football career in 1975. Reid then returned to his keyboard and music, as a performing songwriter.

Through the 1980s, Reid was responsible for eleven Number One country songs and garnered a Grammy for Ronnie Milsap's "Stranger In My House." In the '90s, he signed as a solo artist for Columbia Records, scoring several chart successes, the biggest being the Number One "Walk on Faith." The Creator certainly didn't hold back on Reid when handing out talents. With musical skills equal to his athletic gifts, Reid's baritone voice is as rich and soulful as Ray Charles and his keyboard acumen recalls Bruce Hornsby. In the '90s, Mike Reid co-authored incredible hits, like "My Strongest Weakness" for Wynnona, "Everywhere" for Tim McGraw, and possibly my favorite pop song of all time, "I Can't Make You Love Me," recorded by Bonnie Raitt (which has sold six million copies). Then, always eager to find new and greater challenges, Reid threw his helmet into the classical arena and delved wholeheartedly into musical theater. Although his chamber and operatic compositions have garnered hundreds of performances, Reid's musicals, including *The Ballad Of Little Jo* and *Shane*, have fallen just short of making it to Broadway. Rumor has it that Mike Reid has finally waved the white flag of surrender in the direction of the Great White Way.

For decades, Jimmy Webb, too, has endeavored to get a show running on Broadway. No other individual pop songwriter of my lifetime—with the possible exception of Diane Warren—has had more chart success than Jimmy Webb. Yet, his theatrical writing has, thus far, failed to gain what one might call a Jimmy Webb level of industry or commercial acceptance.

One of my dearest friends, Amanda McBroom—writer of one of the most recorded songs of all time, "The Rose"—actually *has* enjoyed some legitimate success composing for the theater. Her musical, *Heartbeats*, was first mounted in 1989 at West Hollywood's Matrix Theater. The initial incarnation of *Heartbeats* was a loosely structured ensemble review, stringing together selections from McBroom's songbook by depicting stages of a couple's relationship, from youth to middle age. Through the course of various productions, McBroom and her creative partners, Jerry Sternbach and Bill Castellino, developed this property into a legitimate musical with a solid book to support her masterful music and lyrics. The show has enjoyed fifteen regional theater productions to date. So, with that feather in her bonnet and having the well-earned reputation as one of the world's premier cabaret and musical performers, one would think McBroom would be primed to conquer the New York stage. Not so much. Amanda's solo, off-Broadway musical, *A Woman of Will,* opened and closed in short order in 2005.

It's not as though tunesmiths haven't achieved hits on the stage. Pop songwriters have written for the theater almost since there were pop songwriters. The great Cole Porter, for instance, penned songs for a number of Broadway shows, as did Irving Berlin. One pop songwriter who took complete ownership of the stage was Lionel Bart. Although Bart started writing for theater with 1959's *Lock Up Your Daughters,* it was his string of hits for English popsters Cliff Richard, Tommy Steele, and Adam Faith that first won him success and recognition. Then, Bart dashed out the music, lyrics—and the book!—for a little Dickensian romp called *Oliver.* This accomplishment is made even more extraordinary by the fact that Bart didn't play an instrument. He came up with his meticulously composed songs using a single finger, plucking out melodies on the piano. Unfortunately, Bart sold all the rights to his song catalog and his musicals and squandered his fortune investing in a series of failures. Slipping into his life's two final decades, plagued by drugs and alcohol, Lionel Bart died in 1999, nearly penniless.

In more recent years, Billy Joel, Bob Gaudio and Bob Crewe, Bennie and Bjorn from ABBA, Jerry Lieber and Mike Stoller, Ellie Greenwich and Jeff Barry, among others have done very well with "jukebox musicals." These are reviews of the most recognizable songs from a single writer's or songwriting team's career structured into a show. This kind of production offers theatrical entrepreneurs a leg up in their efforts to get butts in those pricey seats because the songs are already well-known and beloved by millions of potential theater goers—particularly unsophisticated patrons, not possessing sufficient curiosity to be motivated to see an unfamiliar piece filled with challenging new material. However, there is always the danger that a jukebox musical's story and characters might come off as contrived in order to make those pre-existing songs work in a theatrical context. But, if a show sells tickets, more power to 'em!

At this writing, a tunesmithing pair with a long history of success, composer Steve Dorff and lyricist John Bettis, have two musicals primed to open on Broadway in 2010 and 2011: *Josephine* (the Josephine Baker story) and *Pure Country,* based on the hit 1992 film of the same name, for which Dorff wrote the score and the Number One George Strait hit "I Cross My Heart" (with Eric Kaz). Both shows have been approximately seven years in development. The first musical Dorff and Bettis wrote was *Lunch,* which got a regional tour. "We got hooked, got addicted," Dorff shares. Then, they wrote *Say Goodnight* (the love story of George Burns and Gracie Allen). Dorff confesses that the songs of Broadway were always his favorites, particularly Gershwin, Cole Porter, Lerner and Loewe. As it turned out, his most frequent collaborator, Bettis, idolized those lyricists. Dorff confides that it isn't easy: "Nobody pays you to do it. And, if you do it right, it takes a lot of time. It's very frustrating; hardest thing I've ever done. Not the creative part—that's fun—to actualize it. To get someone to write the check for all the years of work—*that's* the hard part." With the level of risk entailed in supporting this kind of endeavor, there is no wonder why investors in musical theater are called "angels."

As we've surmised, getting an original show on Broadway is a massive and potentially dangerous feat. In spite of the numerous shortfalls, missteps, near misses for tune crafters at all levels of success, the theater has been exceptionally kind to some songwriters. The point being, those who have found success on the theatrical stage have been well compensated through the time-honored concept of grand rights.

Grand rights would also be the way you would be compensated if one or more of your songs were to be incorporated into a Las Vegas revue, a Cirque du Soleil–like extravaganza, a traveling Ice Capades show, or a Sesame Street live tour.

Most Favored Nations

If you were to place a song (or songs) into one of these kinds of live productions, one of the terms you would probably be looking for in your grand rights contract is something called "most favored nations" (MFN). MFN means that, if another songwriter negotiates more favorable terms, your terms would automatically increase to match. In other words, let's suppose that your contract for your song in a Las Vegas revue states that you will receive, for the sake of simplicity, one percent of gross ticket sales. Another writer negotiates a 1¼ percent rate for his song. If you have a MFN clause in your contract, your participation would automatically increase to match the other writer's agreement.

MFN clauses are very common in sync license and soundtrack agreements as well. Now, it wouldn't exactly be realistic to expect an unknown song or a master by a brand new artist to command the same licensing fee as a major copyright by an established star hitmaker. If all of the songs included are by unknowns, however, then you could reasonably pursue MFN. If you license a song and master for use in a movie for which they will be releasing a compilation soundtrack album, you would be wise to seek MFN status for your royalty rate, so that you are always guaranteed to receive the highest royalty payment that the traffic will bear. It's not always possible to get MFN, but it's always worth asking for.

CHAPTER 8
What Should You Expect From a Publisher?

From my experience, both as a writer and as a publisher, I have developed an instinctive distrust of single-song contracts. To me, these agreements rarely represent any genuine commitment on the publisher's part, nor does their real benefit to the writer outweigh the sacrifice the writer must make.

There are certainly exceptions to this sweeping statement, but consider this: Supposing you've put your nose to the grindstone and worked really hard on a song for months. You're pretty dang sure it's your best composition to date, solidly written, unique, hooky. You've even produced a state-of-the-art demo—on your own dime. You have a strong inkling that this song has legs; this might just be the one that has a real chance of winning you some attention. You bravely pick up the phone and make some appointments with publishers. Soon, you're in your first meeting, with Publisher A. There they are, hanging in the air, beautiful, warm, and fuzzy, the very words you've been longing hear, maybe even for years. Even though you're extremely confident in your new masterwork, you can hardly believe what "A" just said: "Man, that song is a hit! I *know* I can get that song cut!" He plays the demo again, playing desk-drums and singing along. Maybe he even invites one of his colleagues or one of his staff writers in from the hallway for a third listen. "Yeah!" he exclaims, "I've got to publish that song" You can't help yourself; the grin of pride spreading across your face is uncontrollable. Your belly is churning with excitement. This is incredible, a dream come true!

"A" offers to have his company lawyer draw up the standard, single-song agreement, pronto. In fact, he tells you, you can come 'round tomorrow afternoon and put your John Hancock on it. He's making a list of pitch ideas. Only prime pitches, first-line artists for this tune, he pledges. His enthusiasm seems absolutely genuine. You leave a CD copy of the demo with him. Then, you float out of the office, with your feet six inches off the ground.

What just happened? And, more importantly, what does this really mean? Sorry to be Mr. Bummer, but here is the most likely reality: "A" has a pitch meeting in a couple of days with producer du jour, Mr. Big Time. "A" has inside info that Big Time is looking for a certain kind of song as the next single for an established superstar or the most-talked-about new act on the scene. "A" doesn't have any songs that fit that exact description in his catalog. You've just walked in and played him what he thinks just might be *the* song. No skin of his nose. He'll sign your song and pitch it this once. If he gets a pass, the song will more than likely get dumped in with the thousands of other tunes in his catalog, many of whom are by squeaky-wheel writers who are in his face and in his consciousness, day after day. If he gets a cut with your tune, he's a hero. After all, he's discovered and signed your song at no investment whatsoever. All of the effort to conceive and develop the song, along with the expense of demoing it has been yours. (Oh, I forgot to mention, his standard agreement ties your song up exclusively for five years, or, worse yet, maybe even for the life of the copyright.)

When something like this happens, it's tough to resist. You're flattered and excited, envisioning your song on the *Billboard* chart, you and your loved one red-carpeting at the Grammys, your bank account exploding with cash. But, you really need to step back and evaluate the situation rationally. It sure couldn't hurt to have "A" play the song for Mr. Big Time. Then, if he actually scores the cut, you shouldn't hesitate to sign over the publisher's portion of the copyright—or, at the very least, a share of it. I would have no quarrel whatsoever with that notion. "A" would definitely deserve to participate in the song's success, and it would be unscrupulous for any writer not to acknowledge his creative vision, effort, and risk of professional reputation by making him a legal partner in the copyright and its income. But, to sign an exclusive, five-year, single-song agreement on a song that you've just had validation might be your golden ticket? I'd think more than twice about that.

This is a hypothetical situation that really applies, to one degree or another, to most potential single-song agreements. It also hearkens back to the question that inspired this book in the first place: "How do I get my songs heard?" Should you be fortunate enough to solicit the honest enthusiasm of any publisher, reputable song-plugger, or A&R person, you cannot (I repeat, you *cannot*) afford to sit back and wait for that music-biz pro to make it happen for you. It's not that they are in any way insincere. (Although, some truly are scoundrels, particularly the song pluggers who prey on eager out-of-town wannabes and charge steep monthly retainers just for dropping CDs at record companies.) It's just that each of these people have their own lives, careers, and priorities—priorities that include those aforementioned staff writers and their continually growing catalogs. Unfortunately, as excited as "A" is today, when you're out of sight, you're liable to be out of mind. Whereas, you and your interests are never out of *your* mind, are they? So, as we will be discussing thoroughly in these pages, you need to continue to be proactive on behalf of your career and your songs, always putting in the effort to prime the pump of activity.

The real lay of the land is this: The odds of an unproven, unknown writer getting a major cut via a pitch are roughly equivalent to finding a four-leaf clover in the middle of the Sahara. It might happen, but it ain't gonna happen often. Songs by established hit writers sometimes get cut through pitches; songs pitched on golf courses, by highly connected pals might find their way into the studio. So, unless you cowrote your song with one of the select few writers whose name is synonymous with chart success, or "A" and Mr. Big Time are about to tee off for their weekly 18 holes, your song (regardless of how great it may be) already has two strikes against it: the fact that you wrote it, and that this particular plugger has no real personal pull with Mr. Big Time (above and beyond the ability to get a sit-down appointment).

So, being aware of this, and knowing that you are making real creative progress in your craft, why would you be inclined to sign over your best song for the purpose of one long-shot pitch—or, at most, a handful of pitches (before those first half a dozen passes inevitably take the wind out of your song's sails and "A" anchors it in languid Song Harbor, where it will sit, bobbing on the swells and taking on water for the next five years)? "A" is bound to get a crush on another new song next week. He's a music lover, for Pete's sake! At least he *should* have a passion for music, if he's any kind of publisher at all.

Now, let's say you've wisely asked "A" for some time to think over his generous offer, and you've kept your appointment with Publisher "B." Once again, your new demo gets a positive response, although not quite as over-the-moon as the first one. In fact, "B" makes no proclamations that the song is a for-sure hit, nor does she make any verbal guarantees that she can get it cut. However, your song has intrigued "B;" so much so, that she asks to hear some more material. Dag nab it, a couple of your other compositions pique her interest. In fact, "B" has some constructive feedback to share on those songs. You can immediately see how her suggestions might even bring those tunes up to the level of your newest masterpiece. As you shake hands on your way out, she invites you to come back, when you've done some rewriting on those compositions.

So, you smartly take "B" up on it. After all, you now have access to a pro who is willing to make her expertise available to help you develop your material. There is no downside to this relationship, only an upside regardless of whether it pans out as a business partnership. You and your cowriter buckle down to address "B's" comments and suggestions. A couple of weeks later, you're back in "B's" office, guitar in lap, playing the new and improved versions. "B" is impressed with your willingness to take her feedback and apply it constructively to solidify your songs and make them more competitive. She likes most of what you've done and invites you back for a third appointment to play what you both hope will be your final tweaks. "B" is now invested in you, your songs, and your career. Her ego is attached to your success.

After visit number three, your two rewrites pass with flying colors. "B" suggests that, if you're interested, she'd be willing to produce and finance demos on these two songs, in exchange for you signing over the publishing share of your copyrights to her company. How does *that* sit? In this scenario, Publisher "B" has already acted in one of the primary roles of music publisher: that of a creative sounding board, to help you develop and improve your songs for the marketplace. In that way, she has invested her talent and professional experience in you. Now, in addition, she is offering to lay down a substantial hunk of cash to make quality demos so that your now-improved songs will be presentable to the industry. Note: Publisher "B" did not jump up and down and declare your songs bona fide hits. She, in fact, made no definite claim that she would even be able to exploit them.

Which of these hypothetical situations seems more beneficial to you? To me, it's a no brainer. The commitment of Publisher "A", in spite of his enthusiasm level, is nowhere near that of Publisher "B." Publisher "B's" offer is one I would seriously consider, while "A's" gives me trepidation.

Let's weigh the pros and cons of the single-song agreement proposed by Publisher "A."

Pros:

1. You and your song are getting genuine endorsement from an industry pro. (Bottom line, that is great for the old ego.)
2. Your song will be getting more exposure to the industry through pitches.
3. You claim bragging rights for getting published by a legitimate publisher.
4. You might just get a cut, or even score a hit!

Cons:

1. It is not a good idea to get married just because somebody says you're pretty.
2. The likelihood of an unknown, unproven writer getting a cut with a major-label artist from a pitch is somewhere between slim and forget about it.
3. Should the publisher's pitches not get an immediate positive response, he is liable to lose his enthusiasm and move on to other songs (probably songs by staff writers he sees in his office every day).
4. You'll be tying up one of your best copyrights, not to mention a demo *you* financed, for years or more.

Furthermore, anybody who claims to know with certainty which song is a hit and which song isn't, anybody who declares definitively that he or she can get your song cut, is quite frankly blowing smoke. It's fun to hear; but I wouldn't believe it—not even for a micro-second. That's a guarantee that no one can make in good faith.

Now, let's examine the pros and cons for the single-song offers from Publisher "B."

Pros:

1. You and your songs are getting genuine endorsement from an industry pro.Your songs and writing are improving and becoming more competitive through professional, constructive feedback.
2. You are developing an ongoing, creative, writer-publisher relationship.
3. Your songs are likely to get more industry exposure through pitches.
4. The company is putting its resources on the line.
5. You have been welcomed into Publisher "B's" office almost as if you are on staff.

Cons:

1. Aside from "What ifs," I can't see a single, logical reason why not. (By "What ifs," I mean the same insecurities one might feel in any business relationship. "What if this turns out to be the wrong company for me?" "What if another, even-better deal appears after I sign this one?")

What other circumstances might arise that might indicate it's to your advantage to sign a single-song agreement?

1. An artist, producer, or production company agrees to record and release your song, in exchange for their participation in publishing ownership or co-ownership.
2. A feature film or TV placement requires you to sign over a portion of the copyright.
3. A plugger (or publisher) has worked on spec and placed your song with a major artist.

Publishing Deals

When I first arrived in Nashville in 1993, EMI Music had about 100 writers on staff. Sony/Tree, Warner Brothers, Polygram, and BMG had near that number or more. Every other building on 16th, 17th, 18th and 19th Avenues housed a publisher with a dozen writers. That doesn't even count the companies in Berryhill or on Hayes Street. The advance money being doled out by these outfits was very respectable, too. Those were the freakin' days! How times have changed. As I write this book, there are only about 300 pro-writer slots in all of Music City, and typical draws are not enough for any one person to live on, let alone a family. But, let's suppose you are one of the fortunate few. You've culled an offer to sign an exclusive contract with a music publisher. What can you expect? What should you be aware of?

Publishing deals come in all shapes and sizes. However, a traditional, first-time publishing agreement goes something like this: First, you will be expected to sign over every available, unpublished copyright. These will comprise your *Schedule A* songs. (This is negotiable, and I always think it's wise to limit the number of titles on your Schedule A, or to have as many of them as possible revert back to you at the termination of the deal.) You will be under exclusive contract to the publisher for an initial "term" (usually one year, sometimes eighteen months or two years), during which time you will be obliged to write and deliver a certain, minimum number of acceptable songs to the company. In exchange, they will pay for company-approved demos and provide you with a certain weekly or monthly advance (draw), which will count against your future royalties. The publisher will have the option to renew your contract for a second year, and then a third. If they do not inform you before a specified date (usually 60 or 90 days before the end of each term) that they do not intend to pick up your option, then your contract will automatically be renewed for the upcoming year-long term.

The publisher will own every song you write during each term of the deal in perpetuity (meaning for the life of the copyright and all copyright renewals). If your minimum delivery commitment is twelve whole copyrights (pretty common), that means you're responsible for delivering twelve solo-written songs, or 24 two-way cowrites, or 36 three-ways, or any combination thereof adding up to twelve whole copyrights. If you fail to deliver your minimum commitment, the company reserves the right to suspend your contract, meaning you will remain under exclusive contract to the company without pay, until such time as you meet your minimum commitment. The professional staff will determine which of your songs are acceptable against your delivery commitment, and which of your songs (if any) the company is willing to pay to demo. Your contract will more than likely indicate a maximum cost the company will be willing to spend per demo.

Remember that your advances and demo expenses will be recoupable against (be paid back by) any royalties earned by the songs you write for the company. You will recoup only at "your rate." Only the proportion of revenue representing your share will go to pay back your advances and demo expenses. At such time as your songs begin earning royalties, the company will mail you royalty statements (either quarterly or bi-annually) showing how much each song has earned on a pro-rata basis and crediting your portion of the income against the total of your advances and expenses. If your share of your songs' total income exceeds the advances you've received and expenses incurred, your statement should be accompanied by a check representing the balance over the sum that has been recouped.

The way you recoup is important to keep in mind. Writers under traditional deals often never break even and recoup. This is because, even though the publisher can't force the writers to pay them back for their investment, in essence the writers are borrowing their own future income at a usurious 100 percent interest rate. This is also why writers aspire to negotiate copublishing deals. With a copub, a writer is due 75 percent of their songs' income (the writer's 50 percent plus half of the publisher share, another 25 percent), so ostensibly, a copub deal can recoup a successful writer much faster than a traditional 50/50 deal can.

Who Deserves To Be a Publisher?

The law of the land is that an unpublished writer owns his or her own copyright lock, stock, and barrel. That's only fair. Until you assign a copyright or a portion thereof to a publisher, you *should* own 100 percent of your creative property. However, simply owning copyrights doesn't mean that every songwriter is a legitimate music publisher. Since becoming a co-owner of a music publishing company and seeing first hand the complexities of the publishing business, I now believe that songwriters have to earn the right to be publishers. They do this by acting like publishers: paying for demos, pitching songs (and/or hiring a song plugger), being proactive, creating opportunities to exploit the copyrights, keeping clean files containing lyrics, charts, registrations, union contracts, licensing agreements, demos, and so on. Just because the law says you own something doesn't necessarily make you a professional. You may own an NFL football, but that doesn't qualify you to drive down to Paul Brown Stadium to suit up and play for The Bengals.

So, keep this in mind when you set out to get an appointment to cowrite with your favorite Top Dog tunesmith. Your cowriters have two interests: that you be ready to cut the creative mustard and contribute to writing a strong, competitive song; and that you bring something legitimate to the table business-wise as well. As an unknown, unproven writer, no matter how talented you are, if you can't deliver opportunities for your cowrites to create commerce, you will not be all that interesting to a more established writer with a major publishing deal. And, just because you now know the difference between a traditional 50/50 pub deal and a copub, that doesn't mean you deserve to be a copublisher. That's a privilege you will need to earn, through years of hard work, scoring a string of successes, and gaining a reputation for taking care of business.

At the end of the day, this is all you can reasonably expect from any publisher. You should be more than happy if they simply deliver on these key obligations:

1. Provide you with a positive environment to be creative.
2. Pay your advances promptly.
3. Finance a reasonable number of demos.
4. Manage the catalog and keep clean books.
5. Collect your songs' income and account accurately to you for your share of it

If they go above and beyond by giving you constructive feedback to help you improve your songs; actively pitching your songs; setting up strategic cowrites; or, pie in the bright-blue sky, actually get you cuts and create meaningful activity for your songs, that's all gravy. Most of this stuff will be your own responsibility—publisher or no publisher—as you will soon find out.

PART THREE:

THE HEAD SPACE

CHAPTER 9
Why Write?

If you don't know *why* you write, how can you possibly know *what* to write?

Do you remember why you first became inspired to become a songwriter?

I guess some folks are just born writing music. "I was one of these very strange kids who heard and saw music from the time I was very little," recalls Steve Dorff. "I was playing piano at three. At seven years old, I was in a snowball fight with a bunch of kids. All my friends were running from the ice hitting them in the head. But, I just sat there musicalizing the whole thing. I assumed that everybody did that. It was a gift." Despite what little Steve Dorff may have thought back then, not every songwriter has his kind of genius endowed upon them at birth.

Kent Blazy's first creative inspirations began to reveal themselves in the bohemian, artistic community of Woodstock, New York. "Even as a little kid," Blazy muses, "I can remember going to people's houses who had a painting they were working on or gave me a signed book they'd written. Somewhere in my universe I knew that these people were doing something different—and they were making a living at it." I marvel that, even at six years old, Kent took note of how artists were marketing their work and creating commerce with it.

I started writing songs in 1965. I often say it was "a matter of necessity." What I mean by that is this: As a young turk assembling my very first rock outfit, it immediately became obvious that it would be of substantial importance to include a tunesmith in my ensemble. Why? Because, if a band didn't have original songs in the mid 1960s, it just simply wasn't cool. The blame for that stigma fell solidly on the shoulders of one Mr. Robert Zimmerman (aka Bob Dylan) and a little Liverpool combo, fronted by the ultra-gifted, prolific songwriting duo, John Lennon and Paul McCartney. Pete Townshend, Ray Davies, Brian Wilson, and Bob Gaudio had certainly answered that call and snatched up their own, legitimate tunesmithing credentials. In my teenaged mind, I *had* to be just as cool as those guys. Being 15, cocky as hell, and envisioning myself as the very essence of hipness, I volunteered to be my band's principle source of original songs, even though I'd never written one in my life. Necessity, in my case, was not only the mother of invention, she was the mother of composition.

In retrospect, however, it was more than mere pragmatics that led me to huddle away in some private corner with guitar in lap, pencil, and paper to commence making up songs. Some kismet was involved, too. I find some genuine irony here: That initial, ego-driven calling to pen pop songs would, in due course, play a very providential part in guiding me to my true destiny—through the very original compositions I began compulsively piecing together out of scattered fragments of inspiration. Songwriting, the pursuit I began purely because my band needed original material, was fated to guide me to my true fate. I knew bupkiss about craft, nor did I care a dot about developing it. I wasn't inspired with any particular, profound message I felt the world needed to hear. I was just filled with the certainty that I could do it, and I suspected that doing it would bring attention and recognition my way, while giving me more sway over my bandmates and our mutual musical direction. After all, I was the eldest of five talented brothers. I was quite used to getting the upper hand and being the star of the show—thank you very much!

This reasoning was spelled out even more clearly in the summer between my only two years of college. Since seventh grade, I had been torn between a pair of equally impractical career aspirations: stage actor or rock star. I had no back-up plan whatsoever. The towheaded, pink-cheeked, pretty boy I saw in the mirror was headed for fortune and fame, either as a thespian, as a pop preener, or both. No doubt in my mind about that. In the summer of 1968, as an apprentice in the acting company of the Oregon Shakespeare Festival, my boyish looks and scant classical-theater résumé (meaning I could not claim a single, legitimate Shakespeare credit) unsurprisingly resulted in me failing to win major roles. Not having pages of dialog to memorize or lengthy rehearsals to attend, I passed many of my idol hours jamming privately on my acoustic guitar. Many of those improvisations took the shape of new, original songs. The difference was that these new compositions came from a more personal place. They, in fact, reflected my own honest emotions: joy, alienation, loneliness, heartbreak.

A ham at heart, and my ego not enjoying adequate time basking in the theatrical footlights, I sought out a spot to share my new confessional repertoire, mixed in with those old reliable, standard, pop and folk arrangements I'd performed for years. After the plays let out, at a coffee house on the banks of Lithia Creek, I strummed, sang, and passed the hat. I rapidly took on the smell of a big fish in that small, Ashland, Oregon pond, while lining my pockets with spending money. My fellow company members—and even a director or two—began coming in to check out my musical offerings. The esteem I culled from thespians who, only an hour before, had received standing-ovation curtain calls gave me thoughts. *Aha,* I began to figure, *maybe this singer/songwriter thing is the way to go. An actor has to wait for a meaty part to come round,* I further reasoned. *A songwriter creates his or her own vehicles and can usually find a stage somewhere to pick and grin.* That realization clarified my plans. *I can always go back to acting—in my 40s, when my face takes on more character*—I decided.

And, it was then that I also discovered the fundamental fulfillment of being a writer: We get to lay our heads on our pillows every night, knowing we created something that wasn't there before! Of course, that being understood and appreciated, what I didn't take into account was this: A working actor usually gets a paycheck (as meager as it might be; or, in rare cases, as *massive*)! A songwriter can warble, scribble, and raise blisters on his fingers every day until the four horsemen usher in the apocalypse and still not see a dime for his labors. Through the interim decades, I've found many reasons to write: materialistic and spiritual, egoistic and altruistic. You, too, may discover, as the calendar pages turn, that your motivations for writing change or evolve. Regardless, I think it's of some importance for each one of us to begin our journey to success by recognizing why we do what we do. So, I'd like to suggest that you ask yourself the following questions:

- What was it that attracted or motivated me to become a songwriter?
- Why was it that I felt I had something special to offer as a songwriter?
- What is it that motivates me to continue pursuing songwriting?

These probing questions have no wrong answers. You don't have to come up with some deep, earth-shaking justification for expressing yourself in song. Maybe you started writing because your greatest desire is to buy a yacht and cruise the South Pacific. Material gain is a great motivator and makes for a perfectly legitimate reason. (However, you'd be a lot more assured of acquiring and sailing that aforementioned yacht if you ventured into real estate or investment banking.) Maybe you get off on getting hundreds of boots scootin' and booties shakin' out there on the dance floor. Perhaps getting your heart shattered into bits inspired a dozen sad, bitter, or pissed-off love songs. Maybe it was the crush you had on the girl next door, or the boy across the street that got you singin' and rhymin'. These are all perfectly good reasons to write. You don't have to petition for world peace or express praise for an omnipotent God. (Although, plenty of incredibly inspired songwriters answer those passions, too.)

Speaking of passions, emotion is the essence of every song. Songs communicate first and foremost on an emotional level. Emotions are honest. So, the people who write songs should be honest about why they are writing and know what exactly it is they are trying to communicate.

Without that emotional honesty, your songs are going have a hard time connecting with anybody else. What I'm saying is this: write about what *you* care about, not about what you think somebody *else* might care about. If you're composing dance music, write something that makes *you* want to get up and dance. If you feel the need to wail about a heartbreak, do it from your gut, honestly, loudly, and proudly. Say it how you feel it. Use names and details. (Okay, you can change names, times, and places with a wink and a nod.) Dredge up your honest emotions and let 'em out for the whole world to hear!

Twisting the words of the Bard: Songwriter, know thyself. A self-aware songwriter is a better songwriter. A songwriter who dares to express his or her honest emotions through melody and words is a far better songwriter than one who simply chooses to target a certain demographic with a clever idea. If you care about what you write about, you have a heck of a lot better chance that others will care about the songs you write. You may be able to put one or two contrived, disingenuous ditties over on your peeps, but you will not find it easy to make a career out of it. Often, it's the song that a writer just *had* to write, the one that he or she never in a million years thought would ever achieve mass success that does just that. Music fans know sincerity when they hear it—and sincerity is exactly what they want to hear. Liz Rose was a music publisher when she began brainstorming ideas with one of her writers, Kim Patton (now Kim McLean). As Patton began incorporating Rose's concepts into her songs, the two women became collaborators. Now a Grammy–winning songwriter (2009's Country Song of the Year, Taylor Swift's "White Horse"), Rose's first single release as a writer was a Patton/Rose cowrite recorded by Billy Gillman, entitled "Elizabeth." "We never wrote 'Elizabeth' to be cut," Rose recollects. "I just wrote it because my niece was very ill, and I just had to get it out that day."

People often ask me if I knew "My List" was a hit when Tim James and I cowrote it in my attic studio. "No," I always respond. "I knew it was a good song, a solidly written song with a wholesome message." Quite honestly, it was a message that *I* needed to hear myself. At that moment in time, I was writing for my life. Having been dropped from my publishing deal, my savings were dwindling, and I was focused on nothing else but saving my songwriting career. At the time, I had no way of knowing that very song would be the one to do just that—and so much more.

After we finished "My List," James—a bit of a wise guy himself—asked me, "So, now that we've written this song, are you gonna slow down a little and start livin'?"

"Are you kiddin'?" I joked. "I don't have time for that. I'm tryin' to make it in show business!" I began to get an inkling of the power of the song when I played it out at writers' nights. On one such show, the audience (none of whom had ever heard it before) burst into spontaneous applause as I ended the first chorus with the words, "start livin', that's the next thing on my list." My fellow songwriters would often express sincere admiration for that song. However, for two years, the industry paid no attention to it whatsoever. After Toby Keith released "My List" as a single in 2002, James and I started hearing from people all across the country—folks who felt the need to share how Toby's record had helped them through an illness or a job loss, how the song's message nudged them to take a hard look at their lives and put their priorities straight. James suggested that we write a book based on the song. *My List, 24 Reflections on Life's Priorities*, was published by McGraw Hill, in 2003. It was my first book. This one is my fourth. Since then, I've also written three screenplays, a stage play, blogs, essays, and numerous letters to the editor. So, "My List" didn't just sustain my songwriting career for more than a decade. That song opened up new vistas of creative fulfillment by inspiring me to stretch out beyond the finite boundaries of the three-minute song.

Did I know it was a hit when we wrote it? Absolutely not. But, because it was a song that resonated deeply in the hearts of the two men who felt compelled to put its message to music, a superstar artist felt its passion, and he gave it the chance to reach the hearts of millions of music fans. Many lives were changed—not the least of which was mine. This is not to say that you should be dedicating your song craft exclusively to writing songs that change the course of people's lives. In actuality, you don't even have to try because *all* successful songs do just that to some degree. The effect may be momentary, impermanent, fleeting, as in a tune with a great groove and a simple, party theme that helps folks unwind after a grueling week on the job. Or, the effect might be profound and lasting. The important thing is that the inspiration for the song came from an honest place; the writers really meant it when they wrote it. Only writers who strive for self knowledge and honor their true instincts can write sincere, truthful songs. Unless a song is rooted in someone's version of the truth, it will not find an audience.

CHAPTER 10
Call Yourself a Songwriter

First, we find ourselves inspired to make up songs. This impulse might be sparked by records we hear on the radio, production numbers we see in a movie or theater production, or a particularly unforgettable, live concert performance. Maybe we have a relative or a family friend who performs music or even writes songs. Somewhere, somehow, something has touched us, and we've been moved to create music and/or lyrics. We find ourselves scribbling rhymes on a scrap of paper or noodling a phrase of melody, strumming a guitar, or formulating an original sequence of chords on the keys. By honoring this urge and taking action on it, we start the process of becoming songwriters. If we continue to scratch that itch to the extent that we begin building a repertoire of finished, original tunes, we can actually pin the "songwriter" badge to our chests. No one can stand in our way or deny us that right. It's our creative inspiration; and it's our choice.

Regardless of what you do to pay the rent, if it's your calling, your most compelling aspiration, call yourself a songwriter. You may teach school, sell used cars, mow lawns, or wait tables. But if, in your heart of hearts, your greatest desire is to write songs, and you are doing just that every time you get the chance, then the answer should be, "I'm a songwriter." Your day job may be a lab technician or a dog walker, but at the end of the day, if you see yourself writing songs for a living and you're actively laying the groundwork to make that your reality, a songwriter is who you are. Saying "I'm a songwriter" is the first personal affirmation and the first public declaration that will set you on the path to success.

This is not a business for dilettantes. It's not often that we hear of a cashier in Boise, a nurse in Tucson, or a forklift operator in Birmingham spontaneously jotting a lyric down on a napkin or singing a melody into a cell-phone memo, then, through an amazing string of serendipitous events, suddenly seeing their original song bullet to the top of the charts. There's good reason why that never happens. The people who succeed as songwriters are dedicated to following their inspiration and applying their craft on a daily basis. They assemble the tools of the trade and endeavor to learn how to use them. They study the works of the masters and become aware of how the interlocking gears of the music business turn to create commerce.

Becoming a pop songwriter does not require a degree. It only requires a strong desire to do it, a little bit of native talent, the stick-to-it-ive-ness to start and finish song after song, and thick enough skin to withstand what will surely amount to thousands of rejections. However, becoming a *successful* pop songwriter almost always requires an education. I'm not talking about the kind of schooling that culminates with you marching to

"Pomp and Circumstance," although going to school is not only an option, higher education can be a huge benefit for some aspirants. A songwriter's classroom can be one of his or her own making, a place of his or her own choice—a bedroom, a garage, or a basement—some private place, where those organic, creative juices are allowed and encouraged to flow and mix. A songwriter's education doesn't stop at the classroom door, either. Life itself is the campus, and every encounter, from the mundane to the extraordinary, should contribute to the unique ideas and personal perspective reflected in a writer's work.

Songwriters who embark strategically toward achieving success usually do so in two major stages. First comes the part we've been discussing through the entire first half of this book: the education stage. After all, just because you own the CD box set of *L.A. Law* or have memorized hundreds of *Perry Mason* dramas, doesn't mean you can go down to the courthouse and pull off a capable murder defense. Nothing prevents you from defending the accused (as long as you don't actually purport to be a lawyer). Of course, there are no statutes either against you writing songs, demoing, and pitching them. However, lawyers do have briefs to file, arcane terms to master, and protocols they should be familiar with. It's helpful for a lawyer to have a knowledge of all applicable precedents, comparable cases that could affect their current case's outcome. Legal precedents are the golden oldies of the courtroom, the chart toppers of the past, the major copyrights of jurisprudence, the historical benchmarks (pun intended) that brought the law to where it is today. So, for those excellent reasons—and many more, I'm sure—most who seek successful careers as attorneys attend law schools and endeavor to pass those grueling bar exams. Only after running that gauntlet will a newly minted member of the bar apply for a job as a public defender, try to win a starting position at a law firm, or hang up that shingle and start chasing ambulances.

It would seem irresponsible—not to mention jumping the proverbial gun by a few years—for the guy on the forklift in Birmingham to pack his family in a converted van and drive up Interstate 65 to Nashville, armed with only one hastily warbled song on his cell phone. (I mean, he has to have *some* recollection of the training and certification he was required to go through before he was trusted to move that first stack of boxes with his forklift, right? Every job requires *some* training, for Pete's sake!) Without having thoroughly learned his new trade or assembling any tools of it; without having studied the business he aspires to break into; without knowing a soul who might give him an in, impulsively scootin' off to Music City, wife and kids in tow, would obviously be, well, crazy. Yet, it happens (maybe not to the extreme of this example, but close).

My friend, David Preston, is one of a half dozen folks in songwriter/publisher relations working out of the world headquarters of BMI in Nashville. Over lunch, David told me about one such feller, who'd showed up that morning from out of town, pulling his car and a U-Haul trailer into a guest parking spot. This guy walked boldly into the building, up to the reception desk and asked to see somebody about becoming a hit songwriter. He didn't have a songwriting credit to his name or a single industry phone number, let alone know anybody in the business. All he had was a beat-up guitar and some original tunes. He explained to David that he'd quit his job back home and was serious about getting his songs cut by the biggest stars in the country-music pantheon.

Now that, in and of itself, is not so extraordinary. In fact, scenarios like this repeat at least once every day in Music City. Some guy or gal with a few tunes and visions of glory pulls into town, steps off a plane, or jumps down from a Greyhound bus, fully expecting to score a hit record in quick order, without a clue as to how to go about it. Here's the kicker: Waiting in his vehicle in the BMI guest lot were this man's wife, kids, dog, cat, and most of their worldly possessions. It broke David's heart. I'm hoping that everyone who reads this book has more sense than that. It's great to have a dream, to feel compelled to create songs, and to visualize yourself as being successful. It's also helpful to have a realistic plan to make it happen. That plan should start with getting your education.

During the education stage, the writer builds a solid foundation, preparing to face the opportunities he or she will create and encounter in the second stage: the practical stage or the "doing business" stage. The education stage involves learning, practicing, and developing a craft, while simultaneously studying the history, traditions, and machinations of the industry. And, quite honestly, that education should never cease. It should continue until you hang up your instruments, unplug your computer, put your tortured muse at ease, and cast your retirement lure into the lake. There is always something new to learn, something else to discover. "Professional songwriters never stop learning or think they know it all," says Danny Arena of SongU. Physicians, executives, attorneys, professional people of all stripes—even hairdressers—attend seminars, read trade publications, belong to online communities, and so on to keep up on the newest technology and the latest theories, to freshen their basic knowledge, and to stay on the cutting edge. Their interest is not just curiosity, it demonstrates passion for the work, an open mind, and a willingness to progress and improve. Even though the basic craft of pop songwriting goes back centuries, those who do it today should also be keeping themselves apprised of the new tools and the latest trends, if only to avoid creating disposable work that might be hip today but obsolete tomorrow.

So now, assuming that you've committed yourself to your continuing education, we're moving on to stage two in our journey to songwriting success: the stage in which it all starts to happen. Excited? I knew you would be.

Hold your horsepower, pal, because we're not ready to hit the highway just yet. First we need to take a good, hard look under the hood, check for leaks, make sure your plugs are firing, your block is solid, and your cylinders have plenty of compression.

CHAPTER 11
Attitude Adjustment (The Mental Tune-Up)

Have you heard about the songwriter who won the lottery? Somebody asked what he was going to do with all that money. The lucky fellow pondered the question for a long ten seconds. "Well," he finally replied, "I guess I'll just keep writin' 'til it's gone."

Sad—and yet, hi*larious*—this, my favorite songwriter joke, is instructive for two reasons. First and foremost, regardless of your level of songwriting success or your stature in the business, it's never healthy to focus exclusively on, or become emotionally dependent on actual results for your personal fulfillment. If you're not happy unless you have a song bulleting up the charts, you can probably look forward to some pretty miserable days ahead. The need to express yourself, a passion for the process, and a genuine appreciation for each opportunity you get to stretch your creative muscles and grow your God-given talents should be your primary motivations for strumming those strings and scribbling those rhymes. If you can't find satisfaction enough as a writer without achieving constant industry recognition, you might consider trying another profession, one that offers a steady paycheck and "employee of the month" accolades. That said, let's return to our hypothetical lottery winner. In addition to the suddenly fortunate lad's admirable lack of concern that his labor bears fruit, his punch-line response reveals that this dude has a pretty darn good attitude. At least, it's my impression that he has.

It's brutally competitive out there in Songwriterland, for sure. In spite of the hard realities with which you and I are faced on a daily basis, there is one absolutely essential personality trait we would be well advised to put forward at all times: a chipper, upbeat demeanor.

I have a little scrap of blue paper on my desk. I've saved it for years. On it I scrawled:

> ***"I wouldn't be a writer if I wasn't blinded by optimism."***

I honestly don't remember whether that was something I came up with on my own, I heard somebody else say it, or I read it somewhere. If that phrase didn't originate in my own head, I sincerely apologize to the person who is actually responsible for those ten words. However, regardless of its source, this is a sentence that speaks volumes about the inimitable, "always hopeful," song-dog nature we discussed in depth pages ago. Because we songwriters are such optimists at heart, my proposition is this:

Let's take that unflappable, dogged character and put it on display.

If you're thinking, *Well, that's just not me. I'm not some naïve, pie-eyed Pollyana*, then you've found kinship here. I, too, don't come by a sunny disposition naturally. Fact of the matter is, my personal climate tends toward partly cloudy, with a threat of cantankerousness. I'm constantly drawn toward the con and *not* the pro side of the ledger. I'm most content when I'm by myself, immersed in my private, creative thoughts, getting something done. My loved ones have learned to avoid interrupting my flow, because doing that will invariably provoke a snarl from this old Song Dog. Maybe that's why, back in the late 1960s, I loved Neil Diamond's first hit, "Solitary Man," so much.

"What a beautiful day," my nearly always upbeat wife remarks.

"Yeah," I agree. (How can I not, with that sun blazing down from a crystal blue sky?) And yet, I can't help but stick a pin in the balloon. "But, it's supposed to rain tomorrow." That's why, for years, she nicknamed me "Mr. Worst-Case-Scenario Man." Maybe I should have pursued a law degree, because when somebody mentions a possibility, I can always dig up a reason why it won't work.

A full half of my bloodline flows from the frigid tundra of Lapland, so I am easily pulled into morose, pensive introspection. A craving for strong, numbing alcohol runs in my Finnish veins, carried along on a sluggish current of pessimism. Years ago, I was stunned by an episode of *60 Minutes*. The lens of the video camera revealed distant cousin after distant cousin zombie-walking down a Helsinki sidewalk. Each and every face blankly reflected what looked to be a countenance of depression and despair. There was not a smile or even an upturned corner of a lip to be seen. The segment would have been comical, had the pervasive melancholy there on the TV screen not been that of my mother's lineage.

Ironically, music was at the core of this TV article. These morose pedestrians were on their way to participate in a particularly Finnish phenom: lunch-time tango dancing. I'm not kidding. It turns out that thousands of Finns devote their lunch hours to going to clubs and dancing the tango. However, the piece went on to explain that it's not the sensual, languid, Latin strains of the Argentine that move my long-lost relatives to dance, but a more appropriate repertoire for the Northern climes: minor-keyed dirges, with themes of dark depression, murder, and suicide. That, in a straight *60 Minutes* shot glass, seemed to unravel the mystery of my heritage. Like those Helsinki-ites, I've never found it easy or instinctive to smile for the camera. Even on those occasions when I *think* I'm making my maximum effort to project an outward friendliness and enthusiasm, it often doesn't seem to translate to the world outside of my Scandinavian skin. Back in high school, I had a reputation for being "conceited." My schoolmates presumed that I snubbed them because of an out-of-control ego; but, the bubble I'd placed around myself was more about a compulsively creative teenager being constantly lost in his own vivid imagination, making up songs, putting together set-lists, rehearsing rock-star moves in his own head, in some parallel reality, light years away from the bustling hallways of Lake Oswego High.

Why am I unpacking my personal baggage and airing my stinky socks like this? Because I think a lot of creative folks confront similar challenges. You, too, may possess character traits that can stand in the way of your success. For instance, like me, you may automatically kick into to this default mode: leaping ahead, getting busy developing the next creative idea, instead of doing the work necessary to give the just-completed idea any genuine opportunity to find success. Songwriting mentor, Barbara Cloyd, has observed that many deserving, talented writers don't give themselves the chance to succeed because they make the mistake of spending too much time working in isolation. (Let's sing along with Mr. Diamond: "I'll be what I am, a solitary man.") While showcasing thousands of performing writers week after week at the world-famous Bluebird Café, Cloyd has also seen first hand how a writer can diminish his or her prospects with a cocky, surly, impatient, egocentric, or self-righteous attitude. Worse yet is the writer who is bent on complaining—about *every*thing.

A songwriter dies. As her life pretty much straddled the line between sin and salvation, St. Peter gives the dearly departed tunesmith the opportunity to choose between an afterlife in Heaven or everlasting Hell. "Well, I guess it wouldn't hurt to check out the basement first," she kids, probably thinking she'll encounter some familiar faces down there. In Hell, an angel/guide shows our late writer to a conference room, where a bunch of other tunesmith/spirits sit around, drinking coffee, smoking cigarettes, and conducting a pity party. One after the other complains about his or her songs not getting enough pitches, and how it seems impossible to get a cut. "This is just like life," our newly deceased song scribe observes, "I certainly don't want to spend eternity here." So, they take the elevator up to Heaven. There, they find precisely the same scene: a group of disgruntled songwriter/angels kvetching about not getting enough pitches or cuts. "Wait a minute," the writer says, "this is exactly like Hell."

"No, no, no," the guide corrects her. "These writers all have copub deals." Ba-da-bum!

The point is this: As a rule, songwriters love to complain. Here in Nashville, you can't swing a cat without hitting one grumbling songwriter carping to another. Certainly, the uneven lay of the land, the built-in unfairness of the game gives 'em plenty to grouse about. But, let's face it, you can find nits to pick in any business, if that's where you choose to place your focus. The real trick is to recognize how tough it is, yet knock that chip off your shoulder and direct your energies in a positive direction, with a smile on your face. If you get to spend your time makin' stuff up, you're living a pretty charmed life. As far as I'm concerned, regardless of the rewards—short of actually starving to death—living a creative life certainly beats hard labor. And believe me, I've done enough of both to make that distinction.

Being well liked can turbo-charge your launch to the stars. People like friendly, upbeat people. For the most part, positive, affable people are more successful than negative, morose people. Positive people are always attracted to other positive people—and vice versa. Therefore, it follows that putting forward a positive demeanor gives each of us a better chance of succeeding. Bottom line, your attitude is a choice that not only affects your actual experience, it changes your perception *of* your experience—for the better. It's the cup half empty versus the cup half full. It's the same dang cup, with the same amount of liquid in it. Looking at it one way makes you sad; looking at it the other makes you happy. How do you choose to look at it? That, my friend, is entirely up to you.

We've all met somebody we thought was extremely successful, but who still didn't seem to be content or fulfilled. Even the biggest winners can find something to grouse about. A few years back, I re-encountered one of the most successful songwriters of any era, a fellow who has been responsible over the last 50 years for penning dozens of pop music's most memorable hits. It just so happened that I was collaborating on a couple of songs with his most-frequent co-writer. When I suggested that maybe the three of us might team up on something, he grumbled that it wouldn't be any use. "I can't get arrested anymore," the multi-millionaire legend moaned, wallowing in self-pity. "Nobody's interested in my songs." The first time I met this guy, he was bubbling with vigor and positive energy. I found him charming and charismatic; he seemed open and eager for new experiences. Now, despite the enormity of his life's accomplishments, he was feeling beaten, bedraggled, unfit even. One would think that a music-business vet would recognize and accept its built-in, cyclical ups and downs. As Heidi Klum says so famously in her opening bit on *Project Runway,* "One day you are in. And the next day, you are out." Who's to say that, on a third day, you're not back—and stronger than ever? Ask Barry "Teflon" Gibb about that. That cat has had how many lives? And, really, what good does success do you anyway, if you're not capable of taking joy in it?

On the flip side, some among us can be just a little too energetic, to the point of being overbearing. Your goal should be to be pleasant, friendly, likable, and fun to be around. To be obnoxious, boorish, ultra-intense, getting right up in people's faces will not work to your advantage. Being aggressive, no matter how positive you are, can wear out your welcome in a New York minute. (I choose this particular analogy for good reason, because some New Yorkers have been known to be pushy, if ya know what I mean. Actual anecdotal evidence of that cultural syndrome will come later.)

Regardless of which part of the country we hail from, many of us creative types demonstrate another self-defeating tendency as well: dangling imaginary, golden carrots out there in the future, those watermark achievements we think will provide us with that elusive (and illusive) contentment we crave. "When I get a cut by a major label artist, then I can die happy." "When I have my first number one, my life's work will be complete." "If I could only have one Top Five song every year, that would make my career." But, the whole concept of "I'll be really happy when..." doesn't make any sense, does it? For "When I...then I" people, there will always be another, bigger, shinier carrot hanging just out of reach. That attitude makes every satisfaction, contentment, and fulfillment transitory, if not actually impossible. Taking a hard look at the previous example of the unnamed, discontented hit maker should be evidence enough: believing that "success breeds happiness" is illogical, unsound, and downright risky. The opposite actually rings much more true to real life experience: "Happiness breeds success." If you always keep *that* credo in mind, change your attitude, and act accordingly, you'll start gettin' somewhere.

Is happiness important? Should it always be our goal? Or, should we try to make it our continual state? After all, there is a hell of a lot of sadness, disillusionment, and grief in this life, too; not to mention unrequited desire, illness, bad luck, and tragedy. Still, knowing that the road ahead will not always be covered with rose petals, the answers to the above questions are, in order, "Yes," "Yes," and "yes." After being alive for more than 60 years, I have arrived at this conclusion: Happiness is evolutionary. Happiness directs us how to thrive and survive. Happiness is not just some intangible pie in the sky. It is the motivating force compelling us to do the very things that keep us growing and evolving, generation after generation. What are some of our happiest experiences? Right off the top of my head, how about this brief list of big-ticket items: love, warmth, nourishment, being together, genuine communication. If not for at least occasional encounters with these pleasurable, nurturing experiences, we wouldn't last very long as individuals, or as a species, would we? Love drives us to procreate and to take care of our children—and each other. Warmth and nourishment, of course, are essential to our good health and well being, therefore critical to our very survival. Being together and communicating with each other gives our hearts a natural buzz and inspires us to bond as families, to create neighborhoods, to form communities and ultimately nations, the common entities that protect us, while providing essential infrastructure and services. So, to one degree or another, we are all born with the natural desire to have happy experiences because they are the experiences that keep us alive.

I don't know about you, but getting creative, concocting something beautiful, and/or truthful, and/or funny, something that wasn't there before I came up with it, something that springs from my own unique perspective and is shaped by my own special talents; *that* gives me a heck of a lot of happiness. So, that's *gotta* be a good thing!

The first thing a born sourpuss like me needs to address is that bad attitude. A negative outlook, as we've surmised, is not conducive to surviving or evolving. A poor point of view colors and ultimately defines our perception of life. Changing one's perception of the experience of life can actually change one's life experience, because being and acting happy actually attracts more of the experiences that bring us happiness. So, although I did derive some personal consolation from that *60 Minutes* broadcast—it helped me understand myself much better and, suddenly, I didn't feel so alone in my darkness—I certainly wasn't satisfied to remain a charter member of the Sad Sack Club. Seeing those somehow all-too-familiar, perennially miserable faces inspired me to alter the expression on mine—completely. If I was gonna dance the tango of life, I decided, it would be a joyous and successful one, not a suicidal dirge. Lastly, I realized I had been erecting impediments that were keeping me from my own success; so I set out to change my native instincts. "How did you do that?" you query.

"I'm glad you asked," I respond. Daily, I began reciting positive, affirmative statements about myself. During every waking hour, I paid full attention to my thoughts and words, consciously canceling and erasing anything and everything that was at all negative. I started to visualize a sunnier, more pleasant life experience, imagining circumstances that manifested my own positive recognition and abundance. I recognized my unique talents and proclaimed the worthiness of my work. Over time, not only did the corners of my mouth become less weighty, I began attracting more positive people into my life; and, just as miraculously, the grouches who didn't share my newfound positivity began to drop away. The cynics stopped calling, no longer loitered around. Eventually, I began noticing that I was having a more hopeful, fulfilling life, surrounded by more supportive friends, meeting more influential people, and attracting more real opportunities for real success and following through on those opportunities.

Once again, this ain't five-minute abs, folks. It takes time, focus, and lots of spiritual elbow grease to reprogram your habitually negative thoughts and reverse the polls of your energy. By choosing self-awareness and by applying conscious effort, you, too, can change the way you think, how you express and project yourself. And then, you will also change the way your peers and industry decision-makers perceive you, which in turn will enable you to attract other positive, successful people into your world, and thus change your life experience. *Voila!*

We've all heard about the Law of Attraction. The movie and book sensation, *The Secret,* is based on this concept. Actually, this idea goes back through the millennia to the Golden Rule, the teachings of a carpenter/rabbi from Nazareth, and the mystery schools that preceded Him, centuries before He trekked the arid Middle East, healing lepers, and turning water into wine. "No one lights a lamp and puts it in a place where it will be hidden…" Jesus proclaimed. "Instead, he puts it on its stand, so that those who come in may see the light." These words actually go hand in hand with the latest theories of quantum mechanics. Some scientists have compiled what they call empirical evidence that human consciousness or intent can manipulate outcome, thus affecting reality. In the hybrid documentary/drama *What The Bleep? (Down The Rabbit Hole),* jars of water were labeled with different phrases, from the most peaceful and positive language, to the most negative and violent. These jars were set out in a public place. The thoughts of people viewing them, after reading the posted text, actually changed the molecular structure of the water within. Under the microscope, the molecules from jars labeled with violent, negative phrases had become jagged and barbed, while molecules labeled with loving, nurturing words remained rounded and soft. At long last, in some purely scientific circles, it has become an acceptable assertion that our thoughts are capable of creating or changing reality—or at least our perception of reality. And, after all, what else really matters but perception? If you think and believe in your heart of hearts that you are successful, happy, and fulfilled, then that is the experience you will attract.

So, let's light a campfire and have a hootenanny! Everybody sing along! "This little light of mine, I'm gonna let it shine!" "Don't worry, be happy…" "…accent-uate the positive, elim-inate the negative." "…on the sunny side of the street."

But, you can't stop there! No. You do have to take action, too. I once was in a performing duo with a partner who spent too much time working on her headspace and devoted too little real energy to getting the job done. At an afternoon rehearsal, I enquired "Did you call everybody on your contact list to remind them about our gig tonight?"

"No," she replied, dreamily. "But, I visualized them all there."

"Maybe some phone calls might have been more effective," I remarked. I was right about that. The turnout that night was disappointing. Okay, reputedly Ari Geller could bend a silver spoon with his mind, but some metaphysical types take the concept of "thought creating reality" a little too far. You really can't expect to walk out in front of a speeding bus believing you won't be struck down. The bus will have no trouble winning that duel. Surely, Art Linkletter's daughter believed to her core that she could fly, when, tripping on LSD, she leapt from a third story balcony. No matter what she believed in that misguided moment, she was incapable of taking wing. In fact, she perished in the fall. As you and I are survivors, this should be our game plan: reprogram our minds to think positively; see our success in the here and now; speak successfully; and do the things consistent with our new attitude.

What type of person do you like hanging with? Are you attracted to the bitter cynic who always sees and refers to that aforementioned glass as half empty? How about the constant complainer? Or the victim? Or the habitual loser, resigned to waving the white flag of surrender at some point during the course of every challenge? If those are the kinds of people you prefer being around, then you're thinking self-destructive thoughts, speaking perversely, and you are most likely stuck on a treadmill of failure. It's easy to be negative and sarcastic. It's easy to believe that life is unfair, to see yourself as just another pawn in a chess match you'll never win. However, you have a choice between living your life as a victim of circumstance or becoming the master of your fate.

Change your mind and you will change your experience. Develop a positive attitude and you will attract positive people—people who will, in turn, help you succeed. Endeavor to become a person who is fun to be with, who is always ready with a smile and a kind word, who listens to others compassionately and encourages them. Be a living demonstration that life is great and that each day on top of the ground is a good one. If you do that, you will stop building those walls that protect you from one thing only—your own success. And, each day on top of the ground will literally bring you one more step closer to your loftiest aspirations. Pollyanna? Yeah, maybe, but positive energy wins over negative—every time!

Hit writer and renown song-craft teacher, Jason Blume, expounds on his early career...

"First I should tell you I was so positive, such an optimist," confesses Blume. "I absolutely knew that I would have a Mercedes in my driveway in a year." Arriving in Hollywood with all of $400, young Blume moved into a rented room, in a very scary section of town, and was sharing a hallway bathroom with drug dealers and prostitutes. I'd say he had every reason to whine and complain about his lot in life. But, no chip on Blume's shoulder. He just kept putting his cheery disposition out there for the world to see.

Low and behold, brothers and sisters, part of Jason Blume's positive visualization became reality as, within that year, he sat in the driver's seat of a top-of-the-line Mercedes, just one of the many expensive cars he drove through a car wash in the performance of his day job. It actually took 11 years for him to get his first cut and sign a staff-writing contract with Zomba

Music. That publishing deal led to cuts with some of pop music's biggest artists and sales in the tens of millions. In turn, those successes positioned Blume to become one of the most respected songwriting coaches around. Why? For several obvious reasons: He learned his craft, for starters; he persevered through more than ten years of rejections, set-backs, and disappointments; and, he did all of that with a smile on his face.

There are no guarantees that you will ever find Jason Blume's level of songwriting success, even if you have a divine, superior gift for setting lyrics to music, or vice versa. However, it certainly doesn't hurt your chances to make the effort to be pleasant, likable, and optimistic, without being overbearing. If you practice a positive outlook every day, you will more than likely start having a lot more fun, as you travel the bumpy, winding road ahead. And, the other people in your life will have more fun, too.

If this crusty ol' Finn can do it, so can you.

CHAPTER 12
Gratitude

One of the most unsettling, unavoidable aspects of pursuing a songwriting career is that, for extended periods of time, we have absolutely no way of gauging our progress. While we're putting one foot in front of the other, going through the necessary motions—writing, re-writing, playing out, meeting people, and so on—months or even years can slip away, while nothing apparently seems to change. At least, nothing seems to change for the good. We may look at that face in the mirror and detect a few more wrinkles or a gray hair or two; but, when we crank up the radio, we still don't hear one of our songs blasting out of the speakers. It takes a whole lot of trust in forces beyond our immediate control to keep on believing that every day actually brings us a little bit closer to our goals, especially when there are no signs along the highway indicating precisely how many more miles we have to travel before we reach the city limits of Hitsville.

Of course there are positive indicators that imply forward progress. Getting a song in the hands of a key industry decision maker may feel like a milestone worthy of celebration. That same industry pro putting that song "on hold" is definitely a good sign. Certainly getting a cut is an enormous encouragement. Finally, having a song released means you're actually in business. However, it's only when, at long last, you're able to see that composition getting added to radio-station playlists, when you can actually watch something you created climbing the charts, that you actually have a real-time barometer by which you can weigh your success.

I used to believe that rejoicing too soon could jinx the mojo; I thought that all festivities should be postponed until there was something tangible to shout about. Even a cut wasn't quite enough. A release might be something to toast. A single on the radio could warrant a bit of a shout out. Due to that credo, I didn't do a whole lot of celebrating. Getting a pitch (especially a high-level one) is definitely a good thing. It means you got up to bat. *Yay!* Other than being an indication that your song is competitive in the marketplace, getting a hold really only means that one single person (someone who is supposed to possess a credible level of expertise in what a good, commercial song is) likes it—today. A hold doesn't mean you'll get the cut; in fact, it doesn't even guarantee that the song will ever be heard by the producer or the artist. While neither of these preliminary benchmarks are worthy of a fireworks display, there is nothing really wrong with what my ex-business partner, Steve Bloch, calls "premature celebration." After all, a hold may be the only thing a writer will *have* to celebrate for a very long time. Might as well make merry while the possibility still exists that the song is going to make the artist's session.

Go ahead and *paaaaarty!* Be encouraged and thankful that your song has garnered some serious consideration. But, please don't hold your breath for an ASCAP Award. There are so many more hoops to jump through, and you'll need all the oxygen your lungs can absorb.

Inevitably, we all meet up with disappointments and disillusionments along the way, those "almosts," "near misses," and "so closes" that are part and parcel of a game of inches. One of my favorite Jimmy Webb quotes (from his fabulous songwriting manifesto, *Tunesmith*) goes something like this: "We've chosen a profession in which, best case scenario, ninety percent of our work will be completely ignored." By "best case scenario," I will choose to assume that Webb is referring to a writer of his own stature getting one out of ten songs cut. How can I gauge my fortunes against that of one of the most prolific hit makers of the last four decades? Well, over the 40 years of my career, I've had close to 250 cuts and releases. Let's say that, on average, during every one those years, I cranked out about 50 songs. That would make a grand total of approximately 2,000 titles. Having scored 250 cuts out of 2,000 total compositions would mean that I'm doing even better than Jimmy Webb's definition of "best case scenario."

(On second thought, maybe I left some important words out of the Webb quote. Maybe he said, "...ninety percent of our work will be completely ignored *by the public*." If that is indeed what he really said, since at least half of my cuts never got radio play, failed to chart, or didn't enjoy what you might call substantial commercial or even critical acceptance, that would mean my success level is far below one-in-ten. Regardless, having 250 cuts and releases is pretty decent by anyone's standards. I haven't, however, been responsible for at least a dozen of the most-performed and recorded pop songs of the era as Webb has.)

My relatively high batting average doesn't mean that I haven't endured my fair share of abuse. Believe me, my songs have been kicked around plenty; and my ego and professional pride have been pummeled and bruised right along with those babies. It's very easy to take it personally when a tune you've labored over, nursed, coddled, and sent out into the big bad world is not received positively. It's like somebody making disparaging remarks about your child. In the spring of 2002, during one of the five consecutive weeks that "My List" topped *Billboard*'s Hot Country Singles chart, one particular voicemail message cut me to the quick. With the Toby Keith single climbing steadily, I had distributed a compilation CD to record companies—sort of an audio calling card to re-introduce myself to various industry movers and shakers as "Music Row's latest number-one songwriter." I closed the CD with the demo of "My List," the homemade recording that had actually enticed Keith to cut the song. "This is Bryan, intern at Sony Records," the message began. "I'm calling to inform you that we've chosen to pass on the following songs: 'How Cool Would That Be,' 'Trouble With Trouble,' 'Better Than That,' and 'My List.'" An intern, an underling, a nonsalaried, record-company slave called and left a message telling me that he had passed on a song that was not only sitting at the top of the charts at that very moment, but a song that went on to become country radio's most-played single for the entire year. It was a completely ignorant thing to do on his part, something that he should be embarrassed by for the rest of his life. Yet, my feelings were still hurt—because my song had been rejected. Sad, I know. But, that's how sensitive we songwriters can be sometimes.

Try to look at it this way: Every time one of your songs receives a pass, you're a little bit closer to getting a cut. After all, you can't strike out unless you get into the batter's box. You can't miss a free throw unless you've driven the lane and gotten hacked on the arm. I'm sure you get my drift. Getting hundreds of passes, losing dozens of holds, having a Tracy Bird cut not make his greatest hits CD, my Carolina Rain single getting pulled after two disappointing weeks, my David Ball single flopping: every one of those disappointments meant that I was out there on the field of play, getting my uniform muddy. You cannot win if you don't play. This is a "never give up" business. Never give up writing. Never give up rewriting. Never give up improving your demos. Never give up playing your songs publicly. Never give up making contacts and expanding your network. Let the shortfalls go. Forget about 'em. Move on. NEVER! GIVE! UP!

A pass on a song is not necessarily a reflection on the song itself, or on you as its writer. Here is the best way to interpret each and every pass: This particular song is not the exact one the person you're playing it for wants to hear at this very moment. Unless the A&R person actually says something to the effect of, "Never play me that song again," or, in the middle of the second chorus, she reaches for a barf bag and tosses her cookies, that song will live on to be pitched another day. (If it continues to be soundly rejected, then it might just need some rest or some major surgery, but that doesn't mean it's a lame song or that you are an unworthy songwriter.) When a youngster declares his or her intention to pursue a career as a tunesmith or singer/songwriter, I say this: "Better get some thick skin. You're gonna hear the word No a lot."

Steve Dorff, a composer who has found the highest level of success on country and pop radio, television, in feature films, and on the musical theater stage, shares this: "If you don't have the ability to pick yourself up and dust yourself off a hundred times a day, you're probably not suited for this business." So, with that reality in mind, how does a songwriter standing outside the gate prepare to cope day after day with the sound of that heavy door being slammed and double-bolted shut? The same way every successful songwriter has learned to cope: by staying busy, improving craft, making new friends, maintaining existing friendships, faking a smile (when those lips seem heavy and uncooperative)—and finally, by being grateful.

"What's there to be grateful for?" you might ask. "This is a rigged game, and we're playing against a hundred-mile-an-hour headwind. It's not fair!"

"You're absolutely right," I agree. "It *isn't* fair." I know exactly what you mean. You see, I felt that same way, for years in fact. And it was my refusal to find and express gratitude that turned out to be the very reason I wasn't achieving everything I hoped to achieve. This very important lesson, one I finally learned, as they say, "better late than never," made all the difference in my career *and* in my life.

When I first started out, I was incredibly lucky, receiving opportunity after opportunity to shoot for my life's goal of rock stardom. At 20, as a member of the band, Roxy, I signed my first major label contract with Elektra Records. From that point, either in bands, duos, or as a solo artist, I secured record deal after record deal for the next 14 years. By 24, I was producing records as well. From 1970 to 1984, a week seldom passed when I didn't have an album, a single, or a feature-film soundtrack in the marketplace. I was very fortunate to have all those opportunities: touring, writing, and recording with talented artists, producers, and engineers. However, I never reached the level of success or stardom I had assumed would be mine—back when I was a cocky teenager with visions (and presumptions) of grandeur.

After my final major-label artist project failed to take off, I jumped to the other side of the desk, taking an A&R/producer/songwriter position. In that capacity, I was able to collaborate with icons of the music history. In addition, I had the chance to discover, develop, and produce some very gifted, new artists. One of my compositions was honored with a Grammy nomination, and several of my tunes rose to the top of the charts on gold and platinum albums. But still, I wasn't satisfied or fulfilled. Living in Los Angeles, where it's all about the car you drive, the neighborhood you live in, and the face your plastic surgeon lifted last, I lived in constant envy and resentment for the people I saw every day, traversing the city streets in their luxury vehicles—the people who I assumed had achieved so much more success than I had.

I allowed my many career disappointments—along with a debilitating health challenge—to overshadow what seemed to me to be only sporadic victories. Facing my second divorce (both with young children: ouch!) I hit my absolute, emotional, rock bottom. It was then that I made the choice to reclaim my lost self-esteem. I started the long climb from the ground up, paying attention to my attitude and striving to change it, building my confidence, trying to see my own worthiness. It wasn't easy. By then, in Hollywood years, this pup, who had swept into town with such swagger and promise, was over the hill—nearing my 40s—but I began to see some light at the end of the tunnel. My faith kept growing. My work began reflecting this new higher awareness, taking on deeper meaning and (if I do say so myself) greater beauty. Even though I was regaining my belief in myself, a bitter resentment still festered in my heart. Instead of acknowledging how blessed I was to have so many wonderful creative opportunities, I felt exploited by those who put their trust and resources behind me. Instead of cheering for my friends who were finding their own successes, I compared my talents to theirs and questioned their worthiness.

Finding gratitude is about looking for the good in every experience. Although we may have every reason to be dissatisfied with the way things are now, there are still reasons to be thankful. Every situation, from the most triumphant to the most tragic, offers every one of us a chance to express gratitude. Until we choose to look for things to be grateful for, I believe we cannot move ahead to a greater experience. This principle goes back to the theories of quantum mechanics mentioned in the previous chapter. According to those time-honored truths, whatever we focus our minds on will be manifested as our reality. So, if my thoughts are constantly repeating *I can't get a break; life is unfair; the cards are stacked against me; I am a poor, helpless victim of a system that won't allow me to succeed*, that's exactly the experience I'm going to continue to have. If those are the mantras my conscious mind is chanting, that is exactly what my subconscious is absorbing and believing. My subconscious will align circumstances to make sure my thoughts are telling the truth.

So, if I can find nothing else to be grateful for, at least I can give sincere thanks for a new dawn, for another day to use my talents, for the chance to create something that wasn't there before. By focusing on being grateful, instead of being disgruntled, I can open myself up to something greater, and actually program myself for a more positive life experience. It's about changing the vernacular of your inner chatter. For instance: you could sigh and moan and grieve about the hold you just lost, *or* you could choose to appreciate that your song got such a positive response, while expressing thanks that you were in contention. Sure, you're disappointed. You have every right to be. But, how do you explain the circumstance to yourself? What's your choice? Is it about what *didn't* happen or is it about what *almost* happened? What's your inner dialog? *Life's just not fair*! Or, are you saying, *Man, it's so great that I came so close to scoring a cut*?

As soon as I started paying attention to and giving thanks for the things in my life for which I am eternally grateful—my wife, my kids, my parents, all of my family, my collaborators, my business partners, my community, my church, my home, my pets, my creative inspirations, my talents, my intelligence, my fortitude, my tools and resources, every opportunity I've had or will ever have to express my unique point of view, and so on—I began creating, noticing, and experiencing *more* things to be grateful for. The game itself didn't become any fairer. The competition wasn't any less brutal, but I was no longer letting the biased playing field and the long odds get me down or stand in the way of my progress. I could recognize how difficult it is, while not making it even more difficult. I was paying attention to how very fortunate I truly am: fortunate to have talents, inspirations, opportunities and the means to express them; fortunate to have people who love me and support my creative efforts; fortunate for the roof over my head; fortunate to have a dynamic range of priceless life experiences to show for it.

Life *should* be a dynamic experience. Growing up in the Pacific Northwest, I became accustomed to the changing seasons. Every year would begin in the midst of winter chill, with scant sunshine, and short, damp, dark days. Then came that spring awakening, more sun, greater warmth, and the return of migratory birds. Summer ushered in glorious, torpid, languid days spent on the lake, or at the seaside. Then, fall brought back the cool dampness, sent those birds winging southward again, and closed out the year, by welcoming back the winter chill. Without those cold, sometimes torrential days, the clear, bright ones wouldn't have seemed so glorious. Many people are attracted to a climate that tends to stay within a certain range of beautiful. Certainly, Southern California has one of the most pleasant and idyllic seasonal arcs, offering far more sunshine than clouds and an average temperature and humidity that usually allows shirtsleeves year round. Living there for 20 years of my life, this half Finn from Oregon found this seasonless clime disorienting. My clock was thrown off. The years just seemed to evaporate, one into the next, coming and going without any beginning or end. The seasons were only delineated by the angle of the constant sunshine and a few degrees one way or the other. So, I became bored by the sun. I didn't appreciate its warmth—because it was always there.

It's not that I wish for the rain and cold of my youth, but I do thrive on real seasons, the dynamics that give life its rhythm, that take our emotions to high tide and low, the extremes that necessitate the expansion of our wardrobe. There are wonderful ways to enjoy every season. We didn't wait around all year, cowering and shivering, until summer offered us a chance to water ski on the lake or dip our toes in the Pacific Ocean. We bundled up and strapped on skis in the winter, or skidded down the slopes on a sled. We hiked and biked in the months between. We adapted to the changing temperatures, used umbrellas, and found ways to make good, productive use of all of it. You can't change the weather. Either you can accept it, deal with it, and make the best of it; or, you can rail at Heaven for sending you something you didn't want. Your choice.

While my natural demeanor leans strongly in the direction of my mother's Finnish-ness—hard working, stoic, pensive and contemplative, always prepared for the worst—I am a product of the paternal branch of the family tree, too. My musical and writing talents come from Mom; but, my song-dog nature is all Dad. Western-European mutts, the Bishops are resilient, indomitable, eternal optimists, always eager and willing to seek out the upside in every situation. To this day, my father, now in his mid-

80s, finds a reason to be excited and grateful, even in the face of a string of health and financial challenges that have sniped at him for twenty years. His dad, my paternal grandfather, was the most optimistic person I ever knew. And that's saying something, because Pop's exuberant heart failed him at 59, as he lay on the bench seat of a Jeep, on the showroom floor of the Portland, Oregon auto dealership he managed. I was just four years old.

The year before, Pop had taken me, his favorite grandson, to Portland's biggest annual celebration, the Rose Parade. (There was nothing in the world my granddad loved more than a parade.) Not uncharacteristically, the Oregon skies were not cooperating. In fact, buckets of rain cascaded from the dark, cumulous clouds that billowed from horizon to horizon. He had hoisted me onto his shoulders to get a better view of the floats and bands as they slogged past on Broadway, my towhead shielded from the deluge by a sagging, drenched section of *The Oregonian*. It was miserable. No one could deny it. Suddenly, Pop rose to his tiptoes and pointed toward a tiny patch of blue way off on the far edge of the sky. "Look!" he exclaimed. "We're gonna get a break! I *knew* it! We're gonna get a break!"

There we were, standing on the sidewalk, trapped in a downtown crowd, with nowhere to hide from the relentless ferocity of that downpour. I don't ever remember hearing the man complain. Instead, he focused on a speck of hope out there on the horizon. My grandfather was not only the world's most optimistic man, he was grateful for every parade, regardless of the weather. That's exactly the spirit we should all emulate as we face the changing seasons ahead. If winter lasts for a very long time, that means it's time to bundle up, break out the old sled, and climb to the top of the nearest hill. *Or*, you could wrap yourself in a blanket, light the fire and wait it out. Either way, find a way to be grateful, and you will encounter more joy in the experience and more success along the way.

Now, at last, let's start makin' friends...

PART FOUR:

NETWORKING

CHAPTER 13
How Cuts Happen

We'd all love to believe that we're playing on a level field, that once someone has made the team, if he or she attends the practices, does the workouts, and dons the uniform on game day, the best performer will get some good, quality P.T. (that's "playing time," for all of you unfamiliar with Dick Vitale lingo). Unfortunately, in the songwriting game—just like in many businesses—that is not necessarily the case. In fact, a tunesmith could be the most gifted and schooled pop-song craftsperson in the history of the planet, cranking out masterpiece after tour de force, and still never receive a chance to get out on the field on game day.

At one point or another, most of us have been pleasantly surprised to discover an out-of-the-ordinary product, some miraculous concoction that seems to far out-perform the name-brand merchandise dominating the marketplace. Maybe it was some rare, off-brand toothpaste that *really* made your teeth sparkle; a tile cleaner that miraculously lifted stains right out of the grout; a headache medication capable of taking away the pain in a matter of minutes. When that happens, surely we remark to ourselves, "Wow! Why isn't *this* stuff the number-one seller?" After all, here in the U.S. of A., the "free market" is supposed to decide winners and losers. That's what we've always been told, anyway. If one particular cream, pill, powder, or ointment is actually superior to every other cream, pill, powder, or ointment available, the superior one should naturally win the race. Although a case could surely be made for that ideal scenario, that's certainly not the way it happens all the time. In fact, the quality or functionality of any given product is not the ultimate determining factor in its commercial acceptance, market share, or in the profitability of its manufacturer/distributor. Without a doubt, it helps to produce a toothpaste that, if applied properly and regularly enough, renders teeth clean and breath fresh, and helps prevent tooth decay. Assuming a company has achieved that minimum benchmark, success then becomes more about the way the product is branded and marketed, how it's perceived by the public, and in the long run, whether it's sitting in a highly visible place when we walk into the store.

Like those incredible off-brand products, great songs can languish in obscurity, too, forever. Literally thousands upon thousands of brilliantly honed gems will remain undiscovered, sitting idly in publishing catalogs all over the world. And it's not necessarily because nobody has heard them (although getting songs out there for industry pros to check out can certainly be an important pump primer).

Let's get hypothetical. Let's say that Kroger Grocery only stocks a half dozen tubes of the far-superior Rarebrand Toothpaste and adds insult to injury by sticking them down on the bottom shelf, in the shadow of the athlete's foot powder. How is Rarebrand supposed to complete with row after row of colorful name-brand items sitting at eye level? (What does this have to do with getting your songs cut? Hold on, I'm getting to that.) Even though it's a fantastic product and a clear cut above its more-popular competitors, Rarebrand is at the same disadvantage when it comes to drawing attention away from the big brands as your songs are against those written by that select group of writers and powerhouse publishers who, at any given time, get most of the cuts and score nearly all of the singles. Basically, what we have here is one of those ornery Catch-22 situations. Kroger won't order more Rarebrand unless it sells more; and it can't sell more, because it's a relatively unknown quantity that the store simply doesn't display prominently.

You see, name-brands pay rent to Kroger for their prime positions on the shelves—the same way major labels pay promo staffs to coax stingy radio stations into adding new single releases to their playlists. Really, kids, this is Marketing 101. It's about putting the product in the public's sightline—or, in the case of radio promotion, within earshot—as much as possible. But, since we're dreamers, let's imagine something that would never happen in a hundred years: Kroger suddenly becomes magnanimous and gives Rarebrand Toothpaste a key spot, on a middle shelf, right between the Colgate and the Crest. As there are only six tubes of Rarebrand versus grosses of the biggies, this might be the equivalent of one of your songs getting an extra pitch per week. Although that additional exposure might somewhat reduce the long odds against you, it still leaves you getting lapped time and time again by established, brand-name writers. Back to toothpaste: Even if all six tubes of Rarebrand were to sell out in a matter of days, it's distributor would be limited to moving a maximum of those half dozen units between deliveries until Kroger chooses to order more product (which would, in turn, require more pricey square inches on the shelves to stock the additional tubes of Rarebrand, thus taking away that same space from Colgate and/or Crest). There is only so much display space, just as there are only so many minutes of radio airplay available every hour. One product can't acquire more without depriving another. It is, as they say, a dog-eat-dog world.

So, how could Rarebrand possibly get a leg up in the ultra-competitive toothpaste game? Not being a marketing genius, I'll just do some spitballing here: How about shooting for a celebrity endorsement? Convincing a likeable, well-known actor or athlete—preferably with a big-toothed smile—to throw his or her star power and reputation behind Rarebrand would surely raise awareness and make demand rise. With more demand, Kroger would start ordering more tubes and be more inclined to put 'em where its customers could actually find 'em.

We'll even go pie-in-the-sky. Supposing Angelina Jolie were to discover the splendorous effects of Rarebrand Toothpaste. She might just be willing to shout to the rooftops about how that product makes her inimitable smile brighter and her enormous mouth tingle every time she slathers those minty suds on her world-famous teeth. If, while perusing the oral-hygiene aisle, Kroger shoppers were to be greeted by a life-sized, cardboard cut-out of the comely Ms. Jolie, grinning for all the world to see, teeth sparkling, with a world bubble over her head, declaring, "I squeeze Rarebrand. What do you squeeze?" I think folks might just pay attention. Who knows how Rarebrand gets Jolie to try their product, but they do. (Something about bribing a volunteer at the Palm Springs Film Festival to slip a complimentary sample into the actress' goody bag.) Anyway, Rarebrand Toothpaste is the best by far; so naturally, Angie loves the stuff. She even spontaneously testifies to millions of viewers on *Leno* that she's discovered the world's most miraculous new toothpaste (which, at this time, in spite of Jay's goading, still remains nameless—although legions of fans are blogging and tweeting their fingertips off, rumoring and speculating what Angie could possibly be brushing with these days).

This, by the way, would be kind of like one of your tunes getting a strong hold with the hottest act of the day (for fun, let's call her Shania Swift), then finding out that lovely Shania has even gone to the extent of working it up with her band. "I'm gonna be rich!" you might conclude. Not so fast, pal. You and your song just might have a few more bridges to cross.

Now, Angelina's agent, Charley Hollywood, enters the picture. "You want Angie Baby to endorse your toothpaste?" Charley queries. "Sure, she loves the stuff. But, I got one question for ya. What's in it for my client?"

"Hmm…" it begins to dawn on the peeps at Rarebrand, "maybe, just maybe, we'd better consider cutting Ms. Jolie in on the action."

This racket is called the music *business* for good reason. We are not in this thing simply to express ourselves creatively. Self-expression is a great and wonderful part of it, without question, but at the end of the day, we have every intention of turning a tidy profit, just like the friendly folks at Rarebrand Toothpaste. And, like you and me—when we come up with a song we're extra pleased to put our names on—those toothpaste purveyors must be proud as punch to have cooked up and packaged a superb product. It doesn't stop there. The next step is drawing attention to that product and getting as much of it into as many stores as possible, placed right smack dab in view of every average American with a mouthful of teeth. Pure and simple, we're just trying to make a dent in the marketplace, to move some merchandise here, and there ain't a dang thing wrong with that. Few songwriters are islands. In order to grease the wheels of commerce, it helps a whole lot to build a team. Every effective member of that team deserves to know that there will be a reward for whatever he or she contributes to your product's success. Kroger demands rent for the shelf space. Angelina and her agent require a piece of the action in exchange for the star's public endorsement. Likewise, Shania Swift and "her people" just may need a little nudge to close the deal.

Angelina Jolie is thrilled with Rarebrand Toothpaste; Shania Swift loves your song. Angelina testifies to millions on *Leno* about the wonders of Rarebrand; Shania is rehearsing your tune with her band. Now, finally, we've arrived at the bottom line. In order to get the toothpaste endorsement—*or* to secure the cut—Charley Hollywood's question rings out loud and clear: "What's in it for my client?" Maybe Rarebrand gives Angelina stock in the company or a percentage of gross sales—or both. Whatever Rarebrand needs to do to get the box-office queen's smile associated with their toothpaste, they'd be wise to consider it. Business, after all, *is* business. Similarly, you as a songwriter should leverage your position to give your song its best chance at success. Sometimes that means sharing your potential success with those who could figure heavily in making it happen. Am I advising you to *bribe* your song into the studio and onto the charts? Not in a million years. We're talking strategic partnerships here—no different from the enticements a toothpaste company would consider to lure a superstar endorsement or to get more prime shelf space. After all, what's really the difference between getting a song cut and released by a major recording star and a superstar toothpaste endorsement? What's the difference between a song reaching the top of the charts and a brand of toothpaste gaining market share? Not much; not much at all.

A Tale of Two Writers

Let's just examine the exemplary career of my friend, Tom Snow. A jazz-piano aficionado, Snow emerged from a Princeton, New Jersey high school in the mid 1960s with, as Snow confesses, "the romantic intention of becoming the next Bill Evans." Upon entering Berklee College of Music in Cambridge, Massachusetts, he took note of his competition, was "immediately disabused of that notion," and promptly switched his major from performance to composition. Snow started playing keys and cowriting with a performer who was just starting to make a name for himself around town, a talented, charismatic cat named Gram Parsons. Gram, who would go on to become a performing songwriter of legend himself, was assembling his International Submarine Band to record for RCA. Parsons asked Snow to join the ensemble, but according to Snow, "Vietnam was raging at the time," and he declined the invite in order to keep his college draft deferment. However, the Parsons collaboration opened up what seemed to be a more realistic avenue for Snow's musical talents and ambitions by whetting his interest in pop songwriting. After graduating with a composition degree and harboring an admiration for the writers he calls "the usual suspects, Burt Bacharach and The Beatles," Snow moved to L.A. to chase the singer/songwriter thing.

Two record deals and four albums later, Snow had been battling it out in the L.A. trenches for more than a half dozen years, with little to show for his bumps and bruises, except a few obscure cuts, some commercial-flop releases, and an industry buzz as a burgeoning melodist. Finally, good fortune knocked, when Rita Coolidge covered a tune from one of Tom's Capitol solo LPs. That song, entitled "You," was a turntable hit and won Snow a BMI Award. At the awards banquet, he worked up the gumption to make the connection that would alter the angle of his career trajectory (in a very good way)—and forever change his life.

Composer Barry Mann and lyricist Cynthia Weil had long ago risen to god and goddess stature on songwriting's Mt. Olympus. Together—and separately—this married couple had penned some of the biggest copyrights of the rock era. "I did something I'm not prone to doing," Snow says of that night at the BMI banquet, "because I'm not a real self-promoter. I ginned up the courage, went over and introduced myself." Before committing to cowriting with Snow, Weil did a sort of background check on him, discovering that he was indeed more than capable of writing commercially. After that, Weil agreed to put her precise, conversational, and extremely singable lyrics to Snow's soaring, memorable melodies. "I entered the fraternity, so to speak," Snow shares. "Things really started clickin' for me." Snow and Weil's very first cowrite, "Holdin' Out For Love," was recorded numerous times, most notably by Angela Bofill.

When an opportunity to collaborate with hot pop star Leo Sayer offered itself, a more businesslike partnership brought Snow to his next, professional plateau. "I was cajoled, persuaded" he says, "by the Richard Perry folks to sign a copublishing deal." (Perry, one of the most successful producers of the day, was helming Sayer's sessions.) It might seem, especially considering Snow's tactful verb choices, that Perry strong-armed the songwriter into "giving away his publishing" to his Braintree Music in exchange for collaborating with the hit artist. Regardless of how it may have looked at the time, this arrangement turned into a win/win that resulted in massive mutual success for Snow, Perry, and Sayer. As it turned out, this strategic pact also became a boon for a veteran, female, vocal quartet, a Perry production client, and not-so-coincidentally signed to Perry's label, Planet Records. The composition, "He's So Shy"—a song Tom Snow and Cynthia Weil had originally custom-crafted for Leo Sayer under the title, "She's So Shy"—shot to Number Three for the Pointer Sisters. "It was the first time I'd actually written a melody that I knew in my heart was a smash," Snow confides.

So, what we have just observed in this real-life tale is the convergence of all of the elements that add up to songwriting success: a talented writer applying himself to learning his craft; that same writer persevering through some serious dues paying; professional connections, creative collaboration, industry relationships opening doors; and, finally, a highly connected decision maker who had every incentive to record, release, and promote the writer's material. Of course, if Snow's songs didn't have that magical "it" quality, they wouldn't have climbed to the top of the charts to become some of the most lucrative and performed copyrights of the last four decades. Tom Snow went on to collaborate with Mann and Weil on the immaculate Linda Ronstadt/Aaron Neville duet, "I Don't Know Much." Snow's signature piece most certainly is Deniece Williams's Number One "Let's Here It For The Boy," from the film, *Footloose* and its 1984 Grammy-winning soundtrack album. I know that Snow won that Grammy (along with Dean Pitchford, Kenny Loggins, and the other *Footloose* writers) because I was nominated that same year for Paramount's *Saturday Night Fever* sequel, *Staying Alive*. My contribution to that soundtrack was "So Close To The Fire," a song I produced and cowrote with the artist, Tommy Faragher. Faragher and I, of course, lost (along with the Bee Gees, Frank Stallone, and others).

Many of the breadcrumbs along my own career path parallel Tom Snow's. We both studied composition at top music colleges. (No degree for me, however. I only spent two semesters at Oberlin.) We entered the L.A. scene around the same time, both played the Monday-night hoots at the Troubadour, and signed our first major-label record deals with bands that went on to achieve scant commercial success. In spite of getting stalled at nearly every turn in our performing careers, Snow and I both started to win reputations as promising writers. That's where our paths diverged somewhat. I pointed much of my energies and aspirations toward a production career, writing primarily *with* artists, while Snow concentrated on developing high-profile, professional writing partnerships and penning hit songs *for* other artists.

Since we're revealing how cuts really happen, we should take note of another strong comparison between the careers of Snow and Bishop. Like Snow, I benefited tremendously from a publishing partnership with an entrepreneurial producer. Here's how it happened for me: After my final major-label artist project fizzled—the rockin' *Dangerous Infatuation* album for Pasha/CBS in 1983—I segued very conveniently into an A&R/staff producer position at the Pasha label. My creative collaborations with Pasha head man, Spencer Proffer, stretched back to 1976, when he produced my solo singles for A&M. Since those very first sessions, Proffer had called on me time and time again as a go-to utility man—pulling duties as a studio background vocalist, occasional coproducer, and frequent cowriter. Like Richard Perry, Proffer is a producer with an impressive discography *and* a wheeler-dealer of exceptional skills. *Un*like Perry, however, Proffer is a very capable songwriter himself. Our first three-way collaborations were with Allan Clarke, the man who gave voice to all those soaring Hollies' hits: "Bus Stop," "Carrie Ann," "Air That I Breathe," "He Ain't Heavy," and "Long, Cool Woman." Together, the three of us wrote much of Clarke's first solo effort on Atlantic Records. I also became Clarke's surrogate Graham Nash in the studio, wailing those high harmonies above his piercing, knife-like lead vocals.

In addition to my A&R/staff-production position (no salary, by the way; all I got was a handshake, a stack of business cards, and a converted storage-room office), I signed an exclusive publishing contract with Pasha. In spite of its modest advance ($24,000 per year), this deal, like Tom Snow's with Richard Perry's Braintree Music, turned into a substantial windfall for my songwriting career. Now Proffer, as my publisher—with a clever head for making money in the music business balancing on his shoulders—had every incentive to plug me into as many projects as possible as a writer and/or producer. So, because Proffer had so much to gain from every new feather in my songwriting cap, I starting collecting some proud plumage. I scored cuts with the Beach Boys, Heart, and Cheap Trick in Proffer's production of the film soundtrack to *Up the Creek*. I wrote with Peter Noone for a solo project as well as Carmine Appice and Mark Stein for their Vanilla Fudge reunion (*Mystery* on Atlantic Records). I ghost wrote two albums with King Kobra, under the nom de plume, H. Banger. An outtake from platinum-selling, Canadian ensemble, Streetheart, called "Hot Cherie"—I penned the provocative lyric—became a regional hit for singer Danny Spanos. Some years later, a cover of "Hot Cherie" by Hardline, featuring Neal Schon from Journey, hit the national charts and figured in bringing me to Nashville. I coproduced an album (and cowrote several of the songs) for Southern-rock legends, The Outlaws. In the same capacity, I went gold with Canadian metal band, Kick Axe's *Welcome to the Club* album. It was at Pasha that I endured one of the most traumatic—and ultimately rewarding—adventures of my creative lifetime, working with screenwriter/director, Sylvester Stallone. That I have a framed piece of fine, linen paper on my wall, confirming that I was nominated for a Grammy Award for *Staying Alive* (the movie soundtrack, not the Bee Gee's song), in my opinion, is one of the profound ironies of this journeyman songwriter's journey.

Tom Snow—after having enjoyed one of the most exemplary songwriting careers of the last 40 years—spends most of his time on the idyllic golf courses of the California coast, near Santa Barbara. He no longer writes songs. For me, I couldn't imagine hanging up my tools, ignoring my creative calling. But, then again, I don't have the royalty stream Snow no doubt still reaps from his legacy of hits. Songwriting, for me, is still "a matter of necessity" and survival.

I hope you're getting the picture here. Tom Snow and I traveled similar, sometimes almost parallel paths. For both of us, our most visible successes came from collaborations with artists and other equally motivated cowriters, and/or they were produced by entrepreneurial producer/publishers who had something substantial to gain from deciding to include our material in their projects. We both had talent. Both of us had developed our song craft with drive and focus, while surviving plenty of near misses and even some abject failures. But, that wasn't enough. Neither of us met some music mogul in an elevator and put a tape in his hand. This is what it really boils down to: Two talented men possessed strong enough survival instincts and managed to put themselves in the position (i.e., made the friendships, created the partnerships) that eventually enabled their individual talents to thrive in the marketplace. That is how this game is played. And, that's the story you will be hearing over and over again in this book.

The Extra Mile

One afternoon in 1978, I was eagerly thumbing through the latest issue of *Billboard Magazine,* trying to locate a full-page ad announcing a feature-film soundtrack I'd produced. Finally, a page or two past the Hot 100, I found it, in gorgeous, full color, on the left panel. Feeling proud to see my work and my name advertised in that prestigious, glossy, industry, trade mag, I took a glance at the opposite page. There was another full-page ad, this one taken out personally by Tom Snow—to thank the 70 or so artists who, to date, had recorded his songs. It's never healthy to weigh one's own level of success against that of a contemporary—especially when that contemporary has what looks to be a great deal more to brag about. Drawing that contrast can bring out an ugly jealousy, a toxic resentment capable of eating away at one's creative soul, a nibble at a time. As we examined in Part Three of this book, having an envious, bitter attitude is not at all consistent with a consciousness of abundance. But, sometimes we just can't help feeling those unbecoming, self-defeating pangs, can we.

I remember wondering what qualities Snow had that I didn't. What was it that enabled Tom (bleepin') Snow to score so many more prestige cuts and chart successes than I had? I thought about our talents (comparable), backgrounds (similar), and career paths (nearly parallel). Then, in one "Aha!" moment, a possible explanation began to formulate in my covetous head. While I was content to spend 90 percent of my time hiding away in a dark, studio cave, Tom Snow seemed to be popping up everywhere. On the rare occasions when I extricated myself from those endless recording sessions to get out and about, to see and be seen, I never recalled attending a single industry function where Snow wasn't shaking hands, working the room, conversing confidently with the most important and influential people in attendance. Every other trade mag I picked up seemed to feature a photo of Snow's smiling, bearded visage. Yep, there's Snow again—posing, his arm around the shoulder of some superstar, big-time producer, agent, manager, or record company exec. Observing the seemingly ubiquitous Snow had left me with the impression that he was not only a songwriter of enormous gifts, but a skillful self-promoter with unique networking skills, a cunning, political animal, with a natural instinct for keeping the lens of the camera focused in his direction.

Snow doesn't remember it that way at all. In fact, he doesn't consider himself a savvy schmoozer at all, nor does he particularly enjoy the industry glad hand. He gives Mary Belle, his wife of 38 years, credit for constantly giving him that gentle shove, persuading him to shake all those hands and keep smiling for the camera. By urging her husband to do such a basic and essential thing, Mary Belle might have played a role in Tom's success equal to that of Cynthia Weil and Richard Perry. Here, we've discovered one additional piece to stack on a teetering pile of evidence, making the case for each of us to seek out partners and teammates who compensate for our innate weaknesses, who dare us to face our worst fears, who take up the slack when we fall short, and who find fulfillment in doing those necessary things we find uncomfortable, uninspiring, or uninteresting. And if, as he now claims, Tom Snow wasn't born with that innate, winning temperament I once thought I observed in him, surely it was refining his craft and striving for excellence that always moved and motivated him. "What *was* in my nature," he observes now in retrospect, "was to get up every morning and do it."

CHAPTER 14
What Is Networking?

Actor, author, talk-show host, and notorious curmudgeon, Charles Grodin commences his very entertaining memoir, *It Would Be So Nice If You Weren't Here* (New York: Vintage Books USA, 1990), by stating that the only profession possibly more difficult than being an actor would be "selling poetry door to door."

Imagine spending your evenings weaving lines of language, spilling out your most intimate pains, exuding your greatest joys, concocting precise and personal observations about the world around you, making it all rhyme, and then waking up in the morning to spend the day walking around random cul de sacs, ringing doorbells, and making your sales pitch. "Good day, Ma'am. Wouldn't your day be brightened just a little by an original poem?" Sound familiar? Well, it should. Because that, in a parabolic nutshell, pretty much describes the profession of every tunesmith. You see, we're not only responsible for crafting our inspirations into commercially viable products, each of us is also automatically drafted as the first-line rep for that line of goods. If *we* don't do it, odds are no one else will. That would inevitably result in no results, which you'll probably agree is a long way from the most desirable result. At the very least, we write 'em so that people will listen to 'em. We express ourselves with the hope that somebody is somehow affected by our expression. If we don't take the initiative to ask folks for a few minutes of their time, our songs won't have the opportunity to do what we created them to do: to communicate; to move people.

Suppose your job and your livelihood actually did require you to pack up a sample case, go out, and make sales calls to hawk your poetical inspirations. How exactly would you tackle that assignment? First, you'd make sure to have a solid selection of demonstration models on hand: poems to suit every occasion; or, if you're more of a stylist, a dynamic range of high-quality items representing your specialty (birthday, wedding, grief, whatever). Then, you'd start putting together a list of legitimate leads, compiling contact info for potential customers who might be interested in hearing about your product line. You'd then start making calls, setting up appointments to do your song and dance. If you were really on top of your game, you'd be constantly replenishing your list of leads. In every conversation, you'd slyly slip in the question, "Who do you know that really loves poetry?" That way, you could be adding new names, addresses, phone numbers, and email addresses to widen your network. You'd be smart, too, to do some research about each prospective client, taking note of his personal interests, political and/or religious leanings, schools he or his kids attended, and so on. That knowledge could help you put him at ease, might enable you to avoid an unnecessary faux pas, and would give you a better chance of picking out demonstration poems that might speak to him personally.

Entrepreneurs who are serious about launching and expanding their businesses also join civic organizations and service groups. Kiwanis, Rotary, Toastmasters, Knights of Columbus, Bible-study groups, PTA, charitable causes, Chambers of Commerce. Why do they spend time and energy going to meetings, doing charity work, and marching in parades? Well, it's not just because they're purely magnanimous, altruistic people, or because their calendars need filling up, either. They get real professional benefits from involving themselves in these organizations, causes, and interest groups. In those gatherings, they make friends, gain connections, and begin to develop the kinds of trusting relationships that can be all important to increasing one's chances of sustained success. Nobody's all that comfortable with the idea of buying life insurance. But say you've hammered nails for Habitat for Humanity alongside Fred, the local agent from Prudential. Fred's a good guy. The dreaded subject comes up (because, after all, Fred knows an opportunity when he sees one), and you find yourself signing on a dotted line and handing over a fat check made out to The Rock. For generations, that's exactly how a whole lot of business has proliferated in the good ol' U.S. of A.

Now, why didn't Fred just put the hard sell on you the first day the two of you strapped on your tool belts? Why did he wait to broach the subject of life insurance until you got to know him personally, until the two of you developed a rapport, until he detected that you felt at ease with him? Because Fred's a smart salesman. He knows that life insurance is not a wham-bam-thank-you-ma'am product. The relationship between a client and his life-insurance agent is long-term. The two of you will be meeting periodically, year after year, updating and adjusting your coverage as your situation changes.

If Fred were in vacuum cleaner sales, his credo would be ABC, for "Always Be Closing." Why is that? Because a household typically makes a new vacuum-cleaner purchase every ten years or so. Once you've taken possession of the Hoover, once he's cleverly gleaned a couple of hot references from you and collected his commission, your sales person/client dance has pretty much played itself out. By comparison, as in the life-insurance game, songwriters are ostensibly knocking on the same doors, month after month, for years to come. So ABC doesn't work for us. Our immediate goal—with every industry relationship we approach—is not to close the deal (although that certainly would be *great*). Like Fred from Prudential, we seek to engender trust, to put contacts at ease; in essence, we are striving to be liked. So, our first goal is not to make the sale. Our first goal is to be welcomed into the conversation next time, to become part of the inner circle. We are out to cultivate relationships that we can only hope will help facilitate some success; if not today, at least sometime in the future.

Emerge from Under Your Rock

I was born with a good bit of innate talent, a healthy ego, tons of ambition, a lively imagination, and a compelling desire to create. Those qualities, however, were mitigated by my natural inclination for brooding perfectionism. I'm much more comfortable sitting alone—just me, my creative thoughts, and a guitar or a keyboard—than I am subjecting myself to any awkward, intimidating, unpredictable, social, and/or professional situation, where I'm forced to introduce myself to strangers, remember people's names, and put on an outwardly friendly face. Just my surly, self-righteous luck! Those are exactly the kinds of situations that offer every one of us the greatest opportunities to further our careers.

It should be obvious as to how our careers could potentially benefit from mixing it up. It's the "see and be seen" thing, the "I'm a player" thing, the "let's do lunch" thing. It's the handshake, the eye contact, the elevator speech, the business-card exchange, the promise to keep in touch, *and* the all-important follow up. This is where we serendipitously meet someone who makes all the difference, offers the perfect suggestion, introduces us to the very connection we've been looking for. This is how we strengthen our bonds with those upwardly mobile peers. This is when we have a chance to make that pivotal, positive impression on an industry bigwig. All of this good stuff had an opportunity to take place because—and *only* because—we got out there, showed up, and jumped in with a pleasant, positive attitude.

Private time might be essential to your ability to develop your creative inspirations into works of undeniable genius. Too much isolation, however, can become the biggest drag on your career's ascent. Many compulsively creative persons—present company included—do not take naturally to social situations. Sometimes I actually get light headed and disoriented upon entering a room buzzing with industry peers, especially when I've just come directly from hours pondering over a lyric or concentrating on the nuances of a mix. The sudden leap from the east side to the west side of my gray matter completely throws me. So, my instinct is to avoid awkward entrances by steering clear of these kinds of events altogether. My default mode is to stay in the creative realm, if at all possible. Activities like refining language, jamming out a musical transition, or programming a high-hat pattern can easily lure my attention, so that I can avoid picking up the phone to make a strategic call or, Heaven forbid, showering, shaving, and making an entrance into a public place.

I mean, who wants to be standing there, red-faced, baffled, and tongue-tied, while a peer greets you with that simple, sometimes unanswerable question: "Hey, man, how ya doin'? Life treatin' you well?" This, however, is the absolute, so-help-me-God truth: I'm always glad I did it, that I swallowed that bitter pill, bathed, turned the key on my Highlander, and drove down to the showcase, the party, the reception because something good *always* happens there. Some connection is made; a door is opened; I see an old pal; or, at the very least, a new idea creatively inspires me. Although, being naturally antisocial is not the only syndrome that can stand in your way. Songwriters have other potentially negative temperaments as well. I've known quite a number of writers who, wittingly or not, find themselves cursed by a very different, but equally self-defeating trait. These are the gregarious souls who are far too inclined to glad hand, slap backs, and engage in boisterous repartee, while not spending enough time backing up their obvious bravado with strong, fundamental skills and competitive craft. There has to be a healthy, proper balance between right- and left-brain activity.

Thus, in the next few chapters, we will discuss one of the most fundamentally important tools every successful songwriter should have ready and available on his tool belt: the ability to network. Getting out there, showing your face, being a vibrant part of a community, politicking, shaking hands, exchanging business cards, appearing to be happy and successful, and making the continual impression that you have something substantial to offer are all equally as important as spending contemplative hours in your cave, honing your masterpieces. Why is that? Evidence follows.

With more than 40 years of writing songs under my belt, the vast majority of my nearly 250 releases happened due to one or more of the following reasons:

- I was the artist, or one of the artists.
- I was the producer, or one of the producers.
- I wrote the song with the artist and/or the producer.
- The producer, the artist, or the production company published or copublished the song.
- I was a friend (or friend of a friend) to the artist, producer, artist manager, or somebody trusted by those people (somebody who had direct access to the project).

I hope you're taking note that I *did not mention* that I got lots of my cuts because some determined song plugger refused to take "No" for an answer. Why did I choose to omit that? Because only a handful of my cuts were the result of a pitch. Literally. Only a *handful!* Is my experience much different from most other successful songwriters? I really don't think so. You see, if you look at numbers 1 through 5 above, each reason shares a common factor. That common factor adds up to this: My songs made the sessions because somebody involved in the project, usually in a decision-making role, had something to gain from preferring my song over yours.

Getting a song cut from a pitch is extremely rare. However, it does happen on occasion. When it does happen, invariably the reason is the plugger is on a friendly basis with a producer and/or A&R person, artist manager, artist, or record company exec and not because the song is necessarily superior to every other composition under consideration. An even more common reason why a pitch might result in a cut is that the writer has achieved such a level of success and has developed such a lofty reputation for penning hit songs that his or her name speaks louder than the quality of the song itself. Putting a hold on a new Diane Warren or the latest Jeffery Steele song is a no-brainer that would put a feather in any A&R person's headdress. It's a shoo-in for guaranteed kudos. Favoring songs by proven, hit writers also provides a built-in flak shield for the A&R person—should the cut stiff. "Hey, Craig Wiseman and Rivers Rutherford wrote it," she explains. "It sounded like a hit to me." No one ever got fired from a cushy label job for championing a song composed by a proven hit maker. Sticking one's neck out a little too far for an unproven tunesmith, however, might just get a head chopped off.

At any point in time, there seem to be a group of song scribes whose names actually become chart redundancies, as they seem to be attached to hit after hit after hit. Obviously, these folks are blessed with oodles of talent and, surely, they work their heinies off. But, Lord knows, they can't possibly come up with a smash every time out. Still, these writers have established a brand that implies "hit," so a much higher percentage of their songs get recorded. Thus, more of their cuts end up climbing the charts. In the songwriting game, as in most businesses (especially show biz), success breeds more opportunity for more success.

This is akin to the habitual behavior of Hollywood film studios. Movie execs are often more willing to give the green light to a big-budget project because a top box-office star is attached than to approve a far-less expensive production that has no star. The star's name and brand presumably gives the movie the clout to open big on that crucial first weekend of release. By the same token, releasing a single written by a recognized hit maker can ensure adds on a lot of radio playlists. So, why should the label take a chance on a song by a rookie, even if that song is as good or better? There's only one reason: because a decision maker closely tied to the project has something to gain from choosing the more-obscure writer's song. How one gets to the level of those select-few songwriters whose (please pardon my French) "s**t don't stink" is a genuine mystery. There is no formula for that. It's a combination of everything I espouse on these pages, combined with some divine blessing from the gods of Hit Heaven. We can only dream of reaching that pinnacle, while continuing to work very hard to make it so.

What I've described is the real nature of the music business. It has always been the nature of the music business. And, it always will be. You can pretend it isn't so, but that won't change this undeniable reality. You can bridle at it, complain about it, drag your feet, throw a tantrum, scream to those gods all you want. You can refuse to play the game and keep insisting that the best song will always win. Or, you can accept the rules without a shred of denial. If you are ready to take Jack Nicholson's dare and "handle the truth"—assuming you're really serious about increasing your chances to scoop up some of the few remaining cuts available—what does this reality tell you about where you should be placing your energies? How about this hypothetical: Suppose a writer has applied his or her God-given talents responsibly, worked conscientiously to hone those creative skills, written at least a few very special, bulletproof songs, and produced some extremely catchy, state-of-the-art demos. What, now, is the one and only missing ingredient to the recipe for success? You have ten seconds to answer for a chance to move on to the next round!

Okay, the clock is ticking. Ten, nine, eight.... The drum roll crescendos. The curtain is rising to reveal that one missing ingredient. Two, one.... "What's the correct answer, Bob?"

"Relationships!"

That's right! If you said relationships, you could be on your way to join that exclusive club of hit makers. But wait a minute. Knowing you need to know somebody isn't enough. In and of itself, being aware that you should be cultivating key industry relationships and alliances won't make it happen, but you have to start somewhere! So, those of us who are willing to cast the rose-colored glasses aside and stare this cruel business right in the eyes always come to the only logical conclusion: Up near the very top of every songwriter's list of priorities—right after developing song craft—should be initiating, nurturing, and maintaining relationships, friendships, and partnerships that will give our songs their best opportunity to get the exposure and the all-important endorsements that will eventually lead us to cuts and hits. To that end, here are your goals:

1. Make contacts
2. Make friends
3. Cultivate relationships
4. Maintain relationships

How are those goals achieved? Through the fine art of networking. Let's get it on!

CHAPTER 15
Do As I Say, Not As I Did!

As we've concluded, most songs get recorded because of mutually beneficial relationships. The people you meet; the industry peers and pros who get to know you, like you, and trust you; the friendships and partnerships you develop and cultivate as the years go by will ultimately figure heavily in your success. Through those relationships, your opportunities for success will be multiplied because each relationship can lead to additional relationships. The resulting key alliances will eventually come together to create the necessary confluence of factors required for success to take place. Of course, you can only take advantage of those opportunities if you're ready to tackle the job, if you've sharpened your tools, and have a positive, team-oriented attitude. Through my career, I've enjoyed a good deal of success through these exact kinds of partnerships. However, at this juncture, I feel moved and obliged to confess that I haven't always made the right moves. In fact, over my show-biz journey, I messed up big time, more than once. Here are just a couple of the regrettable, boneheaded misjudgments I made over the last four decades. Maybe you can glean something from these cautionary tales that will help you avoid similar missteps.

In January of 1975, I was in the South of France on assignment to "baby sit" a production client, a blond, pouty-lipped, husky-voiced, French/Canadian chanteuse with a Swedish name, Anne Anderrsen. One of Anderrsen's scheduled appearances was just a postcard-scenic hop, skip, and a scoot down the Cote d'Azur to the principality of Monaco. It turned out to be one of those laughably tacky, European lip-sync TV shows, featuring one after another marginally talented but always pert, pretty, tanned, and bleached-blond pop aspirant. However, one of the other young performers on the broadcast defied the platinum-hair cliché. Only moments before, this African/American songstress had mimed her way through one of the most ludicrous and insipid, high-concept recordings I'd ever heard (something involving a phone call from an extortionist demanding ransom for the release of the singer's husband). I think the song was called "Kidnap." Her pop/rock, multimedia segment was replete with a set right out of *Double Indemnity* (the songstress portraying the Barbara Stanwyck role), with a sofa and end table, on which sat a lamp and a telephone. The track commenced with a throbbing rhythm and a ringing phone. The singer picked up the receiver and answered in sultry, Boston-accented English. "Helllllo."

"If you ever want to see your husband again," responded the sinister, filtered voice on the other end of the line, "you'll listen carefully to what I have to say."

That intro was followed by the singer demonstrating overwrought, silent-movie faces, while wailing her hiccupping alto in dismay over this newly revealed dilemma. "Kidnap," she cried. "They've got my husband!" (Or some such operatic exposition.) More specific instructions were then given by the kidnapper—where to leave how much money, etc., followed by more wailing and consternation. Evidently, in that jaw-dropping moment, the way-beyond-corny melodrama of the record's concept and production must have distracted me from the vocal prowess of the artist. After the taping, the Bostonian diva of the ludicrous "Kidnap" recording approached me. After expressing her admiration for the single my artist, Anne Anderssen, had lip-synched on the show, Ms. Kidnap asked me if I'd consider producing an English-language version of Anne's song for her. Haughtily, I turned the girl down flat, barely holding back a scoffing chuckle at the very suggestion that I would stoop to such an embarrassment. "If I ever did an English version," I said curtly, "it would be with my own artist." Within the next year, that same young singer, Donna Summer, had ascended to the throne, anointed as reigning queen of the disco world, and was quickly putting together what would become a long string of international smashes.

By then, my first wife, Melanie, and I had moved to Los Angeles (from Montreal). We were at some kind of industry reception for Bruce Johnston (of the Beach Boys) at the Beverly Hills Hotel, having a grand ol' time, scooping up free eats, and sippin' on schooners of excellent vino. Suddenly, my highly tuned ears identified an extraordinarily rich and powerful sound coming from the direction of the grand piano. *Wasn't that the same voice that, for months and months, had saturated the airwaves with the refrain, "Oooooooo, love to love ya, baby"?* Sure enough, sitting on the bench at the Steinway keys was Donna Summer, smiling big-time and rendering a tune from the Aretha Franklin songbook (more than credibly, I might add). As she finished her performance, I did my part to instigate a boisterous ovation. Summer remembered me on sight and we quickly reacquainted ourselves. Then, I sat down at the keys, and the lady and I ripped into a pretty fantastic, totally improvised version of "Do Right Woman," wowing the kibitzers on hand. After our stirring duet, Summer took an immediate shine to Melanie, we exchanged phone numbers, cheek kissed, and promised a get-together soon.

Time enough passed for Melanie and me to separate (another story; another book). I was damning my poor fortune, pondering life and show business, wondering what fate might befall me next, eating a barefooted lunch, alone, in my Hollywood Hills studio apartment. The phone rang. "Randy?" the female voice asked.

"Yes," I responded, chewing a mouthful of spinach salad.

"Donna Summer," she identified herself. Small talk. Summer seemed genuinely disappointed to hear that Mel and I had split. "Listen, the reason

I'm calling," she said, switching to a more business-like tone, "is that I'm going into rehearsals for a big show in Las Vegas, and I'm looking for a keyboard player." My heartbeat quickened. *Is this my big break?* I wondered. In my mind's eye, I saw myself scooping up the big bucks, playing a Vegas showroom, and cowriting the next worldwide hit for the diva of the decade. Then, Summer quickly popped my fantasy balloon. "If you have any ideas, I'd really appreciate you sending somebody my way." The shoe was on the other foot now, and it was a stiletto heel poking directly into my remorseful heart. I knew what this phone call meant, or at least what it meant to me. Back in Monaco, I had not-so-subtly implied that Summer didn't live up to my lofty standards. Now, she was taking the opportunity to return the dig and more. Ouch!

These sort of things happen in show business. It's not healthy to beat oneself up over dynamiting a potential gold-mine relationship before the first pan of treasure was even sifted. Everyone has a crucial lapse in judgment now and then. It could happen to anybody. Right? I mean, how many despondent record execs could make the claim, "I passed on The Beatles?" However, you might think that "the Donna Summer experience" would have inspired me to heighten my radar, sharpen my wits, that an error that large might have made me at least a little bit smarter. This assumption, however, does not hold water. Certainly it won't after you read this next tale of self-imposed woe.

Later that same year, 1976, I signed a solo deal with A&M Records to record six sides and release two singles. Booked on every session was a hotshot guitar slinger named Jay Graydon. Graydon's nickname was "The Rake," a moniker that had nothing to do with his exemplary musicianship, while saying a mouthful about this particular picker being the in-demand dude on the L.A. session scene. The joke around town was that Graydon was "raking" so much union cash, instead of being paid by the hour, he was compensated "by the note." The Rake played the lead break on Steely Dan's "Peg," for Pete's sake, a prestigious credit if there ever was one. He also had the confident, wise-guy attitude that naturally goes with reaching the pinnacle of a very competitive profession in its capital city. Every time we worked together, The Rake was on my case, suggesting that he and I get together and cowrite. "Come on, man," he goaded, in his nasal, musician-jive speak, "I've got some great ideas. Let's book some time." But, I ignored him. He was just a musician, a studio player. I was a recording artist, a legitimate songwriter. He was just trying to crack into my world, trying to take a ride on my ascending rocket ship. That's how I saw it, anyway, at the time.

By 1981, Graydon had written Chicago's brilliant hit, "Hard Habit To Break" (with transplanted Canadian production genius David Foster and my background-vocal pal and occasional cowriter Steve Kipner). Then, Graydon went on to compose and produce big records by jazz/pop superstar acts, George Benson, Al Jarreau, and Manhattan Transfer, and other pop successes of the day, including DeBarge. A multiple Grammy winner, he has contributed songs to more than 50 feature films and has become a true production and songwriting legend. I could have been part of The Rake's inner creative circle. He put the invite out there. I was simply too flippant and arrogant to take him up on it.

In 1988, I produced some tracks in Graydon's state-of-the-art home studio. He took advantage of that reunion to remind me of those many invitations I'd spurned. He told me that the way I'd repeatedly disregarded his entrees had hurt his feelings. Burned bridges? Yeah, I've blown a few to bits in my day.

However, in spite of my occasionally poor calculations, I also benefited in huge ways from the relationships I developed over the years. In one chapter of *Makin' Stuff Up,* I recall the many "Hoot Nights" at West Hollywood's famous Troubadour, hanging out with future Eagles, Glenn Frey and Bernie Leadon, J.D. Souther, Jackson Browne, Linda Ronstadt, The Dillards, and producer John Boylan. Those Monday-night showcases and friendly peer rivalries led to my first songwriting success, when hip bluegrassers, The Dillards, performed my Bob Segarini cowrite, "St. Peter," on the Troub stage and later on Johnny Cash's CBS variety show.

Most every town offers some similar kind of opportunity for songwriters to get up on stage and try out their original material in front of an audience. While the local participants may not be future Rock and Roll Hall of Famers, these showcases are where you can find out how your work is stacking up against other writers in your area. Before and after your 15 minutes on stage, gatherings like this are where peer and industry relationships are born. Every interchange gives you the chance to make a positive impression on a talented peer, while you can simultaneously suss out those who may (or may not) be compatible with your own network of peers. The members of The Eagles first bonded in the Troubadour bar, while Jackson Browne and J.D. Souther became trusted "go-to" sources for such classic tunes as "Take It Easy" and "New Kid in Town."

In my last book, I shared one of my favorite anecdotes of one-upsmanship over Glenn Frey (who ceaselessly prowled the Troub bar like a territorial, sexual predator) in which my girlfriend/future wife so glibly put down Frey's clichéd pick-up line, resulting in his consequential slinking away to lick his wounds. I have a second little "gotcha" moment that I omitted from those pages. So, please indulge me as I brag about that. This story involves another industry relationship that—had different choices been made—might have spelled long-term career benefits for me as a songwriter.

When I signed my first recording contract in 1969, as a member of the band, Roxy, David Anderle was head of West Coast A&R at Elektra Records. Along with Roxy frontman, Bob Segarini, and a core group of industry sports fans, including producer/engineer Val Garay, I spent most every Sunday afternoon of the 1969/'70 NFL season in front of Anderle's TV, watching games, swilling beer, and joking around. Through those weeks, we all naturally bonded as trusted pals.

Anderle had designs on producing records. Elektra, however, wanted him to concentrate on his duties as an executive. Having plucked exotic, long-legged, throaty, heartthrob, Rita Coolidge out of the supergroup, Delanie and Bonnie and Friends, Anderle bailed from Elektra and signed his future star to A&M. He was rewarded with a staff producer position and installed in an office on the old Charlie Chaplin film lot on LaBrea that housed the A&M campus. By this time, Roxy had lost two members. (Our drummer bagged Hollywood and rock and roll for Stockton and jazz; our keyboard player had been converted to Scientology, and was devoting all his energies to becoming "clear.") That left Segarini, myself, and our lead guitarist, who, as gifted a player as he was, seemed far more interested in sucking down bottle after bottle of Wild Turkey, chain-smoking, and playing solitaire than in pursuing a music career. So, attrition had reduced our electric, concert-rock band to a folkie, acoustic duo called Segarini and Bishop. In that minimal configuration, we continued to write together and hang out at the Troub to play those infamous Monday-night hoots.

Segarini and I began visiting David Anderle frequently at his A&M office to play him our new songs. David, in turn, began showing genuine interest in signing our duo to the label: football-and-beer buddies considering a new creative partnership; relationships at work. Dontcha just love it? Anderle suggested that Segarini and I drop by a tracking session for Rita Coolidge's first album. There in Sunset Sound Studio A, producer Anderle had assembled the cream of American roots rock: Jim Keltner on the skins, Chris Etheridge tag-teaming with Duck Dunn on bass, Booker T. Jones on keys, Ry Cooder and James Burton on guitar. They were cutting a cover of Van Morrison's "Crazy Love." On the spot, Segarini and I worked out a little background-vocal part. Booker T. joined in on a third harmony. The lovely Rita asked us to return the following week to replicate that same vocal blend on the master. Around that same time, Segarini and my relationship with Anderle nearly gave us a winning lotto ticket, when he introduced us to Jack Daugherty, the Carpenter's producer. Segarini and Bishop came within a hair's breadth of getting a cut with that bro/sis dynamo.

Again, partly due to our friendship with Anderle, we got an invite to view a movie-in-progress screening on the A&M lot. *Vanishing Point* was real 1970s filmmaking—raw, existential, counter-culture—and the producers wanted to score the movie with tunes from the hippest new artists on the L.A scene. Inspired by the footage we saw that day, Segarini and I custom-penned a couple of tunes and submitted demos recorded in a Sunset Sound side closet, on ¼-inch four track, on the sly, with an ambitious second engineer. Both songs were chosen for the soundtrack. If that wasn't cool enough, I got to play acoustic guitar on the Jimmy Bowen–produced tracks, alongside session stalwart, Al Casey, and a broad-faced, hillbilly picker by the name of Glen Campbell.

So, there I was, the straggles of my first beard sprouting erratically from my pink cheeks, git-box in lap, positioned at the microphone. And who should swagger up but Glenn Frey. Seeing me on the session, he stopped and put his thumbs in the belt loops of his favorite bellbottoms. (It should be explained that this was pre-Eagles; Frey, at the time, was part of a duo himself, called Longbranch Pennywhistle, partnered with J.D. Souther.) "Hey, man," Frey greeted me. I did a salutation back. "Yeah," he boasted, "Longbranch has a song in the movie." At that moment of typical Frey cockiness, I don't know whether he was aware that I was not merely a hired hand on that date; that I was actually also one of the recording artists, but I set him straight pretty quickly.

"Oh, really, Glenn?" I said, adjusting the tuning on my D string. "Segarini and Bishop have *two* songs in the film." The blush on Frey's face broadcasted his envy. We were rivals, competitive in every way: with the women at the Troub bar, with our hoot-night performances, and now, for spots on the *Vanishing Point* soundtrack. That two-to-one score, however, was my final victory over Glenn Frey. He, of course, went on to a ridiculous level of fortune and fame with The Eagles, while I continued my journeyman career in relative obscurity.

With Segarini and Bishop's two featured tracks on the soundtrack and our momentum picking up steam, David Anderle had even more ammunition to present our duo to A&M. He had one signing he wanted to consummate first. He introduced us to a hulking, pock-marked cat from Eureka, near the most northern tip of California. Mike Stull was as talented as any human God has ever created and just as self-destructive, too. Stull's passion for the whiskey bottle rivaled Hank Williams, and he loved to skid his Mini Cooper around the logging roads outside of his hometown like he was out to win a Grand Prix race. But, there was no mystery why Anderle had offered Mike Stull a solo deal. The cat from Eureka sang like Ray Charles, picked guitar like Eric Clapton, and played piano as well as any full-time keyboardist. After Coolidge's album was completed, Stull was to be Anderle's next project. After that, we all thought, would be Segarini's and Bishop's turn. Now, with all of this good stuff going for us, this was where Segarini, Stull, and I hit a fork in the road and impulsively veered off in a completely different direction.

It all started with Stull's invitation and it happened in his hometown. Segarini and I motored up Highway 1, past the rolling cliffs of Mendocino and the ominous sequoia forests, marveling at the grandeur of this damp, moss-laden wonderland. In Stull's mother's clapboard, Victorian house, Stull, Segarini, and I jammed and sang together. The sound we made with our three-voice blend was unearthly (in a good way). Later, we commandeered the stage at a dive bar called the Purple Haze and spent several transcendent hours, playing Chuck Berry, Muddy Waters, Rolling Stones, anything and everything we could reconstruct from memory. That night marked the birth of a new musical partnership, and we contracted as the house band at that very dive bar six nights a week, seven sets a night. Talk about trial by fire! Stull backed out of his A&M commitment. Understandably, Anderle was not pleased. Another bridge burned. Eventually joined by bassist/singer, Kootch Trochim and drummer, Spencer T. (Ernie) Earnshaw, our ensemble signed with Jac Holzman's Elektra Records and made several albums together—as The Wackers.

CHAPTER 16
Peer Networking

Here's what the Bluebird Café's Barbara Cloyd says: "It is essential to surround yourself with people whose creativity and diligence excite and inspire you regardless of their level of success."

Achieving commercial songwriting success is never a solo effort. Eventually, somebody high up on the industry totem pole will have to play a part. It's also likely that more than a few assistant chiefs will be involved before the Big Kahuna raises that magical scepter and, in one omnipotent motion, declares you and your work worthy of royal attention. However, as a songwriter waits for that lucky tumbling of the dice to roll the right number, the most typical misassumption would be this one: "I just need to get my songs heard." Oh, if it were only that simple!

Undeniably, somebody important will have to hear, fall in love with, and endorse your songs for them to even have the tiniest chance of becoming the hits they aspire to be. However, it's not just that they need to be heard; they need to be heard within a certain context, in an atmosphere that draws the proper attention to them and gives them power. Only when you've put your all your ducks in a row and the stars fall into alignment will any one of your songs be positioned to discover its true potential. You begin this positioning process by assembling or joining an informal group of peers: cosponsors, colleagues, and cohorts, each of whom sign a virtual petition, declaring their unanimous belief that you are ready to play on their team. This declaration is reinforced by their willingness to line up on your side of the ball, as your brothers and sisters in arms, your comrades. On their own, our songs are 98-pound weaklings, just waiting for bullying industry naysayers to kick sand in their eyes. However, with a muscle-bound brigade of die-hards standing by to defend them, those very same compositions can become as powerful as Atlas, unstoppable, and poised to dominate the airwaves.

Speaking of getting songs heard, here's a quick, autobiographical tidbit for you, and it's absolutely true. This was in the late 1980s, shortly after I signed Rhythm Corps to Pasha Records and produced their Number One AOR (album-oriented, FM rock) record, *Common Ground.* A major-label A&R rep invited me to submit an artist package on behalf of an extraordinary singer I was producing and writing for. This particular A&R guy was relatively new on the job, but he had quickly won himself 15 minutes of industry fame, due to his discovery and signing of a very deserving and critically acclaimed alt-rock band. As per his instructions, I delivered a comp CD, the artist's photo and bio—with a cover letter attached—to his office. About a month later, a single, business-sized envelope arrived in my home mailbox, with the A&R dude's name on the return address.

Inside the envelope, I found his response to my submission. On the same cover letter I had typed to him—now, carelessly refolded, tattered, and worse for wear—he had scrawled these six words in the margin: "Sorry, Rand. I didn't here it." I swear to God, that was the sum total of his expert assessment, incorrect spelling and all. What does that say about the level of professionalism, respect, care—not to mention the literacy—of some of the people who make creative decisions at major record companies? Don't *even* get me started!

Industry decision-makers are not all as ignorant or discourteous as that particular A&R rep. Many are caring, passionate, intelligent people who, day in and day out, champion great music and the people who create it. By themselves, though, they can only do so much to expose the music they care about to the world. I heard tell of one such A&R person, who became so frustrated at not getting the attention and respect she sought from artists and producers, that she started throwing cassette tapes against her office wall. As the plastic cases shattered and thin, brown ribbons of tape streamed to the floor, she screamed, "These are great songs! And, I can't get a single [bleepin'] one of 'em cut!" So much for getting your songs heard. More often that not, the very people you want to hear them can't get anybody else to listen to them either.

Yes, we all aspire to know and be known by the captains of our industry, the mighty moguls of commerce, the creative forces who drive the trends, the recognized experts who, with a single nod, can ensure automatic platinum. It's as rare as a snowy day in Jamaica when some assumed nobody from Nowheresville catches the attention of the top brass, takes a detour around the winding, treacherous game-board path, and gets a free pass to the head of the class. It happens once or twice in a generation. Overnight successes never really happen overnight. Almost without exception, a long, steady progression led to what just appears from the outside to be a frog leap to the biggest lily pad. Realistically, that slow progression is usually a very healthy thing; if a certain amount of dues paying, maturity, and growth hadn't taken place over those interim years of hard work, the writer would likely not be prepared to survive the jump or to sustain the trek that waits on the other side of the chasm.

I was impatient, too. In my 20s, I saw my big break coming right around every next corner. I knew in my heart of hearts that I'd be skyrocketed in short order from the far fringe of the biz directly to the loftiest pinnacle at its epicenter. I did have *some* successes, even before I was 25. So, if you'd asked me—at 25—I would have informed you that I had already paid my dues. (And, oh, how wrong I would have been!). In my head, I was poised to claim my spot atop the Hot 100; I was ready to cash some six-figure BMI checks; I was composing and rehearsing Grammy speeches. One day, in the later 1970s, my friend and lawyer, John T. Frankenheimer, introduced me to an industry bigwig as one of the up-and-coming pop songwriters of the day. My lawyer described how my career was likely to progress: from the Long John Baldry cut I'd scored the year before, to maybe a Bonnie Raitt cut this year (Raitt was still a cult, blues artist at the time), then on to a recording by one of the hottest acts of the day, the Pointer Sisters. *Bonnie Raitt?* I thought to myself. *I'm ready for Aretha—at least!* My ego saw no reason to dawdle around with minor leaguers like Bonnie Raitt. Now, I'd commit high crimes and misdemeanors to hear Raitt's voice sing one of my songs—once. The lesson here is this: You never know who is going to be the next superstar. Don Schlitz (who already had Kenny Rogers' "The Gambler" under his belt) complained to high Heaven when an upstart, former dishwasher, named Randy Travis cut "On The Other Hand." The rest, as they say, is history: a history Schlitz would not change for the world.

Aw, but I meander. Let's get back to the subject at hand. Assuming that a writer has laid the groundwork—by recognizing his or her own innate instincts, honoring those creative compulsions, and has begun conscientiously refining his or her unique abilities—the next step is as natural as assembling the neighborhood gang to play cops and robbers, setting the table for a dolly tea party, or organizing a game of kick the can. Well, it might take a little more consideration than those childhood activities, but what I'm saying is this: Creating a peer network is something most of us just do, without a lot of thinking about it. Yet, thinking about it might be a lot more worthwhile than you may think it is because there is a strategic way to go about it. What is a peer network? What is peer networking? Why is putting a peer network together one of the most important steps in your strategy for potential success?

At last, you're probably saying to yourself, *this blowhard is finally getting to the point.* Well, here it is: Your peer network is your posse, a core group of creative friends and partners comprising the other talented people with whom you choose to associate regularly, meaning the friends you write with, record with, and perform with. These are the people with whom—and because of whom—you will most likely gain your initial recognition. There is power in numbers. When the chemistry between the characters is working, that power can be logarithmic. My good buddy, Grammy-nominated songwriter, Tim James, says it so succinctly: "If you're starting this business fresh, I don't think you can set out and say, 'I'm gonna make friends with So-and-So.' You might as well find a group of people that are at your level and your age and everybody kinda works together. And then, you hope and pray that in ten years, if you're still around, that one of your boys has made it, or that *you've* made it." Amen, Brother James!

Hit songwriter, top song-craft coach, and mother hen of the Bluebird Café, Barbara Cloyd, says it this way: "Talented, hard-working writers get noticed by the industry, and as you and your friends make contacts in the business, you can introduce each other to them." You know people. Everyone else in your core group knows people, too. That's why it's called a network, because your peers' friends, acquaintances, fans, and supporters can become yours and vice versa. By being part of a group, your world is multiplied by the people in your group and many times over by all the people they know! That's the logarithm I was referring to. A peer network, to one degree or another, is a songwriting-career pyramid scheme. However, it doesn't cost anybody a dime, even though you just might stand to gain substantial riches at some as-yet unknown date in the misty future.

When I ponder the concept of peer networks, I can't help but think about the late Gary Usher. A self-avowed genius with transparent, pale-blue eyes, and a gaze as piercing as an eagle's, Usher produced the first two albums for my second Elektra band, The Wackers. It was by observing Usher in charge of those sessions that I learned most everything I know about music production. Although, working with my band is not even significant enough to be a footnote to his amazing career. Usher had been a music-business legend for most of a decade when I met him in 1971. His first big songwriting success was "409" by the Beach Boys, cowritten with Brian Wilson, with whom he also penned the beautiful and pensive "In My Room." He closed out the 1960s by producing three brilliant albums by The Byrds: *Younger Than Yesterday*, *The Notorious Byrd Brothers*, and *Sweethearts of the Rodeo*, with the latter arguably being the first successful country/rock album and the project that gave a world-wide stage to a charismatic, self-destructive whiz kid, named Gram Parsons.

By Usher's account, during the early '60s, a quartet of ambitious, Southern California songwriters would cruise up and down Pacific Coast Highway, mining the beach culture for ideas. On those expeditions, this core group—Gary Usher, Brian Wilson (Beach Boy mastermind), Terry Melcher (Doris Day's son, Paul Revere and The Raiders' producer) and Jan Berry (Jan, of Jan and Dean)—brainstormed on the concepts that became chart records by a number of made-up groups; acts they named The Hondells, The Surfaris, The Knights, the Kick Stands, and the Super Stocks. It was pretty much the same studio band and the same singers on all of these records, gathering at Gold Star Studios in Hollywood for quickie, low-budget sessions. If the record took off, they would audition players and singers, assemble a performing unit, and send them out on the road. In one single year, Usher told me, he participated in more than 30 Top 40 hits using this template.

Let's assume that, like Usher, you are part of a tight-knit quartet of talented aspirants. This would be your core group, your peer network. Each one of your three compatriots has his or her own set of assets. Your strength might be as lyricist or a melody writer, or maybe you kick out the hottest guitar riffs ever. Another in your group has a knack for coming up with brilliant hooks, and/or invents cleverly inverted chords that help make a melody soar. Energies combine many times over between the members of your core group, according to how each relates to the others. The members of a good core group enhance each other's work by sharing complimentary tools and talents. At the same time, as we mentioned earlier, they benefit from each other's contacts. This automatically multiplies the exposure for every member. A good core group dares each member to greater accomplishment and holds each member accountable for his or her talents. Ideally, as one member of the group achieves recognition, the others lift their game to keep up. No one is taking a free ride. Everybody pulls his or her own weight and more.

That's when achievement becomes contagious. For instance: one member of the group—let's call her Frankie—has culled some positive interest from ABC Publishing. A rep from ABC shows up to your core group's writers' round to check Frankie out in a live setting. That gives the other three an opportunity to impress, too. Frankie's strong performance draws attention to songs she cowrote with the others. Another group member showcases his passionate vocal chops; maybe you blow the crowd away with some hot guitar licks. That puts a positive buzz on the street: "So-and-So, from ABC came out to see Frankie and her boys last night. Looks like she's gonna get a deal." Now, this core group, or peer network, becomes a unit that more and more publishers and industry mucky mucks will be showing up to see.

I've seen this phenomenon happen time and time again. I call it the Graduating Class. Barbara Cloyd refers to it as "moving up with your class." Assembling a strong, highly visible peer network is something that the industry notices. Chris Oglesby, former publisher, now a top manager of Music Row songwriters, says this: "Somehow the talented ones find each other and hang together." Then, Oglesby remarks that, when he signs a writer, he often works with other members of that writer's core group, too.

One of the first songwriter rounds I ever attended (in 1994) was at Nashville's Douglass Corner. On the docket were Chuck Cannon, Lari White, Verlon Thompson, and Suzy Ragsdale. They were a supportive group of creative peers. Thompson had already released one critically acclaimed—but radio-ignored—album (on Capitol Records, 1990). He then toured and recorded extensively with the legendary Guy Clark. As a songwriter, Thompson's cut list has grown into a country-music who's who: Jimmy Buffet, Alan Jackson, Trisha Yearwood, and so on. Chuck Cannon went on to write a string of big hits, including "I Love The Way You Love Me," performed by John Michael Montgomery (which also crossed over to R&B with Irish boyband, Boyzone), "We Were In Love," "How Do You Like Me Now," and several others by Toby Keith. Multitalented White soon signed to BMG Records, then moved on to Lyric Street, scoring chart success as an artist/writer, before taking on movie and Broadway acting roles. White even coproduced Toby Keith's first album for his own Show Dog label. The daughter of Country Hall of Famer, Ray Stevens, Suzy Ragsdale claims some impressive cuts as writer and credits as a background singer. (Not everyone in every peer network is destined to achieve the same level of success. But, every member ideally should benefit, in one way or another, from the success of the others. In fact, to support that theory, Ragsdale's most impressive songwriting credits are as a cowriter with Thompson and White.)

The Cannon/White/Thompson/Ragsdale performing round was a typical demonstration of a Nashville peer network at work. In the later '90s, I recall Chris Wallin and Rivers Rutherford playing together regularly at a club called The Broken Spoke. From the exposure they helped each other create, both went on to become juggernaut hit makers. To this day, I observe a natural camaraderie between talented, aspiring writers that, in turn, creates a power base to boost every individual Musketeer's career. However, a writer's peer network can take any number of shapes and sizes. It could revolve around a performing band, a recording studio, a nightclub or coffee house, an organization, a publishing company, or a local music scene. And a writer's peer network can evolve from one center to another, according to the circumstances and the relative success level of the various writers involved.

Take the stellar career of Mr. Kent Blazy for example. Blazy recalls first being inspired to pursue a creative life as a youngster in the creative hotbed of Woodstock, New York. Even before he was of an age to enter school, he observed regional artists, poets, and musicians expressing their God-given abilities. Later, growing up in Lexington, Kentucky, Blazy thought he, too, might go the Picasso route, with a palette, paints, and canvas. As a teen, he began dabbling in poetry, but it was the jangly vitality of electric folk-rock, emerging from a mono AM radio speaker that lit the torch and set his course. "After I heard Roger McGuinn and the Byrds and that electric 12-string guitar, I thought, 'That's what I want to be,'" recalls Blazy. "I got a little funky guitar for Christmas, and immediately started aiming to put the music and the words together." He joined the Columbia Record Club (much to his parents' chagrin) and studied the LPs that would arrive monthly. He took notice of a guy named Bob Dylan, whose songs were being recorded by The Byrds, The Turtles, and Sonny and Cher. Even then, he remembers thinking, "That would be a great way to make a living." So, from the moment he picked up the guitar, Blazy was thinking in terms of being a professional songwriter. His developing song craft and guitar chops naturally led Blazy to gigging whenever and with whomever he could, in a series of local rock, jazz, and country bands.

The Lexington scene had some impressive native sons, most-notably Exile, the band that, in 1978, exploded with the international pop smash, "Kiss You All Over." Exile's Sonny LeMaire and Mark Gray (very successful tunesmiths themselves) expressed admiration for Blazy's originals, as did other local musicians. Simultaneously, playing as a sideman, Blazy's writing received a powerful endorsement from Canadian folk-legend, Ian Tyson (writer of "Four Strong Winds" and "Someday Soon"). For the most part, it was the friendships Blazy made in the local Lexington music scene that provided the young guitarist/writer with his first real peer network. As other Lexington-based ensembles began performing Blazy's original tunes, industry recognition followed. Harry Warner, from BMI, scouted one such local group. They were invited to cut some demo sides for RCA Records in Nashville, including four Kent Blazy songs. Although that outfit lost out to another group called Wild Country (who went on to become Alabama), Blazy's songs were getting attention in the capital city of country music and all because of a network of peers in his hometown.

So, this is a perfect example of how a writer's career is born. He begins developing his musicianship and knowledge of solid song craft by playing along with records in his bedroom. He feels compelled to put his own words to music and form songs. He uses his guitar chops and original tunes to make a name for himself in a local music scene, while allying himself with equally talented peers. Thus, his songs begin attracting attention. Kent Blazy's peer networking didn't stop at the city limits of Lexington, Kentucky. "There was this apex of people sayin', 'You need to move to Nashville,'" he shares. "That's what I did in 1980." The move to Music City required finding a new core group, making new connections, while hanging on to his hometown relationships. A brief writing deal with a small company, run by a friend of a friend, a fellow named Jim Dowell, led Blazy to take his first ride up the country charts. Blazy's and Dowell's "Headed For a Heartache," recorded by Gary Morris (Dowell played softball with Morris; need I say more?) hit the Top Five. Kent was suddenly hot. Within a period of weeks, he scored a handful of cuts with Morris, Moe Bandy, his old pals Exile, along with a couple of others. He'd only been living in Nashville for a year and a half. "I thought, 'Wow, this is easy!' WRONG!" Blazy laughs boisterously, remembering that erroneous, youthful assumption. "It happened a lot faster that I thought it would happen. But, then there was a long stretch of getting things cut that never came out or being on hold and not getting the cut. I was playing in bands, and I was writing and doing studio work for other people and doing everything I could to keep it going."

Tiring of the drudgery of the road and seeing his publisher of four years about to close down, Blazy went to the bank, borrowed money to put together his own studio, and began cutting demos for other writers. This move provided Blazy with the most impressive and significant peer network of his career. "I was playing in a band with Billy Dean; so, he was my main guy singer. And Trisha Yearwood sang most of the female demos," he explains. "Bob Doyle, who had signed me to ASCAP called me about a guy who was looking for studio work." In November of 1987, Bob Doyle brought Oklahoma native Garth Brooks over to meet Kent Blazy. At the time, young Brooks was selling boots and cleaning churches for a living.

Blazy liked Brooks' voice and promised to use him on some sessions. Blazy continues, "I still remember, as Bob and Garth were walking out the door, Bob said, 'Well, you know, Garth writes a little bit, too.' So, I said, 'Let's set up a time and give it a shot.'"

At their first writing date on February 1, 1988, Brooks said, "Well, I've got this idea that I've run by probably 25 other writers and nobody's interested in it." He played a rough verse and chorus of "If Tomorrow Never Comes." It may have taken 25 blank looks, but Brooks had finally found the one collaborator who really understood the potential of this concept. As the superstar recalls it, Blazy just "spewed out a first verse." He then moved Brooks' first verse to the second, and a country classic was on its way to completion.

"We thought we'd written a really good song," Blazy says now. "So, we did a great little worktape of it, just a guitar and vocal of Garth, and pitched it around for about eight or nine months. But, nobody was really interested. So, we started thinking maybe it wasn't so good after all." In that next year, Brooks got his record deal and recorded "If Tomorrow Never Comes." That song became Brooks' second single and the first number one for both the artist and Kent Blazy. Garth Brooks is a really loyal guy. So, he's made sure that Blazy had at least one song on nearly every one of his albums, ever since. As a result, they've had five number ones together. Many of the demo singers who passed through Blazy's studio—including Billy Dean and Trisha Yearwood—have also gone on to big careers and recorded Blazy's songs.

Could any one of us replicate this model? Not necessarily. We might not be fortunate enough to grow up in a town where a band of buddies suddenly break with an international smash hit. We might not be lucky enough to have the next Garth Brooks walk into our studio asking for session work and a chance to cowrite. But, by putting ourselves out there, meeting and teaming up with a core group of talented contemporaries, we can all benefit from those strategic combinations of creative energies, those mutually supportive relationships, and create and expand the connections that will naturally come from a network of peers.

CHAPTER 17
Creating Your Own Peer Network

We're all inclined to make friends based on common interests and activities, the things we're mutually excited about. A passion for sports bonds some. The theater brings other contemporaries together. Astronomy, environmentalism, stamp collecting, Dungeons and Dragons, any of these shared pursuits might bring a peer network together. To a certain degree, a peer network is a clique inside a subculture, which, in turn, exists within society at large. High schools, colleges, and churches have special-interest organizations, such as clubs that speak foreign languages, go hiking, or help the homeless. Within those clubs, chemistry happens and personal friendships naturally burgeon. People just hit it off and start hanging together, and begin spending time sharing those common interests and sometimes doing other things besides speaking Russian or doing Civil War reenactments. That's exactly how a peer network is born.

Musicians commonly depend on other musicians to create a full sound, playing off one another in an interchange of rhythm, harmonics, and dynamics. It's only by making music together do most players learn and grow to their ultimate potential. While I'm sure there must be exceptions, you probably won't find a lot of bass players who are satisfied to play exclusively alone in a bedroom, with headphones on. Bass players want to plug into an amp, feel the floorboards vibrate, and jam with drummers. Drummers and bass players usually like to be joined by keyboardists and guitarists. That's how individual musicians combine to form rhythm sections. That natural process is similar to how songwriters assemble peer networks.

Don't get me wrong. Woodshedding by oneself is a good thing. Working singly can definitely sharpen your instincts and improve your craft. A capable songwriter can make a lot of creative progress in self-imposed solitary confinement. Given enough inspiration and perseverance, a solo tunesmith can construct a pop masterpiece with just a pencil and a pad of paper (or even with just some ultra-reliable brain cells). Certainly Jimmy Webb and Diane Warren have done just fine, sitting alone at the keys. However, in order for that brilliant composition to realize its highest potential—whether that potential is getting millions of boots scootin' across hardwood floors, or an equal number of eyes tearing up—that tour de force needs more than scribbles on paper and the unaccompanied warblings of the genius responsible. So, staying locked away in a room does a songwriter's career just about as much good and provides equivalent satisfaction as it does for that bass player with the headphones. We need—and our songs need—friends. To pull this caper off, we need partners in crime.

Where would rock and roll be if Keith Richards had kept the riff to "Satisfaction" to himself? What if Stevie Wonder just sang "You are the sunshine of my life" into a cassette recorder, then slid the tape into a drawer and moved on to his next inspiration, without sharing those warm rays of musical magic? Luckily, most of us not only feel driven to make up songs, but to share them with each other as well. After all, that's what songs are about: communication. Without the chance to communicate, a song is a tree falling in a forest for no one to hear; it is the sound of one hand clapping. Am I getting too deep here? Sorry.

So, who hears your songs or your song ideas first? Is it Clive Davis? Not all that likely. It's usually the fellow sojourner, the pal who dares to share your vision and aspiration to songwriting greatness. Maybe it's that quirky new friend, the cat you're thinking might just be the perfect candidate for the as-yet-unspoken suggestion, "Hey, let's start a band." It might be that schoolmate or workmate who took the initiative to master every parameter of GarageBand and has been cranking out MySpace hits from a suburban bedroom. That's where your peer network begins. But before you can team up, you have to meet these people first.

In assembling your core group, you'll be seeking out others who are equally as passionate about their musical goals as you are about yours, who are at about the same talent and success level, or even slightly ahead of you. Regardless of the talent level, seek out positive people. Steer clear of those folks who begin every sentence by telling you what they don't want, but can't seem to articulate what it is they *do* want. Of course, you're better off with cats and chicks you actually like hanging out with (life's too short to work with a**holes). Although a go-for-it temperament is a plus, stick with people your gut tells you are trustworthy and not so brutally ambitious that they're likely to use you as a wrung on their ladder to the stars. (There is absolutely no guarantee here; but use your radar and trust it. You're bound to be hurt and disillusioned by a "user" or two along the way. But, that's show-biz, kids. No, on second thought, that's just life.) Keeping an open heart is crucial to reaching your highest creative potential, but you don't want to set your ticker out there for it to be trod upon time and time again. Be smart. Use discretion. However, don't be snap-judgmental to the extent that you would exclude somebody from consideration just because he or she doesn't wear the coolest jeans, is overweight, has a bad haircut, or doesn't drive a cool car.

It's extremely helpful if each teammate has a special talent that compliments the group. One might be a great singer; one a hotshot guitar picker; one a great MIDI sequencer, or drummer, keyboardist, and so on. At least one person with home recording equipment and production/engineering skills provides a huge upside. You, too, will need to bring something unique to the party. Of course, you *are* the songwriter, the visionary, the creative genius, aren't you? But, also be that great singer, or that hot, guitar god, or that ProTools engineer. If nothing else, be the best MySpacer, YouTuber, Tweeter, or Facebooker of all time. Ultimately, that talent might be the most essential one of all.

Songwriter Events

Most every city, town, or region of the country has a songwriter association and/or a local venue that offers aspiring songwriters a chance to get up and share their newest compositions. If your town doesn't, maybe you should take the initiative to start one. Make a commitment to show up at every event where other songwriters and musicians are likely to be hanging out. Show your face (and put a smile on it). Wipe the sweat off of your nervous palm and shake some hands. You'll be surprised at how easy this gets once you get over your initial shyness. Be friendly and unpretentious. Be gracious. Most of all, be prepared with a succinct sentence of introduction that sounds intriguing, but not egotistical. You need to be aware that one version or another of a certain question will be coming up often and you need to be ready to answer it. Work on your line in your car on the way there. Rehearse it *before* you get caught off guard. Here it comes:

"Hey, man, how ya doin'? Whachoo been up to?"
"Oh, I've been writing up a storm."
Or, *"I've been in the studio cutting some new demos."*
Or, *"I've been auditioning guitar players."*

Or, all of the above.

Maybe today, you can't boast about a new cut by a big artist or claim authorship of a single bulleting up the charts. Sure, though, you can find something positive to say that speaks of forward progress. Responding with a "Not much" is either needless false modesty or an admission that you are floundering, directionless, drifting on a leaky boat to nowhere. Remember that you took a shower, put on a pair of clean jeans, and left the house for a reason: to make as positive impression as possible on as many people as possible, to make yourself—and your talents—attractive to others. Nobody wants to hitch his or her ascending star to an anchor. Have your intro line ready to go, on the tip of your tongue. Don't make false claims, but don't sell yourself short, either.

If you're introducing yourself to someone for the first time, be prepared. Say hello, give your name clearly, offer a handshake, and immediately look for a way to be complimentary: "You have a great smile!" Or, "What a cool T-shirt!" If you're approaching the singer who just came off stage, mention something specific that lets him or her know you were listening and appreciating the performance, such as "Man, the last verse of that third song knocked me out," or, "You have an incredible range." Who doesn't like a kind word or a good review? Who doesn't thrive on the admiration of a peer?

Then, you will need to have your own elevator career speech on the tip of your tongue. When he or she asks what it is that you do, you'll be ready: "I'm a songwriter, and a bass player [or a singer or a butcher or a night watchman]. I'm putting together my own band right now," or, "I've been cutting some demos at So-and-So Studio." Give your full attention when they talk. Be genuinely interested. Try to absorb the details and remember them. Look the person you're talking to in the eye.

Here's a chronic bad habit shared by a good number of the inhabitants of the mysterious Land of Show-Biz. There we are, at one or another industry function, engaged in conversation, but each lending only half an ear. Our eyes are darting over the other person's shoulders, scanning the room for somebody more important. Instead of looking at each other, we're continually making mental notes of which people we intend to approach next. This, I think you'll agree, is disingenuous, self-serving, and shallow, not to mention, downright rude.

Once, at an after-concert reception, backstage at L.A.'s Greek Theater, I was quaffing white wine and sampling catered eats. And, *holy moly*, the opportunity presented itself for me to have a chat with that evening's headliner, David Byrne, lead singer and chief songwriter of Talking Heads. I was sharing a story that to me, at the time, seemed particularly profound. It had to do with sitting in my parked car, in a supermarket parking lot, listening to one of my favorite Talking Heads tunes. Suddenly, I was struck by a chime-like sound on the record that I had never noticed before, in perfect tune and rhythm with the track. As the recording began to fade, the chime cadence continued at the same volume as before. As it turned out, this added production came from bells ringing in a nearby church tower.

The disappointing part of this conversation—for me—was that it was virtually one-sided. My story was true and revealing, involved real-life serendipity and Byrne's music, and told of what felt to me like a near-religious experience. But, as I shared this personal epiphany, the artist was impatiently looking past me, giving my recollection a partial listen at best. As I shared my church-bell punch line, Byrne failed to respond at all. Wounded, I turned my head to see the subject of his curiosity. There, about ten yards behind me, wine glass in hand, smiling and fully immersed in repartee, was David Bowie. Without so much as a smidge of acknowledgment for my confessional anecdote, Byrne proceeded to muscle through the crowd to schmooze Bowie. Hey, who could blame him? However, that sure let the air out my balloon. I guess the point I'm trying to make is this: Don't do that.

To one degree or another, I think we've all been guilty of this kind of blatant discourtesy. Behavior like this demonstrates that we really have no sincere interest in the person we're talking to, unless, of course, he or she implies that they might be able to open a door, make an introduction, and/or help us get a leg up. Only showing interest at that point would be pretty transparent to just about anyone. Even though, admittedly, we are there in the first place to meet and greet, to make our faces visible and put our names in people's consciousness, and to connect with those who can benefit our careers, we cannot afford to come off as self-serving. We need to show genuine interest in whomever we are talking with, listening intently, remembering names, and storing a detail or two that might come in handy in a next encounter. You never know if this very person might be the contact that, somewhere down the road, might turn the key for you. If you work to win a reputation as a nice person, friendly, attentive, considerate, somebody who remembers names and even a thing or two about other people's lives, you will go much further much faster. It's kind to pay attention. Be kind.

Here's some great advice from Doak Turner, the publisher of the popular online music-event listings publication *The Nashville Muse*, "Friends don't let friends play to an empty room." A master networker, this is taken from Doak's essay "Networking in the Songwriting Business": "Take an interest in the other person. DO NOT tell them what a great songwriter YOU are, or hand them your CD and ask them to listen to your songs! This is a relationship business, and you need to show an interest in other people, take the time to get to know them, and the time will be right to play your songs for that person."

Business Cards

Do not impose your business card, a flyer, a brochure, a CD, or any paraphernalia on anyone else without asking permission. A simple, "Would it be okay [or do you mind] if I gave you my card?" suffices. Listen for the answer and read body language. It's only common courtesy. Of course, you would be wise to have a stack of business cards on hand whenever you go out, even if it's only to the bank, the post office, or the grocery store. You never, ever know who you might run into. Your business cards should have all the pertinent info printed in an easy-to-read, large-enough font (name, company, phone number, email address, and Website). They should also be well enough conceived that they recall who you are when the people you give them to get home and unload their pockets. Countless times, I've found a nondescript calling card and had no recollection of the name or the person who gave it to me.

Turner has this advice on business cards: "You want to be prepared and do not want to fumble through a pocket full of everyone else's cards collected that particular day, trying to find one of your cards that does not have scribbled notes on it. Have *your* business cards in your *left* pocket, and everyone else's cards in your right pocket. Always have a pen and take notes from your conversation—after you have said your 'See you around town, or 'I will call you next week.'" This is excellent, pragmatic, and helpful advice.

Here's the biggest thing to remember about networking: Whether you're connecting with peers, with more successful writers, or with industry higher ups, your goal is not to book the appointment, to score the cut, to sign the deal. You're goal is to make a positive impression, so that the next time you encounter this person, you will be warmly welcomed. You want people to feel comfortable with you. You want them to know that you can be trusted, that you're mature and professional, that your motives are not exploitive or manipulative, that you're in the game for the long haul, and that you're not so desperate as to ever attempt to pressure someone or instigate an awkward encounter. After a certain comfort level is achieved, you will have opened the door to reveal your talents. Being a nice, pleasant, fun person comes first.

Creating a peer network often starts with cowriting. Remember, you never know which of your peers is going to pop through. Kent Blazy, he of five Garth Brooks Number Ones, says this: "One thing I learned from working with Garth, it's a good idea to give everybody at least one chance and sit in the room with 'em." But when you do get the opportunity to write, be ready and be professional. Blazy continues, "I do know this, though: When I get together with a young artist, and they don't have a pencil, a piece of paper, a computer, an instrument, or an idea, I probably won't get with 'em again. I mean what part of songwriting are you bringing to this room?"

After you meet somebody with whom you feel a rapport, someone you think you might want to get to know better, follow up within 24 hours (otherwise it's out of sight, out of mind). I think email is the best method for follow up; just a simple, "Hey, it was great meeting you last night at the SESAC mixer. How about getting together for coffee?" At that point, it would be perfectly fine to paste a link to your MySpace page or your Website. That way, if that person is at all interested, he or she can conveniently check out some of your work, to see if coffee (or even a cowriting session) might be something to consider. Don't be presumptuous enough to send an unsolicited MP3 and/or request the person's opinion about one or more of your songs. I really hate it when someone assumes that I'm interested enough and have time to listen to their stuff. It's even worse when they ask me for my opinion. That's an impossible position to be put in. Ask me for my opinion, and I'm gonna give it to ya. The first opinion I'll be sharing is that you shouldn't impose your music on anybody else, either by pushing an unrequested CD into somebody's hand or sending an audio file via email. If I do listen, I'll be brutally honest. But, it's more likely that I will toss your CD or trash your MP3. Give people the option. Let them come to you. If you've made a positive enough impression, they will make the effort to spend some time listening to your stuff. If they don't listen or get back to you, then they aren't good candidates for your peer network anyway.

Remember, you're looking for personal and creative compatibility, for other writers with complimentary talents to yours, people you take a liking to, who seem trustworthy, mature, responsible, and are dedicated to their craft and careers. You shouldn't be trying to hook up with a writer whose career is light years ahead of yours. That's probably not going happen unless you happen to be a young performer with exceptional promise. However, you do want to find other writers who are more talented than you are, who can inspire you and teach you a thing or two, but who are basically at the same level in their career progress. Hall of Fame songwriter, Rory Bourke, says this: "There's nothing you can learn by yourself." Get out and team up for success. Start now. Time's a'wastin'!

CHAPTER 18
My Graduating Class

As it pertains to my own songwriting career—especially its most recent and most successful "Nashville" phase—I find some irony in the term "graduating class." I say this because when I first set foot here, I was well into my 40s, already had more than 150 songwriting credits, had produced dozens of records and film soundtracks, and received several nominations and awards. I had benefited from membership in a number of peer networks: bandmates and fellow performers I lived, toured, and recorded with; communities centered around recording studios, record labels, and publishing houses; and a Mighty Mouse of a record/production company that provided me with myriad connections and opportunities. These centers of activity stretched from the southernmost to the northernmost ends of the West Coast all the way to Eastern Canada. I had kicked around stages and clubs all across North America and been kicked around in nearly every classroom and hallway of the school of hard knocks.

After arriving in Nashville, I quickly learned, however, that writing for the country-music market requires its own particular vernacular, both musically and lyrically, one that I had not yet mastered. Although a great pop song is a great pop song, most all of the musical subgenres that employ pop song craft also impose their own, peculiar, stylistic demands and limitations on the tunesmith. So, even though I had considerable professional experience and one could say I'd long since earned my degree, I had to pursue my "MBA" (Masters in Bubba Attitude) in writing for country artists and country radio. I did this by collaborating with and paying close attention to writers who were already enjoying success in the genre. As my track record opened doors for me that most new arrivals in Music City typically don't have access to, it wasn't absolutely necessary for me to join up with a posse of pals to get noticed, to break in, to "get my songs heard." I did, however, have a group of contemporaries I particularly admired and with whom I felt a certain kinship. Some I wrote and performed with regularly. Some were merely industry friends.

So, in a manner of speaking, I, too, am part of an unofficial, Nashville "graduating class." My classmates include such noteworthy successes as Michael Peterson, Dave Berg, and Tim James. We all first showed our faces on Music Row within a few years of each other and continue to be friendly and supportive to this day as industry peers. Through conscientious writing and networking, Berg and James have become reliable Music Row hit men. Berg has numerous Number One songs to his credit, while Grammy-nominated James' list of cuts and his string of Top Ten chart successes grows year after year. Peterson initially took the major-label artist route, breaking onto the charts with "Drink, Swear, Cheat, and Lie," followed by the Number One "From Here To Eternity."

I'll never forget the day EMI Music's Pat Finch played me a song called "That's What They Said About the Buffalo." It was 1995. For me, that exquisite composition and its singer set the bar at a new level. The music, lyric, and performance had the sincerity of Garth Brooks, but with even more substance and resonance. "Who is that?" I demanded.

"His name is Michael Peterson," Finch revealed. Soon thereafter, one of my favorite Nashville characters, the affable, omni-talented Robert Ellis Orrall, introduced me to this towering, broad-shouldered, always-smiling man. I took a liking to Peterson right away. Orrall confided that he was setting all else aside to put Peterson on the map in Music City. That's really saying something because, at the time, Orrall had a successful recording career himself with the duo Orrall and Wright ("Boom! It Was Over"). Michael Peterson was already a star, in high schools across North America. He'd been performing his "Who Cares?" motivational presentations for 12 years. Due to his imposing presence, undeniable talent, and star quality—not to mention the efforts of producers Orrall and Josh Leo—the former national champion collegiate football player scored a deal with Warner Brothers Records and then with Monument. Peterson continues to write, record, and perform as an independent artist. He is a multiple Grammy and CMA nominee, and his songs have been recorded by Travis Tritt, Ty Herndon, and John Berry, among others.

I first met Dave Berg under what turned out to be the most ironic of circumstances. It was at Nashville's Commodore Lounge, moments before I was to share a writers' round with two other songwriter cronies, Bob Cheevers and Craig Corothers. This was the very day the scandalous news had broken about Ty Herndon's arrest for exposing himself to a Dallas police officer. Herndon, with his movie-star looks, passionate baritone, and smoldering stage presence, had been hailed as "the next Garth Brooks." His version of Gary Burr's and Vince Malamed's phenomenal "What Matters Most" had rocketed to the top of the Hot Country Singles chart. It was clear to everyone that a new country star was born. Although fans of country music are by and large a pretty conservative lot, they've traditionally been willing to forgive any number of transgressions, such as alcohol and drug problems, marital issues, even criminal behavior. However, sexual deviance is a taboo that is, well, beyond the pale for the vast majority of this crowd. My assumption was that Herndon's lack of self-control, lapse in judgment—whatever you want to call it—spelled a premature demise to a very promising career.

On the way to the Commodore Lounge show, I remarked, with wry empathy, "Who I really feel sorry for are the guys who wrote Ty's second single." I was assuming, after that incident, Herndon's records would be banned from the airwaves. As we unpacked our acoustics in the wings of the venue, a friendly fellow with stringy, blond hair and a toothy grin approached Corothers. They seemed to be well acquainted. Strapping on my Taylor jumbo, I approached the pair as they back-slapped and laughed.

"Hey, Rand," Corothers said, "I'd like you to meet a fellow Portlander. This is Dave Berg. He's got Ty Herndon's new single."

As I shook Dave's hand, I said, "I'm sorry."

My new acquaintance smiled, blushed, scratched his head, and shuffled his feet, searching for a response. "Yeah. Oh, well," he mumbled. But, even with the scandal, aided by an extremely skillful publicity dance, Sony's crack promo staff was able to push Berg's "I Want My Goodbye Back" (cowritten with the record's producer, and head of Epic A&R, Doug Johnson) into the Top Five. Regardless of my sympathies, that hit gave Dave Berg's name a certain cachet on the Row. However, he would have to wait a very long time for his next chart success. After Herndon's single, Dave pursued the solo-acoustic, alt-country route, making his own indie recordings and building a solid rep as a performer of sharp wit and intelligence. All the while, he kept penning tunes with his favorite collaborators, building up his country catalog. The pump-priming, major break came pretty much out of the blue, when Canadian country band, Emerson Drive, revived its career by cutting his long-languishing Sam and Annie Tate collaboration, "Moments," for short-lived Midas Records. "Moments" climbed to Number One. Suddenly, Berg was hot. He followed that record with Reba McIntire's "Somebody" (also cowritten with the Tates) and Rodney Atkins breakthrough (CMA and Billboard's airplay 2006 airplay champ), "If You're Goin' Through Hell." Those three chart-toppers resulted in Berg being awarded NSAI's Songwriter of the Year in 2007. Crafty songwriting, constant performing, persistence, fortitude, and savvy networking had positioned Berg to become one of the most consistent hit writers on the Row. Berg has been on a roll ever since, scoring with Keith Urban ("Stupid Boy"), Chris Cagle ("What Kind of Gone"), and again with Atkins ("These Are My People"). Dave also cowrote Bucky Covington's Top Ten "It's Good to Be Us"—with a gentleman named Tim James.

Tim James grew up in Mufreesboro, Tennessee, a college town just 30 miles down Interstate 24 from Nashville. Ironically, James didn't begin his songwriting career in Music City, but in Los Angeles. He headed off to California after realizing that his life-long dream of playing professional basketball was not going to pan out. "At MTSU [Middle Tennessee State University], the first time I drove the lane," James confesses, "I looked up and some six-ten dude had pinned the ball against the backboard, going... [he completes the sentence with a kind of Augie Doggie snickering sound]." With no plan at all, James headed for California ,"Because," as he says, "I'd never been on a plane."

In L.A., through the remainder of his 20s, James used his considerable charm to make a living as a pharmaceutical salesman and fell into some high-profile company, palling around with up-and-coming actors like George Clooney and a coterie of club comics. Along the way, he also discovered an instinct for songwriting and some personal satisfaction in the process. As he reached his early 30s, his wife, an actress, scored a role in the musical, *Lunch,* written by Steve Dorff and John Bettis. "At some point," James recalls, "I cornered Dorff like an angry rat and asked him if he'd listen to some of my stuff." The vaunted pop composer's initial response wasn't very positive; but James kept sending him his work. Finally, Steve Dorff put a melody to one of Tim James' lyrics. With a real pro cowrite under his belt, and with his wife's encouragement, James began commuting home to Tennessee on a regular basis to cowrite with established Music Row writers. He fit right in: Southern, easygoing, funny, confident, with a rare instinct for the marketplace. James has a nose for finding subjects, creating characters, and telling stories that appeal directly to country music fans, in a language they can completely understand.

Even though he displayed such undeniable native talents, Nashville didn't give James the red-carpet treatment. Legendary publisher, "The Mayor of Music Row," Charlie Monk basically told James that he'd never amount to anything as a songwriter. Being the ultra-competitive sort, James took Monk's assessment as a dare, and flew back to L.A. even more determined to find success as a songwriter, if only to spite Charlie Monk. Introduced by a mutual friend, James and I began cowriting every time he returned to Nashville. This was about 1997, during the three years that I had a copublishing deal with Mike Curb Music. James and I developed a good creative and personal rapport, and he became one of my most-trusted and reliable collaborators. Then, after suffering a divorce, James moved back to Tennessee to lick his wounds and pursue his songwriting career full time. Norman DeVasure at HoriPro Music loved his stuff and tried to sign him but couldn't get the company to go for it. So, DeVasure introduced James to Kelly King at Don Schlitz's company, Hayes Street Music, who signed James to his first, entry-level publishing deal, at $17,500 per year. I invited James to join a Tuesday-night basketball league, made up of songwriters, publishers, producers, and artists. Observing his personal charisma, coupled with his athletic skills and competitive nature, I was able to see the whole person. *This guy would be a success,* I determined, *regardless of which career path he chose.*

In the fall of 1999, James and I wrote a song together that would change both of our lives. At that juncture, he and I had both been dropped by our publishers. For that matter, all of Music Row was in sorry shape. Investors were scattering like rats; money was scarce; publishing companies were closing left and right; "For Rent" signs lined 16th and 17th Avenues. James was painting houses between writing appointments. My savings were evaporating, and I was looking at the specter—for the first time in years—of having to find a job in the real world. In essence, we were writing for our lives. Sitting in the attic studio of my rented, brick, Tudor-style house on Natchez Trace Avenue, James said, "Every day I make a list of things to do. Let's write a song about it." That was all I needed to hear.

My fingers found the descending, finger-picking chords, and the first line of the song just kind of spilled out, "Under an old, brass paperweight is my list of things to do today." Even with the dense language of that song, James and I completed 95 percent of "My List" in one sitting. That's one of the values of a trusted, long-term cowriting relationship. You don't find yourselves second-guessing each other or quibbling over where the song is going. You tend to tag-team and brainstorm, collaborating fluidly, with the assurance that you're heading for the same goal, using complimentary skill sets, while sharing the same, uncompromising standards. With one important lyrical tweak—accomplished via telephone the next day—I barreled ahead to produce a home demo, playing all the parts and singing the vocals myself. Then, the song sat there for two years.

I put "My List" on a comp CD of a dozen new songs. In that group of tunes, it failed to gain any special attention from the many publishers, producers, and artists who heard it. The one exception was the late Dan Seals, who liked it, considered recording it, but found three other songs in my catalog that he decided to record instead. I did get a kick out of playing "My List" at writers' nights; it invariably garnered a good audience response and kudos from my fellow songwriters. To make a buck, I went to work as a crew leader for Census 2000. After that stint, I started my own enterprise, selling legal plans to families and small businesses. I was doing quite well—thank you, very much—building my new venture steadily. I found real satisfaction in facing my fears, picking up the phone, getting out there and meeting people, building my contacts, while helping folks solve real problems. As far as I was concerned, I'd retired from the music business, grateful for the myriad amazing opportunities over a nearly 35-year pro career, the incredible people I'd worked with, for every victory, large or small—and even for all those near misses and heart-crushing disappointments.

Tim James, however, paint-stained and stubborn as the dickens, kept knocking on Music Row doors, pitching his songs to any A&R person, producer, or publisher who would give him a few minutes. After four years of slogging it out on the Row, scoring a modest pub deal and getting dropped, he had one credit to show for it. Tim Rushlow, ex-lead singer of Little Texas, cut a three-way cowrite called "The World Turns." Meanwhile, I tried to persuade James to go into the legal plan business with me. "Hey, I'm doin' really well," I said, as we warmed up for Tuesday-night basketball, "and it beats painting houses, no matter how you cut it." He thought about it for about 30 seconds; but, thank God he turned me down and gutted out what I didn't have the heart to do anymore. Through shear pluck and perseverance, James became the first writer Rob Hendon signed to the new Toby Keith–owned publishing company, Paddock Music. With only a half dozen or so demoed songs to bring into the new arrangement, "My List" stood out. Keith heard something in that song that every other publisher, producer, and artist failed to identify; he was convinced that "My List" was a hit. So, being a supporter of good songwriting, a responsible publisher, and an extremely shrewd businessman, Keith began pitching our song to other acts on his tour. Much to his frustration, no one bit. Not being one to be refused—especially when he has a strong notion in his head—the superstar decided, if nobody else could hear what he heard in "My List," he'd cut the dang thing his own dang self.

Here's the point I'm trying to make. Had Tim James not been part of my peer network, had we not developed a trusted writing relationship, as well as a strong friendship, I would probably not have enjoyed the biggest success of my creative life so far. Had I not recognized James as a writer with solid instincts—as well as a guy who combined personality, wit, confidence and indomitable fortitude—I might still be selling legal policies. (Not that there's a single thing wrong with that. It's just that makin' stuff up is the most blessed job in the world.) And, above all, had Tim James not stuck with his game plan, enduring through Music Row's darkest hours, I might still be renting a house, instead of living in this beautiful, vintage Craftsman cottage in the Belmont district.

Now, on the other hand, had I not been receptive to the song concept and taken an active and professional role in shaping the idea into a polished piece; had I not taken the initiative to use my instruments, musicianship, vocal talents, and engineering acumen to produce a palatable demo, James might still be painting houses. I doubt it, though, because, as I said before—in all sincerity—James would be successful, regardless. He does all the right things. He's likeable, makes friends easily, and plays competitively (yet fairly) in every game in which he participates. This is a perfect example of a peer network working naturally for the benefit of the team. These are the kind of symbiotic relationships you should be striving to create as you assemble your core group of creative allies.

As he built his reputation (despite the erroneous assessment of Charlie Monk), James began burgeoning a friendship with ASCAP's Chris DuBois (son of songwriter/producer/record-company guru, Tim DuBois). For years, Matt Wade, an L.A. buddy had been urging James to get in touch with Wade's young cousin from South Carolina. "He started his own company in Nashville," Wade insisted, "and I think he's kickin' some ass."

James, however, was still concentrating on making connections with top pros, not with relative newcomers like himself. "Just like playin' ball," he explains. "The only way you're gonna get better is to play with the guys who are better." So, assuming that Matt Wade's South Carolina cousin was probably just another struggling wannabe, James never followed up. Meanwhile, Chris DuBois left ASCAP, started writing songs, and had some pretty quick success with a fresh, new country traditionalist named Brad Paisley. In partnership with Paisley's producer, Frank Rogers, DuBois started Sea Gayle Music, as a coventure with EMI. With a cowriting appointment coming up, Dubois asked James if his partner could join them. After hearing about James' California background, small, sturdily built Rogers mentioned that he had a cousin out west. His L.A. cousin's name? Matt Wade. James chortled at this serendipity, "Oh, so *you're* the short guy from South Carolina he's been tellin' me about all that time! We've been friends ever since, and that relationship has been very beneficial." Unknowingly, James had arrived in a creative vortex that would be extremely pivotal to his future success.

Tim James is now a Grammy-nominee for Trace Adkins' "All I Ask for Anymore," produced by (you guessed it) Frank Rogers. Over the first ten years of their friendship, the producer cut eight of the writer's songs. "Frank's not gonna do anybody any favors. I already know that for a fact," James says. "I don't call once a week; or, for that matter, once a month, and say 'Hey, man, I got somethin' for ya.' But, since we're friends, if I get something that's a homerun, I'll call." Year by year, James continues to expand his list of credits. Those cuts have resulted in four good-sized hits since our Number One with Toby Keith. Mark Mason of BMI paired James with Stokes Neilson of The Lost Trailers. Their cowrite, "Holler Back," made it into the Top Ten. "It's Good To Be Us" spent 32 weeks on the charts because of a chance meeting with Dale Oliver, an industry acquaintance, who happened to be co-producing American Idol finalist, Bucky Covington. James cowrote Lee Brice's "Love Like Crazy" with the record's producer, Doug Johnson. So, every financially meaningful, chart-making cut James has gotten has come from a personal relationship—not from a publisher's pitch. "I think you gotta do your own work," Tim says. "You've gotta be your own best advocate."

I hope you recognize the trend here. It's consistent, across the board. As they say, the writing is on the wall. The songwriter will nearly always have to do the heavy lifting to get his or her songs out there, to put those compositions in a position to be heard within a context that allows them a chance to shine. Building a team of cohorts, gaining a reputation together, and benefiting from each other's progress helps enormously in creating that context. It's brutally competitive, so you will always have to write inspired, solidly crafted songs. It helps an awful lot to write them with the "right" people and have a friend or two in possession of the keys to the castle. Obviously, you can't presume to get cowrites with established hit crafters from the get-go or become buddy-buddy overnight with the Producer of the Year. Like you, those folks started at the bottom and came up through the ranks with their own groups of pals, helping each from one rung of the ladder to the next. By surrounding yourself with your own network of talented, dedicated, and ambitious peers, you can give yourself a far greater chance of achieving your goals. Craft first. Friends second. With those two equally important factors in place, you'll know that when luck happens, your songs will be poised to take advantage of the good fortune and bask in the light of success.

In the mid 1990s, I remember seeing a long, lanky, dark-bearded songwriter at various writers' nights. He didn't sing all that well, and he certainly wasn't the most accomplished musician I'd ever witnessed. But, Mark D. Sanders was just then breaking into the top echelon of Nashville songwriters. A journalist asked him to reveal the magic potion responsible for his sudden string of hits. "Are you writing better songs?" the journalist inquired.

"No, my writing hasn't changed," Sanders reflected. "Now my friends are in a position to say 'Yes.'" The classmates Sanders had struggled beside during his developing years were now the established producers, record company execs, recording artists, managers, and so on, the very decision makers who could now wave a wand and give one song preference over all the rest. That illustrates the importance of creating a peer network.

CHAPTER 19
Industry Networking

One of my dearest songwriter friends is a bona fide Manhattanite. This guy personifies all of the hyper-kinetic intensity and assertiveness that inhabitants of the most-competitive urban jungle naturally develop in order to survive and succeed. (He's a lovely person, really—smart, friendly, positive, and talented—just a little too urgent and gregarious for the sweet-molasses pace of Nashville.) In his defense, on the island of Manhattan, being overly gracious, polite, or even passive can result in a person disappearing into the wallpaper, or, worse yet, being devoured alive by those king-sized, big-city rats (figuratively speaking, of course). Acquiring a more aggressive demeanor is Darwin's law at work; it's how the fittest survive in the Big Apple. Anyway, in spite of the town's outward-welcoming nature, Nashville (and the South at large) tends to distrust outsiders from the get-go. It's probably always been that way at least since that post–Civil War era, when slick-talkin' carpetbaggers swept through the South intent on taking advantage of the disarray. That Southern skepticism put my East Coast friend at a serious disadvantage; and he apparently wasn't even aware that one of his New York traits was creating a serious impediment to his potential Nashville success.

This was back in 1995. The Manhattanite and I had satisfactorily completed that day's 10 a.m. to 4 p.m. writing appointment in my office, on the second floor of my small, boutique publisher's Music Row digs. After bidding him a fond "see ya next time," I continued to work for awhile, maybe 45 minutes or so, compiling lyrics or updating a worktape. Then, feeling the need to stretch my legs and clear my head, I bounded down the stairs to warm up a cup of tea. As I approached the microwave, mug in hand, I encountered a frightening sight. There in the tape-copy room, I saw my publisher's face, despondent and desperate, her deer-in-the-headlights eyes crying out, "Please, help me!" My friend, Mr. Manhattan, had pinned this woman against the Xerox machine and was yakking away right in her face. Who knows how long she'd had to suffer this intense, impulsive motor mouthing? After I came to her rescue and my cowriter had schlepped his guitar case out of the building, the deeply disturbed woman declared, "If you want to write with that guy in the future, please do it elsewhere." I had been assigned the very uncomfortable duty of informing my pal that he wasn't welcome in that building anymore, not because he was a jerk, a scoundrel, or a ne'er-do-well, but because he was just *too* dang enthusiastic, assertive, and insensitive to how his energy affected the other people around him. That, brothers and sisters, is your parable for the day from the *Book of Rand*. Now, please open your hymnals and sing along with "Abuseth Not Thy Industry Contacts." Just kidding (about the hymn, *not* about abusing contacts)!

Cultivating industry relationships is a delicate balancing act. You are smart to let them develop naturally. Yet, you are also smart to take full advantage of any opportunity that may present itself to make a positive impression. By "naturally," what I mean is that you will meet people of import through your own network (as my New York friend did, meeting my publisher through me). A publisher might begin seriously courting one of your cowriters; or, a burgeoning artist/cowriter might get some interest from a top management company. Maybe you'll walk into a showcase, and one of your crew will be conversing with a label exec or a big-time producer. Obviously, since this person is your cohort, you have every right to approach and put your face in front of Mr. Bigwig. Other happenstance opportunities for a handshake and a spontaneous intro, however, need to be handled with a great deal of sensitivity and discretion, especially when it comes to chance meetings in public places. There are times when it would be absolutely cool to walk right up and introduce yourself, when you'd actually be remiss in your professional responsibilities not to take advantage; and, there are other times when making an approach could be the absolute worst thing you could possibly do.

Please remember this: Music-business movers and shakers are getting hit on 24 hours a day. Pretty much everybody they meet with or talk to all day long is out to get something from them. Publishers are hounding A&R people and managers to hear their songs. Songwriters pester publishers and A&R people to listen to their songs. Managers are after record company execs to sign their acts and/or put more promotion behind artist/clients already signed. Artists harass managers and agents to get them more money for their concerts or to book more concerts; or, they're urging them to get a bigger promo commitment from the label execs. It's an endless cycle of neediness. By definition, being a music-industry decision maker means you are being badgered during every waking moment. So, if you see a publisher, a label executive, a producer, or a manager out to dinner with his or her family, don't walk up to their table and attempt to engage them in casual repartee. That would be an extremely rude intrusion. He or she deserves some private time with the family.

However, if you're standing in line at Starbucks, next to a producer or a top-dog songwriter you admire—or even the president of a label or a publishing company—it wouldn't be that uncool to say, "Hi," offer your hand, and mention your own name. Don't be surprised if you don't get a "What are you up to?" in response. He or she knows that even a flicker of interest—feigned or sincere—might endanger cracking the door for an unwanted solicitation. If your introductory gesture seems well received, try to follow up by engaging in a little conversation—maybe asking the exec a question about how it's going at the label or the publishing company, express admiration for one of the songwriter's songs, or inquire about a project the producer has just finished—something that indicates you have an interest in that person and some knowledge of the business. Try to make your query intelligent. Think about it for a few seconds before you pop off with something that will leave you tasting your own foot. For instance, it would be a mistake to ask Mike Dungan of Capitol Records about what Faith Hill is up to because Hill is on Warner Brothers. Don't say anything about war, politics, religion, or anything controversial. Don't say anything negative, cynical, or sarcastic that could be misinterpreted. This is an opportunity for you to associate your name and face with a positive, pleasant experience. So, by all means, go for it.

Above all else, even though your little heart may be palpitating as if this very moment might be your biggest chance yet to take a quantum leap forward, *do not* force your business card into this person's hand. This is not the time and the place, unless he or she requests it (which will not happen, *unless* you've already made a very good impression). Even more importantly, *don't* take a CD out of your bag and say, "Hey, I know you're busy, but maybe in your spare time you could give a listen to my band." Don't say, as you're handing this person the card you were not invited to give, "Oh, I just posted some killer new tunes on my Reverbnation site. You should check 'em out." If an industry pro has any interest at all in hearing your music, there is no doubt that he or she will figure out a way to do it. Remember, while a magical stroke of serendipity can make all the difference in your career assent, this business is about building relationships for the long haul. Rarely will a single chance encounter result in a meaningful business relationship. Not that it has never happened, as in the following two modern examples of tight-sweatered Lana Turner being discovered in Schwab's Drugstore.

Danielle Peck was waiting on a table of industry muckymucks at a Nashville eatery. Upon discovering that his waitress was a singer, bad-boy promo-whiz and president/founder of Big Machine Records, Scott Borchetta, said, "Well then, why don't you sing us something?" Right there in the restaurant where she toiled daily to serve the people, Danielle Peck sang her lungs out a capella. Sure enough, Borchetta ended up signing her to his label.

Lanky, beautiful, and blond, with attitude to burn, Bluebird Café waitress Danni Leigh charged out into the parking lot after a customer who had mistakenly walked out on his check. This guy turned out to be a top, Music Row, artist manager. "I don't give a s**t who you are, pal," she said as she challenged him outside the club. "Nobody stiffs me!" It wasn't long before Leigh did care a *lot* who this fellow was, because he became *her* manager and was instrumental in her getting signed to Sony Records. Accosting a person in a parking lot is not the recommended way to charm a potential industry contact. However, if you're a waitress, I guess you gotta do what you gotta do to make a living. However, you can't afford to sit back and expect chance encounters like these to happen. Building strategic, industry relationships can take years.

"Plan for a marathon," advises Danny Arena of SongU. "If you plan for the 100-yard dash, you'll run out of steam long before you can reach the finish line." Arena's advice applies to every facet of your career. Standing in the Starbucks line next to an important industry figure means one thing for sure: This is a chance to plant the tiniest seed of recognition. You want this person to walk out thinking, *What a nice kid. I wonder if he (or she) writes good songs.* You certainly don't want to plant this thought: *"I'd better wash my hands quick, or I might catch a case of obnoxious."* There is a term for someone who dares to push an unsolicited CD or a business card on an industry pro. You may have heard it. This word sounds as unflattering as the traits it describes are disrespectful, unpleasant, and un-called-for. You certainly would not want to be known as a "gherm." I don't know whether the verb came before the noun, or vice versa. However, I think you'll have to agree that having an expertise for "gherming" would not contribute anything attractive or admirable to your all-important résumé.

One of Music City's most ubiquitous and universally welcomed personalities is a gent by the name of Doak Turner, who I quoted earlier in these pages. Turner moved to Tennessee from Charlotte, North Carolina, where he was a regional coordinator for NSAI. With a background that included promoting professional tennis tournaments and NASCAR events, Turner knows a thing or two about making a positive impression. Looking to get a leg up himself in the Music Row songwriting game, he started a weekly E-newsletter called *The Nashville Muse*, which now goes out to well over 5,000 subscribers. Turner also hosts a monthly guitar pull at his rented home in West Nashville. At 3 p.m. on the third Sunday of every month, about a hundred locals and passers-through town gather. There, they munch on Church's fried chicken, drink sweet tea, sit in circles, and pass the guitar. Turner's Third Sunday events have engendered a genuine songwriting community, where writers meet, network, and encourage each other. When it comes to giving aspiring Nashville writers advice, Rory Bourke says this: "As far as what I call 'newbies' are concerned, I tell 'em two things. Call Doak Turner and get involved with his group of people who care about each other. Join NSAI, get into their seminars and learn." Coming from a Hall of Fame writer, with a discography that includes some of the most iconic names and titles in pop-music history, those words amount to quite an endorsement. Turner's events caught the attention of the Nashville Chamber of Commerce and the Music City Visitor's Bureau, so much so that his newest venture is a virtual "Welcome Center," now located on the Web at www.MusicStartsHere.org. A "community-, city-, and industry-sponsored initiative," MusicStartsHere.org is jam-packed with resources and info to help newly arriving artists, songwriters, and musicians. Turner calls the new site a "GPS for the Nashville Music Community." It includes more than 100 video interviews with pros. In fact, I happen to be featured on the site, offering some advice for aspiring "newbies."

That being said, Turner's local notoriety and success is all based on his mastery of networking. In this category, there is no question that he reigns among the all-time champs. As I've stressed time and time again, networking is a talent that is equally as important as the ability to write great songs, produce great demos, and entertain a crowd of people. Turner is featured frequently at music-business gatherings as a keynote speaker, where he generously shares his techniques and sage advice.

Turner has some very creative and pragmatic ideas about building an industry identity, including a slyly ingenious technique for getting your business card into that important person's hand, without committing the dreaded gherm: "When you see someone looking for a piece of paper or something to write on, offer your card and a pen (that you should always have in your pocket). Tell that person to use the BACK of your business card to write notes. I do this all the time, and got a call one day from a pro songwriter telling me that he had six of my cards in his wallet from the previous evening's event. I asked him if he thought it was a coincidence. I don't think so!"

Your First A&R Nibble

So, let's say you've become acquainted with an A&R person from Sony/BMG. Maybe it happened because you worked on a benefit for the Leukemia and Lymphoma Society together, ran a half marathon, or tried to pump the last glass of beer from the keg at a mutual friend's birthday party. Whatever the scenario, you guys kind of hit it off. He seems friendly and accessible every time you've seen him since, and it's progressed to the point where you feel he might just be receptive to listening to some of your material. You're out to lunch, maybe with the wife. He's walking past your table and stops to say, "Hi. How ya doin'?" You give him your quick, rosy report (maybe you just cut a great demo, or got a hold, or wrote a song with a name writer—something positive, please!). Then, of course, you introduce him to the spouse. This is your chance. How do you broach the subject?

"Listen, I'd love you to hear this new tune I just demoed. I'm really proud of it." Or, "I understand Kenny Chesney is cutting in April. I'd really love to get the chance to play you something for Kenny." Just be respectful, unpresumptuous, modest. Be confident, just not pushy.

He might respond by telling you he's all booked up till September. If so, you know you haven't made a strong enough impression on him yet. But, hopefully he'll refer you to his assistant to set up an appointment; or, he'll ask you to drop a CD by the office. He may give you instructions as to the maximum number of songs he would want on a CD, maybe give you some kind of code word to put on the label, so it will go directly to him. Do yourself a favor and follow the program. If he (or his assistant) says

"No more than three songs," don't slip a fourth or a fifth on there or boldly drop two CDs. Make a decision. Put your best foot forward. Go with your gut. I know it's torture to make that choice, but if you really search your heart of hearts, you'll know which songs to give him. This is your chance to make a positive impression of another kind. Presumably, he already thinks favorably of you as a person. Now, it's the songwriter he'll be judging. Steer clear of pitching the most up-tempo piece of radio fluff, unless that's your thing and it's your absolute best pitch. Give him strong songs; show him your best writing. Don't try to pitch something just because it resembles Chesney's last single stylistically or thematically. Use your imagination. Come out of left field. Offer an off-the-wall change of pace. Every songwriter in town will be pitching clone songs. (Why would a superstar want to cut something just like the last record anyway?) Regardless of whether you get clear instructions, never include more than three songs on one CD. For me, when I receive a 10-song comp, I often set it aside for weeks or never get to it at all. If there are just few titles, I am much more inclined to throw it in the player right away and give it a spin.

If you're lucky enough to get a sit-down meeting, be prepared with CDs and lyric sheets. Know what you intend to pitch, but have some alternatives in mind, ready to go, just in case there has been a change of direction since you booked the appointment. That happens quite often. There's nothing more disconcerting than to arrive, ready to play your best Springsteen-style songs, only to discover that Chesney is now looking for something that sounds like Modest Mouse. As excruciating as it is to sit there while a music-business pro passes judgment on your songs, pay attention. Observe his body language, and try to listen through his ears. You will learn a great deal from pitching your own compositions. The intros will sound *so* much *longer*. You'll be dying for the verse to get to the chorus and the hook. The turnaround will last forever. The bridge might suddenly sound convoluted, odd, or just plain wrong. You may leave the office feeling like you're not the songwriter you thought you were. Or, one of your songs will sound better than ever. It'll kick ass and take names. Whatever the response, receive it without defensiveness. Never make excuses or try to justify any compromise you may have made along the way. This is *your* work, and you need to stand by it.

Maybe he says, "I can't really hear through that vocal performance."

Don't respond with, "Well, yeah. We really didn't have enough time in the studio to get it right. But believe me, this song is great!" Or, worse yet, don't confess, "We couldn't really afford a demo singer, so my cousin did the vocal. I thought he did a pretty decent job."

Should he inform you that he would have preferred a stronger lyric in the second verse, please don't blurt out, "I knew it. That was my cowriter's idea. I told her it could be better! We'd be happy to change it to whatever you want." It's too late for that (although you certainly have every right to go home, do some rewriting, and return with an improved song on another day, should Mr. A&R be willing to give you a second appointment). It couldn't hurt to ask, "Would you play it for Kenny if we rewrote it and made it better?" No doubt, he would decline to make that promise. However, he could feel some ownership in the song, if you took his feedback to heart and did some effective rewriting. Only do that if you genuinely agree that the suggestion will make your song a better, more competitive song. Don't do it just to please Mr. A&R. Do not argue, explain, complain, or justify. When your time is up, do not ask for three more minutes to play one more song. Do not indicate in any way that you can't take rejection professionally. Just take your lumps, smile graciously, thank him for his time, and ask, "When I have some more material, would it be okay if I called for an appointment?" Again, an "I'm booked up until September" type of response indicates that you have not made the most positive impression. Hopefully, he will advise you to give his assistant a call and promise to do his best to make room in his schedule.

"But, wait a just a darn minute, here, Rand!" you might be expounding in puzzlement. "What if he asks to keep a copy of a song, or puts it on hold?"

To that possibility, I say, "Great! Congratulations!" But, that's not what this chapter is all about. This chapter is about networking, building industry relationships. Surely, if a music-business pro puts one of your songs on hold, you will have permission to return in the future with more stuff. Your goal here, as in every meeting, is not to close the deal, not to get the cut, not to instantly be rocketed into the songwriter stratosphere. Your goal is to be given permission to book another appointment, to be blessed with these magic words: "Ya'all come back, now. Ya hear?" While a hold certainly makes you feel good, indicates that you're making progress, that you're getting somewhere and while it means that this one professional at this point in time likes your song enough to want to listen to it again, it's not all that big of a deal.

Yes, we love to be loved. Yes, we feel all warm and fuzzy when somebody reacts positively to our songs, especially an industry pro. But that, in and of itself, does not pay the mortgage, does not put kids through college; it won't even buy your next mocha grande. Hey, celebrate anyway. Let's toast to progress, to getting your foot in the door, and making it count! Just don't invest your hopes in anything real happening beyond this point with this song. Don't get emotionally attached to any specific outcome. Your A&R pal will be going back through his hold pile to decide which of those songs he's willing to lay down his life for. (Hopefully, you'll survive that first round.) Then, he'll play those selections in the next A&R department meeting, where all the other A&R staffers will be there championing their favorites. Then, if your song gets unanimous support from that panel of experts, Joe Galante will have to sign off on it *before* Kenny Chesney ever even gets to hear it. Then it will depend on whether

Chesney has had a good night's sleep, is in the mood for your kind of song, whether he's written something similar himself, and so on. Good luck! You and your song are going to need it.

The good news is that, unless you blow it, you now have a friend in a position to open the door a crack, so at least you can get a peak at the top of the mountain, even though, for now, it's really still miles and miles away.

Tuning Up for a Publisher Meeting

Publishers are another breed altogether. Many publishers love to find a diamond in the rough, their own special genius, and nurture that talent, pushing him or her to an as-yet-unrealized potential. If you've wrangled a meeting with a publisher, say through your PRO rep, because of a showcase you did, or even due to an unsolicited cold call, you can play songs in a much less developed and unproduced state. Once again, you don't want to make excuses or come off like a whiney, asset-deprived victim, but you can be a little more candid about your work than you would be with a label exec or a producer. Remain positive, however. Talk about your process, what inspires you, where you see yourself five years from now. Whatever you do, do not dwell on what kind of writer or artist you *don't* want to be. I am always wary of creative people who, when I ask about their aspirations, respond with, "Well, I wouldn't want to be like So-and-So!"

Publishers enjoy hearing songs played live with acoustic guitar or keys and vocal. Often a publisher will offer on-the-spot feedback. Once again, don't be defensive or argumentative. The publisher is not only sharing her experience and expertise with you, she is testing to see if you're open-minded, mature, cooperative, and coachable. For a publisher to sign a writer is a huge commitment, emotionally, financially, and in person-power. It's also a massive leap of faith for you as the writer to put your fate in the hands of a publishing company. It's best to take the courtship slowly and not jump right into bed together. Get to know one another well before you start pledging your troth and exchanging rings.

The best way to cultivate a relationship with a publisher is to act as if you're already signed there. After you've had a couple of positive meetings, keep showing up, as much as you feel welcome. If the vibe is good, drop by at the end of the afternoon. Be charming, relaxed, and fun to be around. Make friends with the receptionist. Book writing appointments with some of the writers, and try to cowrite on campus. If your collaborator is planning to play your new cowrite for the publisher, ask if you can tag along to pick and grin. You should have the right to be there, to observe the response first hand and hear any feedback she might hand out. However, if this makes anyone uncomfortable, don't make an issue out of it. You guys are doing a little dance here, seeing if you mesh. If somebody gets his or her toes stepped on, it may be time to back off and sit one out. These are important relationships; and, regardless of whether this particular publishing company is the right one for you, knowing these people can be to your benefit.

In the late 1990s, due to his frequent L.A.-to-Nashville commutes and a lot of hard work on his craft, Tim James was finally starting to get a bit of a buzz around Music Row. Norman DeVasure of Hori Pro Music wanted to sign James, but the brass there wouldn't go for it, because James was still living in California. DeVasure called Kelly King at Hayes Street Music and suggested that she meet with James. What Devasure was unable to pull off at Hori Pro, King did at Hayes Street, signing James to his first publishing deal. A similar scenario took place for young Rory Bourke, way back in the misty eons of the early '70s. At the time, Acuff Rose had a "no advance" policy. When they offered Bourke a deal, Bourke couldn't accept it; he needed a draw. So they recommended him to Henry Hurt, who was opening Chappell's Nashville office. Via that introduction, Chappell became the first publisher of a future Hall of Fame writer. Every single person you befriend along the way could be someone who opens a door for you.

I've already confessed to a massive career faux pas when, in 1975, after a lip-synch TV taping in Monaco, I failed to recognize the potential of a certain, young diva named Donna Summer. However, that same European trip did birth an industry relationship that would become one of the most important of my career. On the short flight between Paris and Nice, I sat next to an unassuming music-business entrepreneur named Seymour Stein. At that moment, Stein had just enjoyed the first major chart success of his Sire/Passport Records venture: the quirky, yodeling, rock instrumental "Hocus Pocus," by a Dutch group called Focus. Stein and I got to chatting. I was pleased to discover that he had been a fan of my band, The Wackers. Stein was also a MIDEM veteran. So, upon our arrival at the event, he generously pointed me in the right direction for registration and suggested that we have a drink or dinner sometime over the week. The friendship that began on a plane over France would eventually open numerous doors for my career: including a gig producing the English group, Original Mirrors, in London, and a cut by one of my all-time favorite bands, The Searchers. Along the way, Stein would also introduce me to Elton John, Freddie Mercury, John Reid, David Byrne, and even Phil Spector. Since that long-ago Focus hit, Seymour Stein has become one of the most revered record company execs in pop music history, by discovering and signing such acts as The Ramones, Talking Heads, Depeche Mode, Pretenders, k.d. lang, and last, but never least, Madonna.

Success seldom happens exactly the way you think it will. It almost always takes much, much longer than you envision. It's impossible to know which of the many seeds you plant will bear fruit. You'll have no idea whether anything at all is germinating beneath the surface. You just have to trust. Then, something blossoms into the light of the sun. Then another sprout peaks out. Water and fertilize. Plant some more seeds. Cross fingers and toes. A bountiful harvest may be on its way. Now, get out there and make some friends!

PART FIVE:

STRATEGIC WRITING

CHAPTER 20
Cowriting

Answering personal inspirations privately by writing your songs alone is most certainly a virtue that demonstrates devotion to one's craft, exhibits a good amount of self-discipline, and reveals a very noble nature. However, writing by oneself is not the most strategic pathway to chart success. There are exceptions to this rule, of course, exceptional exceptions, at that. Diane Warren, the most prolific hitmaker of all time, writes almost exclusively by herself. Jimmy Webb has pretty much always flown solo, as have Hugh Prestwood and Gretchen Peters. In fact, looking back over the history of pop music, numerous individuals have achieved big-time commercial success writing on their own, such as Willie Nelson, Kris Kristofferson, Neil Diamond, Cole Porter, and Irving Berlin, to recall a few.

Of course, the classic, solo, performing singer/songwriter almost always composes in solitude. That makes perfect sense, because he or she is concerned with expressing a unique voice and point of view that could easily be muddled by the input of a second or third opinion. Writing alone also makes sense for the solo artist, because he or she presumably answers that personal muse whenever and wherever inspiration strikes, instead of assigning specific hours and days of the week for creative endeavors. (The exception here is that enigmatic Randy Newman, who has always found it productive to negotiate L.A. traffic, driving to an office to compose, during prescribed office hours.) It would take a special kind of patience to be the regular writing partner of a star (or even a fledgling genius) writer/performer and be expected to answer a 3 a.m. call to help hone a fresh, middle-of-the-night, dream-inspired melody. That might get awkward after awhile. Elton John relied on Bernie Taupin for those amazing lyrics, but Taupin was never in the room when his flamboyant collaborator was attaching notes and chords to the words. So, even though he has always had lyricists/cowriters, Sir Elton is free to work whenever he feels the spark, just the artist, his piano, and a sheet of paper.

From Buddy Holly and Eddie Cochran, through Bob Dylan, Stevie Wonder, Paul Simon, Marvin Gaye, Gordon Lightfoot, Joni Mitchell, Neil Young, David Bowie, Bruce Springsteen, Jackson Browne, Peter Gabriel, Sting, Elvis Costello, Prince, Beck, and so on, the singer/songwriter has typically been solely responsible for creating his or her own songs. These artists have remained creatively independent because they feel compelled to keep an individual voice and because pragmatics and work patterns haven't allowed for collaboration. There are exceptions here as well. The aforementioned John/Taupin team for one. John Mellencamp has often collaborated, in particular with lyricist George Green. Bryan Adams partnered up on many of his hits as well, notably with frequent collaborator

Jim Vallance and super-producer/songwriter Mutt Lange. Alanis Morissette cowrote her entire breakthrough *Jagged Little Pill* album with producer/ songwriter Glen Ballard. Madonna has always depended on discovering the most cutting-edge collaborators. However, here's the real bottom line: *Singer/songwriters don't have to pitch their songs* because, of course, they perform them themselves. Duh! They write them themselves; and then, for the most part, decide—possibly with some feedback from a friend, a spouse, and/ or a business associate or two—which songs will go on each recording project. So, there's no *strategic* advantage whatsoever for them to cowrite. Cowriting could only possibly offer a *creative* benefit to the process. Because singer/songwriters are smart not to dilute their distinctive points of view and they answer the call of creativity at odd times, they usually keep to themselves in this regard.

Two Heads Are Better than One

For you and me, however, if we have designs on seeing our songs rise to the top of the charts—and something tells me that we do—cowriting is definitely the most advantageous way to go. Nearly every writer I've interviewed for this book has touted the advantages of collaboration in song: both for creative reasons and for the purpose of expanding each song's opportunities in the marketplace.

What are the reasons for this unanimity? First, let's discuss the creative advantages. A constructive collaboration can make a song more universal. This is the flipside of the singer/songwriter coin. While the artist conceiving something for himself sets out to make that piece as personal as possible, in a style only he or she can deliver, you and I are out to compose a song that we hope hundreds of artists will want to perform, in a style that is simultaneously fresh and yet, enduring, familiar, and relatable. While the artist might be tempted to challenge his audience by traveling to uncharted territories, discovering unconventional structures, trying out unusual chord changes, and delving into symbolic, lyrical obscurities, you and I will try to write something special, within more traditional structures, using more customary musical, and literal, lyrical motifs. The artist endeavors to put his own stamp, his or her own twist on the song, while you and I want to create a piece of work that as many people as possible will resonate with.

Working from the perspective of one, single songwriter can result in limited objectivity, thus leaving a good number of listeners in the dark. Whereas, if two capable writers agree that a line of lyric speaks directly to the truth of the song, it is far more likely that others will hear that same truth, understand it, and connect with it. Furthermore, if that theory holds water, it stands to reason that three perspectives might even increase the universality of the message that much more. This, of course, presumes that all collaborators are shooting for the same goal and care enough to stick with it until every single phrase is perfect. Warning! This is not always the case. A song's greatest enemy is summed up in the following words: "That's good enough." Good enough, quite honestly, simply is *not* good enough. So, as you go about choosing who you spend your precious time collaborating with, always seek writers who are committed to writing the best song possible—*every time out.* If you and your cowriter(s) have a solid song concept and you dare each other to excellence, you just might find your way to a competitive copyright, even a great one, one that both or all of you will be proud to play for anyone in the business.

Sometimes, even when a pair or trio of dedicated, professional, song crafters come together, it just doesn't click. I've spent more than a few red-faced hours with top writers, sitting in silence, staring at my computer screen. Arranger/composer, and pop-songwriting legend, Steve Dorff says, "I've sat in the room with great writers, big-name writers, where we've just stared at each other for three hours, and we said, 'Let's just go to lunch.'" That's usually no reflection on any one particular person in the room. As in all relationships, chemistry happens, or it doesn't. Ain't nothin' you can do 'bout that.

By comparison, Dorff mentions a song that became a classic for Kenny Rogers. "For 'Through the Years,'" he recalls, "Marty Panzer handed me the lyric, and it was finished in twelve minutes." But, even Steve Dorff struggles sometimes, kids. It's okay for a song to take months, even years to ripen to its full potential. You can't preheat the oven and set the timer on a great song. It takes as long as it takes; simple as that. On rare, magical occasions, it comes spilling out whole, complete, and perfect. Another one may require multiple, excruciating surgeries. The important thing is to roll up your sleeves and work on it until the last note sits in perfect tandem with the final word. What a great feeling that is, to know that you've had a hand in creating something of excellence!

Some days, too, seem more inspired than others. However, at the end of any given day, whether the collaboration cooked on all burners or produced a tepid, uninspired mess, you will always write a very different song when two or more creative talents are focused on the task. And, I think that is something to celebrate. Besides, as Music Row hit man, Kent Blazy says, "It's more fun to be in a room with other people than being alone with yourself."

Taylor Swift's favorite cowriter, Liz Rose, agrees: "I like just sittin' in the room with somebody and talkin' about stuff. It's just more fun, and I'm more disciplined when I have to be there."

For the most part, Blazy and Rose are right. It usually *is* more fun to hang with your creative pals than to battle away at those elusive words and music in solitaire. However, I only wish that was the case every time. From my experience, collaborations are not always hunky dory. I've been locked in rooms all day long, with cranky, negative, self-righteous, and/or disrespectful cowriters. I've felt so unappreciated and frustrated that I've come close to walking out on sessions with people who failed to give my input any serious credence. Ironically, some of the most discomfiting partnerings resulted in major cuts. On occasion, it was me who was the source of the bad vibes in the room. If a song concept is mine, I have a tendency to hold stubbornly to my original vision, no matter how well meaning, courteous, or even how prestigious my cowriter is. When a couple of opinionated writers disagree on where a song should be going, those conflicting views can result in a creative train wreck. When you come to one of those extremely tense situations, something has to give; and I usually refuse to be the one to wave the white flag. A couple of very fruitful, collaborative relationships were forever damaged by my unwillingness to consider my cowriters' strongly held, contrary points of view. However, that's the dynamic nature of the creative process; and sometimes, even conflict contributes to a better song.

"Get with a lot of different people," advises multi-hit writer Tom Snow, "because a collaborator brings something to the table that you don't have. Even if the song isn't good and you want to get rid of the person, *every* collaboration is worthwhile. Some of it is painful, awful. You will find some like-minded folks and even some friction that makes the work better."

A writer can learn a whole heck of a lot by cowriting, especially when joining forces with more skilled and more experienced writers. It's no secret that a developing tunesmith should always try to "write up," meaning that an unproven newcomer's reputation and skill set can get a real boost from booking appointments with bona fide, established writers. However, you shouldn't be offended if a more successful tunesmith turns down your proposal of a co write. Pop songwriting is, after all, not just a means of self-expression, it's a business. "I write to sell," says Dorff. "I mean, I love writing songs. But, that's my trade. It's a commercial endeavor for me and it always has been." A top-pro writer, like Steve Dorff, has to see the upside of spending creative time with you. Unless you're a promising new artist with a burgeoning career, you'll need to bring something more than a few good ideas to the table. Maybe you know an intriguing, up-and-coming, young writer/performer you can plug into the mix. Otherwise, if you're not signed to a publisher, don't employ a plugger, are not equipped with the resources to pay for demos, and your discography is blank, what is it about you—above every other eager, ambitious song scribe—that you think might convince a hit writer to give you a shot? Think about that before you approach an established professional for a chance to cowrite. You'd better have an angle, something pretty special to offer, or your chances to "write up" will remain pretty remote.

It's hard, even for well-known, established writers to get activity with their songs. Rose advises writers to be smart about whom they write with. "It's good when there's a strong publisher and plugger behind your cowriter because it usually takes the writers, the publisher, *and* the plugger to make it happen," she explains. If you're going it on your own, it almost doesn't matter to most pro writers how talented you are. Says Rose, pragmatically: "It takes a damn continent, a whole country to get a song cut!"

When Tim James started commuting back to Tennessee from L.A. to write songs, he relied on a reservoir of personal magnetism and bravado to get cowriting appointments. Then, after getting in the door, his natural instincts and talent carried him through. As he is eminently likeable, James' friends felt no compunction in introducing him to other friends. I can't remember who sent James my way, but I'll be eternally grateful for that referral. In James, I recognized a fun guy, with a great sense of humor and a decent amount of raw talent, who always tried to partner with more successful writers. At first, I thought he was just trying to hitch his star to his collaborators and do a little name dropping, but he set me straight. He tells me now that it was really more about learning his craft. "It's like when you're playin' ball; if you play with better guys, you have to lift your game. Even now, I try to get with people who are better. If I do, I gotta bring it."

Great collaborations can produce a logarithmic curve of creativity. "A lot of times, two heads are better than one," Blazy remarks. Then, he adds, "Cowriting is the breath of Nashville." It wasn't always that way. In fact, only a few decades back, many Nashville publishers actually discouraged their staff writers from cowriting songs, particularly with writers signed to other companies. Publishers had no interest in splitting a copyright with a competitor. Not only would sharing income diminish immediate revenues, it was a common belief that not owning and controlling an entire copyright would make a catalog sale difficult and cumbersome. When writers from two different Music Row operations started getting together, it became commonplace for the two publishers to take turns publishing every other title. In this random roll of the dice, one company might strike gold with 100 percent of a massive hit, while the other publisher missed the boat entirely. In retrospect, this was a pretty self-defeating policy.

Music Row's Father of Cowriting

In Nashville songwriting lore, the writer who is often mentioned as the father of cowriting is a modest, soft-spoken fellow named Rory Michael Bourke. "My grandparents adored Cole Porter and Jerome Kern," Bourke recalls. So, Bourke's childhood was accompanied by 78 RPM discs of the pop classics of the 1920s, '30s and '40s. As they were Irish Catholic, Bing Crosby was a household favorite. Living next door to the manager of a Cleveland movie house, young Rory was exposed to screenings of every MGM musical "...where people seemed so happy, dancing, and singing," he recounts. Sitting in the dark of the Cedar Lee Theater, Bourke looked up at Fred Astaire and Ginger Rogers on the screen, thinking, *Boy, it would be nice to be like that.* Coming from that environment, Bourke developed a strong affinity for music and lyrics and, as a student at Mount St. Mary's College, he started writing his first songs. Returning home to Ohio after graduation, he went to work as a radio promo man for Mercury Records' regional distributor. After two years, Mercury moved Bourke to national promotion in Chicago. There, he befriended a singer/songwriter/producer from Nashville named Norro Wilson. That relationship led to Bourke's first significant cut, which was Wilson's version of Bourke's "Love Comes but Once in a Lifetime."

Bourke ended his 6-year stint with Mercury doing sales and promotion for Jerry Kennedy's Nashville country division. "It was during that time that I met Eddie Rabbitt," Bourke remembers, "who was kind enough to write some songs with me." Rory Bourke was now a full-time tunesmith. "Paul Richey had a company with Pete Drake, and they would pitch my songs. Gayle Barnhill and I wrote one for Mel Tillis called 'Neon Rose'; and it was a pretty big hit for him." That song put Bourke on the charts. On the recommendation of Don Gant of Acuff/Rose, Henry Hurt (who Bourke calls "a terrific guy") signed Bourke to his first publishing deal. It was 1972, and Chappell Music was just opening its Nashville office. When I asked Bourke why it was that so many people seemed to give him credit for opening the cowriting floodgates in Music City, this is how he responded: "I don't know. It's not like Rory Bourke stepped off the bus and said, 'Let's start cowriting.' You're not the first person say that to me. So, all I can say is, yes, I did cowrite. Yes, that's about all I *did* do. I learned pretty quick that, if I was gonna make a living as a songwriter, songs I wrote by myself weren't gonna pay the bills too well."

As it turns out, cowriting *did* pay the bills, *big time.* Because he could hear every song through the ears of a radio program director or a disc jockey, Bourke added a unique perspective to the collaborative process. Here's how he explains it: "I felt that the experience I brought to the table from a record-business perspective was helpful. I knew pretty much what a bad record sounded like and what a great one sounded like. So, in my mind, everything sort of a had to slant away from what people didn't want to play on the radio."

With his old pal, Norro Wilson, Bourke cowrote a song called "The Most Beautiful Girl." Wilson's Joe Stampley production on the tune failed to take off, so Wilson took the song to Billy Sherrill, suggesting that the songwriter/super-producer cut it with Charlie Rich. "Billy felt that the song had some problems, and he fixed 'em," Bourke says now. "I wish I had been in the room because I would have learned something. But, Billy and Norro tweaked it just right." Although Sherrill didn't want to release the Rich recording, the secretaries at Columbia Records badgered him into putting it out as the follow-up to "Behind Closed Doors." "The Most Beautiful Girl" spent three weeks at Number One on the country charts and two weeks atop the Hot 100. Due to the continuous efforts of Al Gallico Publishing, the song has been recorded countless times in numerous languages and continues to this day to be one of those ubiquitous and lucrative copyrights we all dream of creating someday. Rory Michael Bourke was on his way to the Songwriters Hall of Fame, but his cowriting successes didn't stop with one mega-hit.

"'The Most Beautiful Girl' kind of launched me in that sense," Bourke reflects. "But one huge hit can't do it for you. You still have to show more cards on the table in order to keep rising. It's an upward progression. That one song was incredibly important, but I never wrote with Billy and Norro again. So, if I hadn't been working really hard and cowriting with a lot of people, it's possible that might have been *it* for me." Bourke increased his cut list through the remainder of the '70s—songs co-written with Chappell-mates Johnny Wilson, Gene Dobbins, Charlie Black, and Jerry Gillespie—including a string of hits with Ann Murray. In the '80s, Bourke kept cookin' with Mike Reid, with songs recorded by Ronnie Milsap, Tanya Tucker, Sweethearts of the Rodeo, and Shenandoah.

"A lot of it happened," Bourke says, "because Mike was an artist on Columbia and everybody just loved what he was writing. Plus Rob Galbraith was Reid's publisher at Ronnie Milsap's company." Bourke went on to collaborate on some big hits with Phil Vassar, including Jo Dee Messina's "Bye Bye" and Vassar's "Little Red Rodeo." Bourke was inducted into the NSAI Hall of Fame in 1989.

What exactly is it that has kept Rory Bourke coming back to cowriting time and time again? First, collaboration always makes for an entirely different song than writing by oneself. Bourke reflects on his 1986 George Straight Number One, cowritten with Glen Ballard and Kerry Chater: "I really don't think any of the three writers on 'You Look So Good In Love' would have written that song without three writers being there." Even for this veteran hitmaker, cowriting provides a continuous education in craft. "I've learned something from everybody I've ever written with," Bourke explains. "That's hopefully why you cowrite. You learn to be a better writer and a better cowriter." Having sat in a room many times with this legendary song craftsman, I know he's sincere when he says, "I just love music, I love writing, and I like people." This author feels privileged that Bourke might once have thought the following about me: "You never really know. The next person you sit down with could be the really big one. Not the big one. The *REALLY* big one!"

Greater than the Sum of Its Parts

Nowadays, in a town where cowriting was once strongly dissuaded, it's not uncommon for as many as a dozen separate people to climb on stage to collect a BMI, ASCAP, or SESAC award for a single song. If there are three or even four writers, there might also be eight or nine publishers, all of whom own a percentage of the copyright and presumably played some part in its success. I guess the point here is this: Sometimes a hit song really does take a continent, as Liz Rose said. This is where the psychology and politics of the music business really come into play. Let's say three writers write and demo a song. There's a strong likelihood that one of the song's publishers will be more enthused about it than the other two. If the plugger from that first publisher runs right out and gets a hold on the song—with a top producer for a major-artist project—that activity dares the other publishers to wake up, take notice, and match the zeal of the first publisher. It becomes contagious; activity creates more activity. Or, a more common scenario is that all three publishers *claim* to love the song, but none of them actually makes it a priority pitch. If that happens, this song is liable to start collecting dust pretty quickly, unless the writers take the bull by the horns and start scaring up some industry interest. Maybe one of the writers is pals with a hot producer or a newly signed artist. Through that relationship, he gets a hold on the song. Once again, the writer going to bat for himself inspires the rest of the partners to get involved and show what they can do on the song's behalf. It becomes competitive. One person picks up the ball and carries it. That initiative rallies everyone else to get involved and start blocking, or maybe even accept a lateral and run with it for awhile, as the team moves the ball up the field. It doesn't guarantee a score; but having all of this cooperative muscle behind a song can be a big factor in giving it a better chance to cross the goal line.

"Two publishing companies are better than one," Kent Blazy explains. "The more people you have out on the street with a song, the better it could be for you. It kind of ups your chances." It's simple math, the law of probability. The more folks you have putting their enthusiasm into action and pitching a song, the more exposure it gets. The more exposure it gets, the better its chances are of finding the right artist to record it. Once there is real interest and energy around the song, everyone can use his or her own relationships to work toward actualizing the cut and its release. Once a song gets recorded and released, publishers (and even individual songwriters) have been known to invest in supplemental, independent radio promotion and/or trade ads in support of a certain record. Putting five grand into extra promotion can sometimes make the difference between a $20,000 copyright and one worth $200,000—or even $2 million—because PRO income increases many times over with every week a song remains on the charts and with every higher chart position it achieves.

So, to sum up: Cowriting is usually more fun than writing by oneself. Cowriting offers every writer—from the beginner to the most seasoned—an opportunity to learn something valuable from his or her collaborators. Cowriting usually results in a song that has more universal appeal, because if two or more good writers agree that the song is working, it's more likely that the industry and the public will concur. Regardless of how much or how little each collaborator contributes, cowriting certainly always produces a different song than a song written by an individual writer. And, finally—and probably most importantly—cowriting can give a song greater exposure, activity, and backing, because more writers, more publishing partners, and more representatives stand behind it and have something to gain from its potential success.

CHAPTER 21
Writing For Yourself, As The Artist

Maybe you began jamming on chord changes, humming extemporaneous tunes, and grabbing rhymes out of the ether because you had some elation, epiphany, or heartbreak you just had to get out of your system, a gush of emotion that you feared, if left unexpressed, might cause your young heart to explode. Perhaps you felt invisible and unheard and desperately needed to share your deepest thoughts and feelings with the world. You discovered that whispering or wailing words on melody was the most obvious and available means of articulating those passions. Or, like me, you might have seen Mick Jagger on *The Ed Sullivan Show,* shaking a pair of maracas, undulating those slender hips, and quivering his liver lips. The kids in the crowd were going nuts, and you thought, *Hmmm, I'd like to make the girls squirm and scream like that, too.* Whatever the motivation, you now feel the daily compulsion to hunker down with a six-string or a keyboard, dial up your personal muse, and make stuff up, stuff you fully intend to perform someday for thousands, at arenas and stadiums around the world. If so, you are one of the tortured, yet-blessed creatures, the species known as the singer/songwriter.

Without a doubt, being a performing tunesmith requires an innate, blind trust in some form of divine inspiration. After all, those flashes of genius have to come from somewhere out there in the cosmos. However, if you do feel inspired to write 'em for the purpose of pickin' and grinnin' for the people, you should have some strategy behind how you concoct songs for yourself to perform as an artist. You need to pen vehicles that set you apart from the pack, draw maximum attention your way, accelerate your career progress, and build and sustain your success. How do you suppose a nasal-voiced, Minnesota nebbish named Robert Zimmerman became the singer/songwriters' icon of icons, Bob Dylan? Do you honestly think that little Zimmie just magically morphed from a leather-jacketed, teenaged rocker into the world-renowned, Midwestern ramblin'-man, folkie/poet? Surely, that clever, curly-topped fellow put some substantial consideration into that transformation. While divine inspiration certainly played its part, far more than kismet had to be involved in the Zimmerman-to-Dylan transformation. Bruce Springsteen didn't become The Boss just because he felt an undeniable impulse to tell song-stories about growing up in New Jersey. Surely, Springsteen calculated his assets, took a realistic look at his audience, and thought about how his songs could connect directly with them. No doubt that evaluation continues to this day, because The Boss is still The Boss and rockin' on—at 60.

To one degree or another, it's the same truth for every iconic, innovative, and enduring recording artist of the modern pop and rock era, from David Bowie to Madonna, from Marvin Gaye to Usher, from REM to U2, from Pink to Lady Gaga. As you may recall, we started this journey by casting a look over our shoulders to reflect on the songs that had the greatest impact on our youthful hearts. I urged you to list and re-examine those compositions in search of the qualities that first appealed to you strongly, directly, and personally. So, by the same token, if you're a performing songwriter, it might be of some real value to observe what it was about your favorite artists (and their songs) through the years that piqued your curiosity and won your loyalty as a fan. In my case, I could reflect on what it was about the Rolling Stones that compelled me to fork over my hard-earned cash for every single one of their LPs from 1964 to 1970. What was it about Paul Simon, Jackson Browne, Peter Gabriel, and Dire Straits that got me scooting down to the record store to grab a copy each and every time those artists released a new album?

Take a look at the most beloved artists of the last 50 years (names chosen at random and off the top of my head): Michael Jackson, Led Zeppelin, James Taylor, the Bee Gees, Billy Joel, Neil Young, Elton John, Fleetwood Mac, Prince, AC/DC, Al Green, Joni Mitchell, Bon Jovi, Sheryl Crow, Garth Brooks, Tom Waits, Aerosmith, Alanis Morissette, Metallica, Mariah Carey, Eminem, Ricki Lee Jones, the Dixie Chicks, Elvis Costello, Beck, the names could go on for pages. Certainly this brief list covers a gamut of styles and genres. Each act appeals to a different part of the human musical taste bud. There is nothing whatsoever formulaic about any of these artists' music. In other words, nobody could rightly accuse any of these icons of painting by the numbers. While leaning on their individual influences and building on the foundation of their own musical roots, each of these superstars found a one-of-a-kind path on the way to carving his, her, or their place in the pantheon of pop music. What then, at the end of the day, do all of these great artists have in common?

Perhaps you've already taken notice that all of the names I've mentioned so far have been responsible for writing all of or most of their own songs. That's the first thing this elite bunch have in common: They are all singer/songwriters. Now, there are a number of admirable recording artist/performers who are not known as writers, including Ray Charles, Elvis Presley, Aretha Franklin, Linda Ronstadt, George Strait, Barbara Streisand, Tony Bennett, Tim McGraw, Celine Dion, Faith Hill, Bette Midler, Michael Bublé, and Andrea Bocelli. This list, too, could go on and on. These singers all have a shared quality: a talent for identifying songs by outside writers that they can interpret believably and deliver honestly to their fans. But as I am writing a guidebook for songwriting success, I won't delve into a discussion of the nonwriting crowd on these pages, as worthy as they are.

Who Are You?

Singer/songwriters appoint themselves with an added responsibility, and that is to create the vehicles with which they communicate to the world. So, I think it would be safe to presume that those who have found success have made some very essential and very conscious decisions. Presumably, each great songwriter/performer has explored various options along the way, and finally decided what style of music best exhibits his or her most positive and appealing talents, while simultaneously reflecting his or her deepest musical passions. Beyond that, they have all examined what lyrical themes and messages speak honestly and sincerely from their heart of hearts directly to their audience. This process of self-examination has probably taken place almost nonstop, throughout their careers, with every song they write, and with every record they make. The resulting self-awareness—brought about by constant introspection—allows each one of these artists to blend together the most critically important ingredients that ultimately add up to singer/songwriter success: a believable style; a recognizable sound; and, a distinctive point of view. In other words, not only do you know 'em when you hear 'em, you believe what you hear, and you also know where they stand and how they feel about the world they live in. When combined with an intriguing, attractive, and recognizable visual image, that sonic stamp and consistent attitude amount to a potentially perfect recipe for a highly successful career as a performing songwriter. Here's the equation: the look + the sound + the point of view = the singer/songwriter's brand.

Wait a minute, you may be thinking, *this guy's trying to turn me into a product!* No, I'm not. In fact, I couldn't do that to you if I tried. It's too late for that because, my friend, you've already made that decision, by deciding to pursue a performing career. What every artist (songwriter or not) must understand is that they are constantly straddling an invisible line. On one side is the artist persona, the sensitive and vulnerable, or tough and macho, or caring and instructive (whatever your posture or point of view) creative soul, who shares his or her most intimate fears and passions through words and music. On the other side is the package, the commodity, the product. These two seemingly conflicting characters meld together into one, single brand in the eyes of your fans. To them, you are your songs and your songs speak for you. You are your sound and your look. More than anything, you are your attitude. So, although you may think that you're trying to sell your recorded music to the masses—and certainly, hopefully, people will purchase your CDs, your records, your audio files—the reality is this: Your fans are buying *you*, not any one song or a collection of them. Your songs are your advertisements, your audio logos, your musical calling cards. Each one makes a statement as to who you are as a person and what you stand for. But, in the long run, you should be hoping that your devotees are taking you home with them, that they are putting you on their iPod and not just a favorite track.

That's why I bought all those Stones records. Mick and the boys spoke so loudly and clearly to my teenaged heart that I invited them to share my space. Keith Richards motored me with his raw electricity. Brian Jones colored my imagination. Charlie Watts and Bill Wyman laid down a slip-sliding groove for my daily dance. Those guys were bad; it was obvious. This bunch had some nasty secrets, and they let just enough out to keep me completely intrigued: Mick had some Siamese cat of a girl under his thumb; you wouldn't dare play with that dude, 'cause you'd be playin' with fire; he laid a gin-soaked barroom queen in Memphis. I got it. And they had me rushing down to Sears to buy each and every album.

However, every performer has to come from somewhere. The Stones started out in London, playing Chicago blues, Bo Diddley, and Chuck Berry covers at The Crawdaddy Club. The band was already under contract to Decca Records before they penned their first songs, on a dare from manager/producer Andrew Loog Oldham. Oldham considered it a drawback for the band to exclusively perform material written "by middle aged blacks." While Oldham defined their first collaborations as "soppy and imitative," Jagger and Richards eventually developed into one of the most prolific and ground-breaking pop/rock songwriting teams of all time. Why? Because they had a firm foundation in roots R&B and because their songs have always spoken their own truth, revealing how they feel about the real world around them.

A contemporary of the Stones, Graham Nash states, "What we have always tried to do as artists is to reflect what is going on around us and reveal what is going on inside of us." Sage words indeed. You might recall another little British combo, this one from Liverpool. The Beatles got their start playing for locals at tiny clubs like The Cavern. Heavily influenced by the hits of the Everly Brothers, Buddy Holly, and Elvis Presley, the earliest Lennon and McCartney compositions were almost all about young love: "She Loves You," "I Want to Hold Your Hand," "Please, Please Me." This was the same ground that pretty much all the other pop acts of the day were covering, including Leslie Gore, the Four Seasons, the Phil Spector and Brill Building acts, the early Motown artists. So, what made The Beatles' POV fresh and new? First, of course, they made a statement with their image. Their long-haired look was cute and cuddly, while being playfully rebellious. It won them lots of attention. However, those mop tops would have been pure gimmick had the music not related in a very direct way to the teen audience of the day. Why did those songs connect so strongly? I think it was because their music had an urgency about it. It was not only crafty and extremely well written; it was imbibed with genuine, youthful passion and exuberance. The Beatles didn't just sing *about* young love, they replicated the experience itself, as if their own, youthful hearts were about to burst with passion. That urgency made the teens of the day feel like these four fresh Liverpudlians really knew what they were singing about.

The Beatles marked a rebirth, a renaissance of rock and roll because at the very essence of rock music is passion. And there is no more passionate time of anyone's life than those teenage years. First love. Heartbreak. Obsession. Crushes. All that stuff is prime material for songs because songs, in essence, are primarily emotional things.

The Beatles were young, passionate guys. Surely they were falling in and out of love on a weekly basis, getting crushes and suffering broken hearts. They wrote about what they knew about. That's exactly why Taylor Swift has become such a phenomenon. It's certainly not because she's the greatest singer of all time. She writes smart, passionate, well crafted songs about what she and her peers experience, and every other teenaged girl can relate. So, like Ms. Swift and the early Beatles, you as an artist have to be as genuine as you can be in your songwriting. You should be writing songs about subject matter and in a style of music to which you're absolutely committed. Try to refrain from jumping on a bandwagon just because it's trendy, unless that trend represents who you genuinely are as an artist and as a person. Just because you admire a certain performer or are enamored of a certain musical genre doesn't necessarily mean that's the direction you should be going.

I admit it. I was a fickle young performer, who followed trend after trend. Not only did I jump from one style to another—basically on a whim—I also allowed so-called experts to define me. "I see you as the next Billy Joel," an A&R genius might say. *Yes,* I'd excitedly ponder to myself. *I can pull that Billy Joel thing off. Then, when I hit it big, I can show the world who I really am.* Being young, talented, and attractive can be a curse because many people will see an opportunity to manipulate your gifts to their advantage. While you might score a hit or two under the thumb of some Svengali, that is not how real careers are born and you will certainly end up unfulfilled and miserable. Honesty is the best policy. Step back; take stock. Endeavor to write and perform songs that resonate truthfully and emotionally in your heart. Always be aware that your songs inform the world who you are and what you care about. When any artist, at whatever level, reveals the truth of his, her, or their experience in song in a truly genuine and emotional way, there *will* be an audience for that work. If you feel strongly about something and you put it in a song, then perform it in a style that really exposes your natural talents, others out there will respond positively—*if they get the chance to hear it.* The more universal the truth is in your writing and the more accessible your songs are, the larger your potential audience can be.

It comes down to this: Every successful performing songwriter must look in the mirror and recognize his or her own strengths and weaknesses. Knowing what you do well helps you become aware of which personal attributes are most attractive to your fans. Having that knowledge gives you the opportunity to hone your songs to appeal directly to your fans and deliver them in a style and with an attitude they will accept coming from you. In this modern age, we are not in business just to write honest, deeply felt songs and hope they find ears willing to give them a listen. We are in the business of marketing ourselves as products, through the songs we write, record, and perform.

Besides, we're music fans, too. So, let's give ourselves some credit. We know a sincere, heartfelt performance when we hear it; and, we can spot a phony poser from a mile away. The public is equipped with a B.S. detector. So, a smart singer/songwriter doesn't try to contrive anything by setting out to play a part that is unnatural or light years away from his native character. A smart singer/songwriter doesn't try to make statements he doesn't believe, in a style of music he doesn't feel comfortable with. A smart singer/songwriter always knows where that invisible line is and keeps one foot rooted in the truth of who he is and where he came from. Besides, if all goes well, you're going be out there peddling your wares 100 to 300 nights a year, shaking your butt in front of crowds of people for decades to come. Do you really want to be putting yourself up there night after night performing music you don't believe in? I don't think so. That's not a recipe for success. It's more like a prescription for mental illness.

Your Brand: Generic? Hybrid? Groundbreaking?

The modern world honors marketing over music. Marketing oneself can create a bit of a struggle, because the music business, like all of the entertainment industry, likes to think in easily marketable, generic terms. We've all heard the question: "What kind of band are you?"

"Oh, we're alt-country," or "industrial metal," or "post-hardcore," or "progressive folk..." Whatever! Everybody and their mother wants to put you in some specific, neatly definable bag so they'll know what kind of songs they can expect to hear from you, and what core fan base to market you to. Now think of the great, groundbreaking artists of the rock era. There was no heavy metal before Led Zeppelin or Deep Purple or Black Sabbath. There was no power pop before The Beatles, The Hollies, and The Searchers. No glam rock before Bowie, T Rex, and Roxy Music. No art rock before Pink Floyd, King Crimson, and Yes. No punk before The Ramones, Sex Pistols, and The Clash. No grunge before Nirvana, Pearl Jam, and Soundgarden.

How do you define Dave Matthews Band? Before that eclectic, hybrid ensemble arrived on the scene, was there a generic term that called to mind a group with an art-folk lead singer, with a jazzy back-up band, featuring sax *and* fiddle? No, of course not. They created their own unique brand. How does somebody like Lyle Lovett fit in? He's not really country or a traditional acoustic singer/songwriter is he? Or how about Harry Connick, Jr.?

Michael Penn, a brilliant singer/songwriter and producer (and Sean Penn's brother, by the way), said one of the most accurate things I've ever heard about the music business: "Record companies are like cat breeders. They find a cat that sells, then they inbreed it 'til it dies off." It's true of television and movies too. One successful new show or film breeds clone after clone. The ratings bonanza of *Friends,* for instance, sent the networks into a frenzy, creating copycat after copycat featuring young, quirky pals spouting punch lines filled with sexual innuendo. *Napoleon Dynamite* spawned a new genre of goofy, teen-oriented films. Each one was a paler copy of the one before, until what's left is bland, predictable, and virtually worthless. Creed, a band that was unable to get a major record deal, created a genre of what I like to call "shout-rock." (I don't even know what the official name is.) Creed's sonic template inspired a whole bunch of hugely successful impersonator acts, including Nickelback and Hinder.

It's your decision as the artist. (And, there is no right or wrong answer here.) Do you want to go the difficult road of carving your own path by creating your own individual style and stamp? Or, if you feel committed to a certain genre, do you want to go the equally risky path of jumping on some stylistic trend? By risky, I mean that, by the time you get your act together, the capricious pop world may have moved on to some *new* trend. And yet, some genres never seem to die off, do they? Heavy metal, power-pop, acoustic-alternative, jam bands, dance music all just keep hanging in there, generation after generation. These styles may fall in and out of mainstream commercial favor; but a few purveyors of those genres always seem to be in the game to one degree or the other, continuing to reach a mass audience.

So the real risk is in jumping on some temporary, here-today, gone-tomorrow fad, having devoted a lot of your songwriting talent, months, possibly even years of your time, and a whole bunch of resources to developing material that could only work in one trendy genre that might just become passé overnight. On the other hand, if you boldly blur accepted, generic boundaries by trekking into unexplored territory, creating some new hybrid or experimental style, you risk delaying—or, worse yet, never even realizing—the success you seek. Why? Because it will probably take much longer for the public to get used to something new and embrace it, assuming you can find an audience at all. Being an artist is *always* a risky proposition, but if you play it smart by letting your songs help you find and expand your audience, you can increase your chances of reaching your highest potential success level. Just as with the iconic performing songwriters you and I have admired all our lives, the songs you write for yourself to record and perform are of critical importance to the way you're perceived by your fans and by the public at large.

So, even though I strongly urge you to write songs that are emotionally resonate with you, songs that speak truthfully about who you are and what you care about, I also recommend that you really get to know your fans. You don't have to know every one of them personally, by name.

You do, though, have to know what kind of people they are, what they care about, and most of all *why they are devoted to you.* If you don't know these essential things about your following, you can't communicate effectively with them. As your songs are, for the most part, the conduits through which you communicate to your audience, doesn't it make sense that you would be better served to write, record, and perform songs that appeal and connect to your fan base, and to frame those songs in a way that really speaks directly to them? The artists who succeed and sustain careers know who their audience is, what makes them tick, and what kind of songs their audience will believe, coming from them.

How do you suppose Madonna has kept her persona so fascinating to her fan base for nearly 30 years? Here's an artist who has marginal talent as a singer/songwriter. She's not what you'd call a conventional beauty. However, at 50, to a lot of music fans, she is still the hippest thing going. Why? Because she knows her audience and continually remains intriguing to them, by growing and changing just enough to keep them interested, without losing them. Her career demonstrates true artistry, combined with equally brilliant self-marketing, carefully and thoughtfully straddling that invisible line between artist and product.

In country music, no artist has a more solid knowledge of his audience and keeps on delivering the goods to them than Toby Keith. After a brief career as a semipro football player and a wildcatter in the Oklahoma oil fields, Keith grabbed his axe and headed for the country honky-tonk circuit. Lacking the chiseled features of George Strait, the taut physique of Clint Black, or the vocal acumen of Vince Gill, Keith was relegated to last on the bill at the boot-scootin' dancehalls of the Southwest. With a third-rate band, a second-rate voice, and some fairly decent songs, he made it through his sets mainly on bravado. Then, he'd spend hours after those shows, making himself available at his merchandise table until his last fan had left the club. He sold cassettes and T-shirts and posed for snap shots, while he got to know the people. Those visits informed Keith a great deal about what attracted his following to him: his rugged, bigger-than-life, rebel-next-door swagger, his outspoken candor, and his willing, winning smile. It was market research of the most basic kind. The artist began to refine his songwriting style to consistently represent the character his fans found irresistible, which was the likeable, what-you-see-is-what-you-get, genuine article. So, when Music Row tried to give him a makeover, smoothing the rough edges of his image, Keith refused to play that game. The big guy had become keenly aware of his strongest appeal, and he was determined not to allow himself to be homogenized. Almost 20 years later, Toby Keith owns his own empire because his songs have always spoken the truth about who he is and how he views the world.

A superb singer I've used on several demo sessions—a gracious man, with a unique, velvety voice and an attractive look—told me quite a different story. When this dude arrived in Nashville, he was fronting a Southern-rock band, had hair down to his waist and always wore a signature pair of leather pants. It wasn't long before he and his mates attracted a development deal with a mid-major label. By the end of their first contract year, the label had convinced the singer to fire his bandmates, to cut his long hair off, and forego his leather trousers for a pair of jeans. Then, they put him in the studio to cut a bunch of formulaic pabulum. When the label decided not to pick up his first option, an A&R exec had the nerve to say, "You're not the artist we signed. You've changed." Yeah? No s**t!

I saw Ray LaMontagne on an episode of Sundance Channel's concert series, *Inside Abbey Road.* A soulful artist of genuine integrity and a throwback to the singer/songwriters of the 1970s, who defies every contemporary cliché, LaMontagne said something that stuck with me (I'm paraphrasing here): "We work all of our lives to become unique. Then, when that uniqueness gets us a record deal, we have to work for the rest of our careers to hold onto the qualities that attracted the record company in the first place." It's a constant struggle, at every step of the hike, a push-pull between an artist's native instincts and what the industry expects. But, it's the artist who can straddle that line effectively who finds success and holds onto it.

Basically, that's what we're talking about here. It's a very good idea for a writer/performer to put some regular thought behind a very crass and commercial question: How do I use the songs I write to market myself to my core demographic? Even the cerebral Peter Gabriel has had the experience of being sent back to the woodshed for a commercial makeover. When A&R legend, John Kalodner, then of Asylum Records, informed Gabriel that the label didn't hear a single on his *Security* LP, the artist bit the bullet and wrote "Shock The Monkey." That charming, infectious tune made the difference between Gabriel's previous gold, cult status and him achieving multiplatinum as an established hitmaker. Gabriel was clever enough not to abandon his base audience in order to gain a larger one. He kept his unique, obtuse point of view and merely put a more marketable frame around it, by giving this song a playful, danceable rhythm and injecting some quirky sounds and repetitive hooks.

Newcomer Sara Barielles has a similar tale to tell about recording her debut LP, *Little Voice*. Label execs didn't hear a single and suggested that she round out the project with a relationship-themed song. "Love Song" was her retaliation to their meddling. So, in 2007, when we heard the girl sing, "I'm not gonna write you a love song," over the airwaves about three million times, she was singing to the brass at her label, not to a spurned lover. It worked big time, and Barielles has become one of the breakout singer/songwriters of the new millennium. So, it can be done. A savvy performing songwriter can retain his or her core, musical values and still find mass acceptance in the marketplace. Being aware of your own strengths and weakness, having an intimate knowledge of your fans, and recognizing what it is about you that most appeals to them should inform your songwriting. Arming yourself with that information gives you a huge advantage when it comes to finding, growing, and keeping your audience.

CHAPTER 22
WRITING WITH THE ARTIST

What is the most efficient and expedient way for a nonperforming writer to get songs recorded and performed? That answer should be as obvious as middle C on the closest keyboard: by writing songs *with* the artists who record and perform them. It's always to a writer's advantage to circumvent anyone who can possibly say "No" to a song. Writing with the artist eliminates every single one of the gatekeepers. It gets your song into the artist's hands in the most direct and advantageous way possible. Most artists feel extremely eager to participate in creating their own material. Writing their own records gives them cred, not to mention the potential of scads of supplemental income. Some writer/performers are even smart enough to be receptive to other writers' perspectives and ideas, especially the ideas of professionals with hit credentials.

However, you don't have to be a top pro to get cowrites with artists because there are thousands of fledgling artists with whom you can collaborate. Some of those baby acts will become tomorrow's superstars. For obvious reasons—whether writing solo or with a collaborator—artists set out to write songs in their own style, songs they can imagine themselves performing. When it ultimately comes down to deciding between one song and another, most artists naturally tend to favor their own compositions over outside songs. It's a pride-of-ownership thing (not to mention, in many cases, a lack-of-perspective thing). Thus, an artist's collaborator can reap beaucoup dividends from that artist's strong, not-always-objective desire to get his or her own songs on a project. However, this is not merely a one-way street. The artist can also benefit from collaboration, by gaining another point of view. The song can often be improved immensely, through the input and expertise of a second or even a third writer.

Over the last 30-some years, one of the premier, go-to, artist collaborators has been a ridiculously talented gentleman from South Florida named Desmond Child. Growing up poor and hungry, this ultra-gifted lad developed a strong determination to succeed in the music business. After cutting two albums with his own band, Desmond Child and Rouge, he caught the industry's ear as the co-architect of KISS's late-'70s smash, "I Was Made For Lovin' You." Paul Stanley then introduced him to Jon Bon Jovi and Richie Sambora, with whom Child wrote their band's career-launching single, "You Give Love a Bad Name," and follow-ups, "Livin' On a Prayer," and "Bad Medicine." In the '80s, Child scored hit collaborations with Aerosmith on "Angel," "Dude (Looks Like a Lady) ," and "Crazy"; Joan Jett on "I Hate Myself For Lovin' You" and Alice Cooper on the entire album *Trash*. He didn't just have rock hits, though. For Michael Bolton, he produced and penned "How Can We Be Lovers" (with Bolton and Diane

Warren), and he played the same, duel role for Cher's "Just Like Jesse James." In the '90s, Child scored the monster, international, Latin/pop hit, "Livin' La Vida Loca," with Ricky Martin. Since then, he has collaborated with Kelly Clarkson, Joss Stone, David Archuletta, Jesse McCartney, Hilary Duff, and Meat Loaf, among others. As of this writing, Child's most recent cowriter/producer chart-topper is a song I personally consider an instant pop-rock classic, Katy Perry's "Waking Up In Vegas." Jon Bon Jovi says that Desmond Child "taught me the next level of songwriting." It would be difficult to find a writer with more diverse artist cowriting credits than Desmond Child. Most of us would feel proud and grateful to claim even one of the hit copyrights that liberally pepper his discography.

We've already observed how Tom Snow's career profited from cowriting with Leo Sayer, how Kent Blazy hit the mother lode by collaborating with yet-to-be-famous Garth Brooks, and how Tim James reached the Top Ten by getting together with Stokes Neilson of Lost Trailers. I, too, have a good-sized list of credits from linking up with recording artists. I cowrote the title song to the film *Up The Creek* with Cheap Trick's Rick Neilson. I was privileged to collaborate with the artists on albums by Allan Clarke, Peter Noone, Vanilla Fudge, King Kobra, Kick Axe, and The Outlaws, among others. My Grammy-nominated song "So Close To the Fire" was written with the artist, singer/keyboardist Tommy Faragher. More recently, Carolina Rain lead singer Rhean Boyer and I cowrote their single, "Dealin'."

I genuinely enjoy writing with artists, particularly starry-eyed newcomers. In fact, since I've been spending so many of my days writing books, speaking, teaching, and doing workshops, I've had to become much more discrete as to how I use my writing time. So, I limit my cowrites almost exclusively to collaborating with young artists. I do this for several reasons. First, I've seen first-hand, time and time again, how my chances of getting a cut are increased by writing with the performer. Secondly, I know I have something unique to offer, meaning decades of experience, both professional and personal, that can potentially help a receptive, energetic writer/performer put a good song idea in its most attractive frame. Thirdly, if a song I cowrite with an artist should actually figure in launching his or her career, I stand to enjoy a good bit of positive recognition, along with some healthy royalties. However, my actual long-term goal is to become one of the artist's frequent collaborators for years to come. Whenever he, she, or they have an idea they're excited about, I want to be the guy they'll always call upon to help them bring that concept to its completion. Like Kent Blazy, I will usually give a young artist at least one shot at getting together and getting creative. If the chemistry is right and the artist demonstrates real potential for a successful career, I'll continue to carve out time in my schedule. Presently, I collaborate fairly regularly with at least a half dozen, young writer/performers, none of whom had record deals when we first started writing together, but several of whom are now on their way to very visible recording careers.

Keep Tabs on Up-and-Comers

As you go about your peer networking, try to develop a keen radar for youthful talent and star potential. Whether it is at demo sessions, writers' nights, club gigs, showcases, guitar pulls, networking events, barbecues, or clambakes, wherever you happen to be, keep your eyes peeled for that mysterious, charismatic, elusive élan. Remember, too, that raw talent and good looks are not the only important quotients in this equation. Drive, focus, dedication, passion, a willingness to show up anywhere and everywhere to perform, smile, and shake hands are also positive qualities to look for. These days, MySpace, Facebook, and Twitter skills have become an essential part of the whole package. So, if you discover a singer/songwriter with a great look, good chops, who seems to show up everywhere and is getting it done on Facebook, that kid might just be the industry's next darling. If you play your cards right, somewhere on down the line, you could be taking a ride on his or her gravy train.

As we all know, there are no guarantees. More often than not, even the most gifted singers fall short of putting all the ingredients together. Either that, or that fickle dame, Lady Luck, just doesn't arrive in a timely fashion. That's why you might consider writing with as many potential artists as you can get to know. Planting a lot of seeds will increase your chances of a bounteous harvest and will avoid the unfortunate, devastating crash that occurs when someone you've put two years of work into decides to get married and move to Baltimore (that actually happened to me). So keep that radar scanning for talent, but don't forget to water and fertilize the seedlings you've already planted.

Two decades ago, demo singers like Garth Brooks, Trisha Yearwood, and Billy Dean were passing through Kent Blazy's recording studio on a daily basis. These artists, and several others, eventually scored deals and went on to cut Blazy cowrites. If a youthful vocalist is booking sessions, he or she probably has something good going on. It's true, too, that working demo singers are constantly improving their studio chops, in preparation for the day when they'll have a chance to make their own records. You can also assume that, if a popular demo singer is young and attractive and has a proclivity for writing songs, then he or she is meeting writers nearly every day and fielding plenty of invites to collaborate. So, there is no time to waste. If the lady's hot and sings great, if the dude's got the goods, get in there and make the connection, but not aggressively or desperately. Just make it clear that you're open to setting up an appointment. Try to get something on the books, or at least put the subject of cowriting on the table and exchange contact info. The same goes for writers' nights and showcases. If a kid knocks your socks off, stick around after the set and make the approach. Say something sincere and flattering. Follow up with a little elevator speech about what you've been up to, and offer to get together. What's the worst thing that could happen? If you get shut down, you won't be any worse off than you were before (aside from some wounded pride). If you should connect, you've just created another world of possibilities in your writing career.

The Working Relationship

From my experience, writing with the artist requires a very different approach than getting together with a peer to pen something for the general marketplace. Remember, your goal here is to come up with a song that your collaborator will want to put her reputation and her career behind. You want her to emerge from this session feeling certain that, together, you've just come up with *the* song that will launch her career into the stratosphere. In addition, you're out to compose a song that she truly loves to sing and will continue to love performing hundreds of nights a year—for years to come. For the performer to genuinely love singing a song, she needs to resonate at gut-level with it; and, musically, the melody and dynamics need to be right in the center of her wheelhouse, featuring her most natural and appealing vocal qualities. If the song you write incorporates these two essential ingredients, she will feel confident of always delivering a fan-stirring performance, and her commitment to the song just might stay at its maximum.

So, keeping those goals in mind, you commence your session *not* by pitching her your best title, or detailing some well thought-out concept, or sitting right down to play a song fragment that occurred to you on the way to the appointment. You start by *listening* to her. You want to know what's on her mind, where she is emotionally at this very point in time, what she cares about *before* you even make a suggestion. Is she feeling vulnerable? Or is she ready to rock? Did she just suffer a devastating heartbreak? Or is she in the middle of a giddy, head-over-heels crush? Is she distracted or focused, fragile or empowered, bored or excited? Ask her if she has an idea she's dying to write today. If she didn't arrive with a song blooming, keep asking questions, discretely, with sensitivity, until you suss out what tempo, what mood is the right tone for the day. If she did show up with an idea, it's her show, you're just there to help. So, pledge to assist her, as she chases down the best song possible!

Assuming you're still searching for the idea of the day and you don't know her well, ask about where she came from, her siblings, parents, education, and so on. Get a sense of her values. If you do know her, be the concerned psychologist, taking notes on a tablet, asking, "And how did that make you feel?" Listen carefully to her answers and observe her body language. Then, as you continue to pay full attention, start going through your own list of song ideas, eliminating those that don't seem compatible with today's vibe and setting aside those that might fit the bill. If you're really listening (and you're prepared with a folder full of viable, interesting ideas), a concept will more than likely begin to take shape. Something she says might suddenly mesh mysteriously with a lyrical fragment you scribbled on a torn piece of paper yesterday, last week, or five years ago. "I don't know if this is anything you'd be interested in," you might say. "But how does this sound to you?" Then spill it. Whatever you do, don't announce, "This is a sure-fire career-launching smash for you." That's not for you to say. Let her make that determination herself. Her incentive for deciding what to write with you at this moment should be that you've shared an idea that truly resonates with *her* not because *you* think it's a hit idea. Just share the idea and flesh it out a little—the angle, the twist, the characters, the storyline—trying to match her state of mind and current situation. Keep it low key, and don't start pounding on your guitar. If she seems warm to the idea, ask her how she might hear it put it to music. She's the singer. The essential melody should come from her range, in her style, not yours. Encourage her to set the tone. Never impose your will or your style on any artist. If she doesn't hear a melody yet, you might then suggest a fragment of melody. If she likes it, ask her to try singing it in her own key. Odds are, she'll come out with her own interpretation, one that suits her own style. Don't insist that she sing it precisely, note-for-note, the way you've imagined it. Let it evolve naturally, as true collaboration.

A True Life Example

No songwriter I know has better mastered this process or had more success with it than my friend of more than ten years, Liz Rose. Liz arrived in Nashville from Texas, with her husband, Johnny, and their two young daughters, Caitlin and Hayley. Johnny wanted to try breaking into the Music Row songwriting game but instead took a marketing job at a record label. Liz found herself looking for something to do while the kids were at school. She recalls, "I was just doing it [writing] for fun every once in awhile with a couple of writers that I knew." When Johnny and Liz divorced, Liz started pitching songs to make a living. Meeting some very special songwriters along the way naturally led her from being a plugger to starting her own publishing venture, King Lizard Music. Liz started collaborating more and more with one of her writers, Kim Patton (now Kim McLean). "She taught me a lot," Rose says. When Rose's financial partner ran out of funds, former BMI exec and ex-MCA Music president, Jody Williams purchased the catalog. Williams began noticing right away that the Kim Patton/Liz Rose copyrights were some of his King Lizard favorites. He signed Patton and encouraged Rose to continue writing, putting her on the payroll as an independent plugger. After a short stint pitching songs at Encore Entertainment, Keith Follese fired Rose when the roster writers complained that she was pitching her own songs. Rose returned to pitch the Jody Williams Music catalog and keep writing. After a year, Jody said, "I want you writing full time," and he signed her to an exclusive publishing deal.

By this time, Patton and Rose had scored their first cut, "Harmless Heart," recorded by Keith Harling on Giant Records. Rose was part of a highly connected women's song plugging group called Chicks With Hits. At one of their pitch meetings, DreamWorks' Abby Nemesh insisted that Rose play "Harmless Heart" for producer Mark Wright. He cut it on Trisha Yearwood. Then, Patton's and Rose's "Elizabeth" was a single for Billy Gillman. After that, they got a Tim McGraw cut "All We Ever Find," through Missy Gallimore. Rose met 14-year-old Taylor Swift at a songwriters' guitar pull hosted by RCA Records. This is how Rose remembers that fateful day: "She heard a couple of my songs, came up to me, and asked me if I would write with her." Rose started booking a regular, once-a-week, writing appointment with Swift. "Jody told me I was spending too much time on this girl." (At the time, Taylor was between record deals.)

"Where is this going?" Williams wanted to know.

"I don't know," Rose replied, "but Taylor is going to do something. She's amazing, and this is the funnest, easiest thing I do all week long. So, I'm gonna keep doin' it."

Fortunately, Williams didn't stand in Rose's way. "The beautiful thing about writing for Jody Williams," she says, "was that he let me find my voice. He let me do what I wanted to do, and he never got in my way. I was in a situation where they told me to only write up-tempo radio candy, and I just about quit. With Jody, there were no boundaries. So, today, I can write with anybody."

Even back then, Taylor Swift was a very determined and self-aware young lady. "Can't you get her to write more country?" several industry folks challenged Rose.

"You can't get her to do anything," Rose responded. "Taylor writes Taylor's ideas. Taylor doesn't write other people's ideas. Taylor's just telling how she feels."

Six years later, Rose reflects, "That's why she's connected with all these kids—because someone's finally saying how they feel in their language. I loved writing with her. But she was a very strong force, and she knew *exactly* what she wanted to say, how she wanted to say it. And, I was *not* going to argue."

When asked how she goes about writing with an artist, Rose was generous enough to share her approach. "Instead of going in and saying, 'This is what *I* want to say today,' my whole focus is 'What's goin' on in *your* life?' and just getting them to talk," she explains. "And, while they're doing that, I'm not so much writing a song, I'm just writing down what they say. I want to write *their* song, not mine." This is obviously a big reason why Taylor Swift kept writing with Rose, and why songs they wrote during those weekly appointments are still finding their way to the top of the charts.

"I got really lucky with Taylor. But there were a lot of people Taylor quit writing with because they'd say 'Sit there, little girl. Let us write you a song.' They just wanted to get a cut with this artist, instead of really listening to who she was. They weren't smart enough—or dumb enough—to get out of the way. Or lazy—maybe I was just lazy!" Liz says, laughing heartily. "She scared the hell out of me, so I just said 'Okay, whatever you say!'"

Peaceful Collaboration

Once you've found a song idea that reflects the artist's current state of mind, continually defer to her, asking if it feels like the song is going in the right direction. If she's shy or reticent, you'll want to encourage her periodically to engage herself in the process. If she's forceful, be supportive and enthusiastic, and, like Rose did, try to keep up and help shape the song in progress. If it begins to take off in a direction you don't agree with, try to be diplomatic, using phrases like, "Maybe we should consider..." or, "The only thing I'm concerned about is..." Refrain from being abrasive, disrespectful, or argumentative. Do not imply in any way that you think you know more than she does. Just make it clear that you want to consider *all* the possibilities and not be impulsive. If she comes up with a lyric you think is mundane, banal, or cliché, try not to respond in a condescending fashion. Nod, say that you know where she's coming from, and make a suggestion to improve hers.

I remember hearing about one of my favorite songwriters, Gary Burr, who happened to be writing with a female superstar (whose name will remain unmentioned here). Reportedly, this was what was overheard from the adjacent writers' room: The lady star came up with a lyric line that was, in a word, lame. Burr responded by saying, "Good idea. I think what you mean is this..." He honored her contribution, then countered with the perfect line, which had a similar meaning but was a far better lyric. She felt involved in the process, but Burr was keeping control over the song's quality. Writing a song with an artist will not always be a piece of cake. Some artists simply can't see where their ideas are falling short. Some just keep spouting amateurish stuff and sometimes even insist on incorporating substandard lyrics or predictable, lazy phrases of melody into the piece. In those situations, you have got a real challenge, requiring a boatload of tact. It's incumbent upon you to explain why something might not be working by suggesting how it could be improved.

More than a few highly successful pros disdain writing with young artists. They figure that youth and inexperience add up to someone undeserving of an experienced writer's hard-won expertise. Some traditionalists even harbor the quaint notion that writers are writers and singers are singers, and those roles should forever remain separate. There's a famous story about one such hit Nashville writer, whose publisher had booked him to write with a newly signed recording artist. At the appointed time, the hit song scribe arrived with a cassette, around which he'd wrapped a folded lyric sheet, bound with a rubber band. When the excited young performer greeted his famous collaborator at the door, the haughty hitmaker handed the kid the cassette—lyric attached—and said, "Here's the song we wrote together. Have a great day." The pro turned, strutted to his car, and drove off, leaving the baffled—and presumably offended—young artist blushing on the doorstep. Only a writer of the highest stature could get away with such a self-important, disrespectful gesture.

I would never deign to presume my own superiority to any writer, regardless of his or her level of experience. After all, everybody has to start somewhere. For someone as jaded and world-weary as this old guy, it's invigorating to share space with a talented kid who has his whole life and career to look forward to. Song ideas that might seem stale and overused to me take on a fresh coat of paint with each new generation. It's fun to help a fledgling develop an idea that's important to him, to help him craft it into a tightly constructed and very personal statement.

Finding Balance

Some artist/writers will be relatively passive out of respect and deference to a collaborator, from a lack of confidence and experience, or even due to a deficit of ideas. Others, like young Taylor Swift, come in assertively and spearhead the entire process. Many are equal contributors or even do the lion's share of the work, while some are reluctant to speak up, even when urged to do so.

Regardless how much an artist participates in the crafting of a song, he or she always has an influence on the end result, by virtue of his or her presence in the room. You are wise to continually inquire whether the ship is headed in the right direction, and those responses and a regular body-language check, at the very least, should help guide you to a mutually acceptable destination. If he is not taking an active part, it's a very good idea to periodically request that he give a shot at singing what you've written. After brainstorming over a verse and/or a chorus and finding you're on the right track, nothing is more exhilarating than hearing a brand new composition brought to life for the first time by another voice, particularly when it's the voice of a great singer. Conversely, if you're on a wild goose chase, the artist's spontaneous rendering might just reveal that, as well. That revelation could ostensibly enable you to make the proper course adjustment or to scrap the voyage altogether and regroup.

Reaping the Benefits

January 31, 2010. As I watched The 52nd Annual Grammy Award broadcast, I was delighted to see Liz Rose's proud, beaming face in the first few rows of the star-studded Staples Center audience. From one row behind, Rose patted Taylor Swift lovingly on the back, as the shocked 20 year old rose from her chair to climb up on stage and accept her statuette, as the youngest recipient in Grammy history of the night's biggest prize, Album of the Year. It was the kid's fourth win of the night.

A relatively inexperienced songwriter said yes to a highly motivated 14 year old's invitation to cowrite. Despite her publisher's skepticism, Liz Rose kept writing with Taylor Swift. During their weekly appointments, the duo cowrote Swift's future hits, "Tim McGraw," "Teardrops on My Guitar," and "White Horse," among a raft of others. Some six years later, on a momentous night in January 2010, "White Horse" won a Grammy for Country Song of the Year. Imagine what that must have felt like for Liz Rose. In her own words: "I met Taylor in the beginning. We worked really hard. We created a great body of work. She's winning a lot of awards. She's selling a lot of records. We've won a Grammy." Then Rose laughs giddily, "Can you believe it? I won a Grammy!"

Swift and Rose no longer meet every week to write. Taylor's superstar commitments prohibit that. Rose says, "I'm not the kind of person who's going to jump on a bus. That's not me." But Rose makes it clear that her collaborative days with Ms. Swift have not come to an end. "Taylor's the type who, when she looks at something and says, 'I need to write this with Liz,' she'll pick up the phone and we'll write it." It was exactly one of those calls that inspired their reunion to write the crossover mega-hit, 2009's "You Belong To Me."

CHAPTER 23
Profiles of Songwriter/Producers

Next to being the artist who writes his or her own material, the most direct and unencumbered pathway to getting your songs recorded is to produce the record yourself. For decades, multitalented songwriters have asserted their leadership skills, applied their political savvy, and used their studio acumen to get their songs on sessions. As it wasn't until the cusp of the 1950s and '60s that producers were first credited on records, who knows how many songwriters were actively involved in the recording of their own songs prior to that? One has to assume that thousands of recording sessions were helmed by the writers of the songs. We are, after all, a controlling breed and have a vested interest in shaping our creations in a certain way.

The various routes to becoming a songwriter/producer are manifold. Some started out as recording engineers; some as studio musicians; some as arrangers; others as recording artists who sought more control over their creative direction. Some became songwriters after getting established as producers. For others, it was the other way around. For me, and for many songwriter/producers, it was the inevitable frustration of hearing the high percentage of lackluster or off-base interpretations of my material by other producers that led me to seize the chair at the recording console. The ultimate point is this: A songwriter/producer has a much better chance of getting his songs recorded and of being satisfied with the end result than a songwriter who is not involved in the production. What follows are profiles of some of the most notable songwriter/producers of the last 60 years.

Phil Spector

The advent of the star songwriter/producer began in 1958 with an L.A. teenager named Phil Spector, who put together a vocal quartet with three high school friends. The group was called the Teddy Bears, and their hit recording was Spector's composition, "To Know Him Is To Love Him."

Young Phil Spector had a pretty impressive peer network at Fairfax High, which included not only his Teddy Bear mates Marshall Lieb, Harvey Goldstein, and Annette Kleinbard, but also future producer/Ode Records mogul, Lou Adler (the Mamas & the Papas, Carole King), future Beach Boy and hit songwriter Bruce Johnston ("I Write The Songs"), Wrecking Crew sax man Steve Douglas, and star session drummer/instrumentalist Sandy Nelson ("Teen Beat," "Let There Be Drums"). Early on, Spector demonstrated his innate fascination with the recording process by visiting local recording facilities. Producer Stan Ross, co-owner of Gold Star Studios, allowed Spector to hang out at sessions. Under Ross' mentorship, Spector soaked up the vernacular and the techniques of recording and production.

The four members of the Teddy Bears saved up enough money for two hours of studio time and, on their first session, Spector produced his "Don't Worry My Little Pet," which won the cuddly quartet a record contract with the Dore label. Their next session yielded "To Know Him Is To Love Him," which rose to Number One on the *Billboard* pop singles chart. As we all know, Phil Spector went on to create "The Wall of Sound" and furthered the girl-group cause with The Ronettes, The Crystals, and The Blossoms. He produced more than 25 Top 40 hits between 1960 and 1965. In that later year, Spector scored with BMI's most broadcast song of the century, "You've Lost that Lovin' Feelin'," performed by the Righteous Brothers, a song he cowrote with the brilliant, prolific writing team of Barry Mann and Cynthia Weil.

Lieber and Stoller

However, Phil Spector didn't invent the concept of the songwriter/ producer. Blazing the trail for Spector had been a pair of young composers who began writing songs together before rock and roll even had a name. Jerry Lieber (also a Fairfax High alum, by the way) and Mike Stoller started seeing the fruits of their collaborative efforts when Jimmy Witherspoon performed their "Real Ugly Woman" in 1950. In 1952, the duo hit the R&B charts with Charles Brown's version of "Hard Times" and saw the initial release of a song that would go on to become a Lieber/Stoller classic, "Kansas City." That same year, the duo produced their first session: Big Mama Thornton's rendition of "Hound Dog," which spent seven weeks at Number One on the R&B charts in 1953.

Three years later, a manic, greasy-haired, swivel-hipped, R&B/country hybrid from Tupelo, Mississippi exploded onto the national scene with a slightly tamed-down cover of the Thornton record. Lieber and Stoller would go on to score multiple hits with Elvis Presley (as songwriters, not producers), including "Love Me," "Don't," "Loving You," and "Jailhouse Rock." During the remainder of the '50s, this prolific pair became the industry's first independent producers, cowriting an astounding string of hit records by The Robins, The Coasters, and The Drifters. Here are just few of their dozens of timeless offerings: "Smokey Joe's Café," "Riot in Cell Block #9," "Searchin'," "Yakkity Yak," "Love Potion #9," "Stand by Me" (written with Ben E. King), and "On Broadway" (written with Barry Mann and Cynthia Weil). Later, they scored with Patty Page's "Is That All There Is" and "I'm a Woman" and produced Stealers Wheel's "Stuck in the Middle With You."

Burt Bacharach

In the early '60s, Burt Bacharach emerged as one of pop music's preeminent songwriter/producers. A composer with an idiosyncratic and easily identifiable style, Bacharach was fortunate to team up with Hal David, a lyricist with the instinct and craft to attach the perfect words to Bacharach's enigmatic rhythms and sophisticated melodic concepts. Together, Bacharach and David put together an unparalleled body of work. Curiously, this New York team's first hit was a country record: Marty Robbins' 1957 Number One, "The Story of My Life." They hit the pop charts later that same year with Perry Como's version of "Magic Moments."

In 1961, Bacharach began using a young singer named Dionne Warwick to put vocals on the team's demos. That era brought such Bacharach/David smashes as "Baby It's You" by The Shirelles, "Only Love Can Break a Heart" by Gene Pitney, and "Any Day Now," by Chuck Jackson. The writers preferred Warwick's interpretations to a lot of the records they were getting, so they began to create vehicles specifically for her as the artist. Already a proven and capable arranger, working with Warwick gave Bacharach the opportunity to take the production reigns as well. This three-way partnership resulted in phenomenal success, including "Don't Make Me Over," "Anyone Who Had a Heart," "Walk on By," "Do You Know the Way To San Jose," and "Alfie," among many others. Burt Bacharach was already a hit songwriter before he sat in the producer's chair—and he certainly would have remained a successful tunesmith, with or without calling the production shots—but many of his greatest copyrights were custom made for the incredible Dionne Warwick and his innovative, sophisticated production.

Spencer Proffer

My first experience of working with a writer/producer was in 1976, as a solo artist on A&M Records. Michael Gore (Leslie's brother and the writer of the song "Fame") had produced the piano/vocal demos that helped me secure my modest "singles" contract. Justifiably, Gore fully expected to get the opportunity to produce my master sessions for the label. However, West Coast A&R head, Kip Cohen, had other ideas. Enter Spencer Proffer, fresh from an A&R/producer position at United Artists Records, where he had whetted his songwriter/producer whistle by penning and producing the hit duet for Paul Anka and Odia Coates, "I Don't Like To Sleep Alone." Now independent, Proffer brought in a gorgeous, soaring, original ballad called "Daybreak," cowritten with David Pomeranz (Barry Manilow's "Tryin' To Get the Feelin' Again"). Cohen was convinced that "Daybreak" could break me as an artist. The writer/producer told the A&R man that, if Cohen wanted Randy Bishop to cut the song for A&M, he would have to hire Proffer to produce it. Simple as that. Most of us lack the leverage to make that kind of demand of a record executive. The record turned out wonderfully. Quickly and steadily, Proffer's production started to pick up stations across the country. As it looked like Cohen's prediction of a Randy Bishop hit might just be manifesting, the label immediately put me back in the studio with Proffer to cut four more sides toward completing an album. Then—*dag nab it!*—Bette Midler heard my record of "Daybreak," poached the song, and quickly eclipsed my A&M release with her own version on Atlantic Records. Of course, I was disappointed to have the rug pulled out from under my blossoming hit. (Proffer and Pomeranz, however, made some good coin from the Midler rendition.)

I returned to the studio with Proffer to cut another single Cohen was convinced would put me on the map. This little pop masterpiece had already been recorded several times: first by B.J. Thomas, secondly by one of the song's cowriters, Barry Mann, then by the Carpenters. When Kip played me the unreleased Carpenters recording, I immediately recognized great song craft, a solid hook, and an infectious spirit in "Here You Come Again." Proffer and I conceived a 10cc-influenced arrangement for the song and booked time at a studio called One Step Up. For the session, Proffer assembled a first-class bunch of studio dudes, including three guys who would go on to become immensely successful writer/producers themselves: David Foster, Jay Graydon, and Michael Omartian. As with "Daybreak," my second A&M single became the demo for a female superstar. This time it was Dolly Parton, for her breakthrough pop-crossover. Barry Mann and Cynthia Weil had yet another monster hit to add to their discography, not, however, with Randy Bishop. *Sigh!* Spencer Proffer would go on to produce an eclectic array of very successful records with artists like Billy Thorpe, Little River Band, and most especially Quiet Riot. After liquidating his Pasha Records assets in the late '80s, Proffer segued into film music supervision and film production, which is where he continues to exert most of his efforts to this day.

David Foster

Let's flash back to that session at One Step Up. One of the most thrilling and impactful nights of my life was sitting up until three in the morning observing, as the immensely gifted David Foster orchestrated the B-side to "Here You Come Again," "The Passenger," which I cowrote with Proffer and Allan Clarke of The Hollies. Equipped with only a couple of single-timbred synthesizers, Foster wove together a symphony of sonic colors. I learned more about arranging in that one night than in the rest of my thousands of studio hours combined. At that point, the Canadian keyboard genius was trying to win his green card and U.S. residency, which required him to maintain a $100,000 bank balance in a noninterest-bearing account—for a year.

Of course, since that night in 1976, David Foster has gone on to become one of the premiere pop record producers of all time. Two years after my first and only marathon session working with Foster, he achieved his first massive successes as a songwriter/producer in the form of Earth, Wind and Fire's "After the Love Is Gone" and "Got To Be Real." He spent the '80s writing hits and helming sessions for Chicago (three albums, including the chart toppers, "Hard Habit To Break" and "Hard To Say Goodbye"). He contributed to the *Ghostbusters* and *Footloose* soundtracks and produced Peter Cetera, Alice Cooper, Kenny Loggins, Al Jarreau, Olivia Newton-John, Hall and Oates, Kenny Rogers, and Boz Scaggs. In the '90s, Foster teamed up with Celine Dion for her debut Number One, "The Power of Love," produced Natalie Cole's *Unforgettable,* Barbra Streisand's album *Back to Broadway,* Brandy's "Have You Ever," Gloria Estefan and N'Sync's "Music of My Heart," and Tony Braxton's "Unbreak My Heart." In that decade, Foster won three Producer of the Year Grammies. After the turn of the millennium, he cowrote and produced the Andrea Bocelli/Celine Dion duet, "The Prayer," and discovered, wrote for, and produced Josh Groban and Michael Bublé. All in all, David Foster has thus far won 15 Grammies, seven Juno Awards, an Emmy, and is a three-time Oscar nominee. Not bad for a piano player from Canada.

Steve Dorff

Although on most any recording session, David Foster would certainly vie for the title, "the best musician in the room," I would consider him more of an arranger/producer. I'm quite certain that Steve Dorff would be proud to put himself in the arranger/producer category as well. "I was playing piano at three," Dorff recalls. Even as a child in Queens, New York, Steve Dorff heard music in life the way most of us see color in it. "It was a gift. My obligation to that gift was to learn to do something with it. I learned very early on that I needed to create music, and it was as natural for me to create music and hear music as breathing." Discovering The Beatles in junior high, Dorff put together a band of pals to play the original songs he had begun composing. "They didn't play any instruments," he says of his bandmates. "So, I had to teach them how to play. Those were the formulating stages of being an arranger and producer." Studying preveterinary medicine at the University of Georgia in Athens ("My parents didn't want me to be 50 and still collecting tips in a brandy snifter.") the youthful tunesmith would skip classes and drive to Atlanta to visit Bill Lowry, a publisher who worked with Joe South, Billy Joe Royal, and The Classics IV. Lowry signed young Dorff to a publishing contract, and the kid started scoring some cuts with the roster there. Lowry also gave him his first opportunities to arrange and produce.

In 1974, Dorff went out to Los Angeles to write and arrange for top producer, Snuff Garrett (Bobby Vee, Sonny and Cher). That gave Steve what he calls "the jumping off place, where it all started to happen," including cuts by Johnny Mathis, Andy Williams, Anne Murray, Dusty Springfield, and Karen Carpenter. Garrett introduced Dorff to Clint Eastwood and a long collaboration commenced that includes five feature film scores, and a bunch of hit songs (all Dorff arrangements): including, Eddie Rabbitt's "Every Which Way But Loose," Glen Campbell's "Any Which Way You Can," and the Merle Haggard/Clint Eastwood duet, "Barroom Buddies." To date, according to *Billboard Magazine,* Steve Dorff claims more Number One songs from movies than any other composer. Oddly enough, however, he doesn't use his position as producer to get involved in writing the record, in fact it's quite the opposite. Much like Spencer Proffer did with me at A&M, Dorff hopes his song will win him the job of producer: "If I've got something I can get an artist interested in," he explains, "it's my hope that the artist will say, 'Hey, why don't you produce it on me?' And I'll go, 'Great!' But, if that doesn't happen, that's okay, too."

Like me, Dorff has often felt let down by other producers' interpretations of his songs. "I think that's what ultimately got me into producing," he confesses. "Lots of times I felt like the demos were so nailed. The records were being produced by producers who had had a lot of hits, and they so totally missed it. I barely recognized the song." That, incidentally, was the same reason that Jerry Lieber and Mike Stoller started taking charge of the production of their songs in the early '50s. They, too, felt like other producers didn't get the right sound and missed the groove. I'm glad I'm not the only songwriter/producer who has felt that way, more times than I care to remember.

Mutt Lange

Any discussion of songwriter/producers would be far from complete without mentioning a gentleman with the misleading moniker, "Mutt." Robert John "Mutt" Lange was born in Rhodesia (now Zambia). A strict vegetarian, teetotaler, and spiritual follower of Sant Mat, Lange is known as an eccentric, perfectionist recluse, who has not granted an interview in decades. Still, he is, without a doubt, one of the most successful pop music producers of all time. The first songwriting credit I could find for Lange is "If Dreams Came True," on the Outlaws' 1978 critically panned album, *Playin' to Win.* Before Lange became recognized as a songwriter, he had a long list of production credits, including three big albums for Boomtown Rats, Foreigner's classic *4*, and three massively successful LPs for AC/DC: *Highway to Hell, Back in Black,* and *For Those About To Rock We Salute You.*

Mutt Lange's name began to show up as a cowriter on his second Def Leopard project, 1983's *Pyromania.* With various band members, he is credited for writing every track on the album, including the hits, "Photograph," "Rock of Ages," and "Foolin'." The album sold in excess of 16 million copies worldwide. At this point, the ultra-meticulous Lange was known for demanding a year to produce each album. His first solo writing credit shows up in 1985 on his production of Loverboy's "Lovin' Every Minute of It," that Canadian band's last platinum record. Lange is credited as producer/cowriter on every track of Def Leopard's biggest selling album, 1987's *Hysteria* (more than 20 million units), which yielded seven hit singles. The producer cowrote all but three tracks on Bryan Adams' *18 Til' I Die* in '96. In between, Lange widened his musical horizons to add pop and R&B to his rock credits, working with Billy Ocean ("Get Outta My Dreams, Get Into My Car"), Adams ("Everything I Do, I Do For You," from *Robin Hood, Prince of Thieves*, and "Have You Ever Loved a Woman," from *The Mask of Zorro*, written with the artist and film-scorer Michael Kamen), and Michael Bolton's "Said I Loved You, But I Lied." Having grown up as a lifelong fan of country music, Lange had one more genre to conquer, which he did handily with Shania Twain. Under Lange's mentorship, Twain not only became the biggest selling female artist of all time, but the producer/songwriter's wife. (They are now divorced.) Lange's most recent project, as of this writing, is Nickelback's double-platinum 2008 release, *Dark Horse,* on which the producer is credited with cowriting five tracks.

Glenn Ballard

On previous pages, I described how Gary Usher cranked out chart records by fictitious groups in the '60s, how super session guitarist Jay Graydon scored with Manhattan Transfer, Al Jarreau, and others in the '80s, and I waxed in genuine awe over the three-decade reign of the extraordinary Desmond Child. But, for at least 60 years, every pop-music genre has seen numerous immensely successful songwriter/producers. I met Glen Ballard in the mid '80s, when we were tag teaming at Pasha Studio. Ballard was helming the sessions for axeman/singer Jon Butcher. I was producing what turned out to be the last major-label album for the Outlaws, *Soldiers Of Fortune*. A gentle, modest, and thoughtful man, Glen Ballard emerged from Natchez, Mississippi, where he was inspired to learn piano from seeing a cross-town neighbor, Jerry Lee Lewis, perform locally. Ballard's earliest influences were the great Southern R&B records of the day: Irma Thomas, Al Green, and the Allen Toussaint New Orleans sound. Ballard wrote his first song at ten and had assembled a performing band by the fifth grade. After graduating from Ole Miss in 1975, Glen moved to L.A. to pursue music full time. As keyboardist for Kiki Dee, he arrived on the charts, when she cut his song "One Step." That record led to a $100/week writing gig for MCA Publishing, and on to a lengthy and fruitful tutelage under master producer/arranger, Quincy Jones. Through Jones, Ballard scored cuts with George Benson ("What's On Your Mind") and

James Ingram ("Try Your Love Again"). Then, Jones moved Ballard to a well-warmed chair at the recording console to produce and write songs for Evelyn "Champagne" King, Teddy Pendergrass, and soap star/singer Jack Wagner (the Number Two hit, "All I Need," co-written with Clif Magness).

Becoming an independent writer/producer around the time I met him, Ballard saw no borders around his talent. He cowrote a country Song of the Year, George Strait's "You Look So Good In Love" (with Rory Bourke and Kerry Chater) and one of Michael Jackson's most loved pieces, "Man In The Mirror" (with Siedah Garrett), both in 1986. Then, he proceeded to work with pop diva, Paula Abdul on her 1988 breakout album, *Forever Your Girl.* In 1989, I ran into Ballard at a San Fernando Valley club. He was kind enough to buy me a drink, and as we caught up on the last several years, he told me about a pop female vocal trio he was working with. It was a group comprising the talented daughters of two tortured pop geniuses: Brian Wilson of the Beach Boys (Carnie and Wendy), and John Phillips of the Mamas & the Papas (Chynna). The *Wilson Phillips* album, released the next year, became the biggest-selling recording to date for a female group, spawning numerous hit singles, most of which Ballard had a hand in writing. Ballard didn't stop there. A former dance-pop singer and child TV actress from Canada drafted Ballard to cowrite and produce what would become a phenomenon of astounding proportions. *Jagged Little Pill,* by Alanis Morissette, spawned six hit singles, sold 16 million units in the U.S. alone, and 33 million worldwide. Ballard went on to add Aerosmith, Van Halen, The Corrs, and others to his production credits, along with a record label of his own, and the screenplay for the feature film, *Clubland.* Busy, busy boy!

Steve Kipner

Several other acquaintances through the years have achieved major success by producing their own songs. Steve Kipner had already seen chart success with his duo, Tin Tin, ("Toast and Marmalade For Tea"), before I did several years of background vocal sessions with the transplanted Aussie. Kipner and I also cowrote "This Is Our Night," the title song to my 1978 MCA/Infinity duo album, the one I made with Marty Gwinn. After penning "Physical" for Olivia Newton-John (with Terry Shaddick) and "Hard Habit to Break" for Chicago (with Jay Graydon and David Foster), Kipner grabbed the production wheel and hit pay dirt with Christina Aguilera's "Genie In A Bottle." He went on from there to score hits by 98 Degrees, Westlife, Kelly Rowland, Natasha Bedingfield, and American Idol Season Eight winner, Kris Allen. "My plan is almost always," Kipner shared with me on the phone a few years back, "to come in at the last minute with a hit song, when the artist and the label are growing a little tired of what they've already cut. That keeps my song fresh, and I can usually get the first single that way." Pretty clever. If only you and I had access to Clive Davis and could ride in at the eleventh hour with guns a-blazin' and save the day.

Max Martin

Swedish producer/songwriter, Max Martin, too, has put together an impressive legacy of chart successes, beginning with his mid-'90s pop records with Backstreet Boys, N'Sync, and Britney Spears. In the new millennium, Martin reinvented his production style by blending funk, rock, and Euro pop with Kelly Clarkson ("Since U Been Gone," "My Life Would Suck Without You"), Pink ("So What"), Katy Perry ("I Kissed a Girl") and Ke$ha ("Tik Tok").

Music Row

Nashville has always had its share of successful songwriter/producers. Billy Sherrill went from cowriting (with Glenn Sutton) and producing David Houston's nine-week Number One, "Almost Persuaded," to scoring a massive crossover hit with Tammy Wynette's "Stand By Your Man." That led to a string of duet hits with Wynette and her husband George Jones, most of which were produced and/or cowritten by Sherrill (with either Norro Wilson, or Wynette's future hubby, George Richey). Sherrill produced Jones for 19 years, including some of the most enduring country records of all time. He also had huge, crossover success with Charlie Rich ("Behind Closed Doors," "The Most Beautiful Girl," "A Very Special Love Song"). Other notable Music Row songwriter/producers of recent years include Don Cook, Mark Wright, and my friend Doug Johnson, who started out as more of an engineer/producer in his home state of Georgia. Johnson soon saw the advantage of writing for his production clients, applied himself to becoming a solid crafter of contemporary country, and has succeeded in writing seven Number One country songs and 13 Top Tens. Through the '90s, as head of A&R for Epic Records in Nashville, Johnson signed several singers he thought would be good voices for his writing and production. That strategy paid off, as he penned and produced hits for Ty Herndon ("Livin' In A Moment You Would Die For") and James Bonamy ("I Don't Think I Will"). As of this writing, Johnson is head of A&R at Curb/Asylum Records and has Lee Brice's new single climbing the charts, cowritten, incidentally, with my pal and "My List" collaborator Tim James.

Hip-Hop and R&B

Hip-hop has burgeoned as many or more star songwriter/producers than any other genre. In addition to his own rap records, Sean Combs (aka Puff Daddy, P. Diddy, and simply Diddy) has produced Notorious B.I.G., Mary J. Blige, Jodeci, TLC, Usher, Mariah Carey, Boys II Men, SWV, and Aretha Franklin. His entrepreneurial empire includes record companies and his own line of menswear, and he has racked up several feature-film acting credits. Not too shabby for a Harlem-born, college-party promoter, and former intern at Uptown Records.

Kenneth Edmunds got his start playing with Bootsy Collins, who dubbed the youthful keyboardist, "Babyface." He joined up with drummer Antonio "L.A." Reid in the band, The Deele. Edmunds and Reid had their first songwriting success in 1983, with Midnight Star's album track, "Slow Jam." After cowriting and producing hits for Bobby Brown, Pebbles, Paula Abdul, and Sheena Easton, the pair started LaFace Records in 1989, providing a label home for Toni Braxton and TLC. To date, Babyface's production and songwriting credits are far too extensive to list. They include Whitney Houston, Boys II Men, Prince, Michael Jackson, Eric Clapton, Brandy, Mary J. Blige, En Vogue, Fall Out Boy, Celine Dion, and Beyoncé. This is only about 25 percent of this cat's credits. Come on, now, Babyface! Give somebody else a chance!

Shawn Corey Carter is better known as Jay-Z (a cross between his boyhood nickname, Jazzy and the Marcy Street J/Z subway line). As a self-produced artist, Jay-Z's CDs have sold more than 30 million copies in the U.S. alone, and he holds *Billboard Magazine*'s record for the most Number One albums by one artist on the Top 200. As a rapper, he has a lengthy string of notable guest appearances and cowriting credits. Here is just a sampling: Mariah Carey's "Heartbreaker," Beyonce's "Crazy in Love," Rihanna's "Umbrella," and his own "Empire State of Mind," with guest vocal by Alicia Keys. Starting out on the streets of Brooklyn's Bedford/Stuyvesant neighborhood, the freestyle rapper was unable to get a record deal. So, in 1996, with a couple of fellow renegades, he started Roc-A-Fella Records. Getting a distribution deal with Priority, his debut album, *Reasonable Doubt*, reached Number 23 on the charts. *Reasonable Doubt* was listed at Number 248 on *Rolling Stone Magazine*'s list of the 500 greatest albums of all time and would eventually reach platinum sales. Since then, Jay-Z, now the former CEO of Def Jam Records (which absorbed Roc-A-Fella in 2004) has continued to be a major player, with an personal empire that includes ownership of the NBA's New Jersey Nets, the 40/40 Club, and the Rocawear clothing line. You probably wouldn't call Jay Z a traditional record producer. He composes his own raps and partners up with teams of cutting-edge talent to produce collaborative music that the public has been eagerly lapping up for the last 15 years. The result of his combinations of talents has been to achieve success of the highest level.

CHAPTER 24
You As the Producer

There are nearly as many kinds of producers as there are producers. Generally, however, those who pursue music production fall into one—or any combination—of the following categories: arranger/producers, engineer/producers, musician/producers, deal-maker/producers, cheerleader/producers, executive/producers, and of course, songwriter/producers. In other words, it's usually another skill, interest, or natural inclination that leads a creative and/or entrepreneurial soul to get into record production. One doesn't usually set out to become a producer, per se. While taking the producer's chair may be a goal, it's more likely to happen because of the groundwork one has laid over a period of time. A producer is very much like a film director in this regard (and, in the role he or she plays in the recording process). Film directors often begin their movie-making careers behind the camera, working their way up to directors of photography; or they might start out as editors, screenwriters, or even actors. In those capacities, they've presumably spent endless hours on movie sets, observing and participating in the practice of filmmaking. They've learned how the various technical and creative roles combine to amount to the whole. They've seen the process repeated time and time again, in various permutations. Often, they've been taken under the wing of a mentor, who has welcomed them into his or her world to share the secrets of the trade. Then, and *only* then, are they ready to take charge of an immense, almost undoable task that requires critical evaluation, decisive action, diplomacy, objectivity, focus, vision, and the ability to withstand enormous stress and pressure for months at a time. Sounds like a recipe for madness, doesn't it? The risks to one's well being and reputation are extraordinary. But, the rewards can be even greater: creatively, financially, and status-wise.

No academic degree qualifies one to don the record producer's hat. However, being a successful producer requires a certain skill-set that invariably includes a massive reservoir of patience, myopic concentration, and organizational and multitasking abilities. A producer should also possess a knack for recognizing and showcasing an artist's strongest and most appealing qualities by helping to choose the right material, arrangement, and the best team to create the dynamics that one can only hope will add up to a great record. The best producers not only have a musical sensibility, they possess the instincts of a master psychologist: always encouraging, yet stern when necessary. Like writing, producing is about making decisions—from moment to moment, for long hours, day in and day out—until the final mix is finally mastered. *Un*like writing, producing is just as much about urging and helping other creative souls to effectively use *their* talents as it is about using your own.

There has been a lot of discussion through the years (particularly lately) as to what qualifies one to call oneself a music producer, what he or she should be capable of doing, and so on. In recent years, just about anyone with some hot drum loops seems to claim the mantle of producer. Those who oppose this notion stick to the old-school theory that the producer should always be "the best musician in the room." I think there is middle ground here. I've seen producers who involve themselves with every single note, from the writing of the song, through approval of the photo for the CD package. I've also seen producers who just get the contracts signed, obtain the budget, assemble a team, and stay out of the way, aside from an occasional thumbs up. If you're able to put together the tools, the personnel, and the material and you can take responsibility for making the ultimate decisions that lead to an end result, you are a producer (not necessarily a good producer, but a producer nevertheless). If the buck stops with you, you are a producer, whether you can play an instrument, sing a note, write a song, place a microphone, set a compressor, or equalize a banjo.

HOWEVER (capital letters used here purposefully!), you really need to know the language, and you also need to understand one thing: If you're not the artist, the record is *not* about you. Like a film director, you are there to serve the story and the characters, not to draw attention to how talented you are. Sure, a filmmaker can set up a camera angle that will take an audience's breath away, but unless the acting performances are convincing and the story compelling, that stunning footage is wasted film. A record producer is there to serve the song and the artist, not necessarily to create the world's coolest snare drum sound (although that's cool, too). A record producer is responsible for shaping a piece of recorded music in a way that carries out the song's mission, whether that mission is to get booties shakin' on the dance floor, or to move millions to take action to end world hunger.

If you have a burning desire to become a producer, do what young Phil Spector did. Find a studio that will allow you to be a fly on the wall. Shut up and observe. Take notes on the vernacular. Watch how artists, musicians, and engineers relate to each other. See the various ways a basic track can take shape. Observe how each overdub colors and enhances the whole. Watch how different singers approach a vocal, and how background vocals emphasize the song's hooks and orchestrate a record. Take particular notice of the inherent emotional and psychological dynamics of each session. Check out the moments of triumph, when everything's cookin' and comin' together, and stick around for the stressful, difficult hours, when folks don't see eye to eye, when the guitar player can't get in tune, when the drummer is dragging, and when the singer can't reach the high notes.

Ultimately, you will discover that a producer's biggest ally is time. Great production, like great songwriting, has to be given enough of that precious resource for the team to get it right; and it's always the producer's job to make the final decision as to when it *is* right. On rare occasions, it's that first, magical take. Most times, it takes numerous attempts, or an assembled compilation of partial attempts, to hit the bull's eye. Pay attention to how different people do each and every part of the job, from the tracking to the mix, and every two steps forward and one step back in between. Watch the essential choices being made, and only speak when spoken to, whether you agree or disagree with the process you are observing.

If, after a good hundred hours of being invisible in the studio, you're thinking, "Yeah. I could do that. In fact, I *wanna* do that," then, yes, maybe you're ready to give it shot. You probably won't be very good at it at first. That's okay. Like playing full-court basketball for the first time; it's suddenly a 360-degree game. Everybody in the room has his or her own agenda, and you will be tested over and over to make them all feel you can be trusted to deliver so that everyone will be proud of the end result. You'll hear, "Turn me up!" from every corner of the control room. But, you can't turn *everybody* up, can you? That would only make everything louder. You'll learn that even the slightest change in level or equalization on one instrument changes the sound of every other instrument. You'll make some mistakes and come up with some pretty crappy stuff. Just try not to make the same mistake again. Continually correct your course and move ahead. The craft of record production requires a learning curve that never really ends. As soon as you assume you know it all, your work will become mechanical and predictable, and your career will start spiraling downward because, like songwriting, there is always something new to learn about being a producer. At the end of the day, you will either be the hero or the goat. If the record is successful, you'll be heralded as a genius. If it falls short, you'll get all of the blame, not only from the industry, but from the artists and especially the songwriters. So, if you *are* one of the songwriters, you'd better be absolutely certain you always give it a good, solid, responsible effort, or your cowriters might not want to put their trust in you again. No pressure, kids. No pressure at all.

So, although one of the most expeditious methods for you as a writer to get cuts is by placing your own derriere in the producer's chair, only attempt to go that route if you're willing to study the required skills and tools, do the work required, and take full responsibility for the ultimate result and only if you have the demeanor for it. In the long run, you shouldn't try to produce *just* because you want more cuts. You should be compelled to take charge, because you feel you have the best vision for your own songs, and because you have, at the very least, developed the fundamental chops to get the job done. Regardless of whether you ever produce a single session, you and every other songwriter on Earth is well advised to develop the ability to make viable contributions to the production process, above and beyond saying, "Gee, guys, I don't know. I'll know it when I hear it." The ability to clearly articulate what exactly it is you want will help you get more satisfactory results from any recording session, whether you're just one of the writers, or you're helming the session. More times than not, failing to learn some basic production skills will lead you to major creative disappointment.

It certainly couldn't hurt to enroll in an intensive audio engineering and/or production course at a qualified trade school or university. This would give you hands-on experience working with fellow students on their projects. When I was learning the studio ropes, there were no such institutions. The secrets to audio engineering and production were only passed down from mentor to apprentice. Now, late-night television is filled with ads for schools promising glamorous careers recording exciting superstars. Don't be fooled by that deception. Crafting a quality recording can be a very tedious and laborious process. They don't call an engineer's pallor a "studio tan" for nothing. When a young person informs me that he or she plans to become a recording engineer, my first question is, "Do you like to pee?" The rest of the team can take a break, but the engineer is always left to do the thankless work: the vocal comping, the editing, the mixing. However, it can be truly fulfilling to be such an integral part of the production process. This is the essence of "flow activity," when you're doing a job for which you have the expertise, making measurable progress, and losing all track of time.

Short of enrolling in Full Sail University, or AES, or any one of the many audio engineering programs now available, it would be a very good idea to invest in a home recording facility and do some hands-on work crafting your own home productions. If you're not the best manual reader in the world, you should strongly consider hiring a personal tutor for a few days to educate you in the nuances of your equipment and software. A few hundred dollars of personalized training can accelerate your progress enormously, and you'll always have a number to call when you get yourself in a pickle—and you will invariably find yourself flummoxed at some future juncture. However, all the schooling in the world won't prepare you for the experience of helming a real project. Remember, to be a producer, you don't necessarily have to be a recording engineer. You just need to have the means to hire the best cat available and have some ability to speak his language.

Do You Have What It Takes?

To one degree or another, any kid who listens to the radio with a curious and discerning ear, wondering *How did they do that?* is showing production potential. Every high schooler who picks up a guitar, sits down at a keyboard, or grabs a pair of drum sticks, and recruits some pals to come over and jam out some simple chord changes or learn some classic tunes is demonstrating a glimmer of production spark. Booting up GarageBand and laying down a bass line over some drum loops can be the beginning of an education in production. Even the miraculous process of writing those first songs can plant production's first seeds. If you can hear the rhythm track and the orchestration in your head as you compose the music, you may be an arranger at heart. If you follow a compulsion and figure out how to capture that guitar lick, that groove, and that vocal on tape, or in a digital file, you are showing a proclivity for audio engineering. If you can bring talented friends together and motivate them to work as a team toward a common musical goal, you have leadership skills. If you can't wait to throw a harmony over that vocal and mix the elements together into something that sounds whole and complete, you have the basic elements that can ultimately add up to a producer.

My path to becoming a record producer began with my first recording session at a local AM radio station in Portland, Oregon. My first band, The Turtles (it wasn't long before we were forced to abandon that name, due to the national chart success of a Southern California ensemble using the identical moniker) had some original material we wanted to capture on tape. We actually thought we were destined to duplicate the massive phenomenon of another local combo, The Kingsmen, who had scored big-time with their raw, crudely produced, rock classic, "Louie, Louie." Under the auspices of a recording engineer who was really only qualified to mix prerecorded commercials and monophonic musical beds with a disc jockey's spoken voice, we made some horrific racket that wasn't worth the tape it was recorded on. I was only 16. I realized pretty quickly, though, that it takes more than a couple of microphones and a tape recorder to make a good record. My education in recording advanced somewhat with some sonic experiments engineered by my best friend, Tim Sadler, in his suburban bedroom, on a two-track Revox tape machine. Tim and I would eventually make records together on several continents. He would go on to engineer albums by The Doobie Brothers, Air Supply, and Rod Stewart, before delving into film audio post-production and finally quitting the business over a painful legal wrangle with some partners.

After my the traumatic semesters of college, a Portland recording engineer/producer named Rick Keefer gave me the chance to run amuck in his studio. There, I had several months of on-the-job training, making an introspective, folkie album called *I Sing a Soft Song.* However, my real record-production boot camp began with the two albums my second Elektra band, The Wackers, made under the auspices of Gary Usher. In tandem with engineer Russ Gary, at Wally Heider San Francisco, Usher demonstrated a mastery of the medium, along with a whole kit bag of imaginative, sonic tricks the self-anointed genius had either created himself or borrowed from his brilliant cohorts, Brian Wilson and Terry Melcher. Having produced a plethora of 1960s chart records, culminating with three incredible and groundbreaking Byrds albums, Usher had won his studio cred fair and square. Recognizing and respecting that, I observed the man at work, finally seeing the entire process clearly, from start to completion, including every critical choice in between.

I knew, then and there, without a doubt, that was the role I wanted to play. I had the perfect personality for it. I was a bossy, brooding perfectionist. I was a quick study, and when I put my mind to something, I could muster up a good work ethic. I had strong and definite ideas about how I wanted to hear my own songs recorded, too. In fact, even with all the admiration I had for Gary Usher, I found it impossible to hold my tongue in the studio. One time, I unthinkingly walked up to the recording console holding a box of wooden matches and began shaking it rhythmically next to the producer's ear. "Listen to this," I suggested. "This would work great on this tune!" Past the end of his rope—his was a short one—the intense Usher kicked me (literally kicked me) out of the control room and barricaded the door with a couch, forbidding me from re-entering until he had finished that day's overdub session. Our producer/artist relationship ultimately leapt the rails, when, after an all-night mixing session at Les Studio in Montreal, I haughtily told Usher that he should tear a mix down and start all over. His expression screwed up in a crimson-faced knot, he picked up his coat and brief-case, and he marched out to catch a flight home to L.A. I never worked in the studio with Usher again. However, I did take some personal delight in 1983, when Usher invited me out to his home in a remote Los Angeles–area canyon. That day, my first production mentor pitched me some songs for the Outlaws album I was producing. Respectfully, I passed on the songs. Sadly, Usher died of lung cancer in 1990.

My first opportunity to sit in the producer's chair came on an artist demo for my brother Bart's band, Providence. It was a genuine thrill to be officially recognized with the designation, producer; and I relished the role. My production was instrumental in luring Moody Blues producer, Tony Clarke, from London to attend a Providence showcase, and to Clarke signing the band to Threshold Records. I couldn't wait for my next chance to produce, which came shortly after I left The Wackers in 1974. I took a stylistic hard right turn, deciding to forego the punk-glam poses and shoot for the top of the Top 40. I guess the shift worked somewhat, because my first, self-produced solo single, "Don't You Worry," became a Canadian, national, airplay hit. That record led to contracts to produce a couple of French-Canadian acts and set in motion a trial-by-fire education in record production. Some of my early productions are simply awful. A few I remain proud of today. However, those studio experiences convinced me this much: In order to feel truly fulfilled as a singer/songwriter, I needed to exert my production input as much as possible. If I participated in the production process, I was much more likely to take pride in the end result. So, it wasn't so much my desire to see my songs recorded that drove me to take the production reigns, as it was my need to control how those songs were produced.

From the perspective of 40 years in this business, having been on both sides of the desk—as an artist, as a producer, as a songwriter, and as a publisher—I will share the following piece of hard-earned wisdom. If you are the recording artist, you are—whether you are credited or not—an important contributor to the production process. If, as the artist, you are also the writer of the songs, you are involved in the production by proxy, because you did the most essential and fundamental job—matching the material to the artist and arranging it in the most appropriate style for the artist to perform. So, regardless of whom is actually sitting in the producer's chair, you have every right to participate in every decision that goes into the production of your record. Therefore, I urge you to speak up. Never let anything slip by that you might consider a creative compromise. If you don't exercise your fundamental right to guide your own destiny, there's a high probability that you will be disappointed in the final product. If you're not proud to have your own name attached to your own records, it's very likely that those records will not be received well by the public because music fans can usually tell whether a performance is sincere or faked. However, if the public happens to embrace a record that you feel doesn't truly reflect who you are as an artist, you will be stuck with it forever. Now, *there's* a recipe for madness!

This is not to giving you permission to be obnoxious, unreasonable, and continually demanding in the studio. You do have to pick your battles carefully and not make every single production choice an arduous one for all involved. As you make your case, be firm, but diplomatic. Try never to make a public scene by challenging or calling anyone out on the carpet. That will only result in a digging in of the heels. Take your producer aside and voice your concerns in a calm and rational tone. Let him or her be the one to tell the guitar player that his tone is too over-the-top, his solo is too bland, ornate, or dissonant. Above all, at the end of the day, make sure that you're completely satisfied with your vocal performance. Don't let your producer blow smoke where the sun don't shine and tell you that something is incredible, when you know it can be better. At the end of the day, you will not win every skirmish, nor should you, because your producer probably knows at least a thing or two. Production always ends up including common ground that wouldn't exist if it were not for the varying views of the creative people involved. Remember this: Your producer will walk away from your project and go on to working with another artist, while you'll be left to live with this recording for the rest of your life. This is *your* record, *your* career, *your* reputation, *your* life. Take care to ensure that you can live with it proudly.

The Production Process: An Overview

If you're already working as a producer, I hope you'll pardon me for covering some well trodden ground here. I think, though, for a lot of readers, it might be helpful to take an overview of the production process.

A record production usually follows these basic steps:

1. Preproduction
2. Basic tracking and overdubs
3. Vocals
4. Background vocals
5. Sweetening
6. Mixing
7. Mastering

Traditionally, preproduction provides essential time for the producer and the artist(s) to get to know each other and agree on a common direction for the project. During this early stage, the team considers all of the available material, deciding which songs they plan to record (whether they be originals, outside songs, covers of standards, or previously recorded obscurities). As each song-candidate is considered, the artist and producer might try out some different arrangement ideas, examining various tempos, grooves, keys, structures, and so on in an effort to find an approach that features the artist in his, her, or their best light. I remember walking into a preproduction session at Wally Heider's in Sausalito. Narada Michael Walden was putting together preproduction arrangements for an Aretha Franklin album. For this purpose, he stood in the middle of five keyboardists, all of whom where simulating different roles, from drums to strings. The group would run through the song. Then the producer instructed each player to make specific adjustments, and they'd play it again. It was very much the way Phil Spector ran his sessions: walking from instrument to instrument, listening, then making comments on how that part was working with the whole. Oft times, in preproduction, the producer and the artist do some demoing, creating templates for the studio band. As home digital recording is now so ubiquitous, affordable, and high quality, frequently preproduction demos are used as the foundation for the master recording. Or, they might become the actual master recording itself. For *Jagged Little Pill,* Glen Ballard and Alanis Morissette would write a song in Ballard's home studio, then record the rudiments of the basic tracks and lead vocals on the same day on their way to making the record. A very similar process resulted in Sheryl Crow's hugely successful debut, *Tuesday Night Music Club.*

Ever since multitrack recording became state of the art in the mid '60s, the most typical way to begin the recording process is by booking time in a tracking room and assembling a group of session players for a basic tracking session (or a series of tracking sessions). In the case of a self-contained band, the session players are usually the members of that band's rhythm section. However, over the course of time, records have been made with multiple combinations of band members and pro ringers. A core group of L.A. session players called the Wrecking Crew served as The Byrds, Beach Boys, The Monkees, The Association, Carpenters, the Mamas & the Papas, the Partridge Family, and many more acts. I failed to cut the mustard as a studio bassist for my first Elektra band, Roxy. So, we hired brilliant Motown bass man, Wilton Felder, to lay down the bottom end for much of our album. Even The Beatles often used other, more versatile and accomplished musicians on their records: Big Jim Sullivan and Eric Clapton on guitar, Allan White on drums. Whatever gets the job done. Typically, it's the producer's decision as to which studio, recording engineer, and the exact players who perform on the record. However, the artist often has some input in these regards as well.

The goal of a basic track is to lay down a well structured, sturdy foundation for the record. Players are usually selected to complement the artist's style and the songs selected for each session. Some producers arrive with full arrangements they expect the band to perform verbatim. Others have a basic boilerplate, but welcome the players' ideas. Then, some producers just let the band work out the songs on the date. I'm always amazed when I hear a songwriter accuse a producer of a lack of imagination by complaining, "He just copied the demo!"

Having been disappointed many too many times by off-base productions of my songs, when a producer thinks enough of my demo to copy it, I say, "Thank God!" In replicating my demo arrangement, I feel that my song has been fully honored. Toby Keith's recording of "My List" was a near-perfect duplicate of the home demo I made in my attic, from the voicing and picking of every chord on Biff Watson's central acoustic guitar to the signature lick (which Brent Rowan cleverly chose to play on sitar/guitar, instead of regular electric six-string).

In the past, bands like The Doors, Moody Blues, and the Doobie Brothers actually went into the studio without writing complete songs. Many of their most popular records were written, preproduced, and produced collaboratively on the fly, with the tape rolling. As studio time in top tracking rooms can be extremely costly, this method of making records is not typical. However, it remains common practice to block-book and lock out a tracking room for weeks at a time to enable the musicians to get into a groove. Once the drums are properly tuned and miked, the guitars are in tune, and the headphone mix is set up to everyone's satisfaction, the players can settle into doing their job: making music. Bands like Credence Clearwater and Fleetwood Mac often did multiple, surgical, two-inch-tape edits on their basic tracks to keep the groove consistent and solid. With digital recording, it's now far easier and far less risky to punch in or simply edit different play lists together to create a solid bed for the song. Digital also makes it quite possible—and therefore not unusual—for the engineer to correct time issues and some pitch problems on each basic-track instrument, rather than hammer away at take after take on the way to an adequate—or hopefully inspired—basic track.

As the basic track is for the purpose of supporting the song, the singer usually renders a guide vocal while the players are laying it down. That helps insure the tempo and pocket are right, the key is ideal, the dynamics work, and the rhythm-track instruments are not stepping on or creating dissonance with the melody. Before and after each take, the producer offers suggestions, encourages the crew, continually makes sure the artist is satisfied, and ultimately decides whether each task along the way has been accomplished.

Since the advent of MIDI (Musical Instrument Digital Interface) in the early '80s, many records have been produced one instrument—or even one note—at a time, to construct basic tracks and full arrangements. MIDI allows sequences of notes to be stored in a computer. Those programmed sequences trigger sampled or synthesized sounds (virtual instruments) with on and off signals at certain velocities and lengths. Using these tools, one single musician or arranger can become a whole band, or even a symphony orchestra. Some genres of music—particularly the stuff that has dominated Top 40 radio for decades, such as pop, hip hop, and dance music—use MIDI production almost exclusively. As drum machines and synthesizers predate MIDI by many years, generations of music fans have little exposure to human beings playing real instruments together. I recall driving on the 101 Freeway in L.A., listening to a David Bowie hit, and my eldest daughter, Emily, remarking, "Gee, people are starting to use violins and harmonicas on records now." For little Em (now in her 30s), what was old was new again.

On another occasion, around 1990, I was doing a background-vocal session at the San Fernando Valley recording studio owned by guitarist/songwriter/producer, Ray Parker, Jr. ("Ghost Busters"). The second engineer said, in absolutely sincere wonderment, "You won't believe what happened in this studio yesterday. A drummer, a bass player, a guitar player, and a keyboard guy set up, and we recorded them all playing at the same time. It was wild!" Around that same time, when Counting Crows traveled South from the Bay Area to cut some demos in L.A., they were frustrated over their inability to capture a sound that reflected their live energy. At a loss for what to do, they shared their consternation with old-school production vet, Nik Venet (The Lettermen, Bobby Darin, Lou Rawls, Linda Ronstadt). Venet suggested what, to the band, was a revolutionary move: "Set up just like you do in the clubs," the old fellow instructed, "and play live, together." No one before had ever mentioned that performing together in the studio was even possible. Their next demo session resulted in a record deal, which led to them to a multiplatinum debut album. About year later, Venet found an envelope in his mailbox containing a thank-you note from Counting Crows and a check for ten thousand dollars, out of gratitude for the most obvious advice ever offered in the music business.

Here in Nashville, record making has remained pretty consistent for decades. First, in preproduction—with input from the label A&R department—the producer and the artist settle on the material, the keys, and the song structure. The producer casts and books the band and a tracking room. The session leader goes through the demos and worktapes and does number charts (more about the Nashville number system later). In a series of three-hour union sessions, they cut basic tracks—usually, with the artist rendering guide vocals. Often the guitarists, keyboardist, and/or utility musicians will come up with overdub and solo ideas on the spot and throw them down on the chosen basic track. On another day, the artist and producer will return to a smaller, more intimate recording facility to capture lead vocals. Those sessions are usually followed on another day by background vocals. Final time is reserved for sweetening: replacing solo breaks when necessary, overdubbing and refining instrumental colors, percussion, and/or orchestration. Then, the project moves to a mixing studio, where a mixer plugs the tracks into his template and cranks out a mix. After the producer, the artist, and everybody else gives approval, the mix then goes to mastering.

Mastering is the final part of the production process. The goal of mastering is to refine the end product by taking off the rough edges, subtly attenuating the equalization to feature the most appealing frequencies, and boosting the apparent level as high as possible. These tasks are accomplished by an engineer with sharply tuned ears, using a very sophisticated battery of high-quality, outboard equipment: equalizers, compressors, limiters, phase distortion devices, and so on. When I first started producing, mastering entailed all of the above, with one final, additional step: sending the stereo signal into a lathe to cut the master disc, from which the stamp would be made to create the actual vinyl records. Now, everything is pretty much done in the digital domain. Ta da!

PART SIX:

THE DEMO

CHAPTER 25
Speaking Studio

There are basically two distinct dialects in Studio Land: Musician and Engineer. As these folks spend so much time working together, most musicians speak pretty fluent engineer and vice versa. When I first arrived in Nashville, I was very impressed to see that every engineer I worked with had the ability to read, follow along with, and refer to a number chart. As most studio musicians spend half of their waking hours in recording studios, they can't help but absorb the engineer's lingo as well. In addition, nearly every player has his or her own digital studio at home, so it goes without saying that most home-studio owners have developed some audio-engineering skills and a familiarity with the terminology.

So, when you walk into the control room—particularly when you're there to get the most out of the personnel and the tools available—it's to your advantage to have some comprehension of the language of the land. It will take you even farther on your quest for a great demo if you at least make the effort to speak that language yourself. Americans returning from Europe often complain about the rudeness of the French. Yes, I've seen that snooty arrogance in some Francophones; but really, this communication issue isn't all their fault. We Americans can be obnoxious, boisterous, presumptuous, ethno-superior, and downright rude ourselves. So, this feud is routinely exacerbated by the innate character of both cultures. From my experience, the root cause is the Yankee refusal to even make an effort to learn even a petite smidge of the French language. Most Americans just assume that everybody in the world speaks English, so they can't be bothered to study another tongue. If a foreigner doesn't get what we're saying, we just say it louder and slower, as if they are hard of hearing, or dimwitted. Or we say it in a foreign accent, which is even more offensive. However, we haven't made the effort to know a person's language, which that person probably speaks fluently. Why in the world should we presume that person has learned ours? I can't recall ever having been approached on the street by a German fellow asking for directions in his mother tongue, and when I couldn't understand his question, have him SHOUT... SLOWLY...THE SAME...QUESTION...AT ME...IN GERMAN. Yet, that's precisely what some ugly Americans do, isn't it?

The same goes for the recording studio. If a songwriter walks in to a studio intent on walking out a few hours later with a great demonstration recording, he might well have either prepared a little by learning the essential vernacular of the environment or have brought along a guide who has some fluency in the lingo. Traveling in France, it always worked much better for me to order an omelette du fromage, or a salad nicoise, rather than a cheese omelette or a tuna salad. Seeing me make the initial effort, even the most pompous French folks would usually meet me half way. After identifying my American accent and noticing my struggle with the language, almost invariably they would be willing to use whatever English they knew, and we could communicate in some blend of caveman Franco/Anglo, without any animosity or condescension. Nobody was made to feel like a dimwit, and we all lived happily ever after. Like the garcon and kitchen staff in any French bistro, studio musicians and recording engineers are there to provide a service, to please you. Here's another example: Supposing you hired a crew to paint your house, yet you couldn't tell them exactly what color you wanted. That would surely be more than a little frustrating for the guys in the white overalls. Behind your back, they might even be tempted to poke a little fun at your expense. Musicians and engineers are not, for the most part, cruel, sadistic people, but if you put your studio ugly-Americanism on display from the get-go, you might just become the subject of some ridicule. A lot of players have strong egos and big personalities, and those guys are capable of tromping all over your song—with cleats.

That being said, the rest of this chapter will detail many of the terms you will be expected to know in the course of producing your song demo.

Engineer Speak

First, we'll delve into recording engineer terminology.

BPM (or beats per minute). Applies to tempo. Ballads are usually 60 to 70 BPM. Mid-tempos are around 80 to 110. Up-tempos usually range from 120 to 150. Choosing an exact tempo is the first and most critical decision you will make in the studio. If the tempo seems too fast or too slow, you could suggest that the guys "take it down [or up] a couple of clicks." *Voila,* you're speaking studio!

EQ (or equalization). An engineer can boost or de-emphasize frequencies using EQ. There are various kinds of EQ: parametric, graphic, hi-pass, lo-pass, and so on. It's not necessary for you to know the ins and outs of how these attenuators work, only to learn to recognize high, low, and midrange frequencies by ear and be able to suggest that those be increased or decreased, as in "Could you put a little more high end on that guitar?" or, "Doesn't the piano have a little too much low end?" If you're able to articulate your question or request well enough, the engineer should be able to answer it and dial in the right EQ to satisfy your needs. Note: Equalization can only actually work on frequencies that are already part of the sonic signal. In other words, you can't boost or take away a frequency that isn't already in the natural recorded sound of an instrument or voice.

Reverb (or reverberation). Reverb is caused naturally when a sound reflects off of surfaces in an enclosed space, thus lengthening the apparent decay of the sound. If you go into a gymnasium and clap your hands, the sound you hear after your clap is the reverberation of your hands coming together as the sound echoes off of the walls, floor, and ceiling multiple times. Every recording studio has reverb units capable of placing a recorded sound in a wide range of virtual ambient spaces, from small rooms to cathedrals. Also commonly referred to as echo, ambience, or "verb" for short, as in "Could you put some verb on the snare?"

Pre-delay. The time between the original signal and the beginning of the reverb. Digital reverb units can be set with a delay between the original recorded sound and the beginning of the reverberation. This delay time is measured in milliseconds. Pre-delay gives a more spacious sound to the reverb, while not muddling the original signal. If you want to keep a certain level of reverb on a vocal without affecting the presence of the singer's voice, perhaps a little longer pre-delay is called for.

Slap or tape slap. One, relatively quick echo of a signal. Slap was first created by recording a signal into the record head of a tape machine, then listening back to the same signal from the playback head. The space between the heads created a single echo. Using a VSO (variable speed oscillator), the speed of the tape passing over the heads could be adjusted to alter the length of the slap, meaning the slower the speed of the tape, the longer the time between the original signal and its echo. The old Elvis Presley records used this effect liberally, especially on Presley's vocals and his acoustic guitar percussion. Tape slap became the signature sound of rockabilly.

Delay. Multiple slaps created by "feedback." A number of echoes (called ping-pong delays) can be adjusted to fit in time with the tempo of the track. Each delay or echo is a little less present than the previous one, but this "feedback" effect can last for a number of seconds. Ping-pong delay is often used on electric guitars and vocals, as in Phil Collins singing, "I can feel it comin' in the air tonight...night...night...night..." The extra "...nights" fading away are caused by delay.

Chorus. A shimmering effect when two almost identical signals are perceived as one. When two similarly timbred sound sources are playing or singing the same part at the same time, yet not perfectly in tune with each other, the result is a chorused sound that appears to the ear like one signal. Chorus often occurs naturally when two voices sing or two instruments play in unison, or when you strum a 12-string guitar. Chorus units are commonly used to create a shimmer on electric guitars (e.g., The Police or The Pretenders) or to give a stack of vocal harmonies a sweeping sheen.

Compression/limiting. Leveling amplification. A compressor/limiter is an amplifier that reduces peak signals and boosts quieter signals, then evens the output to a prescribed mean level. Almost every instrument and vocal requires some compression (and/or limiting) in the recording and mixing process. Next to EQ, compression is the most utilized technical tool in the studio. If properly used, compression is pretty much undetectable to the ear. However, this effect has often been used poorly or over-used by untrained engineers, or intentionally used as a way to color the signal, as in Steven Stills' ultra compressed acoustic guitars on CS&N's "Suite For Judy Blue Eyes."

Panning. Placing a sound in the stereo landscape. A guitar, a tambourine, a keyboard, any recorded sound can be placed in any part of, or even all across, the left-right stereo field. Panning helps instruments and vocals stand out in a mix, without having to turn them up, by getting competing elements out of each others' way. Panning helps instruments complement each other and creates a depth of field that more accurately simulates a live-music experience. Engineers often have their own preferences as to where certain instruments should be panned in a mix. You may have ideas of your own. Generally, lead vocals and bass remain in the center of the mix. Drums are usually in stereo, laid out in a simulation of the drum kit. Pianos can be spread across the spectrum, with the left hand to the left and the right to the right or they can be placed off to one side or the other. Panning is very important to every mix. Pay close attention to it.

Flange. A sweeping effect created by two identical signals playing within 20 milliseconds of each other. Flanging is a much more dramatic effect than chorusing. The term was reputedly coined by John Lennon, when engineer Ken Townsend used this technique as artificial double tracking (ADT) on Beatles' records.

Double tracking. Replicating an existing performance on a separate track. This technique has been used liberally on pop records to create a natural chorus effect, particularly on vocals and guitars. When a vocalist sings in unison with himself or herself, it creates a complex group of harmonics. On lead vocals or lead guitars, "doubling" can add depth and character to the part. On background vocals, "doubling" each part helps vocals blend together, while adding depth and texture. Tracks can be double tracked, triple tracked, or more. Each layer adds another set of harmonics. Queen used multitracked unison vocals to create their massive vocal sound (e.g., "Bohemian Rhapsody"). The Beatles often double tracked lead and background vocals ("Paperback Writer") and lead electric guitars ("Something").

Overdubbing. Adding an instrument or vocal, usually on a separate track of a multitrack recorder. After a live basic track has been recorded, every additional part added will be an overdub. In a MIDI production, often every single part beyond the first scratch tracks is technically an overdub.

Gate. A compressor that opens up at a certain velocity level and shuts off any signal below that level. This is used to automatically eliminate noise, leakage, or unwanted ambience between essential parts. A gate can also be used as an effect, as on a snare drum. Gated snares were very popular in the '80s.

Musician Speak

I will make the assumption that, as a songwriter, you are already more than familiar with the basic terminology of song structure: what constitutes an intro, a verse, a chorus, a refrain, a bridge, and a tag. That nomenclature is pretty much a universal language in recording studios all over the world.

Chart. A studio or live musician's map. This comprises the chords or chord numbers written out by the session bandleader as a guide for the players. Learn how to read charts. It could be one of the most important things you ever do.

Coda. A section of the song the musicians return to after following through the basic chart, notated by an oval with a diagonal line drawn through it. Could be any section of the song repeated or a newly introduced piece of music, like a tag on a last chorus or an extra bridgelike piece that allows the song to make a final statement.

Pedal. A drone or repeated note played under, within, or over a series of changing chords. For instance, a bass pedal could be the tonic (root) note played under the one (C) and four (F) chords. A guitar pedal could be the fifth or ninth of the tonic chord that plays within the four, the five, the minor six, and the flat seven. Pedals can make a routine chord progression sound hipper. Producer Ted Templeman used to use a right-hand piano octave pedaling all the way through early Doobie Brothers' records. Take a listen to "Listen to the Music," and "Long Train Runnin'" to hear what I mean.

Push. The syncopated, rhythmic anticipation of a note at the top of or within a measure (bar) of music. A push can involve the kick drum, the bass, and the rest of the instruments hitting a beat an eighth or a 16th note early, then sustaining over the anticipated beat, or the kick and bass can remain steady, while the other instruments push.

Tremolo. An effect used on electric guitars, in which the signal is amplified and diminished rhythmically, creating a pulsating sound. This term is borrowed from the rapid reiteration of single notes on a classical stringed instrument.

Backbeat. Rhythmic accentuation, as in where the snare hits on the twos and fours of a bar. "It's got a backbeat, you can't lose it." —Chuck Berry, "Rock and Roll Music."

Downbeat. The beginning of a bar of music. Taken from the downward motion of an orchestra conductor's baton.

Upbeat. An unaccented beat, as in the four-and beat before the beginning of a bar in $\frac{4}{4}$ time. Once again, taken from the up stroke of a conductor's baton.

Twos and fours. The backbeat, where the snare drum usually hits in straight-ahead $\frac{4}{4}$ time.

Nashville Studio Slang

Now let's look at the recording dialect peculiar to the studios of Nashville.

Diamond. A sustained chord over a rhythmic stop (usually played by the entire band). A diamond could last a bar, two bars, or just the length of a half note or even a quarter note. It is notated on the chart as a diamond around the chord number. (An out-of-town songwriter friend kept referring to diamonds as "footballs." That didn't ingratiate him into the Nashville studio community very well.)

Channel. The b-section of a verse or pre-chorus of a song. The part of the verse that builds to the chorus.

Turnaround. The bars of instrumental music between the end of the first chorus and the beginning of the second verse. Usually a repeat of all or part of the intro figure, or it can be a brief, transitional piece of music only played this one time.

If you'd never swung a nine iron, you probably wouldn't carry a bag of golf clubs onto a country club course—at least not without taking a pal along who'd spent a few hours on the links. Why is it that so many songwriters arrive at Studio X ignorant of the vernacular and clueless about the process, yet expect to get great results? The purpose of this chapter is to translate the bare minimum of an arcane language you will be well served to learn before you invest in your next excursion into the strange but wondrous land of the multitrack recording facility. Still, you can read books and see travelogues about far away places, but no words or pictures can replicate the actual sting of salt air on your face as you stand on the White Cliffs of Dover. You have to do it to really know it for yourself.

CHAPTER 26
Producing Your Great Demo, Part I

I hate nostalgia. Nothing turns my tummy quicker than folks looking back through rosy, retro goggles to some fabricated version of history, pining for a previous era they now see as "a simpler time." Those Civil War re-enactors for instance. Have they not perused the blood-soaked, disease-ridden pages of *Red Badge of Courage,* seeing how 12-year-old boys were ripped from family farms to have their limbs blown off, while fighting against their own cousins, one "noble cause" against another? Or, worse yet, those cultural oddities who idealize the Middle Ages, clashing broad swords in city parks, chomping on fire-roasted turkey legs, spouting "thee's" and "thou's," and treating their wenches like...well...you know, wenches. How about the plague, you guys? That was a barrel of fun, I'm sure. A simpler time? Thou must kiddeth me! I always found *Happy Days* and *Grease* comical and patently embarrassing. The '50s? Sure, an exciting, inspired, rebel-without-a-cause brand of music was born, as country music and blues collided to form that tasty peanut butter and chocolate treat, called rock and roll. And, dag nab it, that decade *was* a simpler time. Those pesky colored folks stayed in their place back then, out of the voting booths, in the back of our buses, drinking from their own, separate fountains. Still, they sho-nuff cooperated in providing the world with the roots of great American music: jazz, R&B, and rock and roll. Ah, those were the good ol' days: "Sunday, Monday, Happy Days..." Everybody sing along!

On the flip side, it's equally as laughable to hear an old curmudgeon pontificating about how he had to walk ten miles through ten feet of snow every day to get to a one-room schoolhouse. "You kids are soft. You don't know what hardship is!" Okay, Grandpa. We get it. Life was tough back then. Well, it ain't all peaches and cream in this modern world, either. And, I kind of doubt we'll ever look back at 2010, longing for "a simpler time." There is no doubt about it, we are living in a very complex era, and we're all coping with an enormous amount of stress. We are constantly being bombarded with input, noise, visuals, and constantly changing technology. Back in the Middle Ages, who could have imagined carrying around a hand-held device that, with a wave of a finger, mysteriously brings full-color images through the air and allows people to communicate instantly from half a world away? Back then, of course, they didn't even know the Earth was round. Anybody who prophesized such blasphemy would surely have been burned at the stake. But, it is what it is, folks. We deal with the times we live in. Songwriters, this is a reality you are just going to have to accept: If you want your songs to achieve their highest potential, you will have to learn to produce great demos. This wasn't always so; but it's the way of this modern, shrinking, and very round world.

When I started my songwriting journey, back in the vaunted '60s—I can just hear you chuckling to yourself, "Oh, here he goes, negating his anti-nostalgia rant by getting all weepy for the good ol' days"—anyway (*ahem*, the professor clears his throat), demos were not commonplace, let alone obligatory. The equipment just simply wasn't widely available or affordable, and audio-engineering expertise was the domain of boy scientists with thick spectacles, pen-protectors in their breast pockets, and multiple keys dangling from their belt loops. Recording was facilitated by heavy, reel-to-reel recorders, using spools of analog tape. To schlep around a two-track recorder, a microphone, mic cable, mic stand, and a box of tape would have been awkward and inconvenient, to say the least, even if one could afford to own such sophisticated stuff, let alone accumulate the knowledge to make it all work together. So, writers usually bypassed the demoing process, by sitting down at the piano and performing their songs live. The necessity of songwriters having to pitch their own stuff with a live performance must have spawned legendary tunesmith, Jule Stein's all-too-true declaration: "Without rendition, there is no song."

It's also true that—at least in the pop music world (not so much in blues, R&B, or country)—prior to the '50s, songwriting was pretty much the province of schooled musicians, who knew how to write lead sheets, and lyricists with some legitimate, literary education. So, most tunesmiths were capable of documenting their compositions on paper, enabling other musicians who wanted to interpret their work to sight read the music and lyrics. For better or worse, by the time I started makin' stuff up, all those assumed qualifications had been chucked out of the window, in favor of a more, shall we say, egalitarian musical utopia, in which anyone with an idea, a pencil, and a sheet of paper could call himself or herself a songwriter. It was an amazing period. Nobody told us that we couldn't do it. Furthermore, as the generation gap was ever-widening, wedged by a strong distrust for our elders, we wouldn't have heeded those old imposters anyway. After all, they told us that smoking pot would make us go insane and/or lead us directly to slavery to the needle. As, for the most part, toking on a doob only resulted in a near-terminal case of the giggles and made potato chips taste like nirvana, those old folks didn't have much cred with us. As a result, all over the world, mere teenagers, with little or no musical education, were suddenly penning classic songs. Well, there were *some* classics. There was a whole bunch of worthless, blathering inanity, too. (And since then, not much has changed in that ratio, I'm afraid.)

In the '70s, with the advent of multitrack, analog recording, the most heavily produced song demos typically comprised a basic rhythm section (drums, bass, guitar, piano), a vocal, and maybe a vocal harmony. If a string machine were available, the keyboardist might throw down a pad and the drummer might shake a tambourine, but that would be the extent of it. Other than those "full-out" studio demos, new songs were usually rendered piano/vocal or guitar/vocal. Gradually, however, songwriters and publishers began seeing the upside of investing in more complex, complete demos that more replicated the songs being played on the radio. As these innovators upped the demo ante, others had to keep up to stay competitive. Simultaneously, computer-based digital recording, and various pedal and rack-mounted effects and outboard equipment gave musicians and engineers access to sounds that used to require a great deal of experimentation and/or set-up time to achieve. As producers, A&R people, and artists became more acclimated to these more sophisticated demos, their ears began to expect a more complete production. Certainly, songs do still get cut from piano/vocal or guitar/vocal worktapes. This happens far less often than it used to, though, and usually only when those bare-bones productions are performed by writers with extraordinary voices and exemplary musicianship. Nowadays, it seems that a song must be pitched as though it is already blasting from the 50,000-watt tower of a Top 40 station, for most industry pros to imagine that it might actually do that very thing. So, Jules Stein's quote brought up to date, might go more like this: "Without a master-quality demo, there is no song."

Evaluate Your Goods

You've heard this already, but it bears repeating here. Remember what Steve Dorff says: "Writing a great song is only half the battle. You gotta demo it just right. Then you've got to be ingenious enough to know what to do with it." So, let's examine the middle sentence in this legendary composer/arranger/producer's three-part recipe for songwriting success. "You gotta demo it just right." Dorff goes onto elaborate: "Sometimes you gotta take a few shots at it." That means you might miss the mark the first time out, come up with a vocal that doesn't quite sell it, or a mix that fails to capture the song's true spirit. If the song is great, the demo has to live up to the song—even if it means redoing various elements of the production or even scrapping the whole thing and giving it another try.

As the industry now pretty much demands a demo that replicates "master-quality," we are actually setting out to make a record on the cheap with every demo we produce. In other words, assuming that we've written a song worthy of investing the time, effort, and resources it takes to make a great demo—and, believe me, those investments are nothing to sneeze at—our mission is to come up with a recording that screams "radio hit" from its first intro note through the tag of the final chorus. However, we are not going to try to make our production so flawless, so exemplary, so superior that artists would be intimidated by the demo singer's vocal performance, or a producer might shy away from attempting to duplicate its grandeur. There is a fine line here. Let's keep in mind that the word, demo, is short for "demonstration recording." Its purpose is to demonstrate the potential of the song as a master recording, not necessarily to outdo any possible future productions.

The mistake that writers and publisher make more than any other is demoing too many songs that are either not up to marketplace standards or are simply not ready yet to be demoed. This indiscretion can create an enormous drain on company resources and person power. Some publishers justify this by explaining they have to throw a writer a bone every now and then, financing a demo on an average or mediocre song, just to encourage the writer. I can understand that philosophy, and it may or may not be true, on a case-by-case basis. However, that begs the question: Why did they sign the writer in first place? Furthermore, it assumes the publisher is actually capable of judging when a song is studio-ready or when it still needs more re-working, or even when a song should simply be set aside. What does demoing a substandard song say to its writer? Is he or she supposed to believe that compromising one's writing standards should be standard operating procedure? Also, if the song doesn't really measure up, it's unlikely to get many pitches—if any. In which case, what does the demo's lack of exposure do to the writer's fragile psyche? It's far too expensive and time-consuming to invest in demos unless the songs are truly great songs. Surely hundreds of millions—if not billions—of dollars and multi-millions of human hours have been squandered on demos that never should have been made in the first place. Of course, you won't find the studio musicians, the engineers, or the studio owners complaining about this, nor should they. However, when an investor checks the balance sheet and finds that his indie publishing company remains in the red, he would have every right to listen closely to the demos in the catalog and question where his investment dollars went. (That's where I'd look anyway.)

This is why I (along with Jason Blume and other songwriting coaches) strongly advise writers to get qualified feedback and constructive criticism on every song before they invest in demos. If you don't have a publisher, a plugger, or some reliable, trustworthy industry pro on whom you can depend to give you this kind of perspective, attend workshops, seminars, or classes; or better yet, find a coach online. To me, it seems a far superior plan to spend the extra time and a few bucks to find out if a song has legs, and to get the kind of input that can make it a more solid and competitive piece, than to throw all your chips on the table and roll the dice without testing the water. Of course, it's only natural to be excited about your latest composition. We all have to be enthused about what we're into at this moment, but don't be impulsive about doing demos. You may be absolutely certain now that a song is a hit, but you might have a confusing line in there, or a convoluted structural problem that some feedback can help you fix. If you eschew coaching, there is a strong possibility that someday in the future, you'll listen to the demos you made this year and recognize the reasons why those songs didn't fly. I can't tell you how many times I've listened to a tune from the past, a song I was sure was going to take the industry by storm, and said to myself, "Oh, *now* I get it. That's what was wrong." We all live and learn. It's better to learn now, than to wait years to find out what you could have done to lift your songs up to be marketplace ready.

Choose Your Approach

"Let's record it now, so we can listen to it later!"—Gordon Mote, legendary Nashville keyboardist and Christian recording artist.

There are basically two ways to go when it comes to producing a great demo. In this chapter, we will be discussing option number one: a full-out studio production. In the next, we'll delve into the second method: home recording. Either path can lead to a killer demo that has every potential of knocking industry socks off left and right. These two routes are not, by any means, mutually exclusive of each other. Depending on the song, the available tools, and the resources at hand, any demo can be a hybrid, utilizing one or the other for each separate step of the process. Remember this: The most valuable ingredient to any production is time. By their very nature, demos are low budget and therefore provide for a limited number of studio hours. So, whatever method provides you with adequate time to capture performances that showcase your song in its brightest light and within your budget, is the right way to go. It's a pragmatic challenge to an artistic endeavor, but one that can be overcome by being prepared, making smart decisions, and using all the modern tools available to you.

The Studio Demo

Producing a studio demo is really just a sped-up version of the production process I described in Chapter 24: booking a demo studio to cut a basic track with a session band, doing overdubs on the date, recording lead and background vocals, doing some sweetening, and mixing. Many excellent facilities (especially in Nashville and other music-business capitals) provide all of these services as a package deal. If you prefer, they can book the players, provide the recording and mixing engineer(s), find demo singers, and set aside a proper amount of time for you. Some studios charge a flat fee, while others bill you by the hour. These demos are more elaborate productions than the first multitrack demos we made in the '70s because the players and studios of today have many more tools and tricks at their fingertips. Getting a certain ambience on an electric guitar or a drum set in the '70s and early '80s required quite a bit of experimentation with mic placements or sometimes intricate jury rigging of the studio space. For instance, legend has it that Roy Halee recorded the crashing drum-boom on Simon and Garfunkel's "The Boxer" by miking an elevator shaft. It presumably took a number of hours just to set that up. The budget for a major artist/major label master album would usually provide adequate time to experiment with this type of extra production coloring. Demo studio time, however, needs to be used very expeditiously, so you wouldn't have the luxury of telling the drummer to take a break for a couple of hours, while you hang a mic cable down an elevator shaft, and set up his drums at the bottom. So, in the '70s, that sound would have been impossible to capture on a demo budget. With the digital effects of today, a replication of that same ambience is only a couple of mouse clicks or button pushes away. So, modern demos can take on more production colors, with guitar effects, reverbs, room ambience, synthesizer presets, virtual instruments, and so on all readily available in the racks on both sides of the glass; by that, I mean in the tracking room with the musicians, and in the control room with the engineer. The players and engineers don't have to jump through hoops and take a ton of time to give the writers and publishers exactly what they're looking for.

That's why it's critically important for you to know specifically what it is you're looking for and how to ask for it. In the previous chapter, I explained how to speak and understand studio lingo. It is equally important that you be able to speak "Musician," too. The musicians and the studio staff are there to follow orders, if you're prepared to bark 'em out. You're the boss. You're paying the bills, or your publisher is. The band and the engineer are the wait staff and the chef. You provide the groceries and the recipe. They cook it up and serve it to you. They are there to please you. They want you to walk away happy. If the guitar player cops an attitude or fails to provide you with the sounds and the parts you want, you probably won't want to hire him again. So, next time, he'll be home watching reruns of *Magnum P.I.,* instead of pickin' with the cats and makin' a nice afternoon's paycheck. However, he can't provide you with what you want, if you can't articulate what you want clearly. If you're looking for an electric guitar color like Andy Summers on "De Do Do Do, De Da Da Da" by The Police, there's a good chance your session guitarist has a Summers preset all ready to go, only a push of a button away. However, if you go to him and say, "I want that sound by that British band, you know what I mean. It's kind of nonsense song," I doubt if he's going know which button to push. Both of you will be left confused and frustrated. If you ask the engineer to put "more juice" on the snare drum, he won't know if you're asking for reverb, tape slap, high end, or distortion.

Some years back, I heard a story about Clive Davis asking a recording engineer to put "more purple" on a mix. Davis may know every detail about how records are promoted at radio, every nuance of how product gets to retail. Evidently, there was a time at least when even the most knowledgeable man in the music business didn't know how to communicate in the studio. Communication, my friends, is the key. If you don't know how to speak "Studio" and "Musician," it would be a very good idea for you to find somebody to produce your sessions with some mastery of the language. Even if you walk in with some great songs, if you don't have the ability to win the players' respect and command the session, you run the risk of completely losing control and having the train leap the tracks. If that happens, you will walk away a very unhappy camper. Nobody wants that to happen. The players don't want it. The engineer doesn't want it. Your publisher doesn't want it. And, more than anybody, *you* certainly don't. So, either learn how to communicate in a way that musicians and engineers can understand exactly what it is you want, or bring along someone who can clearly articulate your desires on your behalf. And, if you *do* bring along a producer, only communicate through him. Consult with him, like he was your trial lawyer on *L.A. Law*. Then, after he translates your request, let him push the talk-back and suggest that the drummer use his high hat in the first chorus instead of the ride cymbal.

As the session begins, some writers prefer not to even play a worktape for the band. My good pal Jon Robbin just sits down with his acoustic and picks and sings the song live for the players, demonstrating the groove and structure of the song, the basic guitar figures, and so on. As the band members listen through to his performance, they make notes on their charts. A guitar player, for instance might write out the exact notation of a signature lick, or a drummer might jot down a staccato build, a stop, or a triplet figure, in his own script on his own chart. Other writers (like me for instance) prefer to record a pre-production demo that shows the motifs, the dynamics, and the exact tempo of the song. This way, the players get a real solid impression of where the production is headed.

Speaking "Musician" starts with learning how to read a chart. Studios outside of Nashville generally use chord charts or lead sheets. In Music City, musicians are more accustomed to number charts. You can find a plethora of detailed descriptions of the Nashville Number System on the Internet. Basically, this simple notation technique was first used by the background vocal group, The Jordanaires, in the late '50s and was later refined by multi-instrumentalist, session stalwart, Charlie McCoy. By assigning a number to each chord, starting with the tonic chord as "1," this system makes it easy for the musicians to read the chart in any key. There are usually four bars per line. Chord numbers that are not underlined last an entire bar. Bars that include more than one chord are called split bars or split measures. For split measures, all the chords in that bar are underlined together. As the arrangement is worked out, each musician is free to add as much detail to his chart as he may need in order to remember his own part. As the writer plays the song through, or they listen to the worktape or pre-production demo, the drummer finds the song's tempo with a hand-held click generator.

Once the band has listened to the writer's run through, worktape, or pre-production demo, following along on the chart, they may ask some questions and make some suggestions and comments. There is usually some playful banter as they move into the tracking room to take their places. Everybody is relaxed and upbeat. There is nothing more fun than this. You are about to have your labor of love instantaneously brought to life, magically, by some of the best musicians—and best human beings—in the world.

The engineer sets the tempo and time signature on the digital grid of the multitrack session. Either the engineer or the drummer will generate a click track into the cue system. One of the songwriters or a session singer will go into a vocal booth or stay in the control room to sing the guide vocal. It's important for the players to hear the vocal as they record, so they can apply the proper dynamics, avoid stepping on the vocal, and take turns filling between vocal lines. Sometimes, that first take is close to perfect. More often than not, you'll want to make adjustments. So, you'll be tested to articulate what you might want to try to improve the next take. Supposing you want the band to come to a sudden stop two bars before the chorus, or you want the band to push the first beat of a certain section. If you're unable to explain that in relationship to where the stop or the push comes on the chart, the band will be hard-pressed to comprehend your instructions. If you can't read the chart, your request can be confusing and frustrating to the players and require a lot of discussion and translation. They are there to please you, but they can't be expected to read your mind or read between the lines of your inarticulate ramblings. You might want to adjust the tempo slightly, shorten the turnaround, or try modulating the last chorus. However, don't overload them with a dozen ideas at once. Prioritize your suggestions two or three at a time. Since they've had a pass at the entire song, you now don't have to run the entire piece to make sure the new tempo is right. Just ask them to play a verse or a chorus. If you want a push into the bridge, just ask them to play that transition. Time is money. Each pass through the entire song and the comments that follow can take an accumulated seven to ten minutes. Your goal on most demo tracking sessions is to get at least four, five, or six songs recorded; at three hours, that's between 30 and 45 minutes per basic track. Being indecisive on one track and falling behind schedule can be a disaster for the session, forcing other songs to suffer for lack of that most-precious commodity: time.

More times than not, one or two of the band members will offer some suggestions. Sometimes they'll propose a different chord in one spot, or a cut bar in another, or to put a certain section in a half-time feel. Ask them to try those ideas out. If you really like their ideas, incorporate them. There is no extra charge to use the band's ideas. If you don't care for how they sound, you are under no obligation to accept them. Although these guys are not a bunch of neighborhood bullies, certain musicians will have forceful, persuasive opinions about what's right and what's wrong. You might even come to a strong disagreement with the bass player over the inversion of one certain chord in the bridge. (That's happened to me more than once.) Certainly, these guys are well-schooled, and they play sessions pretty much every day, all year long. Yeah, they know a thing or two. But, remember, this is *your* song. This is *your* session. This is *your* life. Only agree to a change if it feels right to you, if you agree that it improves your song. However, I reiterate: If you can't tell the players exactly what the target is, you can't expect them to hit the exact center of the bull's eye.

Remember that a basic track is only that: a *basic* track. You want to be sure that the pocket sits perfectly for the melody and the lyrics float easily on top of the groove. Everything else can be changed, punched in, and so on. More often than not, one or two of the players will ask for "fixes," meaning they will want the engineer to give them another pass at a certain section of the track. The bass player may want to redo the bridge. The piano may want to try the second verse again. You may have identified a spot where you'd prefer that the guitar player play a simpler pattern. After fixes, the guitar player might want to add another part and overdub his lead. The piano player might want to throw on a Hammond B3 organ, a synth, or a string pad. The drummer might want to put a shaker, hand drums, or tambourine on the track. You might have some definite overdub/sweetening ideas. It's your party. Speak up loud and clear. Prioritize your ideas. And, don't forget, you can take or leave anything the musicians offer to contribute. The engineer will record each part on a separate track, which can be incorporated into the mix or not.

There's a pretty good chance you'll love everything these guys come up with; after all, they're brilliant players. Realize, however, that you're setting yourself up for some hard decisions later on. The sonic spectrum of a mix can only include so much audio information. Something's going to have to give. Otherwise, you're headed for a hodgepodge mix that includes everything *and* the kitchen sink. Remember, you are making a demonstration recording for the purpose of putting the melody and lyrics of your song in its most flattering frame. This is not a showcase for a hired guitar hero or a keyboard genius. A flashy guitar lead or a brilliant piano passage never got a song cut. So, try to be decisive. Don't spend needless time experimenting with a lot of additional, unnecessary parts. If you feel an overdub is off-base, pull the plug on it. Be diplomatic, but move on. These guys will respect your decision. They're big boys, and no real professional will take it personally if you choose to nix any one part. Above all else, avoid the following suggestion: "Hey, let's fade the song out." A fade only indicates that the songwriter has not completed the composition. The accumulated, wasted studio time taken up by a fade can amount to hours, from the tracking, to the overdubbing, to the vocals, to the mix. As this *is* a demo, a favorable or unfavorable impression will have been made long before the final chorus hits the fade. In the history of pop music, there has never, ever been a single case when a producer or an artist said, "Man, I was on the fence about this song, until you got to that cool fade out." Fading a song is lazy. Fading a song is an indulgence you can't afford. A fade out is only suitable for the last track on an album—never for a song demo.

CHAPTER 27
Producing Your Great Demo, Part II

For as long as I can remember, I harbored a private dream: to possess the tools that would enable me to make quality recordings of my own songs at home, even playing and singing all the parts myself. Maybe it was my innate, controlling personality, a seriously overblown ego, or a latent antisocial nature. Although I can be a bit distant and grumpy, I don't think it's the latter, because I nearly always find cutting basic tracks with a band of brilliant players a very special, joyous, and exhilarating experience. However, I do enjoy my own company, as well; and, I treasure any time I get to delve deeply into my subconscious creative inspirations and mold them into dimensional reality. Those hours of solo productivity exemplify "flow," a certain productive state recognized by some researchers as the most fulfilling experience in human life. Here is my off-the-cuff definition of flow: doing a task for which one has training or expertise, making measurable progress, and losing all track of the passage of time in the process. For some people, flow can be achieved while driving a car, ironing a stack of laundry, gardening, or even while doing the most advanced mathematical calculations. For me, I find flow in writing (music, lyrics, or prose) and especially in recording music in my home studio.

A Brief History of Home Recording

Anyway, all my life I've envisioned (some might say fantasized) full-scale extravaganzas in my head. It began with those extemporaneous, epic Peter Pan vs. Captain Hook dagger-and-sword dramas in the suburban backyard of my prepubescent childhood. Now, my grandiose imaginations are being realized in my gray-haired years with the operatic pop pieces I've been producing. For me, it was never just about the child's play, or the chords, the melody, and the words. I always saw my stories in widescreen Technicolor and heard my songs as fully produced records. I actually believed that, given the tools and enough time, I could bring the sonic pictures in my mind to life all by myself. On the cusp of the 1960s and '70s, Stevie Wonder began making those incredible, self-accompanied, solo records. Man, I envied him. Then, Todd Rundgren made his masterful *Something, Anything?,* playing the roles of songwriter, artist, back-up band, producer, *and* engineer. When Paul McCartney came out with "Maybe I'm Amazed," it hardened my determination to someday realize my own sonic visions, without those pricey, pesky musicians daring to have ideas of their own.

Then, in 1974, I got a chance to give it a go. It was an absolute disaster. My first solo single, "Don't You Worry"—a little piece of ear candy I'd produced at a popular Montreal facility called Le Studio Tempo, using a top, local rhythm section—was rising on the Canadian national charts. So the owner of my little label (Good Noise Records), an infinitely generous and likable gentleman named André Perry, gave me a budget to cut a follow up. For a week, I woodshedded at home, planning and rehearsing the parts to "Very Special Places (We Both Know)," until I felt confident enough to pull it off. Greeting me as I carried my guitars into the studio was recording engineer, Nick Blagona, and my studio band: a set of rented drums, a bass, and some keyboard equipment. Where to begin? As planned, I started with rhythm-electric guitar. Although after several passes, I got all they way through, my time was less than rock solid. *Oh, well, I'll fix it later,* I thought. Then I tried laying down a keyboard track; but, once again, I lost the groove here and there. Then, drums. I couldn't keep a solid beat for more than two bars at a time. *How did Stevie do it,* I puzzled? *How did Todd Rundgren achieve such infectious grooves?* Blagona and I scrapped this ill-conceived idea pretty quickly, and I carried my guitars to my car, humiliated at my inability to make a record as a one-man band, knowing that I'd wasted a good hunk of André Perry's money. We recut the track with real musicians. The record reached the Canadian Top Five, and the song won a BMI Award. Those were wonderful achievements, but I had yet to accomplish what I had always wanted to do.

Ten years later in L.A., I went to a demonstration of a digital workstation called the Fairlight. For starters, this amazing invention consisted of a MIDI–controller keyboard and banks of sampled and synthesized sounds: drums, percussion, basses, keyboards, guitars, horns, strings, voices, you name it. The operator could easily call up any or all of these virtual instruments to be triggered by the notes of its keyboard. As the operator played each part, they were programmed into a sequential MIDI file and saved. Then, each sequence could be played back via the Fairlight's onboard computer. Of course, with MIDI, if a note or notes are played out of time, they can be corrected (quantized). They can be made louder or softer (velocity), or shortened or lengthened (duration), as well. And, any sequence of notes can be copied and pasted to any other part of the song. So, here in one unit, was the back-up band I had been waiting to work with, one with a full arsenal of sounds that would obey my every command, without demanding union breaks. Adding to the appeal of this amazing, hybrid, musical instrument/computer was the fact that it was synchronized with eight tracks of digital audio, on which one could record performances in real time: vocals, guitars, saxophones, whatever. Never mind that it was only 16 bit and that the separate hard drives for each track were as big as large bureau drawer and had a fan that made nearly as much noise as a window-mounted air conditioner. This was the very tool that such ultra-hip studio geniuses as Sting, Peter Gabriel, and Kate Bush were using to make their records! Wow! My little heart went pittypat. *This,* I thought, *is a dream come true*! Here's the capper: it only cost a mere $150,000. *If I could only get my hands on this amazing machine,* I convinced myself, *I could surely make that record I'd failed so miserably at a decade earlier.* Owning a Fairlight remained a dream, a fantasy. Had I been able to come up with the scratch, I certainly would have grabbed up one of those contraptions, faster than The Ramones get to the hook of "Rock 'N' Roll High School."

Today, any songwriter can have everything the Fairlight offered—and much, much more—for a few thousand bucks. And when you consider that an average five-song, studio demo session costs between $2,500 and $4,000, why wouldn't a writer consider investing in gear that can save so much money year after year and put him or her in control of which songs get demoed and how, not to mention providing the learning curve that could naturally lead to greater production expertise? For me, it's an absolute no-brainer. This is not to say that every single songwriter is born with the capacity to get excellent results from a home studio alone. Some tunesmiths are better off leaving the nuts and bolts of recording and production to the experts. But, for the vast majority of writers, investing the resources, the time, and seeking the information and mentoring it takes to make a home studio work well can expand the realm of possibilities enormously. It's not only a form of creative liberation, but owning your own home studio enables you to create real assets—in the form of solely-owned master-quality recordings.

As someone who has always aspired to control the destiny of my own compositions, I have had hands-on experience with most every stage of home recording, as it evolved from an impractical rarity to its present level of ubiquity. Unless you live on a South Sea island or on a million-acre ranch in West Texas, there are probably three or four home recording studios within a five-mile radius of where you are right now. I've already mentioned the two-track recording experiments conducted in the mid '60s, with my pal Tim Sadler on his Revox reel-to-reel. My bandmate and first professional-songwriting mentor, Bob Segarini, always had some model of analog tape deck on hand to capture and store his daily musings. In the infancy of our second Elektra Records band, The Wackers (Segarini, Mike Stull, and I) cut some acoustic guitar/vocal home demos on a four-track Tascam machine. Using repeated bounces from track to track, we did live overdubs, mixing on the fly, *a la* The Beatles, layering vocal parts and doubling guitar lines. The loss of generation and resulting natural chorus and flanging added up to some incredibly vibrant sounds. Those were the recordings that inspired Elektra's Jac Holzman to send Gary Usher to remote Eureka, California to check us out. Usher ended up recommending that the label sign us, and he produced our first two albums. As the '70s rolled on, cassette-based, multitrack consoles became affordable. Many songwriters, like David Baerwald and David Ricketts (known as the duo David and David, *Welcome To The Boomtown* on A&M Records) became experts at creating full-sounding productions, using just those four cassette tracks.

Beat boxes that had commonly been used to accompany drumless lounge acts, evolved into more authentic-sounding drum machines, allowing musicians and composers to lay down a solid, musical bed, in an actual bedroom.

Akai expanded (literally) the cassette-based all-in console/recorder by issuing a full-sized mixing desk with a 12-track recorder built in. The tape cartridges resembled Sony Beta videotape. As the tape was much wider and the tape speed considerable faster than a conventional cassette, the fidelity and signal-to-noise ratio was much better. With these machines—plus good mics, preamps, compressors, and outboard effects—a home recording could be lifted pretty close to master quality. Although, the investment was still substantial for the basic gear required. Then, home digital took a quantum leap with the Alesis ADAT. In a rack-mounted, videotape-based, multitrack format, synchronizing several ADAT machines provided a home studio owner with excellent digital sound at a fraction of what digital multitrack recorders had previously cost. At one time or another, I either owned or availed myself of every one of these various home-studio formats to help give my self-produced song demos greater production quality.

In the '90s, almost overnight, digital hard-disk recorders appeared on the market and supplanted tape-based digital. These portable, all-in studio workstations—approximately the size of one of the Fairlight's eight hard drives and one tenth as noisy—provided superb digital sound reproduction along with a battery of digital outboard effects (reverb, compression, chorusing, electric amp simulation, and mic-signal processing, and so on). They also offered something that ADATs didn't have: virtual tracks. Although my Roland VS 880 could only play back eight tracks at a time, it provided 64 tracks on which to record. So, like The Wackers had done with our four-track reel to reel, like David and David had done on their cassette portable studios, like The Beatles had done with such amazing precision, bouncing parts from one tape machine to another to make their later records, multiple individual parts could be recorded on virtual tracks and premixed (bounced) together across the VS 880's eight audible tracks. As these hard-drive recorders featured digital audio, bouncing and premixing created no loss of generation.

Now, we had, in one box, an entire digital recording studio, for less than $3,000. By adding a MIDI controller keyboard, some MIDI sound generators, a decent tube preamp, a passable compressor, and using a conventional condenser mic, it became possible for nearly anyone to make incredible-sounding recordings at home. In 1996, I used my first advance from Mike Curb Music to finance such a home studio, which I installed in the attic of my family's rented house in Nashville. I put that little studio to work immediately, overdubbing vocals and sweetening basic tracks cut in the studio and even creating full productions from scratch. Three years later, in that very attic, I was still goin' with the flow as I constructed the demo of Tim James' and my song "My List." It was a painstaking, sometimes laborious process. One instrument at a time, then one vocal part at a time. Over three days, the production slowly took shape. What a great studio band could accomplish in ten or fifteen minutes—with far greater skill and spontaneity—took me two days. What an accomplished session guitarist could dash off in a couple of takes took me hours. What a pro mixer could crank out in 90 minutes took me eight hours. Maybe my musicianship wasn't up to the quality of the top session cats. Maybe the sound didn't have quite the punch of a live band recorded by a great engineer in a state-of-the-art facility, but the arrangement was solid and the performances were adequate enough. (Of course, I had years of working in the studio to lean on. A writer with less studio experience might require more experimentation and possibly some expert help to accomplish the same task.) In the long run, James and I had a demo of our song, without pulling one penny out of our pockets. If I had waited to accumulate the cash to do a studio demo, or gone around trying to get a publisher to pay for it, "My List" would likely be a distant memory by now, just another good song that never saw the light of day. Because I took the bull by the horns, invested in the equipment, learned how to use those tools efficiently, and spent the time to build the demo, piece by piece, "My List" was given the chance to become a hit song. Over the years, I've produced countless demos for myself and other writers that have not resulted in songs getting cut, and I've made dozens of other demos that did yield cuts, yet didn't come close to matching the success of "My List." However, the point here should be obvious: buying a home studio and learning to use it well can be a very, very good investment.

The music business has arrived at a new sensibility (or lack of sensibility, depending on your point of view). Expectations of demo production have reached their peak. The stakes have grown such that an international hit can reap multimillions in three to five years. Simultaneously, home-recording gear has become so much more affordable, produces such high quality, and is so user-friendly, there is absolutely no reason that a home demo cannot be just as good as, or even superior to a studio demo. More and more smart writers are producing demos at home and/or using their home facility to enhance studio demos, while saving money on demo budgets. You can no longer get a cut by sitting down and playing a song for an A&R person live. In fact, even excellent worktape demos are almost always not sufficient. Kent Blazy recalls a song he wrote with a writer who has since become a mega-success: "I remember one time, before Jeff Steele really took off, we wrote a song, and we did a little recording here at the house with me and him playing guitars and singing harmonies. It was a great little demo, and you know Jeff Steele can sell just about anything. We took it to somebody, a producer or an artist, and he said, 'Oh, I love this song. When you get it demoed, let me hear it.' I thought, You know, it's gonna be the same song—with drums on it."

Pining for the days when most producers could hear a song in its most basic form, Blazy says, "If you can't hear Skip Ewing with a piano and a vocal and get the idea of the song, then there's something wrong." Well there *is* something wrong then because music and lyrics in and of themselves are no longer sufficient to convince most decision makers that a song could indeed become a hit record. Most times, the demo has to sound like a hit. That's just the reality with which we're faced, right or wrong, like it or not. Having production skills can only help you deliver what the industry expects to hear. If you own even a basic home facility and can run it yourself, you have a massive advantage over a writer who depends exclusively on booking outside studios and hiring musicians and engineers to make demos. With a home facility, you can demo more songs for less money. You can control which songs get demoed. However, if you do invest in a studio, prepare to write far fewer songs, because every demo will eat up three or four times as much time as it took to write the song.

The Home-Studio Demo

I abandoned you in the last chapter, just after you finished cutting that basic track and the players did some overdubs. I left you stranded for this reason: Every step of the production process from that point can be accomplished either in a home studio or in a commercial facility. Cutting a basic track in a home studio, however, is usually quite a different process than recording a live session band. What follows is basically my step-by-step procedure for producing a demo at home.

Once a song is written, structured, and the key is set, I boot up a preset, demo-session template in ProTools. In this session setup, I've already created and labeled individual tracks for the standard instrumentation usually used on the basic track of a record (or demo): bass, drums (kick, snare, hat, toms, cymbals, room), acoustic guitar, electric guitar, and keyboards. I've also already programmed a MIDI click track to a default tempo. All I have to do now is to do a "Save Session As" under the title of the new song. Now, I've cloned a session from the demo template. I can create as many clones as I want from that template, as long as I begin by "saving as." Starting each session with a template you can alter and adjust to suit each song saves a lot of set-up time, rather than starting each session from scratch. Next, I adjust the tempo and save it.

(Please note: I work in ProTools, but this process works in any recording format you may choose. Digital files are basically interchangeable between all of the popular multitrack formats: ProTools, Nuendo, Logic, and so on. Some folks favor one kind of software over the other. I chose ProTools because, at the time I purchased it, ProTools was the most widely used, not necessarily because it was superior to any other. Also, once I master one method of recording, I tend to use it for a period of years, simply because I'd much prefer to be writing and recording music than reading manuals, attempting to learn a new program, and constantly updating my system.)

The next step is to record two fundamental, guide elements to the click track: a basic accompaniment instrument (usually either a keyboard or guitar) and a guide vocal. If the song has a steady and/or syncopated groove, the alternative to cutting these guide tracks to click is recording them to a drum or percussion loop. The initial parts will usually be temp (temporary) tracks. They should, however, be performed in-tune, in decent time, and represent the proper structure of the song. Certainly, I always plan to replace the entire vocal later using a production process I'll be describing in this chapter. Once you print these parts, you should set markers at the beginning of each section of the song: Intro, V1, b-section 1, Ch1, etc. This enables you to go right where you want to go with a mouse click and avoid mistakenly recording a part in the wrong section.

If you plan to program drums, it's usually a good idea to at least sketch them out right after printing your guide tracks. Overdubbing parts to a drum track can be very different than playing to a click. Often, I've found that even quantized drums don't sit perfectly with instruments cut to just a click; that's why it can often be a better idea to record over a loop from the get-go. Programming drums can be one of the most time-consuming parts of the production process. If you're looking to replicate an actual drummer's parts with natural, organic-sounding samples, you'll want to take care to "play" your drums the way a drummer would play them. In other words, since a drummer only has four limbs, you'd steer away from your sequence striking more than four instruments in the kit simultaneously. You wouldn't, for instance, play both a ride cymbal and a high hat at the same time because that wouldn't leave your "drummer" a hand to play the snare drum. If you observe the way drummers play, they seldom, if ever, play two rides at the same time: It's either the high hat *or* the ride cymbal—or it could even be a tom-tom ride—in various sections of the song.

After you get at least a good sketch of the drum sequence in a MIDI file, it's entirely up to you as to which instruments you want to overdub next. I'd say you'd probably want to start with the most fundamental piece in the band. If it's a rockin', guitar-driven song, you'd probably do the electric rhythm guitar next. If it's a keyboard ballad—unless you nailed it on the guide track—you'd probably want to record a perfect piano track. Begin to build from here, one instrument at a time, making absolutely certain that each track sits nicely on the drum track, supports the guide vocal, and doesn't fight with the other instruments. This is the fun part, because ideally each instrument creates a new dimension to the production. There will come a time in this process when it will begin to sound exciting, like when a studio band reads through the chart for the first time. The picture will begin to come clear. Some parts will work better than others. You may have to go back and patch up a guitar or a keyboard or a bass line. So, it's always a good idea to take note of your setups (compressor settings, guitar effects, EQ, and so on), so you can easily replicate the sound on a punch in.

Producing Vocals

Once you feel the track is substantial enough, it's time to record the vocal. Various producers and engineers (and singers, too) have different opinions as to what is the best way of capturing the best vocal performance. The most typical method is to let the singer do a full take everybody concurs is pretty solid, then punch in the lines that might need improvement. If the singer is experienced and comfortable with this style of recording, this approach might work fine. Some singers like to record the song a section at a time, or even a line at a time. Some like to get the verses first, before tackling the choruses. The problem with these methods is that you haven't established a dynamic arc for the vocal performance, so the vocal can end up not being cohesive, not flowing naturally from line to line and from section to section; or it might not represent the ultimate dynamic you're seeking for the song. That's why it's always more desirable, if the singer is well enough rehearsed, to start by doing at least a couple of passes from top to bottom. That way, the singer can get a better idea of the song's dynamic, before you start doing it line by line, or section by section.

Also, as a singer myself, I find it difficult to keep the emotional feel of the whole piece, when I'm nervously anticipating a punch in; and, I tend to lose the context of how the punched-in line fits in the song, when I'm concentrating on the exact phrasing and pitch of one particular passage. This is where the term "red-light fever" comes from. A singer may be relaxed and spontaneous, until he or she is informed that you're recording. That's why it's a very good idea to record everything, even the rehearsal passes. You never know what you'll capture. To avoid nervous self-consciousness, and the necessity for lots of potentially awkward punch ins, what follows is almost always my production approach to lead vocals. For me, it works every time, whether I'm the singer or producing another vocalist. Most singers (particularly artists) really seem to like this method; it's the engineer who sometimes takes issue with it. By the way, this technique was originated and developed by producer Peter Asher for Linda Ronstadt, and can work equally well in a commercial studio or in a home facility.

Ronstadt has always much preferred to sing her songs from beginning to end—no stopping, no punch ins. She wants to achieve the natural dynamics of a stage performance. So, Asher would record multiple Ronstadt takes. Then he would bounce the best passages from each performance onto one, final, cohesive, lead-vocal track, which is commonly called a vocal "comp" (for composite). Unfortunately, in the analog domain, the vocal would loose a generation with this method. Fortunately, in the bounce, the levels of the performance could be premixed, so the vocal wouldn't require a lot of compression in order for it to sit nicely in the mix. That would enable Ronstadt's recorded voice to be more present, not so squashed by the compressor, which mitigated the generation loss. Now, however, with digital, there is no degradation of the signal whatsoever when one track is bounced to another. I record three, four, or even five vocal passes on separate play lists. As the singer performs each pass, I carefully make notes on a lyric sheet as to which takes I favor on which lines of the song. This requires a printed lyric sheet that follows the entire lyric of the song from beginning to end, with each chorus written out, regardless of whether the identical lyric repeats.

Between takes, I make suggestions, keeping my feedback down to a manageable amount of information, so as not to tax the singer's brain. It's always a mistake to make a singer think too much because that can take away from the emotion of the performance. If, at the end of those three, four, or five takes, some passages or sections remain wanting, I ask the singer to perform those sections of the song only, pointing out what might need improvement. It might be melody, phrasing, pitch, or enunciation. It might be a lack of emotional conviction or a part she's been taking a little too over the top. For these patches, I usually reuse the playlists on which I haven't made positive notes for that particular section. The advantage to going this route is that the singer will be able to hear the lines prior to the intended punch for context. If I don't have an available playlist for that segment, I will create a new one for this purpose. Sometimes that might require copying and pasting the lines immediately preceding the punch-in from another playlist for context. If a singer is not comfortable with punching in, it could be a good idea to put the track in "input" mode, meaning that you set her performance to be audible whether you're recording or not. Then, you ask her to sing from the top of the whole section (whether it be a verse, b-section, chorus, bridge, whatever). That way the singer won't be nervously anticipating exactly where you'll be punching in and can get the proper microphone proximity, intensity, and pitch well before you actually begin recording.

Once I'm satisfied I've captured at least one good performance of every phrase of the song, I use my notes to paste the best pieces together onto a comp track. During the comp, I may tune the spots that need some help, adjust the gain levels, jostle some phrases a bit in time, and/or extend or shorten a few words. I also create fades between each pasted-together track to avoid the edits being audible. The result is nearly always a seamless, yet natural, and spontaneous-sounding lead vocal, that sits nicely in the track.

You can probably see why a recording engineer might not favor this approach. It takes a lot of control out of his hands. It also requires perfect communication and teamwork between the producer and the engineer. First, you have to make sure that you are speaking the same language when it comes to which vocal takes you're referring to. In other words, the engineer may have recorded the vocals in this order: track 22, then 23, then 24, then 18. So, although you may call the performance captured on track 22 take "1" in your notes, it's critical that you instruct the engineer to use the proper performance. Before you do the comp, agree on your terminology. Know that you're speaking the same language. With total concentration and good communication, this method should work to everyone's complete satisfaction. Then, after the comp is finished, you may still find that certain phrases don't quite fit in context or some of the comping sounds awkward or unnatural. Most singers are more than willing to come back to patch up a section that falls short.

Please note also that on a demo, the lyrics should be enunciated even more clearly than on a record. Make sure you are absolutely and completely satisfied with the lead vocal performance, that it carries the song, and that every word is easily understood by a listener who is *not* reading the lyric. A demo can be rendered ineffective by a single slurred or poorly pronounced word. This can result in an industry decision maker stopping mentally in the middle of your song to figure out a misheard or misunderstood lyric, or, worse yet, asking for a lyric sheet. An A&R person reading along with a lyric sheet on a first listen will almost always read ahead, thereby losing the emotional impact of the song and probably coming to a premature decision, before your demo has had a chance. A person listening to the radio doesn't read a lyric sheet. Songs need to affect the listener first on an emotional level, not bring the listener into his or her head trying to comprehend the words. Remember also that you're looking for a strong, committed vocal performance, but a performance not so out of this world that it either distracts from the song itself or would dissuade another singer from trying to sing the song. It would be a shame to lose a cut because an artist thought, *Jeez, I'd love to cut that gorgeous song, but I could never match that demo singer's performance. I'd only embarrass myself. It would be safer to pass.*

If appropriate to the song, the next production element after the vocal comp might be vocal harmonies, or background vocals. Vocal harmonies have been used for decades as a way to add texture, dynamics, to emphasize the hooks, and even add extra hooks to pop recordings. Although Jim Weatherly certainly wrote a classic in his "Midnight Train to Georgia," some of the most memorable parts of Gladys Knight's smash-hit rendition are those Pips echoing her, and throwing in a "Woo, woooo" when it really counts. Admittedly, a Pips arrangement may be an extreme example of the contribution background vocals can make to a production. Darryl Hall possesses one of the most magnificent and soulful vocal instruments in pop music, as well as being an inspired and superb song craftsman, but Hall never achieved much success as a solo artist. There was something about how John Oates arranged and performed those back-ups that made "Sara Smile," "Rich Girl," "Kiss On My List," "Maneater," "One on

One"—need I go on?—into chart busters. One would be hard pressed to imagine the Fab Four's "She Loves You" or "Paperback Writer," the Beach Boys' "Help Me Rhonda" or "Good Vibrations," The Association's "Cherish," or The Chi Lites' "Have You Seen Her" without the vocal harmonies that are such an integral part of their sound.

However, due to time restraints, demo productions rarely take full advantage of background vocals, due to the added expense of hiring singers and/or the extra studio time it takes to record them. It may also have something to do with a lack of expertise and/or experience in using voices to enhance the production. This points out another reason why owning and operating a home studio provides a great advantage. Since you're not paying for a studio by the hour, you have the luxurious option of trying out some backgrounds and any number of other sweetening elements, for that matter. Even if you've cut your basic track with a live, studio band, nothing prevents you from taking those digital files home to record vocals and do your sweetening. A session can be transferred onto your portable Firewire drive in five minutes and copied into your system just as quickly. This production method will save you at least a couple hundred bucks per demo, as well as providing you with the most valuable ingredient to quality production: time to get the parts just right. When I was doing lots of back-up vocal sessions in Los Angeles, I would often be wowed by how much our vocal harmonies enhanced nearly every production. When we arrived, the track and lead vocal would usually sound strong. By the time we finished our parts, the production was really starting to sound like a record.

When it comes to background vocals, one existential question is "To double or not to double?" Double tracking can produce a natural chorus or flange effect that sends off magical harmonics. Doubling also can help the voices blend together and sit behind the lead. However, the answer to this fundamental, philosophical query really depends on what kind of song it is. Doubling usually sounds more pop. Examples of doubled vocals are: Crosby, Stills, and Nash, Queen, and the Carpenters. Before Shania Twain's huge Mutt Lange–produced hits, it was relatively uncommon for country records to employ a lot of doubled vocal harmonies. Since Twain's enormous success, doubling has become far more common on country radio. It never hurts to try doubling back-ups. As you experiment with this time-proven production technique, you will recognize the effect right away, recalling the vocal parts from many of The Beatles' records (like the aforementioned "Paperback Writer"), CS&N's "Suite for Judy Blue Eyes," or the Carpenters' "Close To You." Most Top 40 pop records utilize some measure of doubled back-ups.

If you're planning to double your background vocals, I have a little production trick to share. Set up the session's BG (background) vocal tracks in pairs, labeled something like lo BG left, lo BG right, hi BG left, hi BG right, etc. Pan those tracks hard left and right (as labeled). Then, when you record, print your first pass on both tracks simultaneously, so the performance is twice as loud in the phones and in the center of the mix. Then, when you start to double, take one of the tracks out of record and tell the singer which side of the phones the new part will be on and which the original part is on. That will help everyone hear any phrasing or pitch discrepancies between the tracks and eliminate a lot of rebalancing the mix in the cue system. Sometimes it's a good idea to use solo, two-part harmony tracks on selected verse lines, then up the ante by going to double-tracked parts in the chorus. If you choose this tactic, then you can keep the verse harmonies printed on both tracks, so they will stay in the center of the mix. Have fun with background vocals. Use them intelligently. You don't want your BGs to dominate your demo unless the song is written for a vocal group. Strategically used back-up parts can add a very impressive sparkle to your demo production.

Frosting

The final frosting, in the form of sweetening overdubs may be percussion (tambourine, shaker, hand drums, and the like); synthesized strings, a lush pad, or organ; lead instruments (guitar, sax, harmonica, and so on); utility instruments (in country: steel guitar, fiddle, dobro, mandolin, accordian, or banjo, for example); doubling or reinforcing lines of the arrangement in octaves or using other colors. Sometimes, in a home studio environment, you might want to premix a little by printing effects on certain spots. I often put a little chorus on "oooos" and "aaaahs" or other special passages of background vocals. Maybe there's a rim shot that wants extra reverb. Do this sparingly, and always keep the original signal intact in case you change your mind later.

As you can see, producing a great demo can be tricky. While you certainly want to keep your expenses as low as possible, you want to keep your quality at its highest level. Knowing how to communicate with studio musicians and engineers helps enormously toward accomplishing this goal. Not only does being able to articulate your desires and your comments clearly make every session go smoother, you will also command the respect of the players and mixers. Because the musicians and engineers are there to serve you, being familiar with the production process, knowing precisely what you want, and having the capability to ask for it increases the chance that everyone will go home happy. Moreover, having a home studio can increase the over-all quality and uniqueness of a production by giving you more time to experiment and get performances and colors perfect. Now we've got it all stored on digital audio, we're on to another critical stage of the process: the mix.

CHAPTER 28
Mixing and Mastering Your Great Demo

Most basic, home-studio set-ups are fully capable of capturing sounds of a quality roughly equivalent to those recorded in a state-of-the art, commercial facility. Or, at least within the context of a mix, there should be little or no discernable difference between a vocal, a fiddle, or a guitar part recorded in a home environment and the same part recorded at a studio that charges several hundred dollars per hour. However, when it comes to the mix, I cannot make the same claim. Mixing a multitrack production is an art in and of itself, one that requires certain, specific skills and its own arsenal of tools. Make no mistake, the mix can make or break any production, master or demo.

Mixing engineers comprise a special breed, blessed with extra-sensitive, discerning ears and extraordinary concentration. These ultra-focused individuals think nothing of spending endless hours in confined spaces, week after week, blending recorded sounds together, doctoring botched productions, and adding a bit more sparkle to well conceived ones. For them, experiencing flow is a way of life. A talented mixer can take a piece of music he's never heard before, recorded on 40 or more tracks, reconstruct it from the ground up, and give it ten times more punch and polish, all in a matter of a few hours. These guys have magic at their fingertips, fairy dust in their pockets, and they aim to please. Each mixer also has his own kit bag of easily accessible tricks. Every top mixer has created and refined proven templates, generic mix sessions he can plug your tracks into to instantly give each, individual element of your production a new sheen, yet help it to fit together in harmony with all the other pieces of the mix puzzle. Then, he has the ability to custom craft this standardized pastiche into a sonic picture that displays your production's best features in a way that could only apply to this one song and no other. It's a bloody miracle, it is. My hat is off to the great mixers of the world. Finding a mixing engineer you like, who really gets you and your writing, and with whom you can work comfortably (both in a creative and business relationship) is priceless.

Mixing a demo is a somewhat different task than mixing a master. As the purpose of a demo is to feature the melody and lyrics of the song in their most flattering light, one certain element needs to be featured above all others: the vocal. With a master, the performance and personality of the artist and the coloration of the production can be equally as important as the song. In a demo mix, sonic perspectives need to be such that everything compliments the melody and lyric and nothing distracts from the composition. As we discussed in the previous chapter, every single syllable of the lyric must be audible, up front and center. Therefore, the vocal in a demo mix will customarily be drier (mixed with less reverb or echo) so that no effect clouds the listener's comprehension, and the vocal will be boosted further above the backing tracks than it would typically be on a record. What makes mixing a demo challenging is keeping the vocal present and in the foreground, while simultaneously trying to retain as much as possible of the vibrancy and spirit of the track and the production, so that it still simulates a hit song on the radio.

You want a mix to have strong dynamics. Remember that post-basic-track outpouring of spontaneous genius by the session band? The guitar player did a couple of very cool overdubs, each with a different sound, and containing its own, off-the-cuff personality. The keyboard player threw on a couple of parts, maybe a string line, a synth pad, or a soulful B3. Perhaps since then, you've overdubbed some utility instruments, a banjo, an accordion, and/or a bouzouki. You have some percussion parts in there, too. Well, I warned you that you were going to have to make some difficult decisions when mix time came around, didn't I? Your time of reckoning has come nigh. This is when your arrangement skills and production expertise will be tested. Yes, your mixing engineer—if you have one—might be able to offer some assistance and opinions in this regard, but you are only complicating his job by handing him responsibility that really shouldn't be entirely his. Unless you come to the mix with a plan, you are already revealing your inexperience and lengthening the process. A seasoned pro would have come to some decisive conclusions long before now. Had you crossed this bridge many times before, you would have instructed the basic-track guitarist to save one part or the other for the second verse, the chorus, or the bridge, as an added or alternative color. Perhaps you would have experimented with various panning and color changes, boldly removing a part from one section, while featuring it in another. At the very least, you would have made some mental notes as to how you envisioned muting and/or highlighting certain parts in the mix. (Also, in retrospect, often times it's a better idea to double a great part in a high dynamic section of the song, instead of overdubbing an entirely different one—even if the new part is the coolest thing ever.) Those are the kinds of decisions that producers learn to make on the spot and live with.

Match the Mix to the Song

To include every recorded instrument (and the kitchen sink) in a mix, from top to bottom, will only leave you with a mess of a production that has no clarity or dynamic arc. If you haven't already done so, the mix is when you'll have to choose which parts will be included in which sections of the song, and mute or de-emphasize the others. It's always a good idea to make a song build, saving its highest intensity for about two-thirds to three-quarters of the way through the song. If you've been paying close attention to records on the radio, you've discovered that, for the most part, up-tempos begin with a strong intro, the instrumentation of the first verse becomes sparser, and then various instruments and additional vocal tracks enter and exit over the course of the song as it builds to its strongest intensity. Many ballads build steadily from the beginning to the end, starting with a simple piano or acoustic guitar intro; the vocal comes in and instruments follow: bass, drums, electric guitars, strings, BG vocals, percussion, and so on, slowly and logically crescendoing to the song's highest dynamic. Power ballads often kick off with a muscular fanfare of sorts that presages a theme from the upcoming song in dramatic fashion, but then they almost immediately strip down to basic instrumentation as the vocal enters in verse one. Once again, as the song develops, other instruments rejoin, building the arrangement, saving the kitchen sink for a highly anticipated moment two minutes and 30 seconds to three minutes down the line.

So, let's get more specific with some hypotheticals. Say you're mixing a high-spirited up-tempo song called "Party Girl," a sultry mid-tempo groove thang called "Oooo, Baby," and a passionate power ballad called "The Pain of Love." Obviously, you will approach the mixes of each of these very different songs quite differently. "Party Girl" kicks off with a lively figure played on electric guitar and doubled by synth, accompanied by a syncopated bass line and balls-to-the-wall drums, incorporating sizzling ride cymbal and lots of crashes. "Oooo, Baby" has a slippery intro, with a horn section playing a hooky figure over a steady drum groove, with tom-tom doubling the snare, bass throbbing underneath, electric guitar punctuating the up beats, Wurlitzer piano and B3, all held together by a shaker, the unnoticed glue. The intro to "The Pain of Love" is a two-bar, multitracked, unison guitar line suggesting a melodic theme to come, with some cymbal crashes and swells. Appearing from underneath the decay of the final, sustained note of the guitar fanfare is a simple, acoustic piano, playing a major add-9 chord on the quarter notes. In all three cases, the vocalist has introduced his or her personality to the songs with some kind of nonlyrical adlib—a "Woe-woe," an "Oooooo," or a little humming. Each song already sounds like a hit.

Now, as these first verses begin, each track empties out into its sparsest instrumentation. "Party Girl" strips down to electric guitar, keys, bass, and drums for the first eight bars, to support the opening lines of verse one. The drummer dials back his velocity somewhat and switches from ride cymbal to high hat. The kick and bass pattern is regular and unsyncopated. As the song progresses into the b-section or prechorus (in Nashville vernacular, the channel), some added color enters. Maybe it's another keyboard pad or an arpeggiated electric guitar and an added tambourine doubling every other snare hit. Perhaps you've put a two-part harmony over the vocal. You are building to the chorus. The first verse of "Oooo, Baby" may begin accompanied by that steady, throbbing drum and bass groove, with just Wurli piano and some sparse electric guitar. The shaker will probably remain throughout. At the channel, you introduce a sweetening coloration: B3, background vocal "Ooooo's," or even a light string pad. Once again, a tambourine on every other beat of the snare might work. You are building to the chorus. With your power ballad, "The Pain of Love," the verse begins with vocal over that forlorn solo piano. The bass slides in unobtrusively on bar three, while high, crying electric guitar notes may swell between lines from a far-away, echo-y place. The high hat may start playing the backbeat. At the prechorus, the drum kit may enter with a sidestick on the rim of the snare and a light hat ride. For sure, a chorused electric guitar and/or a string pad will add texture to the prechorus. You are building to the chorus.

You can see that, although these songs are generically very different, with different instrumentation, they all share one thing in common when it comes to their arrangements, and therefore how you will approach the mix: They all grab the listeners' attention with a catchy intro, empty out in the first verse to let the singer establish his or her personality and get the story started, then begin to bring in elements to color and orchestrate the song as it builds to the first chorus. As "Party Girl" hits that first chorus, the background vocals chime in earnestly, reinforcing the lyrical hooks and echoing various phrases. The drummer goes back to his ride cymbal and gets down to poppin' that snare. The bass line becomes more syncopated. The tambourine is shaking. Every musician in the band has upped his intensity level, all for the purpose of giving muscle to the main refrain of the song. Maybe you were smart enough to double the electric guitar to motor this track along. It's rockin'. With "Oooo, Baby," the chorus also lifts, due to the band's upped intensity. The drummer adds a tom-tom ride. Background vocals chime in, along with those horns padding and punctuating the rhythms. "The Pain of Love" hits hard at its chorus, with electric-guitar power chords, full drum kit, tambourine splashes, and a lush string pad. You may or may not have chosen to introduce background vocals yet. It depends on how personal the lyric is. It always seems odd to have a whole choir singing about being hurt or lonely. You might have chosen to limit the BGs to a two-part harmony in the first chorus.

Remember in all cases, not to shoot your whole wad in the first chorus. Restrain yourself a little. Hold something back. You want your climactic moment to come in the second chorus or later. The first chorus is the highest dynamic yet, but you've still left some headroom for later.

The top of verse two is where the oboe comes in. (I mean that metaphorically, in that it's usually standard procedure in a great arrangement to bring in a new color in the second verse.) For "Party Girl," you could answer the vocal lines with a wah-wah electric guitar, alternated with an analog synth, essentially instruments with personality. Commonly, there are two-part harmonies, "Oooos" or "Ahs" over various lines of verse two. Maybe there is an added percussion color as well. Presumably, you have an interesting buffet of sounds to choose from among those post-basic-track guitar and keyboard overdubs.

Just don't be a glutton and try to eat it all in one sitting. If you add one part, you are more than likely going to want to either mute another, or at least de-emphasize it volume-wise. Often it's better to remove a competitive sound from the sonic spectrum instead of boosting the level of an instrument you want to feature. If you turn one part up, it just may trounce the lead vocal, or dwarf the rhythm track, which is the last thing you want to do, as you attempt to make your mix as dynamic as possible. You'll probably want to keep verse two of "Oooo, Baby" pretty sparse. Maybe you've added some two-part harmonies or some BG padding and/or repeats. A simple, sustained string note might add just enough color, along with a slippery guitar answer here and there. Some flutey, Leslie-affected, B3 noodling often offers a sensual texture to this kind of song. For "The Pain of Love," the second verse should be more lush in its orchestration, yet stay sparse and open rhythmically. Here is where you actually could introduce the "oboe" part, in the form of some theme that plays in counterpoint with the melody. Verse two of a ballad needs to have its own personality, as it builds to an even bigger payoff when the chorus comes round again.

Hopefully, the composition bears the weight here, because that is always the job of the second verse: to make the second chorus even more powerful and more meaningful than the first. The production, the arrangement, and the mix should help facilitate this dynamic. So, as "Party Girl" approaches chorus two, the listener should not be able to stay still. That chorus should have everyone ready to join the party. More voices, more driving guitars, more handclaps, whatever it takes to lift the intensity level another notch. With "Oooo, Baby," it's business as usual. The arrangement is gonna throb on, while the vocalist ups the intensity with some sensual wandering away from the exact melody, as the BG vocals hold down the hook. There could be an extra synth texture or string pad, but the horns repeat their basic pattern, and the drums and bass keep laying down that unrelenting pulse. By the second chorus of "The Pain of

Love," all stops are out. Those background vocals are chiming in, and the additional orchestration, even more powerful power chords, and deeper echo on the snare drum are coming into play. The passion of the vocal performance and the desperation of the lyric are matched with the might of the production. Each song's emotional core is being emphasized and reinforced by the mix, as each song builds toward it's highest dynamic.

Bridges are tricky. Tricky to write and tricky to arrange. Sometimes they just come flowing out and fit naturally into the structure of the arrangement. Sometimes it takes some extensive experimentation to find the right chord progression, the perfect lyrical statement, and a changed feel that doesn't lose the momentum of the song. Not every song needs a bridge. However, a great bridge can almost always make for a better, more intriguing, and more enduring song. So, let's assume that all three of these songs have wonderful bridges. It's usually a good idea to change the sonic landscape in the bridge. Your goal here is to create new and memorable hooks, provide more lyrical information (or reinforce that which has come before), while cleansing the listener's palate. If you do this effectively, your chorus can return refreshed to close the deal one last time. Don't make the mistake of just letting your bridge slip by without offering some new coloration (by adding or removing an instrument or two), a groove alteration (with percussion and/or basic track arrangement), or an ambience change (drier or wetter, whatever's appropriate). A bridge can be made far more effective by using these arrangement and mixing tricks.

Depending on the kind of bridge and/or solo section you've placed in your song, a breakdown could be the way to go for the beginning of the last chorus. Stripping the chorus down to drums and vocal, with the possible support of electric guitar, power chords, and/or a colorful keyboard pattern for the first four bars is a traditional way to add tremendous dynamic and momentum into the climactic part of the final chorus. If a bridge goes into half-time or brings the dynamic down, a breakdown chorus is not usually the way to go. You need to be coming out of an intense section for a breakdown to really be effective. Another consideration would be modulating (changing the key of, usually higher) the last chorus, but obviously that's something you would have had to decide to do way before the mix stage. After a breakdown or modulation, it's no-holds-barred, Katy-bar-the-door, making that last chorus as forceful, as colorful, and as robust as possible for the big finish. And, remember: Don't fade! Write an ending! With a fade out, a mix might take a third again as long, as the mixer has to decide which of the instruments to feature, which vocal adlibs to use, and so on through repeated passes over music that has nothing to do with the success or failure of your demo. I repeat: *Never fade a demo!*

You will want to bounce four separate mixes: a regular mix with a vocal; a vocal-up mix (usually boosting the vocal ½ to one decibel); a TV mix (track with BG vocals, no lead vocal); and, a track mix (no lead or BG vocals). Every one of these mixes just might come in handy. So, it's better to take the extra 15 minutes to do them all now than having to go back and capture something later you could have on the original mixing session.

Mastering

Mastering, the basic concepts of which we discussed in Chapter 24, is another alternative, even for demo mixes. Several companies make very good and very affordable mastering software for computer-based home studios. I use iZotope's Ozone. After I've finished my mix, I go into the audio folder and drag the mix to my desk top. Then I open up a new ProTools session and label it with the song title, followed by the word "master" or the abbreviation, "mstr." I import the audio of the mix into the grid. Then, I open up the Ozone software as an insert. Ozone offers a half dozen options. You can use any one or any combination of these options. I always use the Paragraphic EQ first. As the track plays back, a graph shows the frequency curve of the mix as it plays through. I find it almost always beneficial to roll off the bottom end below 40 cycles. The human ear can't hear notes that low anyway, and phantom noises in the lowest register can cloud a mix or create bottom-end rumbling that is not pretty. Of course, for hip-hop recordings, you wouldn't want to remove any bottom end. Sometimes there's a pile up of low mid-range around 300 hertz. That stuff can also cloud up a mix. If I identify a build up there, I'll take that frequency down a tiny bit, too. A vocal covers a wide frequency range, from 100 hertz to 10 kilohertz. Most singers create sibilance at around seven kHz, but individual voices vary: some are sibilant at three kHz, some at ten, or any frequency in between. Hopefully, you've taken care of excessive sibilance in the mix with a combination of EQ, compression and (if necessary) a de-esser (a limiter that identifies specific high-frequency spikes and automatically turns them down). The cutting-edge articulation of most voices is somewhere around 2 kHz. If the vocal is still not cutting through the mix, it can be helpful to boost a little there to bring out the lyric of the song. The crack of the snare drum is usually somewhere around 8 kHz. You can affect the curve of your mix using this mastering feature, but use it sparingly, always remembering that what you do to one frequency colors the entire sonic spectrum.

Another mastering effect I frequently use on a mix is "loudness." Ozone calls their loudness module the Loudness Maximizer. You want your mix to be at its optimum level from top to bottom so that it will compare favorably with other demo mixes and yet not lose its depth and dynamics. If an A&R person is going through a stack of CDs, or listening to a play list of MP3s, some mixes will sound brighter and louder than others. That's another reason why mastering is so important. It would be a shame if the song you spent so long crafting and refining and the demo you invested so much time and resources in didn't get a fair shot because it was not mastered at optimum level. What loudness does is grab the quiet parts of the song and pull them up to their maximum volume. That way, a ballad that starts with just a piano and a voice can compete next to an up-tempo rocker that has a hot band thrashing from the opening chord. While you want the instrumentation of your demo to be arranged dynamically, you don't want the apparent levels to vary so much that they disappear into the background or fail to cut through in their quiet moments. Classical recordings often have this quality, where an adagio passage will be nearly inaudible; then, when the symphony orchestra suddenly shifts into overdrive, it just about blasts you out of the room. That wide of a dynamic range is not at all desirable in a song demo. So, using the loudness feature of a mastering program is helpful. There are numerous parameters within this section you will need to experiment with, adjusting the character and mode, noting how loudness affects the sound of your mix. However, loudness has no discretion when it comes to frequencies, so the bass notes will be boosted just as much as the high transients and the mid-range frequencies. If your bass is not properly mixed, using loudness can result in an even more bottom-heavy mix or vice versa.

Sometimes, I'll also use the dynamics section of my mastering software, which in Ozone is called "Multiband Dynamics." This is basically a compressor/limiter. Most mixes are compressed to one degree or another. Like loudness, compression also keeps the level of the mix more even, but it also takes some of the rough edges off. Compression lifts the track up between vocal lines, so the production can be featured without swallowing the vocal. However, restrain yourself in your use of compression, because it can definitely color the entire mix, giving the drums a sort of sucking/popping sound and removing some of the most exciting high-end sounds from the sonic spectrum. Ballads generally can take a little more compression than up-tempo songs because of the audible effect compression has on hard-hitting drums and guitars.

I steer away from the other features of my Ozone software. I see no reason to apply more ambience (Mastering Reverb) or stereo spread (Multiband Stereo Imaging) to a demo mix. Some people love the Harmonic Exciter, which adds a high-end sparkle to an entire mix. I find it cheap sounding. If you haven't recorded and mixed your parts with enough pizzazz, it's usually too late to goose the sizzle in the mastering process. And, as far as I'm concerned, when everything in the mix is effected equally, nothing is really gained in boosting what is in essence is phase distortion in the high end.

PART SEVEN:

FINAL THOUGHTS

CHAPTER 29
Pitching Your Own Songs

An ad has been running on TV these days that really cracks me up; it's for the online stock-trading company, E-Trade. A man is intensely scratching the numbers on a lotto ticket with a coin. Observing him from a highchair is a baby, presumably Lotto Man's offspring. In a voice that sounds like a snide, 30-year-old wise guy, the baby remarks to Daddy, "You know, you've got about as much chance of winning as being mauled by a grizzly bear and a polar bear—in the same day." Dad completes his scratch off, scowls in disappointment, and tears up the ticket. "Oh, you didn't win?" the baby asks, mockingly. "This is my surprised face." Then, the little guy makes an expression that looks like he's whistling the highest note ever. I have to laugh every time I see it.

I think I've made it quite clear how remote the chances are of you or me—or most any songwriter, for that matter—getting a cut via pitching our songs through traditional channels. However, in spite of those nearly impossible odds, it's still important for every writer to continue knocking on doors and playing those tunes for folks, because, quite frankly, you just never know. Even if you're fortunate enough to get signed to a publishing deal, to rely exclusively on the company's pluggers to pitch your songs to success can be a major miscalculation. (The same is true if you've contracted an independent plugger to rep your catalog.) Take it from someone who's been there and done that. Every time I've signed with a publisher, had a good, steady advance coming in, and hunkered myself down in my studio to concentrate exclusively on writing and recording, all the while neglecting to do the essential sales job on my own material, my career has skidded to a grinding halt.

In the 1990s, after enjoying numerous hits, Kent Blazy signed a lucrative deal with industry juggernaut, BMG Publishing. He was on the roster with Hugh Prestwood and Marcus Hummon, two writers who were enjoying equivalent success. "In three years, I got 40-something cuts," Blazy recalls, "and BMG got maybe three of those." The 40 others came from cowriting with the artists or from Blazy pitching his tunes directly to producer/friends, manager/friends, or artist/cowriters (who often heard a song from his catalog just because they were in the room together).

"The writer is truly his own best publisher," shares Steve Dorff. "No one cares about the song the way the creator does. It's not the publisher's heart that's in the song." Not only is it often true that we care and believe in our own material more than anyone else on Earth, we also care and believe in our work 24/7/365. You have to be aware that there is always an "out of sight, out of mind" factor. It's human nature, a fact of life. You may be sitting in your publisher's office, and he or she might expound with genuine exuberance and admiration for one of your tunes, even pledging a personal commitment to getting that puppy cut by a major artist. That kind of talk makes you feel good. You get the impression that, finally, something is going to happen here. Well, that passion, that enthusiasm, that allegiance may be absolutely sincere, *in that moment*. However, to be sure, as soon as you walk out the door, another writer is going to walk in. That writer will become the next squeaky wheel demanding love and attention. The commitment you just received is immediately diluted by the rest of the writing staff, all of whom have strong, competitive songs, too, and fragile egos to go with 'em. Out of sight, out of mind.

More often than not, too, publishers have their pet staff writers. That results in one or two on the roster getting the lion's share of the pitches. One of my best songwriter friends happened to be entering his publisher's office, just as a producer/acquaintance was exiting after a pitch meeting. "Did we take care of you?" my friend asked.

"Yeah, man," the producer said, displaying a comp CD, comprised of songs composed exclusively by the company's resident superstar writer.

Disturbed not to see any of his own material on the comp, my friend boldly asked, "Do you mind if I play you some of my stuff?" To the embarrassment of my friend's publisher (who continually discouraged writers from pitching their own material), that query led to a massive radio hit that remained in the Top Ten for multiple weeks.

I always advise writers that the only things you have an absolute right to count on from your publishing company are these: a) They hand you your advances on time, and the checks clear; b) they pay for at least a minimum number of demos; and c) if you *do* have success, they account to you honestly for your share of the royalties. Everything else a publisher does for you is, in a one-word cliché, gravy. Yet, for so many writers, the goal is to get a publishing deal. For so many writers, that exclusive writer/publisher contract is the pie in the sky. Surely it's a tasty slice, but it's really just a nibble of the whole shebang. Yes, a reputable publisher investing in you most certainly boosts your industry prestige and does miracles for your confidence level. Absolutely, receiving a regular paycheck enables you to spend more time writing songs and focusing more of your attention to the task you love. Without question, it's great to have a home away from home, where you can apply your craft and meet and mix with other writers and industry players. Furthermore, if you're fortunate enough to be working with a publisher or a plugger willing to devote some regular time and attention to listening to your works in progress and offering you some helpful, constructive feedback—not just saying, "I love it, dude. Keep writing!"—then you have a priceless relationship, one that certainly should be appreciated and cultivated. However, to depend on *any* other person or persons—no matter how much you like them, or how much they like you—to be as committed as you are to your work, to your success, to you building a legacy in this business? That is *never, ever* a safe bet.

"There are no rules," says Dorff. "Throw them out the window. It's the Wild West when it comes to getting a song recorded. That's the approach I take and the advice I'd give to anybody, new or old. I think if you go the route that you're supposed to take—give it to the publisher and wait for him to put it in the pitch schedule—that's not for me."

Dorff's recipe for getting a cut is three, seemingly simple steps: a) Write a great song; b) make a great demo; and c) get the song as close to the artist as possible. Remember these words of advice from one of the most successful songwriters of our times: "Writing a great song is only half the battle. You gotta demo it just right. *Then* you've got to be ingenious enough to know what to do with it." That almost always means pitching it yourself, by hook or by crook. "If you can find out what hotel room the artist's staying at in Oklahoma City," Dorff hypothesizes, "and you can slip a CD under his door, with a clever note, that makes him go 'This person really went to great lengths to get this song to me,' you've got a far better shot than giving it to your publisher to pitch."

Pitching your own songs, of course, automatically means risking getting your heart crushed by a rejection, or more likely, smashed to bits a piece at a time by numerous and repeated rejections. *Yikes!* In response to that all-too-common trepidation, Dorff adds, "If you don't have the ability to pick yourself up and dust yourself off a hundred times a day, you're probably not suited for this business." His observation comes from a lifetime of negotiating the perilous pathways of the business of which he speaks, along the way to a list of credits that you and I can only dream about. That pathway began with a 16-year-old songwriter traipsing the streets of Manhattan, in search of his first break in the music business. "In high school, I felt like I had a couple of really good songs," Dorff recalls, "so I went into New York City and beat the proverbial bushes, looking for a publisher. I didn't really know what a publisher was. I just knew that I wanted somebody to hear what I was writing." There he was, a naïve, fearless teenager, with some songs he thought were pretty good. Did he sit around waiting for his tunes to be discovered? No, sir-ee-bob! He hit the streets, fully prepared to sit down at the nearest keyboard to sing those fledgling compositions for anyone who'd listen. "I found some people who were interested in me, and they paid for some demos."

At 16, Steve Dorff, from Queens, New York was in the business of songwriting. "They were pretty god-awful," he adds now, speaking of his earliest works, "but I was learning the craft." His first cut came when Herb Bernstein, the hippest arranger of the day, stripped the lyrics from one of the youthful writer's melodies and produced it as an instrumental. The artist was guitar player Al Caiola and his Orchestra, on United Artists Records, best known for his hit single, "Never On Sunday." Soon after that, a female singer, who was being developed in the same publishing office, recorded a Dorff composition (this time, lyrics included) on a little indie label. That female singer was Melissa Manchester, long before she became "Melissa Manchester."

"A lot of songwriters can't handle taking a song to an A&R person," Hall of Famer, Rory Bourke notes. "Songwriters have a hard time distinguishing between themselves and the song. And, if gets turned down, it's about them, because it's their song that came from their gut." It's only natural for a writer to feel emotionally attached to a song. We birth these ideas. These are our babies, ripped from our loins with forceps. We bleed to bring these children into the world. (Okay, I'm way, way over the top on this metaphor; but, that's how some of us feel.) We raise 'em up, teaching them to walk and talk, home schooling them, while drilling some manners into their stubborn, little heads. Then, when we think they're ready, we put them up on stage to do a little tap dance, crossing our fingers and toes that somebody besides Mom and Aunt Matilda will stand up and applaud. Sometimes those little guys trip up. Most times they fail to draw any attention at all. We hope they will perform perfectly. But even if they do give a flawless showing, there is no guarantee that anyone of import will even notice, positively or otherwise.

Tim James says this: "When people say, just go write great songs, it makes you wanna say, 'I got a catalog full of great songs!'" Writing a great song is not enough. Making a great demo of a great song is not enough. Getting a great demo of a great song heard is not enough. But the song sure isn't going to record and release itself. Every pitch is a lottery ticket, and we have as much chance of winning as being mauled by a grizzly bear and a polar bear in the same day. Maybe you might consider that every time you go out there and pitch your stuff. Think of your song as just a number, just a half dozen ping-pong balls rolling around a squirrel cage stuffed with balls, all falling at random. More often than not, your number is just not going to come up.

Fortunately for you, unlike Lotto Dad, you don't have to tear up the ticket. You can leave it in the hopper for as long as you're willing to take a chance on it. However, Rory Bourke says this about pitching: "Don't take more than one song. Take one song you think is a killer."

A devout, Christian man gets down on his knees and prays, "Lord, I've been a good man all my life. I've helped my neighbors, been faithful to my wife, gone to church every Sunday, tithed, worked hard, and supported my family. I've never asked for anything for myself before. But, today, I'm going to make a request, just this once. Please, Lord, let me win the lottery." Weeks go by. The man fails to win the lottery. He's beginning to question his faith. His patience is growing thin. He gets back down on his knees. "Lord, I only asked for one thing. It's been weeks and I still haven't won the lottery."

Suddenly, booming down from the sky is a very exasperated, Earth-shaking voice, "Buy a ticket!" God responds. "*YOU HAVE TO BUY A TICKET!*"

There's only one guarantee, kids: You can't win if you don't play.

"I feel very honored and validated when someone does one of my songs," says Dorff. "They're picking something of mine over literally thousands of other submitted songs. You've got better odds goin' to Vegas and throwin' money down on Red 25."

So then, how does Dorff increase those odds? "Okay," he replies, "I've got a good demo of a good song. Sounds like it might be a great song for George Strait. How am I going to get it to him? I tell people, any way you can! If you happen to know a guy who knows his bus driver, that's probably a better way to get the song in his hand, rather than sending it to an A&R guy at MCA Records where it's going to get thrown in a box with eight thousand other demos and never get heard. It's the nontraditional way that creates the action."

Supposing you do go the traditional way. Nothing wrong with that. After all, you never know. Anyway, you're pitching a song to a junior A&R person—and she likes it. (One of the things you never know is whether this bright, young person is going to be running the label in ten years. This is a relationship you'd be foolish to disregard.) What's next? She is going to have to pitch it again, to her superior. Then, often times, your song will have to be approved by a committee, every member of which has his or her own agenda, personal favorites he or she is promoting for the project. Everybody at the label wants to take credit for discovering a song and getting a George Strait cut. Then, those few, select, surviving tunes that pass the committee's muster—most of which are probably written by name writers with proven track records—will get pitched to the producer and the artist, to compete with the songs the producer and the artist have already found themselves. Why submit your song to that kind of scrutiny, when it's the artist who ultimately makes the decision anyway? "When you're dealing with high-level artists," Dorff says, "they make the decisions. At the end of the day, no executive is gonna tell an artist what song to sing." That's why, he explains, "I've always tried to get the song directly to the artist."

There are some classic stories about how songwriters have gotten their tunes directly to the artist. The most famous is probably helicopter pilot, Kris Kristofferson, landing his chopper in Johnny Cash's garden. When the man in black emerged from his house, Kristofferson handed the star a tape of some of his songs. Cash went on to record "Sunday Morning Comin' Down," not only the breakthrough cut in a Hall of Fame songwriting career, but CMA Song of the Year in 1970. My friend, independent publisher/plugger Scott Lynch, once followed Faith Hill to a mall parking lot in order to hand her a CD. That interchange led to a cut. Remember what Steve Dorff said, "There are no rules. It's the Wild West." Those who adhere to the protocol established by record company hierarchies are limiting themselves to extremely long odds against success, subjecting each of their pitches to three or four subsequent pitches, each of which can easily shoot that song out of contention.

Making a Game Plan

There are two basic philosophies of song plugging. The most typical method is pouring through the pitch sheets on a weekly basis, taking note of which artists, which producers, which labels are looking for material; making calls to set up appointments with the gatekeepers listed; then lastly, sitting down to cast what material to play at those meetings. To me, this particular process is convoluted. It's like procuring display space in the market, then scouring through the warehouse trying to find product to place on the shelves. In my opinion, it's much more effective and motivating to feel certain that you have a product you can stand behind 100 percent, and then find a way to market it.

So, for me, a much more logical method is to approach pitching in the complete opposite direction. First, identify the titles in your catalog that you believe in wholeheartedly, the songs you feel are exemplary and truly worthy of industry attention; then, one song at a time, find a way to get those songs as close to the artist as possible, bypassing as many of the gatekeepers as possible. Of course, it can be helpful to be aware of who is actively looking at any given point in time, and the pitch sheets can be very informative in that regard. For instance, if Tim McGraw has a freshly mixed album in the can, it's probably not worth your while to break your hump to get your latest masterpiece into his hands right now. It would probably make more sense to wait until he's looking again to make your move. Yet, if the opportunity should suddenly present itself, you should take advantage of it—regardless of the timing. Great songs are great songs, whether or not an artist is recording today, next month, or a year from now. It's just that artists are usually much more receptive to listening when they're seeking material than when they're winding a project down. It's human nature to be more excited about the newest thing. Even a great song can lose its sparkle when a newer model hits the showroom floor. Conversely, however, I've had songs cut that were more than ten years old, because a producer or an artist loved the song, put a CD in a drawer, and waited for the perfect moment to put that piece on a session.

Just because we should always attempt to eliminate the "No" people doesn't mean we should disregard A&R departments, management companies, producers—and their assistants—altogether. If we get the chance to pitch to any of those people, we should always jump at it. The smartest way to get that appointment it is to say, "I've got a song I really want to play you. Just one. It'll only take five minutes." Doing that, of course, means you'd better be sure you have a contender. Then, arrive with something you believe in from the souls of your Sketchers to the button of your ball cap. Be ready, of course, to play more on request and come prepared with a couple of other possibilities in advance. In other words, be prepared, but don't expect it to happen. One of my favorite A&R and publisher responses is this one: "I like that. What else have you got?" What exactly does that mean? She likes it, but it's not right? She likes it, but not enough to do anything with it? She likes it, but not for this artist, on this day, or any day for that matter? Well, at least she likes it enough to ask to hear more. That has to be a good thing. So, be prepared.

Be encouraged, but don't read too much into it. "People tell me, 'Hey, they said they really liked my song,'" Bourke says. His response to that is, "Did they tell you they were going down to the bank and taking out a loan on their house over it?" If not, maybe they didn't like it quite enough. And, never, never, *never* beg to play "just one more song." Remember, although you'd just about die for a cut, your goal here is not to make the sale as much as it is to be invited back. Take your lumps with a smile. Once again, listen to Rory Bourke: "You have to get to the point to where people can trust you to take the bad news." Having a reputation as a person of your word is important, too. When you say you only want to play one song, don't push for a second or a third pitch. To do so would risk coming off as pushy, or worse yet, needy. Avoid being that door-to-door encyclopedia salesperson with your foot wedged in the doorway. Don't appear to be someone who would take advantage of access to an industry decision maker. If you do, your next call to book an appointment will go unanswered and unreturned.

Here's the thing about pitching songs. A pass today is only that: a pass *today*. There are songs I've pitched to producers several times, getting little or no positive response. My belief in those songs remains steadfast, though, so I bring them back. Finally, on a third or fourth pitch, he might say, "Why haven't you played me this song before? I love this song." Some industry characters pride themselves on remembering every song they've ever heard. Ridiculous, preposterous, not to mention impossible. When your job entails listening to hundreds of pitches every single week, your mind is going to wander now and then. The memory is a tricky thing. Sometimes that first listen plants the seed, the second germinates it, and the third time around brings that sprout shooting toward the light. By the fourth time, the song sounds familiar and right. True story: A song plugger in a pitch group played the song he believed in most for the producer. The producer passed. The other pluggers played their pitches until it came around again to the first song plugger. He played the same song again. On the second play, the producer put the song on hold. I wouldn't necessarily recommend this policy, but do understand that, if you believe in a song and if this song is your best foot forward, keep putting it out there until somebody tells you to lay off. Here's the mistake all of us make: We think our newest song is our best song. It's fresh. As you continue learning and getting better as a writer, it has to be the best one yet. Right? Many pluggers are like that, too. Songs from the latest session by the most successful writer at the company are the only songs they want to pitch. However, the best pluggers have an objective overview of the entire catalog. They remember which producers, which A&R people, and which artists responded positively to which songs. They keep bringing those songs back because someday, just maybe, it won't be a pass, it will be a capital-letter YES!

Here's something I heard from every single songwriter I interviewed for this book: It's tough; it's hard; it doesn't get any easier. In fact, it's getting harder. There are fewer major labels and fewer major-label artists; fewer slots are open because more and more artists and producers are writing and/or publishing their own material. Radio playlists are growing shorter, and stations are playing fewer new records. Even writers with scads of success are finding it difficult. Bourke taught a weekly songwriting class at ASCAP one year. He recalls a student coming up to him and pleading, "Just tell me this gets easier at some point!"

"No, it doesn't get easier," the instructor responded. "You just get a 'No' faster."

"You could be working ten, twelve years before you see some light," Bourke says. "It's a long, hard road. But, it's the same with any creative art: acting, producing, directing, screenwriting. In most cases those people work ten, twelve, fifteen years before they start to become successful. They earn every dime they make because they've suffered and worked hard."

So, while some of us might actually prefer being mauled by a bear than to be subjected to the strong possibility of our songs being rejected time and time again, somehow, we have to step back emotionally and come to the logical conclusion that each "No" only brings us that much closer to the next "Yes." And, when the "No's" start coming faster, it just might mean you're almost there.

AFTERWORD

Every morning, in my prayer of gratitude, I say these words with enthusiasm: "Thank you, God, that I am able to thrive in this lifetime as a creative person." To me, living a creative life is two things: a privilege that cannot be taken for granted, and a calling that cannot go unanswered. So, whether or not I'm feeling particularly prosperous or successful on an given day—or during any particular year, for that matter—I still have much to be grateful for: my God-given talents, and every single opportunity I get to manifest my unique gifts, inspirations, and points of view into the energy of life. From the start, a creative person must recognize and believe that he or she has a special, individual voice, a one-of-a-kind perspective, as well as an inimitable way of expressing some very personal intuitions. Learning to be grateful, however—even when it seemed that so many others were zooming past me on the highway of success—was the biggest and most important lesson I could have ever learned. And, finding true gratitude was the missing ingredient that transformed this journeyman music pro into a hit songwriter, which in turn led to becoming an author and a teacher.

All of the songwriters I interviewed and profiled in this book have enjoyed far more success than I. Yet, even with their enormous achievements, the acclimation, and the financial rewards that accompany writing multiple hit songs over decades of being Top Dogs in this business, they all share this sense of gratitude. Time and time again, I heard these hit writers say things like, "I was really lucky..." or "I feel honored..." I also heard each one of them confide that they had a calling, that at some point along the way, they recognized singular and undeniable talents for which they felt they had to take responsibility. You may have that same sense, that you have something above and beyond the ordinary to offer and that you feel compelled to share your own individual musings. I hope that is the case. And, I hope that this book has given you some insight into what it takes to realize and manifest your dreams.

Another unanimous refrain in these interviews is this one: "It's hard!" I heard these words time and time again. "It's tough." "It's brutal." And, I'm sorry to say, "It's getting harder." As Steve Dorff—a man with multiple country and pop Number One songs, scores for a dozen TV series, as many films, and has two shows poised to open on Broadway—said in the previous chapter about any one song getting cut: "You've got better odds goin' to Vegas and throwin' money down on Red 25."

Rory Bourke—a Hall of Famer, with hits spread across four decades—says, "I think now it's a harder time than ever. You could be working ten, twelve years before you see some light. It's a long, hard road." It takes persistence, perseverance, stamina, bull-headed determination. You're going to hear a million versions of the word, "No." Sure, you're going to get discouraged. Sometimes, I still feel like I'm slogging hip deep through swamp water, not even knowing where I'm headed, or whether it's worth the effort. When publisher Charlie Monk ("The Mayor of Music Row") told Tim James he'd never make it as a songwriter, James refused to be denied. He was going to find a way, if only to prove Monk wrong. Fifteen years later, James has racked up a five-week Number One, four Top Ten songs, and a very impressive, ever-lengthening discography. If you believe in yourself, if you feel that same drive to continue to express your inspirations into song and share them with the world, keep doing it. Did you hear me? Keep doing it. To recap: Keep doing it.

One of the most infamous commencement speeches was given by Sir Winston Churchill. After an introduction that no doubt listed the great English political figure's many achievements, he arrived on the platform, dressed in top hat, gloves, coat, and wielding a cane. He proceeded ceremoniously by laying his cane aside. Then, he slowly and deliberately removed his hat, gloves, and coat. He stepped up to the lectern and said nine words: "Never give up. Never give up. Never give up!" To the crescendoing applause of the shocked graduates, Churchill put his outer finery back on and stepped down. 'Nuff said.

Grammy winner, Liz Rose—cowriter of most of Taylor Swift's biggest hits—offers this advice: "Write every day, all day long. Go to work. Treat it like job. Show up. Get up and do it. Because you never know when you're gonna write that song."

Tim James says the same thing: "It may sound like a cliché, but go to work. Show up." He recounts a couple of days when he just didn't feel like making the 40-minute commute from Rutherford County to Williamson County. But he's glad he mustered up the gumption to make those treks, because getting together with those writers resulted in songs that are putting the groceries in his family's pantry.

However, please, don't expect to do this by yourself. You may have the ability to write a great song in solitude. That's a wonderful gift. But that song will not find its way to the top of the charts without friends. The music business is a community, a machine with interlocking, interdependent parts. Every single song that somehow rises above a thousand competitors and steals its way into the studio to be recorded had a lot of help. Every song that gets more than a single spin on a radio station has done so with the support of a team. Every song that climbs the charts is being lifted on the wings of a congregation of believers.

Your first real opportunities will more than likely come from your peer network, your talented pals, your creative cohorts. Your success will probably begin with your cowriters, with the musicians and singers you play beside on the weekends, with the ambitious, young, attractive, charismatic performers you meet in clubs and recording studios. Your eventual breaks will come because you have endeavored to make friends;

by being a likable, fun person; a considerate, genuine, concerned listener; someone who is always welcomed into the conversation. You will attract these people because you display something that tells the world you are already successful, that you are on your way to some kind of greatness—not because you *say* it's true, but because you act *as if* it's true. You are not desperate. Quite the contrary, you possess a quiet confidence. You are relaxed in who you are. You can be trusted not to selfishly and blatantly exploit the connections you glean from your peer relationships. You can be trusted not to badmouth a friend or offend someone of import. You know that this is a team sport. So, you're willing to drive the ball to the basket or take the open jumper; and, when you don't have an open shot, you're willing to pass off for a score. Finally, you know that you don't know it all, that there is always something new to learn. SongU guru, Danny Arena says, "Professional songwriters never stop learning or think they know it all."

This truth is borne out by what these tremendously successful, veteran writers all told me: About cowriting, Rose said, "You always learn something." James confided that he always tries to get with more experienced writers because it forces him to lift his game.

"Get with a lot of different people," advises Tom Snow, "because a collaborator brings something to the table that you don't have. *Every* collaboration is worthwhile."

Rory Bourke sums it up: "There's nothing you can learn by yourself." So, who are your teachers? Every single person you ever work with can teach you something. Some lessons will be handy tricks of the trade. Another lesson might amount to a veritable epiphany, a magic key with which you can unlock a whole new creative Universe. Some will help you circumvent self-destruction, as you observe friends, colleagues, and acquaintances making massive, possibly even fatal miscalculations. If you're very fortunate, you will find mentors along the way willing to give you sound advice so you can improve your work and make good, solid decisions. Those relationships can be equally or even more important than those with the industry decision makers who may eventually welcome you into their inner sanctums.

You will find that getting out there in the world, mixing it up with your contemporaries, and meeting industry folks will do wonders for your forward progress. Coming home with a couple of business cards in your pocket, knowing that you've handed several out yourself to potential allies gives you a real good feeling about yourself.

"Get out there and do as many things with as many people as possible," Blazy instructs. "Meeting as many people and playing as many gigs as you can, you never know who you're gonna meet out there, who's gonna come up to you."

You'll learn how to put a positive spin on every smile and handshake and how to compose and give a ten-second elevator speech that says, *I'm a player. I'm in this business to win.* Still, more often than not, you will find it nearly impossible to know for certain whether you are making any progress at all. You'll just have to trust that some of the many seeds you plant every single day will someday blossom into the light.

If you haven't already, you will start putting together a core group of colleagues—your peer network—with whom you will cowrite, perform, hang out, and be seen. You and your peers will dare each other to do your best work. You will dare each other to follow through, to be accountable. You will pass the ball back and forth and slowly work your way up against that seemingly impermeable, industry full-court press. Eventually, one of you will break loose to score, by getting an internship at a record company or a top studio, a job assisting a top producer, an artist-development contract, a hot manager, a publishing deal, or even a cut. By association, all of you will start to get more notice. "Play out a lot," Bourke says. "Find some people who are maybe a couple of steps up in the business, who are maybe going to get a job somewhere someday. Befriend each other."

Remember what Mark D. Sanders said, when he became an "overnight success" after many years of struggling on Music Row. Was he writing better songs? In a word, "No," Sanders candidly confessed, "now, my friends are in a position to say, 'Yes.'" You are not only in the business of building the best song you can. You are also in the business of building strategic relationships. You never know which of those relationships will be the one that will put the spotlight on the right song at the right moment.

"The more people you know and the more you can get directly to people, the better your chances are of getting things recorded," advises Blazy. "Sometimes it works, sometimes it doesn't. You have to have the song with somebody who can hear it at that time. It happens all different ways." What are those ways? Maybe, your cowriter gets signed to a superstar/artist's publishing company, as happened when Tim James signed with Toby Keith's new Paddock Music venture, resulting in our Number One, "My List." Maybe you wrote a song with a young-wannabe singer, back when he was tending bar at a downtown restaurant, which happened for my pal, Jon Robbin, with his Number One, "I Breathe In, I Breathe Out" for Capitol Records artist/ex-bartender, Chris Cagle. Maybe a fledgling producer/friend fell in love with one of your songs ten years ago, kept it in a drawer all this time, and is now in a position to cut it on a big star. Maybe a session singer sings one of your song demos, pledges his undying love for the song, promises to cut it someday when he gets his own record deal, and, when he does get the deal, he actually keeps his word. Maybe you run into a producer/acquaintance in the hallway at your publishing company, and he mentions, "I'm looking for Wynonna. Got anything?" as happened to Jill Colucci, when Tony Brown said that very thing to her in passing one day at EMI Music, resulting in Colucci's Wynonna Number One "No One Else On Earth." Maybe an awkward, gawky, but promising 14-year-old singer/songwriter hears a couple of your songs, approaches you, and asks you to cowrite; your publisher thinks your wasting your time with the kid, but you recognize some real potential, you love writing with the kid, so you keep doing it. Now, six years later, you've had a string of country/pop crossover Number One songs and there's a Grammy on your mantle (the Liz Rose/Taylor Swift story).

You can't possibly know what the exact scenario will be. You don't know now precisely how it will happen for you. You just know that your chances of it happening are enhanced immeasurably by continually working on your craft and through the relationships you are beginning to develop and cultivate today. It's not enough to get your songs heard. They have to be heard by the right person, at the right moment, under the right circumstance. Your songs have to be heard by someone whose "Yes" means something, someone who wants to like them, someone who has some real incentive to prefer your songs above everyone else's, not someone whose job description is to find something wrong with them and respond with a resounding, "No."

You know absolutely that, if you can write a song with the artist, it will give you your best chance of getting a cut. And since it's highly improbably that you'll be able to commandeer a cowriting appointment with Toby Keith, Sheryl Crow, Mariah Carey, or Jesse McCartney, you had better keep your eye out for the next generation of stars, as did Jon Robbin and Liz Rose. It might take years for those cowrites to show up in the marketplace. There is no guarantee that your tunes will ever be performed or heard by anyone, but you knew that coming in and you're in this game for the long haul. You also know without a doubt that, if you can write a song with the producer, you've got a far better chance of scoring a cut. Since you probably won't have the opportunity to get in a room with David Foster, Desmond Child, Frank Rogers, or Mutt Lange, you'd be well advised to watch for the next great producer/songwriter poised to emerge on the scene. If you're really smart, you'll take some young artist you met at a BMI showcase to that young producer and get the three of you writing together. That kind of mix can multiply the possibilities many times over.

You know absolutely that, the closer you can get the song to the artist, the better chance you have of your number coming up in the songwriting lottery. The further down the music-business totem pole you begin your pitch, the more decision makers stand in the way of your song getting through the maze. And since it's the artist who ultimately makes the "Yea" or "Nay" decision, you'd be smart to take the initiative to put it in his or her hand, or at least have it pass through as few hands as possible on its way. So, the bus driver, or the make-up person, or the bass player can often be much more valuable to you than a junior A&R person at the label. However, as the junior A&R person just might be the head of the company someday, that's a relationship you'd better not ignore either.

You also know that you cannot afford to totally depend on anyone else to—or to expect that anyone else will—do your legwork for you. You care about your songs more than anybody else, every waking hour—even in your dreams. So, it's entirely up to you to continue to prime the pump and keep the momentum going by initiating your own activity. By doing that, you will dare your reps, your cowriters, and their pluggers to rise to the occasion, to step up to the plate. No matter how painful it is, no matter how shy and reclusive you are by nature, you need to take full responsibility for your own success. You do this by writing the best song you can write, producing a killer demo, and using your imagination and ingenuity to get the song to the artist in the most direct way possible. Meanwhile, you continue to make friends; cultivate old ones; put your best foot forward publicly; act as if you are successful at all times; you're never pushy or presumptuous; you're always gracious, polite, respectful, pleasant, upbeat, and fun to be around. You have the patience of Job, the strength and stamina of Atlas, the courage and tenacity of David, and the artistic sensibility of Mozart and Shakespeare.

No easy task this songwriting game. To get into this business in the first place, you have to be just a little bit crazy. It's like selling poetry door to door, while trying to step around land mines and dodge sniper fire. Every day, it's as if your rag-tag posse is standing nose to nose opposite a well armed battalion of granite-chinned hard-bodies, all intent on keeping every doubloon of the king's ransom for themselves. "We're not songwriters," Rory Bourke says, "we're song fighters." It's like trying to hit a major-league curve ball with a toothpick, swimming the English Channel with a cinderblock taped around your waist, expecting to beat Roger Federer using a ping-pong paddle and wearing a blindfold. But, dang, kids! It can be a whole heck of a lotta fun, too! Makin' up songs. Recordin' 'em. Listening back to a newly mixed demo, thinkin', *Wow! That's pretty darn good*! What could be better than that? Yeah, I know: seeing that song reach Number One. But for now, living a creative life is an amazing blessing. To be able to make a living as a creative person? That, my friends, is truly divine.

That is why every day I give thanks for my talent, for every opportunity that I receive to use my gifts, to learn and grow, and for every single chance I get to share my creative inspirations with the world. I trust that my work is worthy of notice. I trust that I will be generously rewarded for my work. I trust that my work makes the world a better place. And I know it's entirely up to me to put my work out there to fly or, far more often, to crash. If a song I write fails to find an artist to perform it or an audience to listen, I do not place the blame on anyone else. I never consider myself the victim of a slanted industry playing field. I see the uphill battle, and I accept it, knowing that—in order to have any chance at all—I'll have to be cleverer, more perseverant, and luckier than the game itself.

Although I cannot know with any certainty when and from where my next success will come, I do know that it's on its way. And, I also know that there is only one real guarantee: If I quit trying, I will not succeed.

ACKNOWLEDGMENTS

My first songwriting heroes were Eddie Cochran and Boudleaux and Felice Bryant. "Summertime Blues," "C'mon, Everybody," "Dream, Dream, Dream," and "Wake Up Little Susie" all hit me square in the bull's eye of my young heart, even before I had any inkling of the teenaged angst those songs so precisely expressed. Over the last 60 years, I've had too many idols, mentors, cheerleaders, and patrons to mention here. However, it surely all began with my parents, Norm and Jean Bishop, who cheered me on from my first steps, have believed in me unwaveringly, and never challenged my oft-times questionable decisions. Thank you, Mom and Dad, for your faith in your firstborn son.

I would like to thank Marc Ellington for teaching me how to Cotton pick, Bob Segarini for welcoming me into the professional songwriting world, John T. Frankenheimer for his steadfast advocacy when I didn't have a clue of my own potential, Jac Holzman for allowing me to realize a big part of my dream, André Perry for letting me play with his expensive toys, Spencer Proffer for those myriad opportunities to apply my gifts, and Parker MacDonell for his continuing generosity and friendship. I am grateful to each and every music publisher I've ever worked with: especially Ed Silver, Chuck Kaye, Linda Blum, Meredith Stewart, and Steve Bloch.

I am deeply indebted to the songwriters who donated their time to share their experience and hard-won wisdom for this book: Tom Snow, Steve Dorff, Kent Blazy, Liz Rose, Rory Michael Bourke, and Tim James. Tim James deserves extra kudos from my entire household for his fortitude to keep knockin' on those Music Row doors, when I'd lost the gumption to do it myself. If Tim hadn't gutted it out, I would surely not still be living this blessed creative existence into my seventh decade of life. That leads me to thank every one of the more than 200 artists who have given voice to my songs, especially Toby Keith, who took my song to the top of the charts and gave me the ultimate experience possible for a journeyman songwriter.

I am profoundly grateful to Mike Lawson for shepherding this project from concept to publication, to Link Harnsberger, and everyone at Alfred Music Publishing for putting their resources behind this effort. My editor, Mary Cosola, deserves not only heartfelt thanks but hazard pay for her heroic efforts in so capably getting this book to press in record time.

Lastly, I want to thank my devoted wife, Stacey, and my beautiful daughter, Glendyn, for putting up with my fierce drive to create something every day that wasn't there before. I'm a very lucky man. I know that. And, for that I am eternally grateful.

Rand Bishop
Nashville, Tennessee
March 25, 2010

INDEX

Pop, 2, 4–5, 7, 10, 13, 18, 20–21, 27, 131, 134, 141, 147, 149, 152–153, 158–159, 161, 163–164, 169, 178–185, 196, 202, 206, 213–214, 223–224, 243, 247, 252, 33, 55–57, 68–69, 73, 75, 80, 85, 87–88, 92, 97–98, 109, 111–112, 117, 121, 124, 129

ABOUT THE AUTHOR

It would be difficult to find anyone with more diverse music-business experience than Rand Bishop. A 40-year industry veteran, beginning as a recording artist for Elektra, A&M, MCA, and Epic, Bishop has applied his songwriting and production skills to build an eclectic discography: nearly 250 cuts by such legendary artists as the Beach Boys, Heart, Indigo Girls, and Tim McGraw, numerous Gold and Platinum records and film soundtrack productions, a Grammy nomination, and multiple BMI awards. Bishop has demonstrated his professionalism on "both sides of the desk," as a singer, songwriter, and producer, as well as filling A&R, talent development, and music-publisher roles. "My List," cowritten with Tim James and recorded by Toby Keith, was a five-week *Billboard* Number One and became *Radio & Records'* most-played country single of 2002. Since that hit, Bishop has gone on to become an award-winning screenwriter, a produced playwright, and the author of four books. He is in demand as a speaker and workshop facilitator, and he offers his services as a song-craft coach and talent-development consultant through his Website, http://makinstuffup.net.

Also by Rand Bishop:

My List, 24 Reflections on Life's Priorities (McGraw-Hill, 2003)

Makin' Stuff Up, Secrets of Song-Craft and Survival in the Music-Biz (Weightless Cargo Press, 2008)

Grand Pop, A Memoir by Keefe Taylor as told to Rand Bishop (Strategic Book Publishing, 2010)